WORLD HISTORY

Reading
and Note Taking
Study Guide

PEARSON

Prentice Hall

Boston, Massachusetts
Upper Saddle River, New Jersey

Boston, Massachusetts
Upper Saddle River, New Jersey

ISBN 0-13-133345-3

7 8 9 10   12 11 10 09 08

Contents

How to Use This Book

The **Reading and Note Taking Study Guide** will help you better understand the content of *Prentice Hall World History*. This book will also develop your reading, vocabulary, and note taking skills.

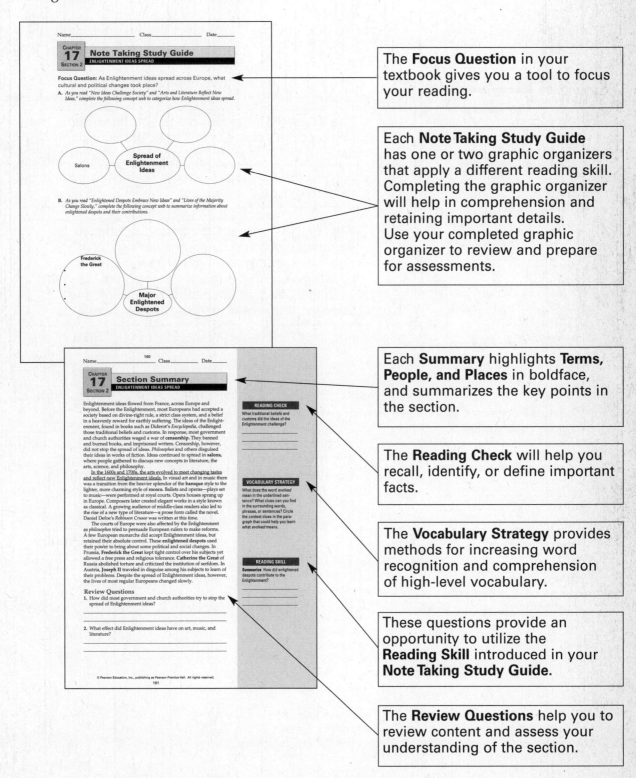

The **Focus Question** in your textbook gives you a tool to focus your reading.

Each **Note Taking Study Guide** has one or two graphic organizers that apply a different reading skill. Completing the graphic organizer will help in comprehension and retaining important details. Use your completed graphic organizer to review and prepare for assessments.

Each **Summary** highlights **Terms, People, and Places** in boldface, and summarizes the key points in the section.

The **Reading Check** will help you recall, identify, or define important facts.

The **Vocabulary Strategy** provides methods for increasing word recognition and comprehension of high-level vocabulary.

These questions provide an opportunity to utilize the **Reading Skill** introduced in your **Note Taking Study Guide.**

The **Review Questions** help you to review content and assess your understanding of the section.

Concept Connector Worksheets support the **Concept Connector** features and the **Concept Connector Cumulative Review** found in each chapter of your text, as well as the **Concept Connector Handbook** found at the end of your textbook. These worksheets will help you to compare key concepts and events and to see patterns and make connections across time. The thematic essay portion of each worksheet will prepare you for social studies exams and assessments.

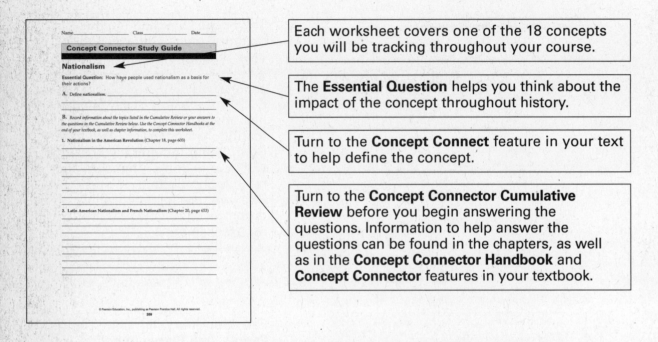

Each worksheet covers one of the 18 concepts you will be tracking throughout your course.

The **Essential Question** helps you think about the impact of the concept throughout history.

Turn to the **Concept Connect** feature in your text to help define the concept.

Turn to the **Concept Connector Cumulative Review** before you begin answering the questions. Information to help answer the questions can be found in the chapters, as well as in the **Concept Connector Handbook** and **Concept Connector** features in your textbook.

Thematic essays are an important part of social studies exams and assessment tests. This portion of the Concept Connector Worksheet provides sample topics for thematic essays.

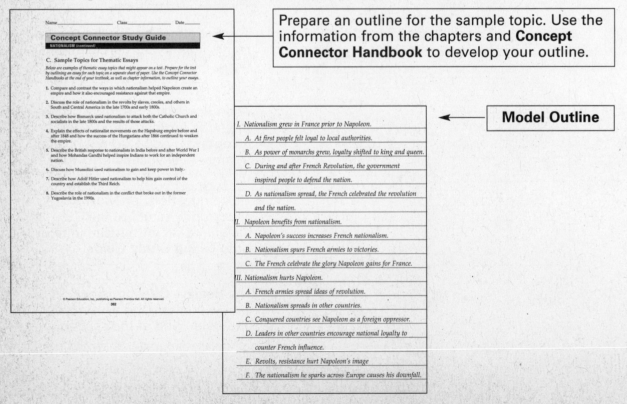

Prepare an outline for the sample topic. Use the information from the chapters and **Concept Connector Handbook** to develop your outline.

Model Outline

Note Taking Study Guide

UNDERSTANDING OUR PAST

Focus Question: What have scholars learned about the ancestors of humans, and how have they done so?

A. *As you read "Studying the Historical Past" and "Investigating Prehistory," complete the following graphic organizer, identifying the types of scholars who study the past. Then summarize what each type does.*

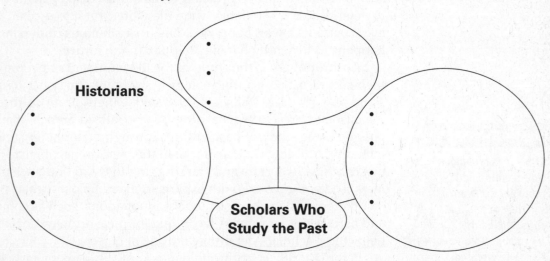

B. *As you read "Discoveries in Africa and Beyond," complete this table by identifying different hominid groups and summarizing what scholars have learned about each group.*

Hominids	
Group	**Summary**
Australopithecines	• • •
	• •
	• • • •
	• • • •

CHAPTER 1 · SECTION 1

Section Summary

UNDERSTANDING OUR PAST

READING CHECK

What is anthropology?

_____

_____

_____

The long period before the invention of writing is called **prehistory.** Then about 5,000 years ago, humans invented writing and recorded history began.

Historians learn details of the past from **artifacts,** such as clothing, coins, and artwork. However, most rely on written evidence, such as letters or tax records. Historians must also evaluate evidence to determine if it is reliable. Then they interpret it to explain why an event, such as a war, happened. Historians help us understand what happens today and what may happen in the future.

Anthropology is the study of the development of people and their societies. Some anthropologists study human bones to understand how physical traits have changed. Others study **cultures** from the past and present. **Archaeology,** a specialized branch of anthropology, is the study of past cultures through material remains, including buildings and artifacts. In the past, archaeologists might just choose a likely site and start digging to try to find ancient artifacts. Today they work with experts in many fields, such as geology and biology. They also use modern innovations, such as computers and aerial photography. A technique for measuring radioactivity helps these scholars determine the age of objects.

Before the 1950s, anthropologists knew little about early humans and their ancestors. Anthropologists **Mary** and **Louis Leakey** searched for clues in East Africa at **Olduvai Gorge.** There they found many ancient stone tools. The tools showed that whoever had made them had developed the skills and tools, or **technology,** to survive. Early human relatives, or hominids, must have made them. Then, in 1959, after two decades of searching, Mary Leakey found the skull of an early hominid. In 1974, anthropologist **Donald Johanson** found pieces of a hominid skeleton in Ethiopia. "Lucy" was at least 3 million years old. Discoveries like these helped establish that a number of different groups of hominids, such as *Homo habilis* and *Homo erectus,* lived over the course of several million years. Two groups of *Homo sapiens* arose. One group—the Neanderthals—disappeared between 50,000 and 30,000 years ago. Early modern humans were then the only hominids on Earth.

VOCABULARY STRATEGY

What does the word *technique* mean in the first underlined sentence? Look for the word *technology* in the second underlined sentence. Notice that these two words have a common root. Use these related words to help learn what *technique* means.

READING SKILL

Summarize In your own words, summarize the important discoveries made by anthropologists Mary and Louis Leakey at Olduvai Gorge.

_____

_____

_____

Review Questions

1. What evidence do historians study to learn about the past?

_____

_____

2. What have stone tools taught anthropologists about early humans?

_____

_____

Note Taking Study Guide

TURNING POINT: THE NEOLITHIC REVOLUTION

Focus Question: How was the introduction of agriculture a turning point in prehistory?

As you read this section in your textbook, complete the following chart to summarize the eras of prehistory before and after the introduction of agriculture.

Eras of Prehistory	
Life Before Farming	**Life After Farming**
• _____ _____	• _____ _____
• _____ _____ _____	• _____ _____ _____
• _____ _____ _____	• _____ _____
• _____ _____ _____	• _____ _____
• _____ _____ _____	• _____ _____
• _____ _____	• _____ _____
• _____ _____ _____	

Section Summary
TURNING POINT: THE NEOLITHIC REVOLUTION

READING CHECK

Into what two eras do scholars divide prehistory?

_____

_____

_____

VOCABULARY STRATEGY

What does the word *transition* mean in the underlined sentence? What clues can you find in the surrounding words, phrases, or sentences? Circle the word below that is a synonym for *transition*.

1. remain

2. change

READING SKILL

Summarize In your own words, summarize how the Neolithic Revolution changed the way people lived.

_____

_____

_____

Scholars have divided prehistory into eras called the **Old Stone Age,** or **Paleolithic Period,** and the **New Stone Age,** or **Neolithic Period.** During both, people made stone tools. However, during the New Stone Age, people began to develop new skills and technologies that led to dramatic changes.

Early modern humans lived toward the end of the Paleolithic Period. They were **nomads** who moved around in small groups, hunting and gathering food. These people made simple tools and weapons, built fires for cooking, and used animal skins for clothing. They also developed spoken language, which helped them cooperate during the hunt. Some people also began to bury their dead. This suggests belief in a spiritual world or life after death. Cave paintings around the world depict animals and humans. Many scholars think that our ancestors believed the world was full of spirits and forces that might reside in animals, objects, or dreams. Such beliefs are known as **animism.**

The New Stone Age began about 12,000 years ago (or about 10,000 B.C.), when nomadic people made a great breakthrough— they learned to farm. By producing their own food, people no longer needed to roam in search of it. As a result, early farmers settled the first permanent villages. <u>This transition from nomadic life to settled farming brought about such dramatic changes in way of life that it is often called the **Neolithic Revolution.**</u> No greater change in human history took place until the Industrial Revolution of the late 1700s. These early farmers were the first to **domesticate** plants and animals.

Archaeologists have unearthed the remains of some early Neolithic villages, including **Çatalhüyük** in modern-day Turkey, and **Jericho,** which exists today in the West Bank. In these settled communities, people accumulated personal property. A council of male elders or elite warriors made the important decisions for all the villagers. To farm successfully, people developed new technologies, such as ways to protect their crops, calendars, and the use of animals for plowing. However, not all technologies were invented everywhere at the same time.

Review Questions

1. What religious beliefs did early modern humans develop during the Old Stone Age?

_____

_____

2. What led to the establishment of the first permanent villages?

_____

_____

Note Taking Study Guide

BEGINNINGS OF CIVILIZATION

Focus Question: How did the world's first civilizations arise and develop?

As you read this section in your textbook, complete the following chart with details from the text to summarize the different phases of the development of civilization.

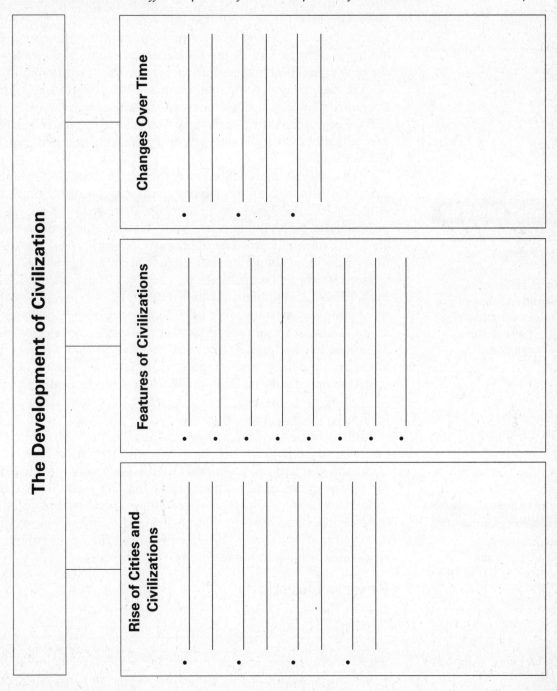

Section Summary

BEGINNINGS OF CIVILIZATION

What is significant about the rise of cities?

_____

_____

VOCABULARY STRATEGY

What does the word *complex* mean in the underlined sentence? Notice the signal word *more* appears before *complex*. In what way do you think writing changed? Use the signal word to help you learn what *complex* means in the sentence.

READING SKILL

Summarize Explain what caused cultural diffusion.

_____

_____

The earliest civilizations developed near major rivers. Rivers provided water, transportation, and food. Floodwaters made the soil fertile. In such rich conditions, farmers produced **surpluses,** which allowed them to store food and feed growing populations. As populations grew, villages expanded into cities. Away from these cities, people lived in farming villages or as nomadic herders on grasslands, or **steppes.** Unlike these **traditional economies,** however, in the new cities some people had jobs other than farming.

The rise of cities is the main feature of **civilization.** In addition to this, historians distinguish other basic features of most early civilizations. They include organized governments, complex religions, job specialization, social classes, arts and architecture, public works, and writing.

In these early civilizations, central governments led by chiefs or elders coordinated large-scale projects such as farming or public works, established laws, and organized defense. Most people were **polytheistic,** believing in many gods. Usually, the gods were associated with natural forces such as the sun or rivers. Also, for the first time, individuals began to specialize in certain jobs. Some became **artisans.** In many civilizations, people's jobs determined their social rank. Priests and nobles usually occupied the top level. Wealthy merchants and artisans were next. Most people were peasants and held the lowest social rank. Art and architecture developed, reflecting the beliefs and values of the civilization. Skilled workers built large, ornate palaces and temples decorated with paintings and statues. Many civilizations also developed writing from **pictographs.** As writing grew more complex, only specially trained people called **scribes** could read and write.

Over time, early civilizations changed. Famine, drought, or other disasters sometimes led people to migrate. Migration, as well as trade and warfare, led to **cultural diffusion.** Trade introduced people to new goods or better methods of making them. In warfare, victorious armies forced their ways of life on conquered peoples while they incorporated aspects of the new cultures into their own. Rulers acquired more territory. This brought about the development of **city-states** and, later, the rise of the first **empires.**

Review Questions

1. Why did early civilizations develop near major rivers?

_____

_____

2. What roles did central governments have in early civilizations?

_____

_____

_____

CHAPTER 2 SECTION 1

Note Taking Study Guide

CITY-STATES OF ANCIENT SUMER

Focus Question: What were the characteristics of the world's first civilization?

As you read this section in your textbook, complete the concept web below to identify the main ideas about the city-states of Sumer under each heading.

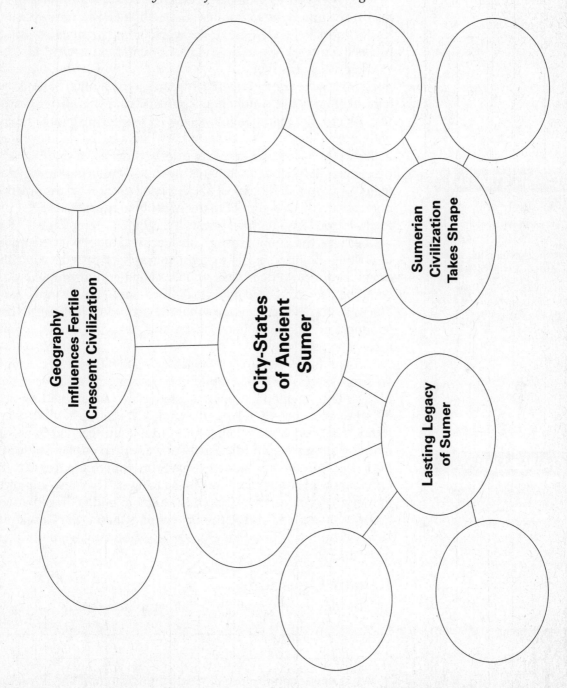

CHAPTER 2 SECTION 1

Section Summary

CITY-STATES OF ANCIENT SUMER

Around 3300 B.C., **Sumer,** the world's first civilization, arose in Southeastern **Mesopotamia.** Mesopotamia lay within the **Fertile Crescent,** between the Tigris and Euphrates rivers. The region's geography affected its people. Frequent flooding forced Sumerians to work together to protect homes and control water for irrigating farms. Although the region had rich soil, it lacked natural resources. Yet, Sumerians built some of the world's first great cities using bricks from readily available clay and water. Sumerians also became traders along the rivers.

Eventually, Sumer had 12 city-states, which often battled over control of land and water. So people turned to war leaders for protection. <u>Over time, this changed when war leadership evolved into hereditary kingship.</u> Sumerian society had a social rank, or **hierarchy,** including an upper class (rulers, priests, officials), a small middle class (lesser priests, scribes, merchants, artisans), and a vast lower class (peasant farmers). Like most ancient peoples, Sumerians practiced polytheism, the worship of many gods. In **ziggurats,** stepped platforms topped by a temple, priests led religious ceremonies.

VOCABULARY STRATEGY

What does the word *evolved* mean in the underlined sentence? What context clues can you find in the surrounding words or phrases? Circle any words or phrases in the paragraph that help you figure out what *evolved* means.

Perhaps the Sumerians' greatest achievement was the invention of writing. Beginning as simple pictographs, by 3200 B.C. writing had developed into wedge-like symbols, called **cuneiform.** Cuneiform could be used to record complex information. People now had access to knowledge beyond what they could remember. Eventually, conquering Akkadian, Babylonian, and Assyrian armies swept across the region.

However, Sumerians left a lasting legacy. Besides creating a writing system, they developed basic astronomy and early mathematics. They created a number system based on six, setting up 60-minute hours and 360-degree circles. We still use this system today. Akkadians, Babylonians, and Assyrians carried Sumerian learning across the Middle East. They adopted cuneiform for their own use. Babylonians recorded the Sumerian oral poem, *The Epic of Gilgamesh,* in cuneiform, thus preserving it. They also expanded on Sumerian learning to develop basic algebra and geometry, to create accurate calendars, and to predict eclipses. Later, the Greeks and Romans built on Sumerian knowledge; then they went on to influence all of Western civilization.

READING SKILL

Identify Main Ideas In the last paragraph of the Summary, which sentence represents the main idea? Write that sentence below.

_____

_____

_____

Review Questions

1. How did its geography help Sumer to develop?

_____

_____

2. What major contibutions to learning were made by Sumerians?

_____

_____

Name_____ Class_____ Date_____

Focus Question: How did various strong rulers unite the lands of the Fertile Crescent into well-organized empires?

As you read this section in your textbook, complete the table below to identify the main ideas about the different empires under each red heading.

Red Heading	Main Idea
First Empires Arise in Mesopotamia	
Conquests Bring New Empires and Ideas	

CHAPTER 2 SECTION 2

Section Summary
INVADERS, TRADERS, AND EMPIRE BUILDERS

Many groups rose to power in ancient Mesopotamia and made long-lasting cultural contributions. Some invaders simply destroyed; others created vast empires. The first invader, in 2300 B.C., was the Akkadian leader, **Sargon.** He conquered Sumer and formed the world's first empire. In 1790 B.C., **Hammurabi,** king of Babylon, unified Mesopotamia. He made the first important attempt to **codify,** or arrange and record, all laws of a state. Hammurabi's Code was carved on public pillars for all to see. It included **civil laws,** which covered private matters, like contracts, taxes, marriage, and divorce, and **criminal laws,** which covered offenses against others, like robbery and murder.

Other conquerors brought new learning to Mesopotamia. Hittites extracted iron from ore to forge strong weapons. Although their empire collapsed around 1200 B.C., ironsmithing spread to Asia, Africa, and Europe, launching the Iron Age. Next, Assyrians, though warlike, created a well-ordered society and founded one of the world's first libraries.

Later, the ruthless Babylonian king **Nebuchadnezzar** controlled the region. He rebuilt and restored the city of Babylon to greatness. His empire eventually stretched from the Persian Gulf to the Mediterranean Sea. However, it fell to Persia in 539 B.C. The Persian empire was enormous. It reached from present-day Turkey to India. Emperor Darius I formed provinces ruled by local governors. Yet, he encouraged unity by building roads across the empire and establishing a single Persian coinage. This helped people move from a **barter economy** toward a **money economy.** Another unifying force came from the Persian prophet **Zoroaster,** who taught belief in a single god and ideas of heaven, hell, and final judgment day. When both Christianity and Islam emerged, or arose, in the Middle East, these new religions stressed similar beliefs.

Not all achievements came from conquerors, however. The Phoenicians were skilled seatraders from the eastern Mediterranean coast. They formed colonies around the Mediterranean. A **colony** is a settlement ruled by people from another land. The Phoenicians spread Middle Eastern culture over a large area. However, perhaps their greatest achievement was the creation of an **alphabet.** The Greeks expanded on this letter system, leading to the alphabet we use today.

Review Questions

1. Who was Sargon?

_____

_____

2. How did Darius I encourage unity?

_____

_____

Name_____ Class_____ Date_____

Note Taking Study Guide

KINGDOM ON THE NILE

Focus Question: How did the Nile influence the rise of the powerful civilization of Egypt?

As you read this section in your textbook, complete the outline below to identify the main ideas about the Nile kingdoms under each heading.

I. _____

    A. _____

    B. _____

II. _____

    A. _____

    B. _____

III. _____

    A. _____

    B. _____

IV. _____

    A. _____

    B. _____

CHAPTER 2 · SECTION 3

Section Summary

KINGDOM ON THE NILE

Fertile land along the Nile brought early peoples to Egypt, and over time, a powerful Egyptian civilization arose. Farming flourished in the rich soil deposits from annual river floods. The surrounding desert served as a buffer from frequent invasions. Early governments formed to organize an irrigation system.

Egypt was made up of two regions. Upper Egypt began at the Nile's first **cataract,** or waterfall, in the south. Lower Egypt covered the Nile's **delta,** the triangular marshland where it emptied into the Mediterranean. About 3100 B.C., King Menes united both regions, forming one of the world's first unified states. Though leadership passed from one **dynasty,** or ruling family, to another, Egypt generally remained united. Egypt's history is divided into three main periods: the Old Kingdom, the Middle Kingdom, and the New Kingdom.

During the Old Kingdom, **pharaohs,** or Egyptian kings, organized a strong central government and established a **bureaucracy,** with different jobs and authority levels. A **vizier,** or chief minister, was the pharaoh's chief of government business. The Great Pyramids stand at Giza today as a lasting reminder of Old Kingdom achievements.

VOCABULARY STRATEGY

What does the word *displaced* mean in the underlined sentence? The prefix *dis-* means "away," or "apart." The root *-place* means "a spot or position." Use these clues to help you figure out what *displaced* means.

The Middle Kingdom saw unpredictable flooding and rebellion. Yet, strong leaders expanded farmable lands, dispatched armies into gold-rich Nubia, and sent traders to the Middle East. However, by about 1700 B.C., foreign invaders, called the Hyksos, conquered the Nile delta using a new military technology: war chariots.

After more than 100 years of Hyksos rule, powerful Egyptian leaders ushered in the New Kingdom, an age of expansion. One of these leaders was **Hatshepsut,** the first female pharaoh. She sent trading expeditions along the eastern Mediterranean and Red Sea. Her stepson, **Thutmose III,** a great military leader, stretched Egypt's borders to their greatest extent. Much later, **Ramses II** pushed north into Syria. During his reign, Egypt battled the Hittites, but ultimately signed a peace treaty. This treaty is the oldest surviving document of its kind.

After 1100 B.C., Egyptian civilization slowly declined. The Assyrians and then the Persians invaded. In 332 B.C., the last Egyptian dynasty ended as Greeks took control. Finally, in 30 B.C., Roman armies displaced the Greeks.

READING SKILL

Identify Supporting Details Find two details in this Summary that support the statement, "Geography helped to shape Egypt."

_____

_____

_____

Review Questions

1. How did Egypt benefit from the Nile River?

_____

_____

2. Who was Hatshepsut?

_____

_____

Note Taking Study Guide
EGYPTIAN CIVILIZATION

Focus Question: How did religion and learning play important roles in ancient Egyptian civilization?

As you read this section in your textbook, complete the chart below to record the main idea about Egyptian civilization under each heading. Include at least two supporting details for each main idea.

Egyptian Civilization	Supporting Detail	Supporting Detail	Main Idea	Red Heading

CHAPTER 2 SECTION 4

Section Summary

EGYPTIAN CIVILIZATION

READING CHECK

How did French scholar Jean Champollion use the Rosetta Stone to decipher the meaning of hieroglyphs?

_____

_____

_____

VOCABULARY STRATEGY

What is the meaning of the word *radical* in the underlined sentence? Look for words or phrases in the surrounding sentences that help you figure out the meaning of the word.

READING SKILL

Identify Supporting Details Identify two details from this Summary that support the main idea that Egyptian civilization made lasting contributions.

_____

_____

_____

Ancient Egyptians made lasting contributions to civilization in many fields. Their religion, written language, art, science, and literature have fascinated people for thousands of years.

During the Old Kingdom, the chief god was the sun god, Re. By the Middle Kingdom, Egyptians called the supreme god **Amon-Re.** Then, around 1380 B.C., pharaoh Amenhotep IV replaced Amon-Re with a minor god, Aton. He then changed his own name to **Akhenaton,** meaning "he who serves Aton." However, priests, nobles, and peasants resisted Akhenaton's revolutionary changes, and his radical ideas failed. Most Egyptians related to the god **Osiris,** who ruled the dead. They also worshipped the goddess **Isis,** who promised life after death. People believed the afterlife was much like life on Earth, so they buried people's possessions with them. The Egyptians also learned to preserve bodies by **mummification,** or embalming and wrapping in cloth, so that the soul could return to the body.

Ancient Egyptians made advances in learning. Their first writing system, **hieroglyphics,** used symbols. Symbols were originally carved in stone. They used a simpler script called hieratic for everyday use. Later, they developed a similar script called demotic. They also developed material to write on, made from **papyrus** plants.

Egyptian civilization eventually declined, yet its written records survived. No one understood them until the early 1800s, when a French scholar, Jean Champollion, **deciphered,** or figured out meanings for, carvings on the **Rosetta Stone.** On this stone, the same passage was written in three ways: hieroglyphics, demotic, and Greek. By comparing these, Champollion decoded the hieroglyphs, allowing later scholars to read thousands of surviving records and inscriptions.

Egyptians also made advances in medicine, astronomy, and mathematics. Egyptian physicians diagnosed illnesses, performed surgeries, and prescribed medicines, some of which are still used today. Priest-astronomers mapped constellations, charted planets, and created a 12-month calendar that became the basis of the modern one. Mathematicians developed basic geometry.

Egyptian artwork has endured for thousands of years. It includes monuments, statues, wall paintings, temple carvings, jewelry, furniture, and other objects. Ancient Egyptian literature includes hymns, practical advice, love poems, and folk tales.

Review Questions

1. What did Egyptians do to prepare for the afterlife?

_____

_____

2. What contributions did ancient Egyptians make to science?

_____

_____

PRENTICE HALL

WORLD HISTORY

Reading and Note Taking Study Guide

PEARSON

Prentice Hall

Boston, Massachusetts
Upper Saddle River, New Jersey

Boston, Massachusetts
Upper Saddle River, New Jersey

ISBN 0-13-133345-3

7 8 9 10   12 11 10 09 08

Contents

How to Use This Book

The **Reading and Note Taking Study Guide** will help you better understand the content of *Prentice Hall World History*. This book will also develop your reading, vocabulary, and note taking skills.

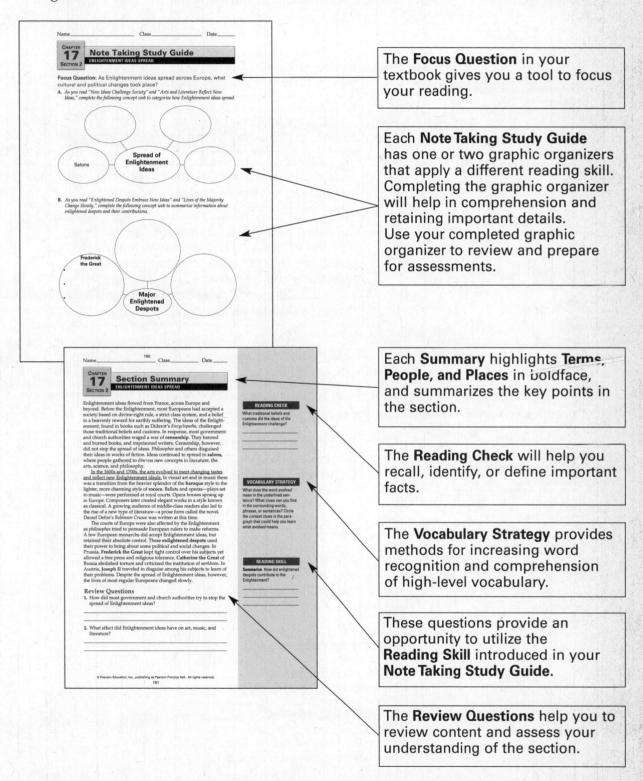

The **Focus Question** in your textbook gives you a tool to focus your reading.

Each **Note Taking Study Guide** has one or two graphic organizers that apply a different reading skill. Completing the graphic organizer will help in comprehension and retaining important details. Use your completed graphic organizer to review and prepare for assessments.

Each **Summary** highlights **Terms, People, and Places** in boldface, and summarizes the key points in the section.

The **Reading Check** will help you recall, identify, or define important facts.

The **Vocabulary Strategy** provides methods for increasing word recognition and comprehension of high-level vocabulary.

These questions provide an opportunity to utilize the **Reading Skill** introduced in your **Note Taking Study Guide**.

The **Review Questions** help you to review content and assess your understanding of the section.

Concept Connector Worksheets support the **Concept Connector** features and the **Concept Connector Cumulative Review** found in each chapter of your text, as well as the **Concept Connector Handbook** found at the end of your textbook. These worksheets will help you to compare key concepts and events and to see patterns and make connections across time. The thematic essay portion of each worksheet will prepare you for social studies exams and assessments.

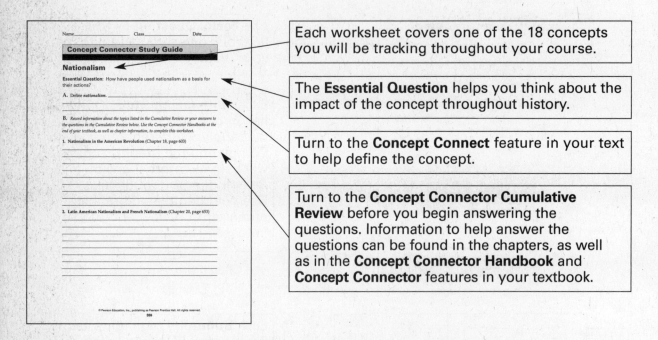

Each worksheet covers one of the 18 concepts you will be tracking throughout your course.

The **Essential Question** helps you think about the impact of the concept throughout history.

Turn to the **Concept Connect** feature in your text to help define the concept.

Turn to the **Concept Connector Cumulative Review** before you begin answering the questions. Information to help answer the questions can be found in the chapters, as well as in the **Concept Connector Handbook** and **Concept Connector** features in your textbook.

Thematic essays are an important part of social studies exams and assessment tests. This portion of the Concept Connector Worksheet provides sample topics for thematic essays.

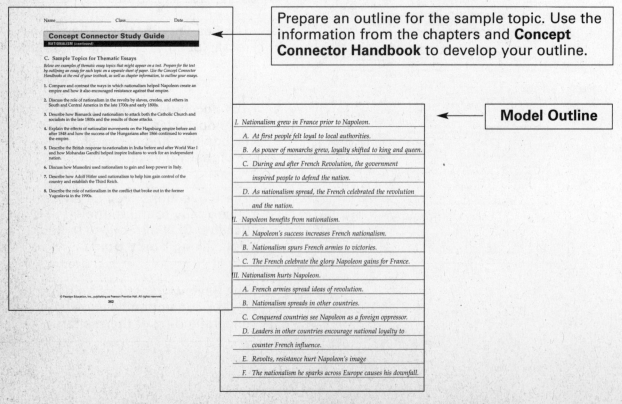

Prepare an outline for the sample topic. Use the information from the chapters and **Concept Connector Handbook** to develop your outline.

Model Outline

I. Nationalism grew in France prior to Napoleon.
  A. At first people felt loyal to local authorities.
  B. As power of monarchs grew, loyalty shifted to king and queen.
  C. During and after French Revolution, the government inspired people to defend the nation.
  D. As nationalism spread, the French celebrated the revolution and the nation.
II. Napoleon benefits from nationalism.
  A. Napoleon's success increases French nationalism.
  B. Nationalism spurs French armies to victories.
  C. The French celebrate the glory Napoleon gains for France.
III. Nationalism hurts Napoleon.
  A. French armies spread ideas of revolution.
  B. Nationalism spreads in other countries.
  C. Conquered countries see Napoleon as a foreign oppressor.
  D. Leaders in other countries encourage national loyalty to counter French influence.
  E. Revolts, resistance hurt Napoleon's image
  F. The nationalism he sparks across Europe causes his downfall.

Note Taking Study Guide
UNDERSTANDING OUR PAST

Focus Question: What have scholars learned about the ancestors of humans, and how have they done so?

A. *As you read "Studying the Historical Past" and "Investigating Prehistory," complete the following graphic organizer, identifying the types of scholars who study the past. Then summarize what each type does.*

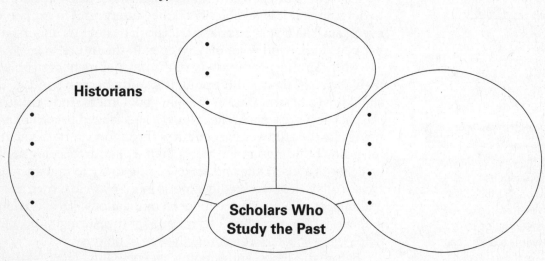

B. *As you read "Discoveries in Africa and Beyond," complete this table by identifying different hominid groups and summarizing what scholars have learned about each group.*

Hominids	
Group	**Summary**
Australopithecines	• • •
	• •
	• • • •
	• • • •

CHAPTER 1 SECTION 1

Section Summary

UNDERSTANDING OUR PAST

READING CHECK

What is anthropology?

_____

_____

_____

VOCABULARY STRATEGY

What does the word *technique* mean in the first underlined sentence? Look for the word *technology* in the second underlined sentence. Notice that these two words have a common root. Use these related words to help learn what *technique* means.

READING SKILL

Summarize In your own words, summarize the important discoveries made by anthropologists Mary and Louis Leakey at Olduvai Gorge.

_____

_____

_____

The long period before the invention of writing is called **prehistory.** Then about 5,000 years ago, humans invented writing and recorded history began.

Historians learn details of the past from **artifacts,** such as clothing, coins, and artwork. However, most rely on written evidence, such as letters or tax records. Historians must also evaluate evidence to determine if it is reliable. Then they interpret it to explain why an event, such as a war, happened. Historians help us understand what happens today and what may happen in the future.

Anthropology is the study of the development of people and their societies. Some anthropologists study human bones to understand how physical traits have changed. Others study **cultures** from the past and present. **Archaeology,** a specialized branch of anthropology, is the study of past cultures through material remains, including buildings and artifacts. In the past, archaeologists might just choose a likely site and start digging to try to find ancient artifacts. Today they work with experts in many fields, such as geology and biology. They also use modern innovations, such as computers and aerial photography. A technique for measuring radioactivity helps these scholars determine the age of objects.

Before the 1950s, anthropologists knew little about early humans and their ancestors. Anthropologists **Mary** and **Louis Leakey** searched for clues in East Africa at **Olduvai Gorge.** There they found many ancient stone tools. The tools showed that whoever had made them had developed the skills and tools, or **technology,** to survive. Early human relatives, or hominids, must have made them. Then, in 1959, after two decades of searching, Mary Leakey found the skull of an early hominid. In 1974, anthropologist **Donald Johanson** found pieces of a hominid skeleton in Ethiopia. "Lucy" was at least 3 million years old. Discoveries like these helped establish that a number of different groups of hominids, such as *Homo habilis* and *Homo erectus,* lived over the course of several million years. Two groups of *Homo sapiens* arose. One group—the Neanderthals—disappeared between 50,000 and 30,000 years ago. Early modern humans were then the only hominids on Earth.

Review Questions

1. What evidence do historians study to learn about the past?

_____

_____

2. What have stone tools taught anthropologists about early humans?

_____

_____

Note Taking Study Guide

TURNING POINT: THE NEOLITHIC REVOLUTION

CHAPTER 1 SECTION 2

Focus Question: How was the introduction of agriculture a turning point in prehistory?

As you read this section in your textbook, complete the following chart to summarize the eras of prehistory before and after the introduction of agriculture.

Eras of Prehistory	
Life Before Farming	**Life After Farming**
• _____ _____	• _____ _____
• _____ _____ _____	• _____ _____ _____
• _____ _____ _____	• _____ _____ _____
• _____ _____ _____	• _____ _____ _____
• _____ _____ _____	• _____ _____ _____
• _____ _____ _____	• _____ _____
• _____ _____ _____	

Section Summary

TURNING POINT: THE NEOLITHIC REVOLUTION

READING CHECK

Into what two eras do scholars divide prehistory?

_____

_____

_____

VOCABULARY STRATEGY

What does the word *transition* mean in the underlined sentence? What clues can you find in the surrounding words, phrases, or sentences? Circle the word below that is a synonym for *transition*.

1. remain

2. change

READING SKILL

Summarize In your own words, summarize how the Neolithic Revolution changed the way people lived.

_____

_____

_____

Scholars have divided prehistory into eras called the **Old Stone Age,** or **Paleolithic Period,** and the **New Stone Age,** or **Neolithic Period.** During both, people made stone tools. However, during the New Stone Age, people began to develop new skills and technologies that led to dramatic changes.

Early modern humans lived toward the end of the Paleolithic Period. They were **nomads** who moved around in small groups, hunting and gathering food. These people made simple tools and weapons, built fires for cooking, and used animal skins for clothing. They also developed spoken language, which helped them cooperate during the hunt. Some people also began to bury their dead. This suggests belief in a spiritual world or life after death. Cave paintings around the world depict animals and humans. Many scholars think that our ancestors believed the world was full of spirits and forces that might reside in animals, objects, or dreams. Such beliefs are known as **animism.**

The New Stone Age began about 12,000 years ago (or about 10,000 B.C.), when nomadic people made a great breakthrough—they learned to farm. By producing their own food, people no longer needed to roam in search of it. As a result, early farmers settled the first permanent villages. This transition from nomadic life to settled farming brought about such dramatic changes in way of life that it is often called the **Neolithic Revolution.** No greater change in human history took place until the Industrial Revolution of the late 1700s. These early farmers were the first to **domesticate** plants and animals.

Archaeologists have unearthed the remains of some early Neolithic villages, including **Çatalhüyük** in modern-day Turkey, and **Jericho,** which exists today in the West Bank. In these settled communities, people accumulated personal property. A council of male elders or elite warriors made the important decisions for all the villagers. To farm successfully, people developed new technologies, such as ways to protect their crops, calendars, and the use of animals for plowing. However, not all technologies were invented everywhere at the same time.

Review Questions

1. What religious beliefs did early modern humans develop during the Old Stone Age?

_____

_____

2. What led to the establishment of the first permanent villages?

_____

_____

CHAPTER 1 SECTION 3

Note Taking Study Guide

BEGINNINGS OF CIVILIZATION

Focus Question: How did the world's first civilizations arise and develop?

As you read this section in your textbook, complete the following chart with details from the text to summarize the different phases of the development of civilization.

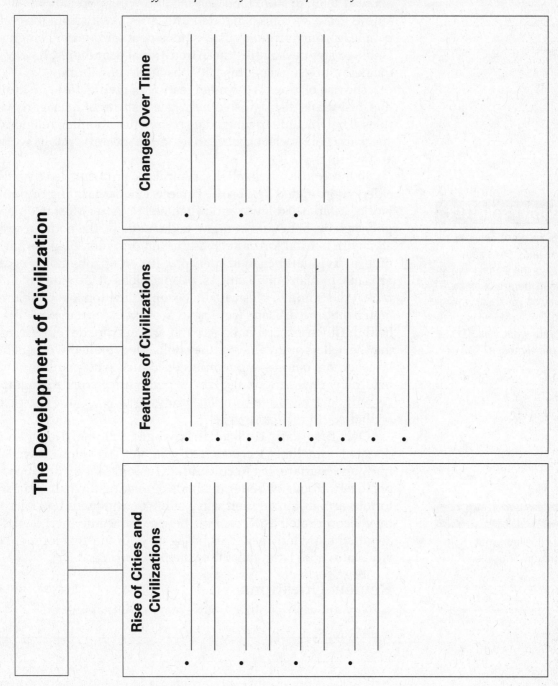

Section Summary

BEGINNINGS OF CIVILIZATION

What is significant about the rise of cities?

_____

_____

What does the word *complex* mean in the underlined sentence? Notice the signal word *more* appears before *complex*. In what way do you think writing changed? Use the signal word to help you learn what *complex* means in the sentence.

Summarize Explain what caused cultural diffusion.

_____

_____

The earliest civilizations developed near major rivers. Rivers provided water, transportation, and food. Floodwaters made the soil fertile. In such rich conditions, farmers produced **surpluses,** which allowed them to store food and feed growing populations. As populations grew, villages expanded into cities. Away from these cities, people lived in farming villages or as nomadic herders on grasslands, or **steppes.** Unlike these **traditional economies,** however, in the new cities some people had jobs other than farming.

The rise of cities is the main feature of **civilization.** In addition to this, historians distinguish other basic features of most early civilizations. They include organized governments, complex religions, job specialization, social classes, arts and architecture, public works, and writing.

In these early civilizations, central governments led by chiefs or elders coordinated large-scale projects such as farming or public works, established laws, and organized defense. Most people were **polytheistic,** believing in many gods. Usually, the gods were associated with natural forces such as the sun or rivers. Also, for the first time, individuals began to specialize in certain jobs. Some became **artisans.** In many civilizations, people's jobs determined their social rank. Priests and nobles usually occupied the top level. Wealthy merchants and artisans were next. Most people were peasants and held the lowest social rank. Art and architecture developed, reflecting the beliefs and values of the civilization. Skilled workers built large, ornate palaces and temples decorated with paintings and statues. Many civilizations also developed writing from **pictographs.** As writing grew more complex, only specially trained people called scribes could read and write.

Over time, early civilizations changed. Famine, drought, or other disasters sometimes led people to migrate. Migration, as well as trade and warfare, led to **cultural diffusion.** Trade introduced people to new goods or better methods of making them. In warfare, victorious armies forced their ways of life on conquered peoples while they incorporated aspects of the new cultures into their own. Rulers acquired more territory. This brought about the development of **city-states** and, later, the rise of the first **empires.**

Review Questions

1. Why did early civilizations develop near major rivers?

_____

_____

2. What roles did central governments have in early civilizations?

_____

_____

Note Taking Study Guide

CITY-STATES OF ANCIENT SUMER

Focus Question: What were the characteristics of the world's first civilization?

As you read this section in your textbook, complete the concept web below to identify the main ideas about the city-states of Sumer under each heading.

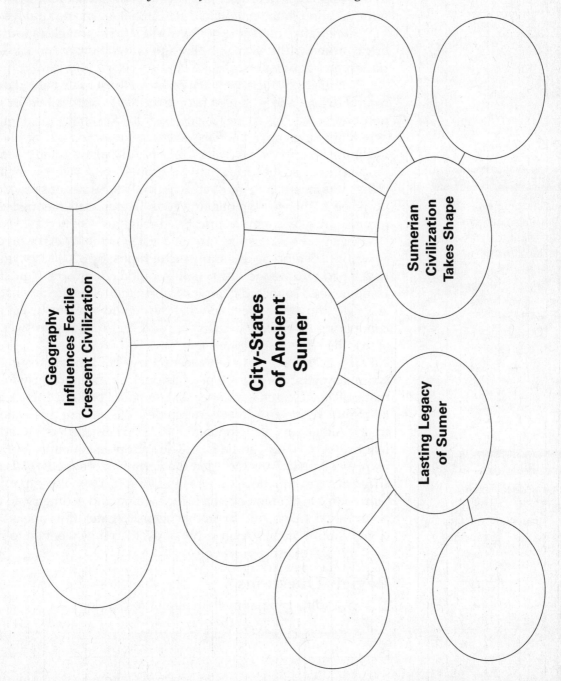

CHAPTER 2 SECTION 1
Section Summary
CITY-STATES OF ANCIENT SUMER

READING CHECK

What were ziggurats?

_____

_____

_____

VOCABULARY STRATEGY

What does the word *evolved* mean in the underlined sentence? What context clues can you find in the surrounding words or phrases? Circle any words or phrases in the paragraph that help you figure out what *evolved* means.

READING SKILL

Identify Main Ideas In the last paragraph of the Summary, which sentence represents the main idea? Write that sentence below.

_____

_____

_____

Around 3300 B.C., **Sumer,** the world's first civilization, arose in Southeastern **Mesopotamia.** Mesopotamia lay within the **Fertile Crescent,** between the Tigris and Euphrates rivers. The region's geography affected its people. Frequent flooding forced Sumerians to work together to protect homes and control water for irrigating farms. Although the region had rich soil, it lacked natural resources. Yet, Sumerians built some of the world's first great cities using bricks from readily available clay and water. Sumerians also became traders along the rivers.

Eventually, Sumer had 12 city-states, which often battled over control of land and water. So people turned to war leaders for protection. <u>Over time, this changed when war leadership evolved into hereditary kingship.</u> Sumerian society had a social rank, or **hierarchy,** including an upper class (rulers, priests, officials), a small middle class (lesser priests, scribes, merchants, artisans), and a vast lower class (peasant farmers). Like most ancient peoples, Sumerians practiced polytheism, the worship of many gods. In **ziggurats,** stepped platforms topped by a temple, priests led religious ceremonies.

Perhaps the Sumerians' greatest achievement was the invention of writing. Beginning as simple pictographs, by 3200 B.C. writing had developed into wedge-like symbols, called **cuneiform.** Cuneiform could be used to record complex information. People now had access to knowledge beyond what they could remember. Eventually, conquering Akkadian, Babylonian, and Assyrian armies swept across the region.

However, Sumerians left a lasting legacy. Besides creating a writing system, they developed basic astronomy and early mathematics. They created a number system based on six, setting up 60-minute hours and 360-degree circles. We still use this system today. Akkadians, Babylonians, and Assyrians carried Sumerian learning across the Middle East. They adopted cuneiform for their own use. Babylonians recorded the Sumerian oral poem, *The Epic of Gilgamesh,* in cuneiform, thus preserving it. They also expanded on Sumerian learning to develop basic algebra and geometry, to create accurate calendars, and to predict eclipses. Later, the Greeks and Romans built on Sumerian knowledge; then they went on to influence all of Western civilization.

Review Questions
1. How did its geography help Sumer to develop?

_____

_____

2. What major contibutions to learning were made by Sumerians?

_____

_____

Note Taking Study Guide
INVADERS, TRADERS, AND EMPIRE BUILDERS

Focus Question: How did various strong rulers unite the lands of the Fertile Crescent into well-organized empires?

As you read this section in your textbook, complete the table below to identify the main ideas about the different empires under each red heading.

Red Heading	Main Idea
First Empires Arise in Mesopotamia	
Conquests Bring New Empires and Ideas	

Section Summary
INVADERS, TRADERS, AND EMPIRE BUILDERS

Many groups rose to power in ancient Mesopotamia and made long-lasting cultural contributions. Some invaders simply destroyed; others created vast empires. The first invader, in 2300 B.C., was the Akkadian leader, **Sargon.** He conquered Sumer and formed the world's first empire. In 1790 B.C., **Hammurabi,** king of Babylon, unified Mesopotamia. He made the first important attempt to **codify,** or arrange and record, all laws of a state. Hammurabi's Code was carved on public pillars for all to see. It included **civil laws,** which covered private matters, like contracts, taxes, marriage, and divorce, and **criminal laws,** which covered offenses against others, like robbery and murder.

Other conquerors brought new learning to Mesopotamia. Hittites extracted iron from ore to forge strong weapons. Although their empire collapsed around 1200 B.C., ironsmithing spread to Asia, Africa, and Europe, launching the Iron Age. Next, Assyrians, though warlike, created a well-ordered society and founded one of the world's first libraries.

Later, the ruthless Babylonian king **Nebuchadnezzar** controlled the region. He rebuilt and restored the city of Babylon to greatness. His empire eventually stretched from the Persian Gulf to the Mediterranean Sea. However, it fell to Persia in 539 B.C. The Persian empire was enormous. It reached from present-day Turkey to India. Emperor Darius I formed provinces ruled by local governors. Yet, he encouraged unity by building roads across the empire and establishing a single Persian coinage. This helped people move from a **barter economy** toward a **money economy.** Another unifying force came from the Persian prophet **Zoroaster,** who taught belief in a single god and ideas of heaven, hell, and final judgment day. <u>When both Christianity and Islam emerged, or arose, in the Middle East, these new religions stressed similar beliefs.</u>

Not all achievements came from conquerors, however. The Phoenicians were skilled seatraders from the eastern Mediterranean coast. They formed colonies around the Mediterranean. A **colony** is a settlement ruled by people from another land. The Phoenicians spread Middle Eastern culture over a large area. However, perhaps their greatest achievement was the creation of an **alphabet.** The Greeks expanded on this letter system, leading to the alphabet we use today.

VOCABULARY STRATEGY

What does the word *emerged* mean in the underlined sentence? The word *arose* in the same sentence is a synonym of *emerged.* Use this synonym to help you figure out the meaning of *emerged.*

READING SKILL

Identify Main Ideas Write a sentence in your own words that gives the main idea of the Summary.

_____

_____

_____

Review Questions
1. Who was Sargon?

_____

_____

2. How did Darius I encourage unity?

_____

_____

Note Taking Study Guide

KINGDOM ON THE NILE

Focus Question: How did the Nile influence the rise of the powerful civilization of Egypt?

As you read this section in your textbook, complete the outline below to identify the main ideas about the Nile kingdoms under each heading.

I. _____

   A. _____

   B. _____

II. _____

   A. _____

   B. _____

III. _____

   A. _____

   B. _____

IV. _____

   A. _____

   B. _____

CHAPTER 2 SECTION 3

Section Summary
KINGDOM ON THE NILE

Fertile land along the Nile brought early peoples to Egypt, and over time, a powerful Egyptian civilization arose. Farming flourished in the rich soil deposits from annual river floods. The surrounding desert served as a buffer from frequent invasions. Early governments formed to organize an irrigation system.

Egypt was made up of two regions. Upper Egypt began at the Nile's first **cataract,** or waterfall, in the south. Lower Egypt covered the Nile's **delta,** the triangular marshland where it emptied into the Mediterranean. About 3100 B.C., King Menes united both regions, forming one of the world's first unified states. Though leadership passed from one **dynasty,** or ruling family, to another, Egypt generally remained united. Egypt's history is divided into three main periods: the Old Kingdom, the Middle Kingdom, and the New Kingdom.

During the Old Kingdom, **pharaohs,** or Egyptian kings, organized a strong central government and established a **bureaucracy,** with different jobs and authority levels. A **vizier,** or chief minister, was the pharaoh's chief of government business. The Great Pyramids stand at Giza today as a lasting reminder of Old Kingdom achievements.

The Middle Kingdom saw unpredictable flooding and rebellion. Yet, strong leaders expanded farmable lands, dispatched armies into gold-rich Nubia, and sent traders to the Middle East. However, by about 1700 B.C., foreign invaders, called the Hyksos, conquered the Nile delta using a new military technology: war chariots.

After more than 100 years of Hyksos rule, powerful Egyptian leaders ushered in the New Kingdom, an age of expansion. One of these leaders was **Hatshepsut,** the first female pharaoh. She sent trading expeditions along the eastern Mediterranean and Red Sea. Her stepson, **Thutmose III,** a great military leader, stretched Egypt's borders to their greatest extent. Much later, **Ramses II** pushed north into Syria. During his reign, Egypt battled the Hittites, but ultimately signed a peace treaty. This treaty is the oldest surviving document of its kind.

After 1100 B.C., Egyptian civilization slowly declined. The Assyrians and then the Persians invaded. In 332 B.C., the last Egyptian dynasty ended as Greeks took control. Finally, in 30 B.C., Roman armies displaced the Greeks.

Review Questions

1. How did Egypt benefit from the Nile River?

_____

_____

2. Who was Hatshepsut?

_____

_____

CHAPTER
2
SECTION 4

Note Taking Study Guide
EGYPTIAN CIVILIZATION

Focus Question: How did religion and learning play important roles in ancient Egyptian civilization?

As you read this section in your textbook, complete the chart below to record the main idea about Egyptian civilization under each heading. Include at least two supporting details for each main idea.

Egyptian Civilization	Supporting Detail	Supporting Detail	Main Idea	Red Heading

Section Summary
EGYPTIAN CIVILIZATION

How did French scholar Jean Champollion use the Rosetta Stone to decipher the meaning of hieroglyphs?

_____

_____

_____

VOCABULARY STRATEGY

What is the meaning of the word *radical* in the underlined sentence? Look for words or phrases in the surrounding sentences that help you figure out the meaning of the word.

_____

_____

_____

READING SKILL

Identify Supporting Details
Identify two details from this Summary that support the main idea that Egyptian civilization made lasting contributions.

_____

_____

_____

Ancient Egyptians made lasting contributions to civilization in many fields. Their religion, written language, art, science, and literature have fascinated people for thousands of years.

During the Old Kingdom, the chief god was the sun god, Re. By the Middle Kingdom, Egyptians called the supreme god **Amon-Re.** Then, around 1380 B.C., pharaoh Amenhotep IV replaced Amon-Re with a minor god, Aton. He then changed his own name to **Akhenaton,** meaning "he who serves Aton." However, priests, nobles, and peasants resisted Akhenaton's revolutionary changes, and his radical ideas failed. Most Egyptians related to the god **Osiris,** who ruled the dead. They also worshipped the goddess **Isis,** who promised life after death. People believed the afterlife was much like life on Earth, so they buried people's possessions with them. The Egyptians also learned to preserve bodies by **mummification,** or embalming and wrapping in cloth, so that the soul could return to the body.

Ancient Egyptians made advances in learning. Their first writing system, **hieroglyphics,** used symbols. Symbols were originally carved in stone. They used a simpler script called hieratic for everyday use. Later, they developed a similar script called demotic. They also developed material to write on, made from **papyrus** plants.

Egyptian civilization eventually declined, yet its written records survived. No one understood them until the early 1800s, when a French scholar, Jean Champollion, **deciphered,** or figured out meanings for, carvings on the **Rosetta Stone.** On this stone, the same passage was written in three ways: hieroglyphics, demotic, and Greek. By comparing these, Champollion decoded the hieroglyphs, allowing later scholars to read thousands of surviving records and inscriptions.

Egyptians also made advances in medicine, astronomy, and mathematics. Egyptian physicians diagnosed illnesses, performed surgeries, and prescribed medicines, some of which are still used today. Priest-astronomers mapped constellations, charted planets, and created a 12-month calendar that became the basis of the modern one. Mathematicians developed basic geometry.

Egyptian artwork has endured for thousands of years. It includes monuments, statues, wall paintings, temple carvings, jewelry, furniture, and other objects. Ancient Egyptian literature includes hymns, practical advice, love poems, and folk tales.

Review Questions
1. What did Egyptians do to prepare for the afterlife?

_____

_____

2. What contributions did ancient Egyptians make to science?

_____

_____

Note Taking Study Guide
ROOTS OF JUDAISM

Focus Question: How did the worship of only one god shape Judaism?

As you read this section in your textbook, complete the chart below to record the main idea about the roots of Judaism under each red heading. Include at least two supporting details for each main idea.

Roots of Judaism

Red Heading:	Red Heading:	Red Heading:
Main Idea:	**Main Idea:**	**Main Idea:**
Supporting Details: 1. 2.	**Supporting Details:** 1. 2.	**Supporting Details:** 1. 2. 3.

CHAPTER 2 SECTION 5

Section Summary
ROOTS OF JUDAISM

READING CHECK

Who is considered the "father of the Israelites"?

_____

_____

_____

VOCABULARY STRATEGY

What does *undertook* mean in the underlined sentence? Read the underlined sentence aloud, but leave out the word *undertook*. What word could you use in its place? Use this strategy to help you figure out the meaning of *undertook*.

READING SKILL

Identify Supporting Details Find two details in the Summary that support the idea that Jews maintained their identity during the Diaspora.

_____

_____

_____

About 4,000 years ago, the ancient Israelites developed Judaism, one of today's major religions. Unlike neighboring peoples, Israelites were **monotheistic,** believing in only one god. They believed every event reflected God's plan. So, they recorded events and laws in the **Torah.** It is the most sacred text of the Israelites, or Jews, and includes the first five books of the Hebrew Bible.

According to the Torah, about 2000 B.C., **Abraham**, and his family migrated to a region called Canaan. Abraham is considered the father of the Israelites. The Israelites believed that God made a **covenant**, or binding agreement, with Abraham. This covenant promised a special relationship with God and a homeland in Canaan. However, famine forced the Israelites into Egypt, where they became slaves. Much later, **Moses** led their exodus, or departure, from Egypt back to Canaan.

There, they established the kingdom of Israel around 1000 B.C. Under the second king, **David,** the feuding 12 tribes of Israel were united into one kingdom. Then, David's son **Solomon** undertook the task of turning Jerusalem into an impressive capital city. He completed a massive temple and increased Israel's influence in the region. However, after his death, the kingdom split and eventually fell to the Assyrians and Babylonians.

Israelite society was **patriarchal,** meaning that men held the greatest authority. Also from early times, law was central to Judaism. The Torah contains laws on such subjects as cleanliness, food preparation, and crime. Also in the Torah is a special set of laws called the Ten Commandments. These laws stress moral conduct and religious duty, such as keeping the **Sabbath,** a holy day of rest and worship. Often in Jewish history, **prophets,** or spiritual leaders, arose. They urged social justice and taught strong codes of **ethics**, or moral standards of behavior.

During a 500-year period called the **Diaspora,** the Jews left or were exiled from Israel, and they spread out around the world. Still, they maintained their identity in close-knit communities, following religious laws and traditions. This helped them to survive centuries of persecution.

Judaism has been an important religion. From that culture and faith, both Christianity and Islam emerged, creating an ethical legacy we call the Judeo-Christian tradition.

Review Questions

1. What is the Torah?

_____

_____

2. What was the Diaspora?

_____

_____

Name_____ Class_____ Date_____

Focus Question: How have scholars learned about India's first two civilizations, the Indus and the Aryan?

As you read this section in your textbook, complete the following chart to sequence important events in early civilizations of India and Pakistan.

Event					
Date					

Section Summary
EARLY CIVILIZATIONS OF INDIA AND PAKISTAN

READING CHECK

What group was at the top of Aryan society?

_____

_____

_____

VOCABULARY STRATEGY

What does the word *embodied* mean in the underlined sentence? The prefix *em-* means "to put or to cover with." What is the root word of *embodied?* Use these clues to help you figure out the meaning of *embodied.*

READING SKILL

Recognize Sequence Number the following in the correct sequence:

____ Aryans migrate to India.

____ Organized government plans Mohenjo-Daro.

____ Aryan beliefs move toward the concept of brahman and mysticism.

____ Flood, earthquake, or other disaster hits Indus civilization.

The Indian **subcontinent** is a large landmass that juts out from Asia. It is divided into three zones: the Gangetic Plain, with rivers that support farming; the Deccan **plateau,** a raised area of level land too dry for farming; and the coastal plains, which receive plenty of rain. Life there is greatly affected by **monsoons,** or winds that bring hot, dry air from the northeast in October and rains from the southwest in mid-June.

Civilization began on the subcontinent around 2600 B.C. in the Indus River valley. Archaeologists believe organized governments helped plan cities such as **Harappa** and **Mohenjo-Daro.** They were built with wide streets, strong building materials, and complex plumbing systems. Most people farmed, although some traded goods by ship with Sumer. People worshiped many gods and regarded certain animals as sacred, perhaps influencing latter Indian beliefs such as the **veneration** of cattle. The civilization declined by about 1900 B.C., possibly as a result of environmental damage, a major flood, or an earthquake.

The Aryans migrated to the subcontinent and established a strong civilization about 1500 B.C. They began as nomadic herders but later settled into farming. Aryan warriors elected leaders called **rajahs.** Some rajahs competed for control of trade and land. The society was divided into four groups. At the top were priests, followed by warriors, farmers and merchants, and workers and servants.

People worshiped gods and goddesses who embodied natural forces, such as the sky and sun. **Indra,** the god of war, was the chief deity and used thunderbolts as weapons. Priests wrote sacred teachings in the **Vedas,** a collection of hymns and religious instructions.

Over time, Aryan beliefs changed. There was a move toward the concept of **brahman,** a single spiritual power beyond the gods of the Vedas and existing in all things. **Mystics** also sought direct communion with divine forces.

By 500 B.C. there were many kingdoms, yet **acculturation** created a common culture by blending traditions. Epic poems were part of the culture. They described early Aryan warfare, important religious beliefs, and valued behavior.

Review Questions

1. Why do archaeologists think organized governments planned Harappa and Mohenjo-Daro?

_____

_____

2. What are the Vedas?

_____

_____

CHAPTER
3
SECTION 2

Note Taking Study Guide

HINDUISM AND BUDDHISM

Focus Question: In what ways were religion and society intertwined in ancient India?

As you read this section in your textbook, complete the following chart to sequence important events in the development of Hinduism and Buddhism.

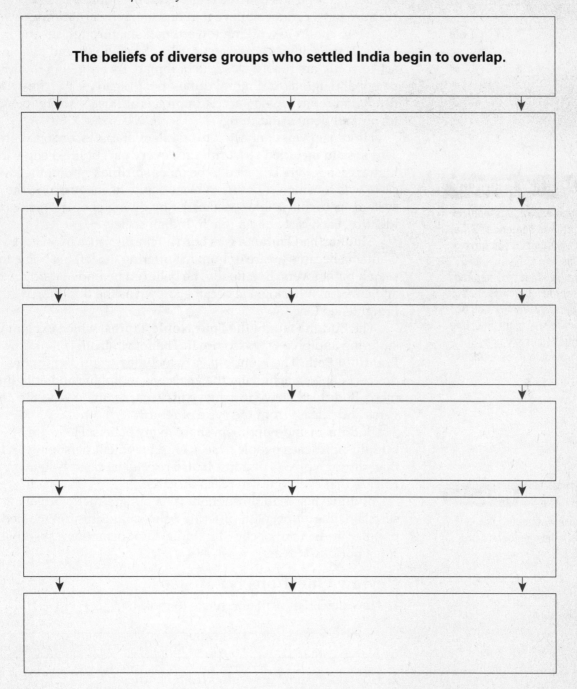

The beliefs of diverse groups who settled India begin to overlap.

CHAPTER 3 SECTION 2
Section Summary
HINDUISM AND BUDDHISM

READING CHECK

Who became known as the "Enlightened One"?

_____

_____

_____

VOCABULARY STRATEGY

What does *aspirations* mean in the underlined sentence? What prior knowledge do you have about this word? If you heard someone say that they *aspired* to a career in medicine, does that mean they want or don't want a career in medicine? Use these clues to help you figure out the meaning of *aspirations*.

READING SKILL

Recognize Sequence Did Buddhism develop before or after Hinduism?

_____

_____

_____

Two major religions, Hinduism and Buddhism, emerged in ancient India. Although Hinduism grew out of the overlapping religious ideas of diverse groups, all Hindus share basic beliefs. One force, the brahman, is the basis of everything. People have an essential self, or **atman.** Their goal is to achieve **moksha,** or union with brahman. Because most cannot achieve it in one life, **reincarnation** allows people to continue working toward moksha through several lifetimes. **Karma** affects a person's fate in the next life, and people who act correctly are reborn closer to brahman. By following **dharma,** or personal religious and moral duties, people can escape the cycle of death and rebirth. One part of dharma is **ahimsa,** or nonviolence, toward all people and things.

Hinduism was connected to a system of **castes,** or social groups. This system included strict rules for every part of life. People in higher castes were believed to be more spiritually pure; the lowest caste was considered untouchable. Despite its inequalities, the caste system ensured a stable social order by giving people a sense of identity. Each caste had a role in Indian society.

Siddhartha Gautama was born a Hindu prince in 563 B.C. When Gautama became aware of human suffering, he left his home to search for answers. Eventually, he believed he understood the cause and cure for suffering. He became known as the Buddha, or "the Enlightened One."

The Buddha taught the **Four Noble Truths,** which explain life as suffering and give ways to cure it. The fourth truth is to follow the **Eightfold Path.** The Eightfold Path includes "right aspirations" and directs people in achieving the goals of a moral life and enlightenment. Buddhists strive to achieve **nirvana,** or union with the universe and release from the cycle of rebirth.

Buddhism and Hinduism share many beliefs. However, Buddhism teaches people to seek enlightenment personally, rather than through priests or gods. It also rejects the caste system and teaches that everyone can reach nirvana.

Buddhism spread throughout Asia but gradually broke into two **sects,** or subgroups, with differing beliefs. Buddhism remained very popular in Asia but declined in India. Hinduism there absorbed some Buddhist ideas.

Review Questions

1. How does reincarnation relate to moksha?

_____

_____

2. How does Buddhism differ from Hinduism?

_____

_____

Note Taking Study Guide
POWERFUL EMPIRES OF INDIA

Focus Question: In what ways did Maurya and Gupta rulers achieve peace and order for ancient India?

As you read this section in your textbook, complete the following timeline to sequence the important events in the Maurya and Gupta periods.

321 B.C.

Section Summary
POWERFUL EMPIRES OF INDIA

Who founded the first Indian empire?

_____

_____

_____

What does the word *status* mean in the underlined sentence? What context clues to its meaning can you find in surrounding sentences? For example, the last sentence says there were more restrictions on women. Use this and other context clues to help you figure out the meaning of *status.*

Recognize Sequence Did nomadic people from Central Asia overrun Gupta India before or after the decline of the Maurya empire?

_____

_____

_____

Chandragupta Maurya founded the first Indian empire in 321 B.C. The Maurya empire's capital had schools, libraries, and palaces. The government built roads and harbors, collected taxes, and managed businesses. A secret police force reported on crime and **dissent,** or ideas opposed to those of the government.

Chandragupta's grandson, **Asoka,** continued to expand the empire. Asoka began ruling in 268 B.C. He became a Buddhist and ruled by moral example. He sent **missionaries** to spread Buddhism throughout Asia. To help his people, Asoka built hospitals and roads. However, the empire declined after his death and ended around 185 B.C.

Rival princes then held power for about 500 years. Each kingdom had its own government and capital. Dravidians in the Deccan spoke different languages and had different traditions from peoples of the Aryan north.

The Gupta dynasty united India from A.D. 320 to about 540. During this time, India enjoyed a period of great cultural achievement called a **golden age.** Prosperity contributed to a flowering of the arts and learning. Universities attracted students from many parts of Asia. Advances in mathematics included the system of numerals that we use today, the concept of zero, and the **decimal system.** Villages had more power than they had under the Mauryas. Eventually, nomadic people from Central Asia overran Gupta India.

For most Indians, everyday life revolved around the rules and duties associated with caste, family, and village. Villages produced most of the food and goods they needed. People regularly interacted with others from nearby villages while attending weddings, visiting relatives, or going to markets. Parents, children, and their offspring shared a common dwelling as a **joint family.** The father or oldest male served as head of the household. Children were trained to do the duties of their caste. Arranging good marriages was important and some families provided a **dowry,** or payment to the bridegroom. Women had had a higher status in early Aryan society than they did now. Over time, Hindu law placed greater restrictions on them.

Review Questions

1. How did Buddhism influence Asoka's rule?

_____

_____

2. What were some of the advances of the Gupta dynasty?

_____

_____

CHAPTER 3 SECTION 4

Note Taking Study Guide

RISE OF CIVILIZATION IN CHINA

Focus Question: What characteristics defined the civilization that developed in China under its early rulers?

As you read this section in your textbook, complete the following outline to sequence the important events in early China.

I. _____
   A. _____
      1. _____
      2. _____
      3. _____
      4. _____
   B. _____
      1. _____
      2. _____

II. _____
   A. _____
   B. _____
      1. _____
      2. _____

III. _____
   A. _____
   B. _____
   C. _____
      1. _____
      2. _____
   D. _____

IV. _____
   A. _____
   B. _____

(Outline continues on the next page.)

(Continued from page 31)

V. _____

   A. _____

   B. _____

   C. _____

VI. _____

   A. _____

   B. _____

   C. _____

     1. _____

     2. _____

   D. _____

CHAPTER 3 SECTION 4

Section Summary
RISE OF CIVILIZATION IN CHINA

The earliest civilization in China grew along the Huang River. This river carries **loess,** or fine windblown yellow soil, which raises the water level. People suffered from the river's frequent floods. The need to control the water likely led to the rise of government.

The Shang dynasty began about 1766 B.C. Kings ruled along with princes. The princes were probably the heads of **clans,** or groups of families claiming a common ancestor. Shang warriors used leather armor, bronze weapons, and horse-drawn chariots. <u>They may have learned of chariots as they interacted with other Asian peoples.</u>

The Zhou people overthrew the Shang in 1122 B.C. They promoted the Mandate of Heaven, or divine right to rule. This idea later expanded to explain the **dynastic cycle,** or rise and fall of dynasties. If rulers became corrupt, heaven would withdraw support and dynasties would fail. The Zhou established **feudalism,** where lords governed their own land but owed military service and support to a ruler. In the 600s B.C., iron tools made farming more productive and the population increased. The Zhou dynasty ended when fighting feudal lords could not be controlled.

During the Shang dynasty, the Chinese prayed to many gods and nature spirits. During the Zhou dynasty, two great thinkers emerged: **Confucius** and **Laozi.** Confucius developed a **philosophy,** or system of ideas, that greatly influenced Chinese civilization. Confucius was concerned with social order and good government. He emphasized five key relationships between people. **Filial piety,** or respect for parents, was everyone's highest duty.

Laozi founded Daoism about the same time. It emphasized that people should live in harmony with nature. They should look beyond everyday cares and focus on the Dao, or "the way."

One great achievement of early China was silk-making. The Chinese kept the technique a secret for many years. They also developed a system of writing at least 4,000 years ago. Questions were written on **oracle bones.** After heating the bones, priests interpreted the answers. Later, a writing system evolved that included thousands of **characters,** or written symbols. The Chinese then turned writing into an art called **calligraphy.**

Review Questions

1. What impact did iron tools have on China?

_____

_____

2. What was the focus of Confucius' teachings?

_____

_____

READING CHECK

What is the dynastic cycle?

_____

_____

_____

VOCABULARY STRATEGY

What does the word *interacted* mean in the underlined sentence? Break the word into parts. The prefix *inter-* means "between," "among," or "with." The word *act* means "to do something." Use these word-part clues to help you figure out the meaning of *interacted.*

READING SKILL

Recognize Sequence Did Confucianism emerge before or after 1122 B.C.?

_____

_____

_____

Note Taking Study Guide

STRONG RULERS UNITE CHINA

Focus Question: How did powerful emperors unite much of China and bring about a golden age of cultural achievement?

As you read this section in your textbook, complete the following chart to sequence the important events of the Qin and Han periods.

Event					
Date					

CHAPTER 3
SECTION 5

Section Summary

STRONG RULERS UNITE CHINA

The Qin Dynasty began in 221 B.C. when the leader of the Qin conquered the Zhou and proclaimed himself **Shi Huangdi,** or First Emperor. He centralized his power by adhering to Legalism, a philosophy that said that strength, not goodness, was a ruler's greatest virtue. He tortured and killed any who opposed his rule. Shi Huangdi replaced feudal states with military districts headed by loyal officials. To promote unity, he standardized weights and measures, coins, and Chinese writing. Under his orders, thousands of workers connected shorter walls to form the one Great Wall against invaders from the north.

The Han Dynasty began in 202 B.C. The most famous Han emperor, **Wudi,** ruled from 141 B.C. to 87 B.C. Instead of Legalism, Wudi made Confucianism the official belief system of the state. He improved transportation, controlled prices, and created a government **monopoly** on iron and salt. His policy of **expansionism** increased the land under Chinese rule. He also opened a network of trade routes, later called the Silk Road.

Han rulers chose Confucian scholars as government officials, or **civil servants.** Young men could advance in government through skill, rather than family influence. <u>They might be tested on their knowledge of the Five Classics, a collection of histories, poems, and handbooks compiled from the works of Confucius and others.</u>

The Han dynasty was a golden age for Chinese culture. Han scientists wrote texts on chemistry, zoology, and botany. The Han invented the seismograph, suspension bridge, rudder, and paper from wood pulp. Medical treatment included **acupuncture** to relieve pain or treat illness. Artisans created products from jade, ceramics, bronze, and silk. Poets and historians wrote about the grandeur of Han cities.

As the Han dynasty aged, emperors could no longer control **warlords,** or local military rulers. Peasants rebelled. The last emperor was overthrown in A.D. 220, after 400 years of Han rule.

Buddhism had spread from India to China by about A.D. 100. It became increasingly popular during the times of crisis that followed the fall of the Han, and by A.D. 400 it had spread throughout China.

Review Questions

1. How did Legalism influence the rule of Shi Huangdi?

_____

_____

2. How was the Han dynasty a golden age for China?

_____

_____

READING CHECK

Which emperor had the Great Wall built?

_____

_____

_____

VOCABULARY STRATEGY

What does the word *compiled* mean in the underlined sentence? Note that the Five Classics contain the works of several people. Use this context clue to help you figure out what *compiled* means.

READING SKILL

Recognize Sequence Sequence the following events:

Buddhism spreads throughout China; warlords overthrow the Han Dynasty; Shi Huangdi standardizes weights, measures, and coins

1. _____

_____

2. _____

_____

3. _____

Note Taking Study Guide
EARLY PEOPLE OF THE AEGEAN

Focus Question: How did the Minoans and Mycenaeans shape early Greek civilizations?

As you read the section in your textbook, complete the table below to record the main ideas about the Minoans, Mycenaeans, and Dorians.

Dorians	
•	• •

Mycenaeans	
• • • • • • •	

Minoans	
• • • • •	

Section Summary

EARLY PEOPLE OF THE AEGEAN

The island of Crete, located on the Aegean Sea, was home to a successful trading civilization known as the Minoan civilization. Minoan rulers lived in a vast palace at **Knossos.** This palace housed rooms for the royal family, banquet halls, and work areas for artisans. It also included religious **shrines,** areas dedicated to the honor of gods and goddesses. The walls were covered with colorful **frescoes**—watercolor paintings done on wet plaster. The frescoes revealed much about Minoan culture by illustrating scenes from daily life.

By about 1400 B.C, the Minoan civilization vanished. The reasons are unclear, but it is certain that invaders played some role in its destruction. These invaders were the Mycenaeans.

The Mycenaeans ruled the Aegean world from about 1400 B.C. to 1200 B.C. They were also sea traders whose civilization reached as far as Sicily, Italy, Egypt, and Mesopotamia. The Mycenaeans learned skills from the Minoans, such as writing. They also absorbed Egyptian and Mesopotamian customs, which they passed on to later Greeks.

The Mycenaeans are remembered for their part in the **Trojan War,** which began about 1250 B.C. The conflict may have started because of economic rivalry between Mycenae and Troy, a rich trading city that controlled the vital **straits,** or narrow water passages, connecting the Mediterranean and Black seas. According to Greek legend, the war erupted when the Mycenaeans, or Greeks, sailed to Troy to rescue the kidnapped wife of the king. The war lasted 10 years, until the Mycenaeans finally burned Troy to the ground.

Much of what we know about the Trojan War and life during this period comes from two epic poems, the *Iliad* and the *Odyssey.* These works are credited to the poet **Homer,** who probably lived about 750 B.C. The *Iliad* and the *Odyssey* reveal much about the values of the ancient Greeks. <u>The poems' heroes display honor, courage, and eloquence.</u>

In about 1100 B.C., invaders from the north known as the Dorians conquered the Mycenaeans. After the Dorian invasions, Greece passed several centuries in obscurity. Over time, a new Greek civilization emerged that would extend its influence across the Western world.

Review Questions

1. What was revealed by the frescoes found at Knossos?

_____

_____

2. What information about Greek culture can be found in Homer's epic poems?

_____

_____

READING CHECK

According to legend, why did the Trojan War begin?

_____

_____

_____

VOCABULARY STRATEGY

What does the word *eloquence* mean in the underlined sentence? The word *eloquence* comes from the Latin word *eloqui,* meaning "to speak out." Based on that information, what do you think *eloquence* means?

READING SKILL

Identify Main Ideas Explain how Mycenaean culture spread.

_____

_____

_____

CHAPTER 4
SECTION 2

Note Taking Study Guide

THE RISE OF GREEK CITY-STATES

Focus Question: How did government and culture develop as Greek city-states grew?

As you read this section in your textbook, complete the outline below to record the main ideas and supporting details in this section.

I. Geography Shapes Greece
  A. Landscape defines political boundaries
    1. _____
    2. _____
  B. Life by the sea
    1. _____
    2. _____
    3. _____
II. _____
  A. _____
    1. _____
    2. _____
    3. _____
  B. _____
    1. _____
    2. _____
    3. _____
  C. _____
    1. _____
    2. _____
    3. _____
    4. _____
III. _____
  A. _____
    1. _____
    2. _____
  B. _____
    1. _____

(Outline continues on the next page.)

(Continued from page 38)

2. _____
3. _____

IV. _____
  A. _____
    1. _____
    2. _____
    3. _____
    4. _____
  B. _____
    1. _____
    2. _____
    3. _____
    4. _____
    5. _____
  C. _____
    1. _____
    2. _____
  D. _____
    1. _____
    2. _____
  E. _____
    1. _____
    2. _____
    3. _____
  F. _____
    1. _____
    2. _____
    3. _____

CHAPTER 4 SECTION 2

Section Summary
THE RISE OF GREEK CITY-STATES

What is a tyrant?

_____

_____

_____

What does the word *imposing* mean in the underlined sentence? It comes from a Latin word that means "to put upon." Use this word-origins clue to help you figure out the meaning of *imposing*.

Identify Supporting Details
What details in the Summary support the main idea that geography had a role in the development of Greece?

_____

_____

_____

Greek city-states were isolated from one another by mountains or water. The seas, however, provided a vital link to the outside world. The Greeks became skilled sailors and traders. As they traveled, they acquired new ideas from foreign lands, which they adapted to their own needs.

As their world expanded, the Greeks evolved a unique version of the city-state, called the **polis.** The polis consisted of a major city or town and its surrounding countryside. The **acropolis,** or high city, with its many temples, stood on a hill. Because the population was small for each city-state, the **citizens** felt a shared sense of responsibility for the triumphs and failures of their polis.

Different forms of government evolved in Greece. At first, there was a **monarchy.** In a monarchy, a hereditary ruler exercises central power. In time, the power shifted to an **aristocracy**—or rule by the landholding elite. As trade expanded and a wealthy middle class emerged, the result was a form of government called an **oligarchy**—where power is in the hands of a small, wealthy elite.

A new method of fighting also emerged. The **phalanx** was a massive tactical formation of heavily armed foot soldiers. In the city-state of **Sparta,** Spartans focused on developing strong military skills, paying less attention to trade, wealth, new ideas, or the arts.

In **Athens,** government evolved from a monarchy into an aristocracy. Under the aristocracy, discontent spread among ordinary citizens. Slowly Athens moved toward **democracy,** or government by the people. Despite government reforms under the leadership of Solon in around 594 B.C., there was still unrest. This led to the rise of **tyrants,** or those who gained power by force. <u>They often won support from the merchant class and the poor by imposing reforms to help these groups.</u> In 507 B.C., the reformer Cleisthenes broadened the role of ordinary citizens in government and made the assembly a genuine **legislature,** or lawmaking body.

Despite divisions among city-states, Greeks shared a common culture. They spoke the same language, honored the same ancient heroes, participated in common festivals, and prayed to the same gods.

Review Questions

1. What different forms of governments evolved in ancient Greece?

_____

_____

2. What reforms did Cleisthenes make?

_____

_____

CHAPTER 4

SECTION 3

Note Taking Study Guide

CONFLICT IN THE GREEK WORLD

Focus Question: How did war with invaders and conflict among Greeks affect the city-states?

As you read the section in your textbook, complete the table below to record some of the supporting details for the main ideas discussed in the section.

Peloponnesian War	• Greeks outside Athens resent Athenian domination.
Athenian Democracy	
Persian Wars	• Athens is victorious at Marathon.

CHAPTER 4 SECTION 3

Section Summary

CONFLICT IN THE GREEK WORLD

READING CHECK

How did Pericles encourage citizens to participate in government?

_____

_____

_____

After 522 B.C., the Persians extended their empire to include the Greek city-states of Ionia in Asia Minor. Although under Persian rule, these Ionian city-states were largely self-governing, they resented Persian control. In 499 B.C., Athens sent ships to help these city-states fight the Persians. This decision led to the Persian Wars.

Eventually, the Greeks were victorious against the Persians. This victory increased the Greeks' sense of uniqueness. Athens emerged from the wars as the most powerful city-state in Greece. Athens formed an alliance, called the Delian League, with other Greek city-states. An **alliance** is a formal agreement to cooperate between two or more nations or powers.

After the Persian Wars ended, a golden age began in Athens under the leadership of **Pericles.** Because of his wisdom and skill, the economy thrived and the government became more democratic. Periclean Athens was a **direct democracy.** Under this system, citizens take part directly in the daily affairs of government. Pericles believed that citizens from all social classes should participate in government. Therefore, Athens began to pay a **stipend,** or fixed salary, to men who served in the Assembly and its Council.

VOCABULARY STRATEGY

What does the word *uniqueness* mean in the underlined sentence? The root, *unique,* comes from the Latin word *unus* meaning "one." Use this word-root clue and any prior knowledge you might have about the word *unique* to help you figure out the meaning of *uniqueness.*

In addition, Athenians served on juries. A **jury** is a panel of citizens who make the final judgment in a trial. Athenian citizens could also vote to banish a public figure they believed was a threat to their democracy. This was called **ostracism.**

Athens prospered during the Age of Pericles. Pericles' efforts helped turn Athens into the cultural center of Greece. The arts were encouraged through public festivals, dramatic competitions, and building programs. Building projects increased Athens' prosperity by creating jobs for artisans and workers.

Many Greeks outside Athens resented Athenian domination. Soon, the Greek world was divided by new rivalries. In 431 B.C., warfare broke out between Athens and Sparta. This conflict, known as the Peloponnesian War, soon engulfed all of Greece. Sparta defeated Athens with the help of Persia. The defeat ended Athenian domination of the Greek world. However, the Athenian economy revived and Athens later regained its place as the cultural center of Greece.

READING SKILL

Identify Supporting Details
How did victory in the Persian Wars strengthen Athens?

_____

_____

Review Questions

1. How did action by Athens bring about the Persian Wars?

_____

_____

2. What is direct democracy?

_____

_____

Note Taking Study Guide

CHAPTER 4 SECTION 4

THE GLORY THAT WAS GREECE

Focus Question: How did Greek thinkers, artists, and writers explore the nature of the universe and people's place in it?

As you read this section in your textbook, complete the concept web below to record the supporting details about Greek achievements discussed in the section.

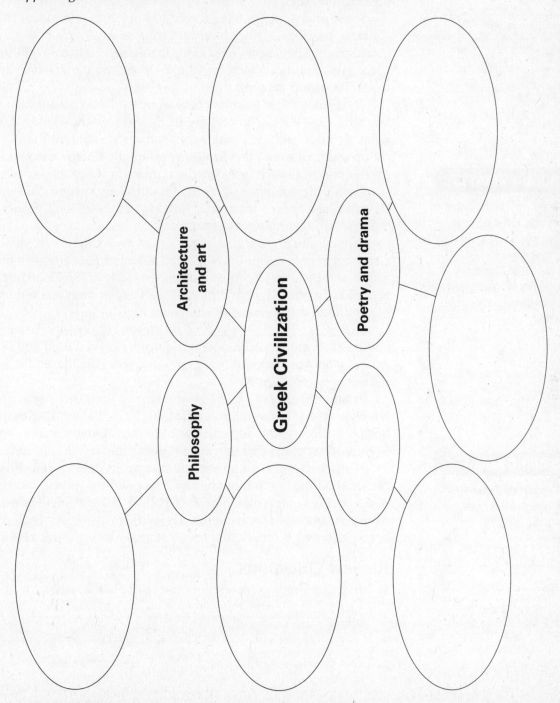

CHAPTER 4 SECTION 4

Section Summary

THE GLORY THAT WAS GREECE

READING CHECK

Who was Herodotus?

_____

_____

_____

Greek thinkers used observation and reason to explain events. These thinkers were called **philosophers,** meaning "lovers of wisdom." Philosophers explored many subjects, from mathematics and music, to **logic,** or rational thinking. They believed that through reason and observation, they could discover laws that governed the universe.

Some philosophers were interested in ethics and morality. In contrast, the Sophists believed that success was more important than moral truth. They developed skills in **rhetoric,** the art of skillful speaking. Ambitious men could use clever and persuasive rhetoric to advance their careers.

The philosopher **Socrates** was an outspoken critic of the Sophists. He believed in seeking truth and self-knowledge. Most of what we know about Socrates comes from his student **Plato.** Plato set up a school called the Academy where he taught his own ideas. Like Socrates, Plato emphasized the importance of reason.

Plato's most famous student, **Aristotle,** also promoted reason as the guiding force for learning. He set up a school, the Lyceum, for the study of all branches of knowledge.

While Plato argued that every object on Earth has an ideal form, Greek artists and architects reflected a similar concern with balance, order, and beauty. The most famous example of Greek architecture is the **Parthenon.** The basic plan of the Parthenon is a simple rectangle, with tall columns supporting a gently sloping roof.

<u>Early Greek sculptors carved figures in rigid poses.</u> Later, they emphasized more natural forms. Sculptors carved their subjects in a way that showed human beings in what was considered their most perfect, graceful form.

In literature, the Greeks also developed their own style. Some Greek playwrights wrote **tragedies**, or plays that tell stories of human suffering, usually ending in disaster. Others wrote **comedies,** or humorous plays that mock customs or that criticize society.

History was also an important study for Greeks. **Herodotus,** often called the "Father of History," stressed the importance of research. He visited many lands to collect and chronicle information from witnesses of actual events. Thucydides also recorded events as he experienced them. Both men set standards for future historians.

VOCABULARY STRATEGY

Find the word *rigid* in the under-lined sentence. What context clues to the word's meaning can you find in the surrounding words or phrases? Circle any context clues in the paragraph that help you figure out what *rigid* means.

READING SKILL

Identify Supporting Details How were the views of Socrates different from those of the Sophists?

_____

_____

_____

Review Questions

1. What did Greek philosophers use to explain events?

_____

_____

2. What two forms of drama did the Greeks develop?

_____

_____

Note Taking Study Guide

ALEXANDER AND THE HELLENISTIC AGE

Focus Question: How did Alexander the Great expand his empire and spread Greek culture throughout the realm?

As you read this section in your textbook, complete the outline below to record the main ideas and supporting details about the empire of Alexander the Great.

I. **The Empire of Alexander the Great**

  A. Philip II conquers Greece

    1. _____

    2. _____

    3. _____

    4. _____

  B. Alexander takes Persia

    1. _____

    2. _____

    3. _____

  C. _____

    1. _____

    2. _____

    3. _____

  D. _____

    1. _____

    2. _____

II. _____

  A. _____

    1. _____

    2. _____

    3. _____

    4. _____

    5. _____

    6. _____

    7. _____

(Outline continues on the next page.)

CHAPTER 4 · SECTION 5

Note Taking Study Guide

ALEXANDER AND THE HELLENISTIC AGE

(Continued from page 45)

B. _____
  1. _____
  2. _____
  3. _____
C. _____
  1. _____
  2. _____
  3. _____
III. _____
  A. _____
    1. _____
    2. _____
  B. _____
    1. _____
    2. _____
    3. _____
    4. _____

Section Summary
ALEXANDER AND THE HELLENISTIC AGE

Soon after Macedonian king **Philip II** gained the throne in 359 B.C., he built a powerful army and eventually brought all of Greece under his control. Philip's next goal was to conquer the Persian empire. However, he was assassinated before he could. **Assassination** is the murder of a public figure, usually for political reasons.

After Philips's death, his son, who came to be known as **Alexander the Great,** acquired the throne and began organizing forces to conquer Persia. Alexander was victorious. Once much of the Persian empire fell under his control, he advanced into India.

Unexpectedly in 323 B.C., Alexander died at the age of 33 in Persia from a fever. Although his empire collapsed soon after, he is credited with spreading Greek culture from Egypt to the borders of India. Local people **assimilated,** or absorbed, Greek ideas. In turn, Greek settlers adopted local customs. Gradually, a new Hellenistic culture emerged that blended Greek, Persian, Egyptian, and Indian influences.

At the very heart of the Hellenistic world stood the magnificent city of **Alexandria,** founded in Egypt by Alexander. Its great library was among the greatest scientific and cultural centers of the age. Like Alexandria, cities of the Hellenistic world employed many architects and artists. Temples, palaces, and other public buildings were larger and grander than the buildings of classical Greece. <u>The elaborate new style reflected the desire of Hellenistic rulers to glorify themselves as godlike.</u>

During the Hellenistic age, scholars built on earlier Greek, Babylonian, and Egyptian knowledge. In mathematics, **Pythagoras** derived a formula to calculate the relationship between the sides of a right triangle. The astronomer Aristarchus developed the theory of a **heliocentric,** or sun-centered, solar system. Another scientist, **Archimedes,** applied the principles of physics to make practical inventions. In the field of medicine, the Greek physician **Hippocrates** studied the causes of illnesses and looked for cures.

Greek works in the arts and sciences set a standard for later Europeans. Greek ideas about law, freedom, justice, and government continue to influence political thinking today.

Review Questions

1. How was Alexandria typical of a Hellenistic city?

_____

_____

2. On what was Hellenistic scholarship based?

_____

_____

READING CHECK

What kept Philip II from trying to conquer Persia?

_____

_____

_____

VOCABULARY STRATEGY

What does the word *elaborate* mean in the underlined sentence? Look for context clues in the underlined sentence. Use the context clues in the surrounding words and phrases to figure out the meaning of *elaborate.*

READING SKILL

Identify Supporting Details
How did Alexander the Great's conquests help create a new Hellenistic culture?

_____

_____

_____

Note Taking Study Guide
THE ROMAN WORLD TAKES SHAPE

Focus Question: What values formed the basis of Roman society and government?

As you read this section, complete the flowchart below to identify causes and effects of important events during the Roman republic.

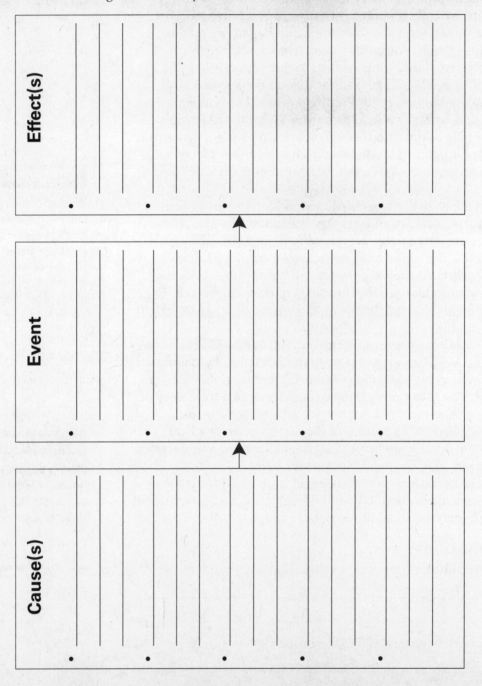

CHAPTER 5 SECTION 1

Section Summary

THE ROMAN WORLD TAKES SHAPE

Rome's location on the Italian peninsula, centrally located in the Mediterranean Sea, benefited the Romans as they expanded. In addition, Italy had wide, fertile plains, which supported a growing population. Rome began on seven hills near the Tiber River.

Romans shared the Italian peninsula with Greek colonists and the **Etruscans**—a people who ruled most of central Italy for a time. The Romans learned from the Etruscans, studying their engineering techniques and adapting their alphabet.

In 509 B.C., the Romans drove out the Etruscans and founded the state of Rome. They put in place a new form of government called a **republic.** To keep any individual from obtaining too much power, the republic was run by officials who represented the people. The most powerful governing body was the senate. Its 300 members were all **patricians,** or members of the landholding upper class. Each year, the senators nominated two **consuls** from the patrician class to supervise the administration and command the armies. Also, in the event of war, the senate might choose a temporary **dictator,** or ruler with complete control over the government.

Initially, all government officials were patricians. **Plebeians,** or common people, had little influence. However, the plebeians fought for the right to elect their own officials, called **tribunes.** The tribunes could **veto,** or block, laws that they felt harmed the plebeians. <u>Although the senate still dominated the government, the plebeians had gained access to power and their rights were protected.</u>

The family was the basic unit of Roman society. Although women could own property and, in later Roman times, run businesses, men had absolute power over the family. Romans also believed in education for all children. Religion, too, was a significant part of Roman society.

By 270 B.C., Rome controlled most of the Italian peninsula. This was due mainly to a well-trained army. The basic military unit was the **legion.** Each legion included about 5,000 citizen-soldiers. As Rome occupied new territories, they treated their defeated enemies well. As long as conquered peoples accepted Roman rule and obeyed certain laws, the Romans allowed them to maintain their own customs and governments.

Review Questions

1. What governing body in the republic had the greatest power?

_____

_____

2. What were the consuls' responsibilities?

_____

_____

READING CHECK

What were the two main social classes in the Roman republic?

_____

_____

_____

VOCABULARY STRATEGY

What does the word *dominated* mean in the underlined sentence? The word *dominate* originates from the Latin word *dominus* which means "master." Use this word-origins clue to help you figure out the meaning of *dominated*.

READING SKILL

Identify Causes and Effects
What was the cause and what was the effect of the establishment of the office of tribune?

_____

_____

_____

CHAPTER 5 SECTION 2

Note Taking Study Guide

FROM REPUBLIC TO EMPIRE

Focus Question: What factors led to the decline of the Roman republic and the rise of the Roman empire?

As you read this section, complete the flowcharts below to help you recognize the causes that led to the decline of the Roman republic and the rise of the Roman empire.

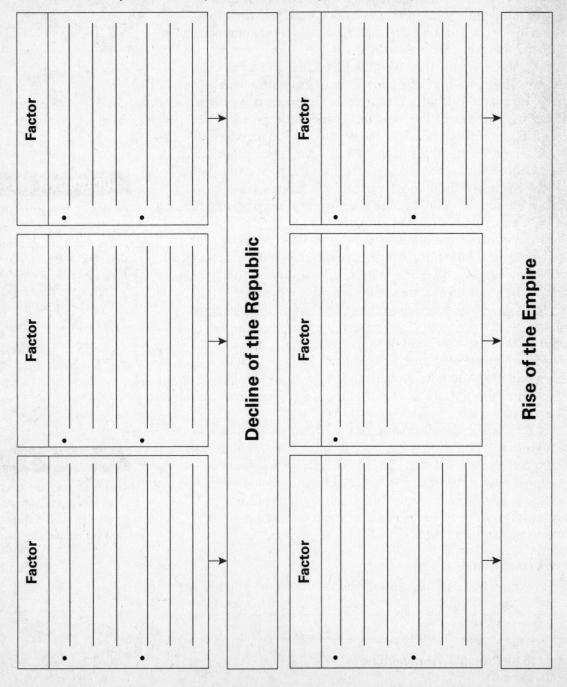

CHAPTER 5 SECTION 2

Section Summary

FROM REPUBLIC TO EMPIRE

As Rome extended its territory, it encountered Carthage, an empire that stretched across North Africa and the western Mediterranean. These two powers battled in three wars. These Punic Wars lasted from 264 B.C. to 146 B.C., when Rome finally destroyed Carthage.

Rome was committed to a policy of **imperialism**—establishing control over foreign lands. Roman power soon spread from Spain to Egypt. Rome soon controlled busy trade routes that brought tremendous riches. Wealthy families purchased large estates, called **latifundia,** and forced war captives to work as their slaves. The gap between rich and poor grew, leading to corruption and riots.

Rome was in need of social and political reform. Young patrician tribunes **Tiberius** and **Gaius Gracchus** were among the first to attempt it. However, the senate felt threatened by their reforms, and in a series of riots, the two brothers and their followers were killed. This power struggle led to a period of civil war.

Out of the chaos emerged **Julius Caesar,** a brilliant military commander. With Caesar's rising fame, a rivalry erupted between him and another general, Pompey. <u>Caesar eventually defeated Pompey and his soldiers and swept around the Mediterranean, suppressing rebellions.</u> Victorious, Caesar returned to Rome and forced the senate to make him dictator for life.

Caesar pushed through a number of reforms to help solve Rome's many problems. Fearing that Caesar would make himself king, however, his enemies killed him in 44 B.C. His friend, Marc Antony, and his nephew, Octavian, joined forces to avenge Caesar. However, they soon battled one another for power, and Octavian defeated Antony.

With this triumph, the senate gave Octavian the title of **Augustus,** or "Exalted One." He was the first emperor of Rome and ruled from 27 B.C. TO A.D. 14. Augustus built a stable government for the empire. He also undertook economic reforms. To make the tax system fair, he ordered a **census,** or population count, of the empire. Another influential Roman emperor was **Hadrian.** He codified Roman law, making it the same for all provinces.

During the *Pax Romana,* Roman rule brought peace, prosperity, and order to the lands it controlled. Spectacular entertainments were popular across the empire. However, social and economic problems hid beneath the general prosperity.

Review Questions

1. Who was Julius Caesar?

_____

_____

2. Who was Octavian?

_____

_____

READING CHECK

What did Tiberius and Gaius Gracchus attempt in Rome?

_____

_____

_____

VOCABULARY STRATEGY

What does the word *suppressing* mean in the underlined sentence? The word *suppress* comes from a Latin word that means "to press under." Use this word-origins clue to help you figure out the meaning of *suppressing.*

READING SKILL

Recognize Multiple Causes How did Augustus come to power?

_____

_____

_____

CHAPTER 5 SECTION 3

Note Taking Study Guide
THE ROMAN ACHIEVEMENT

Focus Question: How did advances in the arts, learning, and the law show the Romans' high regard for cultural and political achievements?

As you read this section in your textbook, complete the concept web below to list developments that show effects of Rome's cultural and political achievements.

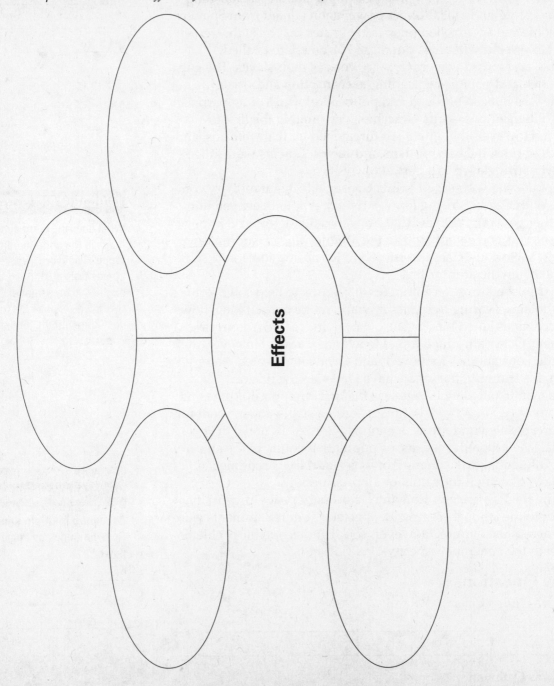

Effects

CHAPTER 5 SECTION 3

Section Summary

THE ROMAN ACHIEVEMENT

Greek art, literature, philosophy, and scientific developments made a significant impact on Rome. Still, the greatest Roman authors wrote in Latin. In his epic poem the *Aeneid,* the Roman poet **Virgil** tried to show that Rome was as heroic as Greece. Others used poetry to **satirize,** or make fun of, Roman society. Roman historians pursued their own theme, recalling Rome's triumphant past in an attempt to renew patriotism. In philosophy, Roman thinkers were impressed with the Hellenistic philosophy of Stoicism.

Like their Greek predecessors, Roman sculptors realistically portrayed their subjects, focusing on every detail. However, the Romans distinguished themselves by also focusing on individual character. Art, too, was an important aspect of Roman culture. Artists depicted scenes from Roman literature and daily life in frescoes and **mosaics**—pictures made from chips of colored stone or glass.

Another distinction that set the Romans apart from the Greeks was their architecture. Unlike the Greeks, the Romans emphasized grandeur. They built immense palaces, temples, and stadiums, which stood as impressive monuments to Roman power. The Romans also improved structures such as columns and arches. Utilizing concrete as a building material, they developed the arched dome as a roof for large spaces.

In addition, the Romans excelled in **engineering,** which is the application of science and mathematics to develop useful structures and machines. Roman engineers built roads, bridges, and harbors throughout the empire. They built many **aqueducts,** or bridge-like stone structures that carried water from the hills into Roman cities.

In general, the Romans entrusted the Greeks, who were by that time citizens of the empire, with scientific research. **Ptolemy,** the astronomer-mathematician, proposed his theory that Earth was at the center of the universe. This mistaken idea was accepted in the Western world for nearly 1,500 years.

Rome was committed to regulating laws and to serving justice. To protect the empire and its citizens, Rome developed the civil law. As Rome expanded, the law of nations was established. This law was applied to both citizens and non-citizens of Rome. When Rome extended citizenship across the empire, the two systems merged.

Review Questions

1. What did Virgil wish to accomplish with his poem the *Aeneid?*

_____

_____

2. What theory did Ptolemy propose?

_____

_____

READING CHECK

How were Greek and Roman architecture different?

_____

_____

_____

VOCABULARY STRATEGY

What does the word *utilizing* mean in the underlined sentence? Use any prior knowledge you might have about the word and a related word, *utility,* to figure out the meaning of *utilizing.*

READING SKILL

Understand Effects What effects did Greek culture have on Roman culture?

_____

_____

_____

Name_____ Class_____ Date_____

Focus question: How did Christianity emerge and then spread to become the official religion of the Roman empire?

As you read this section in your textbook, complete the table below to show the factors that caused the rise of Christianity and its establishment as the official religion of the Roman empire.

Causes	Effects
• _____ _____ • _____ _____ • _____ _____ • _____ _____ • _____ _____ • _____ _____ • _____ _____ • _____ _____ • _____ _____ • _____ _____ • _____ _____	• Rise of Christianity • Establishment of Christianity as empire's official religion

CHAPTER 5 SECTION 4

Section Summary
THE RISE OF CHRISTIANITY

Within the Roman empire, there were various religious beliefs. Rome tolerated these different religions, as long as citizens honored Roman gods, too—including the emperor. Because most people were polytheistic, meaning they believed in more than one god, for a long time this was not a problem.

Later, the followers of Judaism became divided about living under Roman rule. Many began to follow a Jewish man named Jesus. They believed Jesus was the **messiah,** or anointed king sent by God. Jesus chose 12 **apostles,** meaning "persons sent forth," to help him preach his message.

While Jesus' teachings were rooted in Jewish tradition, he also preached new, Christian beliefs. Jesus taught the need for justice, morality, forgiveness, and service to others. After Jesus was put to death, the missionary **Paul** did much to spread Christianity. The message was helped by the *Pax Romana* and the ease of travel on Roman roads. Paul said that those who believed Jesus was the son of God and complied with his teachings would achieve salvation.

Because they did not obey certain Roman practices, many Christians were persecuted. They became known as **martyrs,** or people who suffer or die for their beliefs. Still, Christianity continued to spread. Many found comfort in Jesus' message of love and promise of salvation. Finally, the emperor **Constantine** issued the Edict of Milan in A.D. 313. This granted freedom of worship to all Roman citizens. By the end of that century, Christianity was the official religion of the empire.

Each Christian community and its **clergy**—those who conduct religious services—were grouped together in a diocese. Every community had its own priest. All the priests in a diocese were supervised by a **bishop,** a high Church official. Eventually, bishops from five important cities gained more authority and held the honorary title of **patriarch.**

However, as the Church became more structured, differences arose from within. The bishops of Rome came to be called **popes,** and claimed authority over all other bishops. There was also an emergence of **heresies,** or beliefs said to be contrary to official Church teachings. Important teachers helped to define Christian theology. One of these was **Augustine,** from Hippo in North Africa.

Review Questions

1. Why is the missionary Paul an important figure in Christianity?

_____

_____

2. What did the Edict of Milan accomplish?

_____

_____

READING CHECK

What is a diocese?

_____

_____

_____

VOCABULARY STRATEGY

What does the word *complied* mean in the underlined sentence? The word *disobeyed* is an antonym of *complied.* Use the information about this antonym to figure out the meaning of *complied.*

READING SKILL

Understand Effects How did Christianity spread?

_____

_____

_____

Name_____ Class_____ Date_____

Focus Question: How did military, political, social, and economic factors combine to cause the fall of the western Roman empire?

As you read this section in your textbook, complete the chart below to list the causes of the fall of the western Roman empire.

Causes of the Fall of the Western Roman Empire				
Economic	**Political**	**Social**	**Military**
•	•	•	•
•	•	•	•
•	•	•	•
•	•		•

CHAPTER 5 — SECTION 5

Section Summary
THE LONG DECLINE

In about the A.D. 200s, the Roman empire began to weaken. The golden age of the *Pax Romana* had ended. Rome suffered political and economic turmoil and a decline in the traditional values that had been the empire's foundation.

The oppressive government and corrupt upper class generated hostility among the lower classes. High taxes to support the army and government burdened business people and local farmers. Over and over, emperors were assassinated or overthrown by ambitious generals eager for power. Political violence and instability dominated Rome.

In 284, the emperor **Diocletian** set out to restore order. He divided the empire into two parts. He appointed a co-emperor, Maximian, to rule the western provinces, and he controlled the eastern part. To help strengthen the weak economy, Diocletian slowed **inflation,** or a rapid rise of prices, by establishing fixed prices for many goods and services.

When the emperor Constantine came into power, he continued Diocletian's reforms. In addition, he granted toleration to Christians and moved the empire's capital to **Constantinople,** making the eastern empire the center of power.

While these reforms helped improve the situation in the empire, they failed to stop the long-term decline. Nomadic people from Asia, called **Huns,** were forcing Germanic peoples into Roman territory. Fierce battles ensued. By 410, Rome itself was under attack. By then, the empire had surrendered much of its territories to invaders. Roman power was fading.

There were several reasons for Rome's decline, but the primary reason was the many invasions. Rome's legions were not as strong nor as loyal as they had been. To get more soldiers, Rome hired **mercenaries,** or foreign soldiers serving for pay, to defend its borders. Many were Germanic warriors who did not feel loyalty toward Rome. As Roman citizens were suffering the consequences of a declining empire, patriotism diminished. <u>The upper class, which had once provided leaders, now devoted itself only to luxury and the pursuit of prestige.</u> The Roman empire finally "fell" in 476, when Germanic invaders captured Rome and ousted the emperor. The power of Rome had ended.

Review Questions

1. How did Diocletian help slow inflation?

_____

_____

2. How did the Huns contribute to the fall of Rome?

_____

_____

READING CHECK

How did Diocletian attempt to restore order in the Roman empire?

_____

_____

_____

VOCABULARY STRATEGY

What does the word *prestige* mean in the underlined sentence? Apply your prior knowledge of the word *prestige* and a related word, *prestigious,* to figure out what *prestige* means.

READING SKILL

Recognize Multiple Causes
What are three main reasons for Rome's decline?

_____

_____

_____

Name_____ Class_____ Date_____

Note Taking Study Guide
CIVILIZATIONS OF MESOAMERICA

Focus Question: What factors encouraged the rise of powerful civilizations in Mesoamerica?

A. *As you read "People Settle in the Americas," complete the following chart to record the similarities and differences in how early people adapted to climate and geography in different parts of the Americas.*

Adapting to the Americas	
Climate	**Geography**
• _____ _____ • _____ _____ • _____	• _____ • _____ _____ • _____ • _____

B. *As you read this section in your textbook, complete the following Venn diagram in order to recognize the similarities and differences among the cultures of Mesoamerica.*

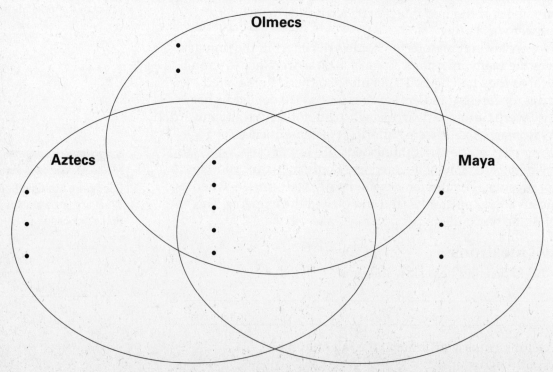

Section Summary
CIVILIZATIONS OF MESOAMERICA

People first came to the Americas from Asia between 60,000 B.C. and 18,000 B.C. They may have walked across a land bridge or come by boat. In **Mesoamerica,** a cultural region including Mexico and Central America, people grew **maize** and other crops. They raised animals and settled into villages by about 1500 B.C. As populations grew, some of the villages developed into the early, great cities of the Americas.

The earliest American civilization, that of the **Olmecs,** developed along the Gulf Coast of Mexico. That civilization lasted from about 1500 B.C. to 400 B.C. A class of priests and nobles led it. Later Mesoamerican peoples, including the Maya and Aztecs, adopted elements of Olmec culture, such as carved stone, hieroglyphs, and the calendar.

Around 300 B.C., the Maya were building large cities in present-day Guatemala. By the time the Mayan golden age began, about A.D. 250, Mayan civilization included large, independent city-states throughout southern Mexico and Central America. The Maya were not united politically as an empire. Instead, cities maintained contact through trade and, sometimes, warfare. Mayan cities included temples, palaces, and **stelae,** which were tall stone monuments decorated with carvings. Scribes carved each stela with historical information, such as the names of rulers and dates. They also wrote about astronomy and religion in books made of bark paper. However, around A.D. 900, the Maya abandoned most of their cities, possibly because of frequent warfare or over-farming.

Aztec civilization began in the **Valley of Mexico.** The Aztecs founded **Tenochtitlán,** their capital city, in A.D. 1325. <u>Because it was located on an island in a lake, they found ingenious ways to create more farmland.</u> They built **chinampas,** which were artificial islands made from mud and reeds.

Unlike the Maya, the Aztecs built an empire. They also fought wars continuously. War brought wealth and power. As their empire grew, the Aztecs used **tribute,** or payment from conquered peoples, to make Tenochtitlán magnificent. They also sacrificed war prisoners to the sun god. Among the gods they worshipped were powerful gods from an earlier culture centered at the city of **Teotihuacán.** Although the city fell, its culture influenced later peoples of Mesoamerica.

Review Questions

1. How were Mayan city-states connected?

_____

_____

2. How did the Aztecs benefit from war?

_____

_____

READING CHECK

Where was the Aztec capital of Tenochtitlán?

_____

_____

_____

VOCABULARY STRATEGY

What does the word *ingenious* mean in the underlined sentence? It comes from a Latin word meaning "natural talent." Use this word-origins clue to help you figure out the meaning of *ingenious.*

READING SKILL

Compare and Contrast Compare and contrast the culture of the Maya with the culture of the Aztecs, including their types of governments and achievements.

_____

_____

_____

Name_____ Class_____ Date_____

Focus Question: What characterized the cultures and civilizations that developed in the Andes?

As you read this section in your textbook, complete the following chart to contrast the cultures of the early peoples of the Andes with the Inca. Use the chart to organize relevant details.

		• • • • • • • •
		• •
Chavín		• • •
Location	**Unique Achievements**	• • •

Section Summary
ANDEAN CULTURES OF SOUTH AMERICA

The first cultures of South America developed in the Andean region. The earliest was the **Chavín** culture, named for the ruins at Chavín de Huantar in Peru. Around 900 B.C., the people built a huge temple complex. Chavín's arts and religion influenced later peoples of Peru. Later, between A.D. 100 and 700, the **Moche** people lived along the north coast of Peru. They improved farming techniques, built roads, and used relay runners to carry messages. They also used **adobe** to build the largest adobe structure in the Americas. Skilled artisans worked in textiles, gold, woodcarving, and ceramics.

The **Nazca** people lived between 500 B.C. and A.D. 500. They are known for the geoglyphs they etched in the desert of southern Peru. East of the Nazca, the city of **Huari** controlled mountains and coastal areas in Peru. To the south, **Tiahuanaco** became a powerful city on Lake Titicaca. The two cities may have been connected through trade or religion because their artistic styles are similar.

The most powerful of the Andean peoples were the Inca. Their civilization began in the 1100s, but greatly expanded its power after 1438. That is when **Pachacuti Inca Yupanqui,** a skilled warrior and leader, declared himself **Sapa Inca,** or emperor. Eventually, the Inca empire controlled 2,500 miles along the Andes, from Ecuador to Chile. The Inca built a network of roads of about 14,000 miles, winding through deserts and over mountains. The roads allowed news and armies to travel quickly throughout the empire. All roads led through the capital **Cuzco.** Various culture groups from all over the empire lived in this city.

The emperor had absolute power and was also the religious leader. Inca rulers ran an efficient government. Nobles ruled provinces, and local officials handled everyday business. Officials kept records on colored, knotted strings called **quipu.** Everyone had to speak the Inca language and follow the Inca religion. Each village, or **ayllu,** had a leader who assigned jobs and organized work for the government. Farmers created terraces to farm the steep hillsides. They spent part of the year farming for their village and part working land for the emperor.

The Inca worshipped many gods, but the chief god was **Inti,** the sun god. Religious festivals occurred each month to celebrate the forces of nature that were important to the Inca.

Review Questions

1. Which group was the most powerful Andean civilization?

_____

_____

2. What was the responsibility of the village leader?

_____

_____

READING CHECK

What three peoples lived in South America before the Inca?

_____

_____

_____

VOCABULARY STRATEGY

What does the word *network* mean in the underlined sentence? *Network* is a compound word. Use the meanings of the two words that make up *network* to help you figure out its meaning.

READING SKILL

Contrast How did the Inca civilization change after 1438?

_____

_____

_____

Note Taking Study Guide
PEOPLES OF NORTH AMERICA

Focus Question: What factors contributed to the growth of diverse cultures in North America?

As you read this section in your textbook, complete the following outline to help you compare and contrast details about various culture areas.

I. **Southwest**
   A. Environment—Desert
   B. Settlement Type
      1. _____
      2. _____

II. **East**
   A. _____
   B. _____
      1. _____
      2. _____
      3. _____

III. _____
   A. _____
      1. _____
      2. _____
      3. _____
   B. _____
      1. _____
      2. _____
      3. _____
   C. _____
      1. _____
      2. _____
      3. _____

CHAPTER 6 SECTION 3
Section Summary
PEOPLES OF NORTH AMERICA

Before A.D. 1500, there were many Native American culture groups in North America. Scholars have organized early people of North America into culture areas based on where they lived. This section covers the following culture areas: Southwest, Southeast, Arctic, Northwest Coast, and Northeast.

In the deserts of the Southwest, around 300 B.C., the Hohokam built canals to carry river water to crops. Between A.D. 1150 and A.D 1300, the Anasazi built homes on cliffs. The largest of these housing complexes, at **Mesa Verde** in present-day Colorado, had more than 200 rooms. The cliffs offered protection from enemies. The Anasazi also built villages on the ground, which they modeled after the cliff dwellings. The Spanish called these villages **pueblos. Pueblo Bonito** was the largest. It still stands in New Mexico. This huge complex was five stories high and had over 800 rooms. In the center was the **kiva**, a round, underground room used for religious ceremonies and meetings.

The Adena and Hopewell of the Northeast farmed in the Ohio and Mississippi river valleys. They built **earthworks,** which were large piles of earth shaped into burial mounds, bases for structures, and defensive walls. By A.D. 800, these cultures had disappeared. A new people of the Southeast, the Mississippians, began to build large towns and ceremonial centers. They also built mounds. The homes of rulers and nobles sat on top of the mounds. By about 1100 A.D., their great city of **Cahokia,** in present-day Illinois, had 20,000 people.

The Inuit adapted to the harsh Arctic climate in about 2000 B.C. They used seals and other animals for food, clothing, tools, and cooking. They built homes from snow and ice and used dogs to pull sleds that carried goods across the ice.

The Northwest Coast provided Native Americans there with plentiful fish and game, and trees for building permanent homes. Wealth gained from trading surplus goods was shared in **potlatch** ceremonies. In this ceremony, a high-ranking person gave gifts to a large number of guests.

Many Native American groups of the Northeast were known as the Iroquois. To stop constant warfare, they formed the **Iroquois League.** This was an alliance of five Iroquois groups, known as the Five Nations.

Review Questions

1. How were the Hohokam able to grow crops in the desert?

_____

_____

2. How did the Inuit adapt to their environment?

_____

_____

READING CHECK

Which Native American culture group built the city of Cahokia?

_____

_____

_____

VOCABULARY STRATEGY

What does the word *complexes* mean in the underlined sentence? Read ahead for context clues. Use these context clues to help you figure out the meaning of *complexes*.

READING SKILL

Compare and Contrast How were the Hopewell and Mississippian cultures similar? How were they different?

_____

_____

_____

CHAPTER 7 SECTION 1 — Note Taking Study Guide
THE EARLY MIDDLE AGES

Focus Question: How did Germanic tribes divide Western Europe into small kingdoms?

A. *As you read this section in your textbook, use the table below to identify main ideas for each red heading.*

Early Medieval Europe	
Heading	**Main Idea**
Western Europe in Decline	
The Rise of the Germanic Kingdoms	
The Age of Charlemagne	
Europe After Charlemagne	

B. *As you read "The Age of Charlemagne," use the table below to identify main ideas about Charlemagne's rule.*

The Age of Charlemagne	
Heading	**Main Idea**
A New Emperor of the Romans	
Creating a Unified Christian Empire	
A Revival of Learning	

CHAPTER 7
SECTION 1

Section Summary
THE EARLY MIDDLE AGES

After the Roman empire fell, Western Europe was cut off from advanced cultures in Asia, overrun by invaders, and divided. The period from 500 to 1000 is sometimes called the Dark Ages. However, it was a time when Greco-Roman, Germanic, and Christian traditions slowly blended to create a new, **medieval** civilization called the Middle Ages.

In the early Middle Ages, Germanic tribes, such as the **Franks,** divided Western Europe. In 486, **Clovis,** king of the Franks, conquered Gaul, later to become France. Clovis followed his own customs but also kept Roman customs and converted to Christianity. In the 600s, Islam began in Arabia. Muslims, or believers in Islam, created a huge and expanding empire. When a Muslim army crossed into France, **Charles Martel** and his Frankish warriors fought them at the **battle of Tours** in 732. Muslims ruled in Spain, but did not advance farther into Western Europe.

In 768, Charles Martel's grandson, also named Charles, became king of the Franks. He built an empire covering what are now France, Germany, and part of Italy, and he was known as **Charlemagne,** or Charles the Great. Later, the pope crowned him the new emperor of the Romans. Charlemagne worked, in his 46-year rule, to unite his kingdom by fighting off invaders, conquering peoples, spreading Christianity, and further blending Germanic, Roman, and Christian traditions. He set up an orderly government, naming nobles to rule locally. <u>Charlemagne regarded education as another way to unify his kingdom.</u> He brought back Latin learning across his empire and encouraged the creation of local schools.

After Charlemagne's death in 814, his sons battled for power and his grandsons split up the empire. About 900, nomads called **Magyars** settled in what is present-day Hungary. They overran Eastern Europe and moved into Germany, France, and Italy, but they were eventually pushed back. Also, in the late 700s the **Vikings** from Scandinavia began to invade towns along coasts and rivers in Europe. The Vikings were skilled sailors and explorers. They settled and mixed with local peoples in England, Ireland, northern France, and parts of Russia, bringing their culture with them.

Review Questions

1. Name three things that Charlemagne did to unify his kingdom.

_____

_____

2. What happened to Charlemagne's empire after his death?

_____

_____

READING CHECK

What traditions blended to form the new, medieval culture?

_____

_____

_____

VOCABULARY STRATEGY

What is the meaning of *unify* in the underlined sentence? The word *uni-* is Latin for "one." Use this information on the origins of *unify* to figure out its meaning.

READING SKILL

Identify Main Ideas Find the sentence at the beginning of the Summary that represents the main idea of the whole section on the early Middle Ages. Write the sentence on the lines below.

_____

_____

_____

CHAPTER

7

SECTION 2

Note Taking Study Guide

FEUDALISM AND THE MANOR ECONOMY

Focus Question: How did feudalism and the manor economy emerge and shape medieval life?

As you read this section in your textbook, use the flowchart below to identify the main ideas for each red heading in the section.

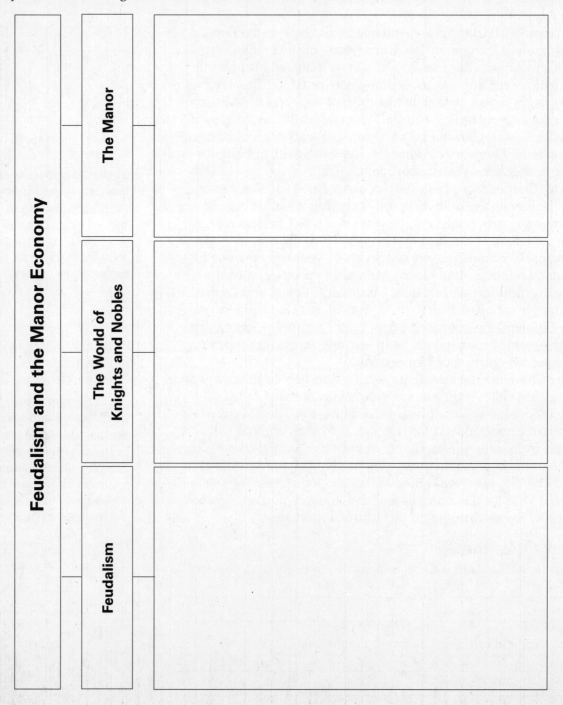

CHAPTER **7** SECTION 2	**Section Summary** FEUDALISM AND THE MANOR ECONOMY

Medieval society was a network of mutual duties. Even kings and nobles exchanged vows of service and loyalty. These vows were part of a new political and legal system called **feudalism,** which was the basis of European life during the Middle Ages.

Feudalism was a structure of lords and lesser lords, called **vassals.** Lords and their vassals exchanged pledges, which was called the **feudal contract.** In this contract, lords expected military service, payments, and loyalty from vassals. In return, they granted vassals protection and parcels of land, called **fiefs,** or estates. By the 1100s, many nobles lived in castles, which served as fortresses.

All aristocrats had a place in this structured society. For nobles, war was a way of life. Many trained from boyhood to become **knights.** They learned to ride horseback, fight, and care for weapons. They competed in mock battles called **tournaments.** Noblewomen, too, participated in the warrior society. They took over estates while their husbands were at war, and might even fight to defend their lands. A few learned to read or write. All were expected to learn spinning, weaving, and the supervising of servants.

Knights were expected to follow a code of ideal conduct, called **chivalry.** It required them to be brave, loyal, and honest, to fight fairly, to treat captured knights well, and to protect the weak. **Troubadours,** or wandering musicians, often sang about knights and ladies. Their songs formed the basis for medieval romances, or epic stories and poems.

The **manor,** or lord's estate, was central to the medieval economy. Manors were self-sufficient, producing all that their people needed. Most peasants on manors were **serfs,** who were bound to the land. Although they were not slaves, serfs could not leave the manor without permission. They had to work the lord's lands several days a week, pay fees, and get permission to marry. In return, they were allowed to farm several acres for themselves and received protection during war. Their work was harsh, and hunger and disease were common. Yet they found times to celebrate, such as Christmas, Easter, and dozens of Christian festivals each year.

Review Questions

1. Describe the feudal contract.

_____

_____

2. What were serfs required to do?

_____

_____

READING CHECK

What was chivalry?

_____

_____

_____

VOCABULARY STRATEGY

What does the word *aristocrats* mean in the underlined sentence? Reread the paragraph and ask yourself which group in society is being discussed. Use that context clue to help you figure out the meaning of *aristocrats*.

READING SKILL

Identify Main Ideas On the lines below, write a sentence that states the main idea of the Summary.

_____

_____

_____

Focus Question: How did the Church play a vital role in medieval life?

As you read this section in your textbook, use the concept web below to identify main ideas for all the headings in the section.

The Medieval Church

CHAPTER 7 SECTION 3

Section Summary

THE MEDIEVAL CHURCH

During the Middle Ages, the Roman Catholic Church controlled the spiritual life of Christians in Western Europe but was also the strongest worldly or **secular** force. Church officials were closely linked to secular rulers. Clergy might even be nobles with lands and armies.

For most people, village churches were the center of community life. Their parish priest celebrated mass and administered **sacraments,** or sacred rites. Church doctrine also taught that men and women were equal before God.

Some chose to live a religious life in monasteries or convents. About 530, a monk named Benedict created rules governing monastery life. They required vows of obedience, poverty, and chastity, or purity. In time, this **Benedictine Rule** was used by monasteries and convents across Europe.

As God's representatives on Earth, medieval popes eventually claimed **papal supremacy,** or authority over kings and emperors. The Church had its own courts and body of laws, known as **canon law,** and issued punishments. One was **excommunication,** or the withholding of sacraments and Christian burial. This condemned a sinner to hell. In addition, rulers could be punished by the pope with an **interdict.** This barred entire towns, regions, or kingdoms from receiving sacraments and Christian burial. The Church also used its authority to end warfare among nobles by declaring times of peace known as the Truce of God.

However, as Church wealth and power grew, so did corruption. Monks and nuns ignored their vows. Throughout the Middle Ages, there were calls for reform. In the early 900s, Abbot Berno of Cluny brought back the Benedictine Rule. Over the next 200 years, monasteries and convents copied these reforms. Other reforms came from **friars,** or monks who traveled and preached to the poor, and did not live in monasteries. The first order of friars, the Franciscans, was founded by **St. Francis of Assisi.** The Franciscans preached poverty, humility, and love of God.

In the Middle Ages, Jewish communities also existed all across Europe. Yet by the late 1000s, prejudice against Jewish people had increased. The Church eventually issued orders forbidding Jews from owning land or having certain jobs.

Review Questions

1. What vows did the Benedictine Rule require?

_____

_____

2. What two actions could the Church take to punish Christians?

_____

_____

READING CHECK

Medieval popes claimed authority over kings and emperors. What was this called?

_____

_____

_____

VOCABULARY STRATEGY

What does *doctrine* mean in the underlined sentence? What clue in the sentence lets you know that it has something to do with teaching? Use context clues to help you figure out the meaning of *doctrine.*

READING

Identify Main Ideas Find and underline the sentences that give the main idea of the Summary.

Note Taking Study Guide
ECONOMIC RECOVERY SPARKS CHANGE

Focus Question: How did changes in agriculture and trade lead to the growth of towns and commerce?

As you read this section in your textbook, identify the main ideas of each heading using the outline below.

Economic Recovery Sparks Change

I. 1000s—agricultural revolution changed Europe.

    A. New technologies allowed farmers to grow more crops.

    B. _____

II. _____

    A. _____

    B. _____

III. _____

    A. _____

    B. _____

IV. _____

    A. _____

    B. _____

    C. _____

V. _____

    A. _____

CHAPTER 7 SECTION 4

Section Summary
ECONOMIC RECOVERY SPARKS CHANGE

New farming methods started a series of changes in medieval Europe. By the 800s, farmers were using iron plows instead of wooden ones, and horses rather than slower oxen. Also, a new crop rotation system improved soil fertility. These changes helped farmers produce more food, and Europe's population nearly tripled between 1000 and 1300.

In the 1100s, trade improved, too, as warfare declined. Demand for goods increased and trade routes expanded. Trade centers arose along the routes and slowly grew into the first medieval cities. Merchants in such towns would ask the local lord or king for a **charter.** This was a document establishing rights and privileges for the town in exchange for a large sum of money, a yearly fee, or both.

As trade expanded, new business practices arose. <u>The need for **capital,** or money for investment, stimulated the growth of banks.</u> In addition, merchants sometimes joined together in **partnerships,** pooling their money to finance large-scale ventures. Other business changes included development of insurance and use of credit rather than cash, allowing merchants to travel without having to carry gold. Overall, however, the use of money increased. Peasants began selling their goods to townspeople for cash. Also, by 1300, most peasants were hired laborers or **tenant farmers,** paying rent for their land.

By 1000, merchants, traders, and artisans had become a powerful social class between nobles and peasants, called the **middle class.** Members of this class formed **guilds,** associations which controlled and protected specific trades or businesses. To become a guild member, people often began in early childhood as **apprentices.** After seven years, an apprentice became a **journeyman,** or salaried worker. Few became guild masters. Unlike in other areas of medieval life, women dominated some trades and even had their own guilds.

Towns and cities expanded rapidly during medieval times. Typical cities were overcrowded, with narrow streets, multistory houses, and no garbage or sewage systems. They were a fire hazard and breeding ground for disease.

Review Questions

1. What advances in agriculture led to greater food production and increased population?

_____

_____

2. What new business practices arose as trade expanded?

_____

_____

READING CHECK

What ranks did a guild member have to pass through to become a master?

_____

_____

_____

VOCABULARY STRATEGY

What does *stimulated* mean in the underlined sentence? Some synonyms for *stimulated* include *awakened, excited,* and *inspired.* Use these synonyms to help you figure out the meaning of *stimulated.*

READING SKILL

Identify Main Ideas Write another title for this Summary that gives the main idea.

_____

_____

Note Taking Study Guide
ROYAL POWER GROWS

Focus Question: How did monarchs in England and France expand royal authority and lay the foundations for united nation-states?

A. *As you read this section in your textbook, use the cause-effect chart to identify the causes for changes in royal power.*

Royal Power Changes

William the Conqueror	Henry II	John
• _____	• _____	• _____
• _____	• _____	• _____
_____	_____	_____
• _____	• _____	• _____
_____	_____	_____
• _____	• _____	• _____
_____		_____

B. *As you read this section in your textbook, use the Venn diagram to compare and contrast the development of royal power in England and France.*

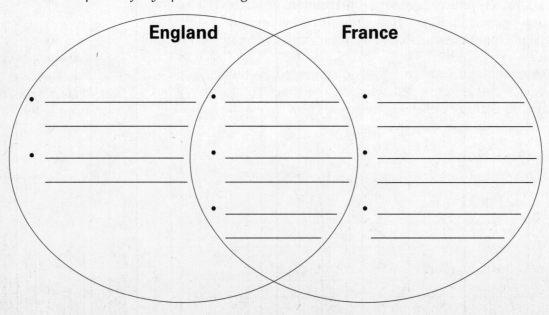

Section Summary

ROYAL POWER GROWS

During the early Middle Ages, European monarchs had limited power. However, from 1000 to 1300, increases in royal power and control gradually established the foundations of modern government.

In 1066, **William the Conqueror** took over England. By 1086, he had completed a census and property survey called the *Domesday Book.* It helped establish an effective taxation system and treasury. In 1154, Henry II ascended the English throne. He expanded the justice system. Royal court decisions became the foundation of English **common law,** a system based on custom and prior rulings. Henry II also set up a **jury** system that was the forerunner of today's grand jury.

Henry's son, **King John,** abused his power and was forced to sign the **Magna Carta,** or Great Charter. It required the king to obey the laws. It also established two important principles: **due process of law,** or protection from arrest without proper legal procedures, and **habeas corpus,** or protection from imprisonment without being charged with a crime. John also agreed not to raise taxes before consulting his Great Council of lords and clergy. Under later rulers, this council evolved into **Parliament,** England's legislature. Parliament eventually controlled the "power of the purse," meaning it would not approve new taxes unless the monarch met certain demands.

Unlike the English, early French monarchs did not rule a united kingdom. Then in 987, Hugh Capet became king and began expanding royal power. The Capetians stabilized the kingdom over the next 300 years. In 1179, Philip II took the throne. <u>He gained control of English lands in Normandy and expanded territories in southern France, adding vast areas to his domain, and becoming Europe's most powerful ruler.</u>

Louis IX came to power in 1226. Although he persecuted heretics and Jews and led crusades against Muslims, he also outlawed private wars, ended serfdom, and expanded royal courts. By the time of his death in 1270, France was a centralized monarchy ruling over a unified state. In 1302, the Estates General was set up, but this council of clergy, nobility, and townspeople never gained the "power of the purse" over French royalty.

Review Questions

1. What did the *Domesday Book* help establish in England?

_____

_____

2. What important English document limited the absolute power of the king?

_____

_____

READING CHECK

How did the Estates General differ from Parliament?

_____

_____

_____

VOCABULARY STRATEGY

What does the word *domain* mean in the underlined sentence? What context clues can you find in the surrounding words or phrases? Circle any words or phrases in the sentence that help you figure out what *domain* means.

_____

_____

_____

READING SKILL

Identify Main Ideas Find the sentence at the beginning of the Summary that states the main idea of the whole summary. Write the sentence on the lines below.

_____

_____

_____

CHAPTER 8 SECTION 2

Note Taking Study Guide

THE HOLY ROMAN EMPIRE AND THE CHURCH

Focus Question: How did explosive conflicts between monarchs and popes affect the balance of power in Europe?

As you read this section in your textbook, record the actions of emperors and popes and the effects of their actions.

Pope or Emperor	Actions	Effects				
Otto I	• Cooperated with Church	• Pope crowned Otto emperor.				

CHAPTER 8 SECTION 2

Section Summary
THE HOLY ROMAN EMPIRE AND THE CHURCH

During the Middle Ages, popes and the Church spread their influence across Europe. European rulers, too, grew more powerful. However, this increase in power often resulted in conflict.

Rulers of the **Holy Roman Empire,** which extended from Germany to Italy, often confronted the pope over the appointment of Church officials. **Pope Gregory VII** wanted the Church free from lay (non-church) control. To do this he banned **lay investiture,** in which the emperor rather than the pope named and installed bishops. However, Holy Roman Emperor **Henry IV** said that bishops held royal lands under his control, so he had the right to appoint them. In 1076 the pope excommunicated him and threatened to crown a new emperor. Henry was forced to humble himself to the pope as a sinner, and Gregory forgave him. Later, Henry led an army to Rome, sending Gregory into exile. Fifty years later, the Concordat of Worms was accepted, giving popes sole power to invest bishops with religious authority and emperors the right to invest them with lands.

Power struggles over land also occurred during the 1100s and 1200s. Holy Roman Emperor Frederick I, called **Frederick Barbarossa** or "Red Beard," fought but failed to capture wealthy northern Italian cities. Instead, he arranged for his son to marry the heiress to Sicily and southern Italy, expanding his control there. His grandson, Frederick II, also sought but failed to control northern Italy. Ultimately, the Holy Roman Empire broke up into separate feudal states, while southern Italy went through centuries of chaos.

By the 1200s, the Church reached its peak of power. In 1198, **Pope Innocent III** took office and claimed supremacy over all other rulers. He excommunicated the English and French kings, and placed their kingdoms under interdict, barring people from religious sacraments. He also launched a holy war against heretics in southern France, killing tens of thousands. After Innocent's death, popes continued to claim supremacy, but they were challenged by the monarchs' growing power. In the late 1200s, France's Philip IV successfully challenged the pope on the issue of taxing the clergy. Philip then went on to engineer the election of a French pope.

Review Questions

1. What did Pope Gregory VII want?

_____

_____

2. What did Innocent III claim?

_____

_____

READING CHECK

What agreement ended power struggles between Holy Roman emperors and popes over lay investiture?

_____

_____

_____

VOCABULARY STRATEGY

What does the word *confronted* mean in the underlined sentence? *Confronted* is made from three word parts: the prefix *con-* means "together"; *front* means "the part of something that is facing forward"; *-ed* is a suffix that indicates past tense. Use these word-part clues to help you figure out the meaning of *confronted.*

READING SKILL

Understand Effects Was the Concordat of Worms a cause or effect of the power struggles between popes and rulers?

_____

_____

_____

Note Taking Study Guide

THE CRUSADES AND THE WIDER WORLD

Focus Question: How did the Crusades change life in Europe and beyond?

As you read this section in your textbook, complete the concept web below showing the causes of the Crusades in the top ovals and the effects of the Crusades in the lower ovals.

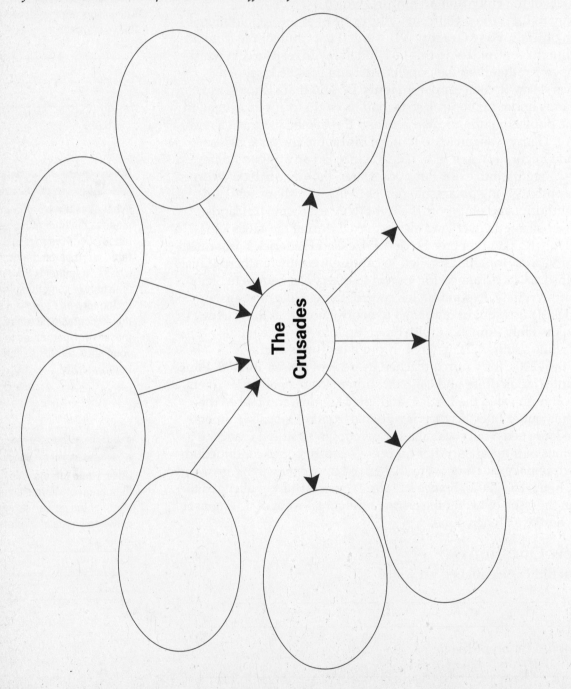

The Crusades

CHAPTER 8 SECTION 3

Section Summary

THE CRUSADES AND THE WIDER WORLD

The **Crusades** were a series of wars in which Christians fought Muslims for control of Middle Eastern lands. The Crusades were destructive, but ultimately opened a wider world to Europeans and increased the pace of change.

In 1071, Seljuk Turks conquered Byzantine lands in Asia Minor and then moved into the **Holy Land.** The Byzantine emperor asked **Pope Urban II** for help, and Urban launched the **Crusades** to free the Holy Land. Only the First Crusade was a success for Christians, who captured Jerusalem in 1099. In the Second Crusade, Jerusalem fell to the great Muslim leader Saladin. He agreed to reopen the city to Christian pilgrims after crusaders failed to take Jerusalem in the Third Crusade. By the Fourth Crusade in 1202, knights were fighting other Christians to help Venice against its Byzantine trade rivals. Crusaders captured and looted the Byzantine capital, Constantinople.

The Crusades left a legacy of hatred in the Middle East and Europe. They also produced vast changes in society. In the Middle East, Muslims began to reunify. In Europe, trade increased. The Crusades encouraged the growth of a money economy. Monarchs gained the right to collect taxes to support the Crusades. The experiences of crusaders in the Muslim world introduced Europeans to new places. In 1271, Venetian **Marco Polo** headed for China and returned home to write a book. His and the crusaders' experiences brought new knowledge to Europe.

Religious zeal continued in Europe, however. Around 1100, Christian kingdoms in Spain began a struggle called the **Reconquista,** or reconquest. The purpose was to expel Muslims, who had lived there since the 700s. In 1469, **Ferdinand and Isabella** married, unifying Spain. They captured the last Muslim stronghold, Granada, in 1492. Under Muslim rule, Christians, Jews, and Muslims had been able to live together. <u>However, Ferdinand and Isabella wanted to impose religious, as well as political, uniformity on their diverse peoples.</u> So, with the help of the **Inquisition,** they launched a brutal campaign against Muslims and Jews. Those found guilty of heresy were burned at the stake. More than 150,000 people, mostly Muslims and Jews, fled Spain, taking their skills and learning with them.

Review Questions

1. How did the Crusades change Europe?

_____

_____

2. What was the Reconquista?

_____

_____

READING CHECK

Which Crusade was the only one to achieve real success?

_____

_____

_____

VOCABULARY STRATEGY

What does *diverse* mean in the underlined sentence? An antonym for *diverse* is *similar.* Use the antonym to help you figure out the meaning of *diverse.*

READING SKILL

Identify Causes and Effects List one cause and one effect of the Inquisition.

_____

_____

_____

Note Taking Study Guide
LEARNING AND CULTURE FLOURISH

Focus Question: What achievements in learning, literature, and the arts characterized the High Middle Ages?

As you read this section in your textbook, fill in the flowchart to recognize the multiple causes of the cultural and intellectual flowering of the Middle Ages.

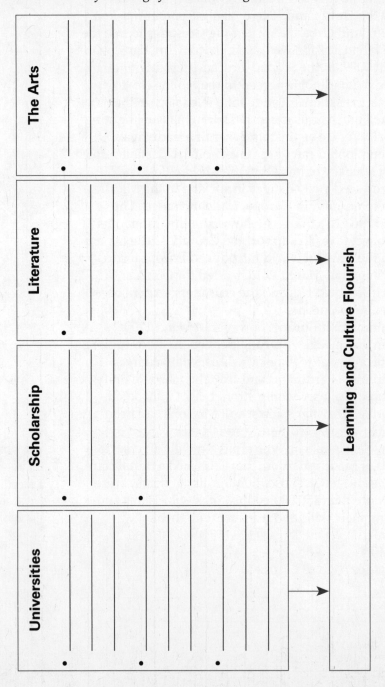

CHAPTER 8 SECTION 4	Section Summary
	LEARNING AND CULTURE FLOURISH

Europe in the High Middle Ages experienced a blossoming of education, literature, and the arts. This was influenced by increased prosperity, contact with other cultures, and the rediscovery of ancient learning.

Education gained importance. By the 1100s, schools sprang up near cathedrals, some evolving into the first universities. Muslim scholars had translated the works of Aristotle and other Greeks into Arabic. In Muslim Spain, they were translated into Latin, the language of European scholars. In the 1100s, the new translations initiated a revolution in learning. The Greek philosophers had used reason to discover truth; Christians believed that the Church was the final authority. Christian scholars struggled with this reason-based, rather than faith-based, approach. To resolve the conflict, they began to use reason to support Christian beliefs. This method is known as **scholasticism.** The most famous scholastic was **Thomas Aquinas.** He wrote *Summa theologica* to prove that faith and reason exist in harmony.

Scientific learning also reached Europe, including translations of Hippocrates on medicine and Euclid on geometry. Europeans adopted the more streamlined Hindu-Arabic numerals over cumbersome Roman numerals, allowing later scientists and mathematicians to make great strides.

Latin remained the language of Europe's scholars and churchmen. However, new literature emerged in the **vernacular,** or everyday languages of ordinary people. This change brought a flowering of literary works, including the *Song of Roland,* a French epic poem of chivalry; *Divine Comedy,* the Italian classic poem of heaven, hell, and purgatory by **Dante Alighieri;** and a portrait of English medieval life, the *Canterbury Tales,* by **Geoffrey Chaucer.**

Architecture and the arts also flourished. Fortress-like Romanesque churches gave way to the **Gothic style.** Its key feature was **flying buttresses**—exterior stone supports that permitted thinner, higher walls and massive windows, bringing light and height to cathedrals. Other arts during the period include stained glass, religious paintings, and woven wall hangings. A famous example is the Bayeux Tapestry, an embroidered illustration of the Norman Conquest of England. The Gothic style was also applied to the decoration of books, known as **illumination.**

Review Questions

1. How did Europeans become aware of Greek thinking?

_____

_____

2. How were Gothic cathedrals different from Romanesque churches?

_____

_____

READING CHECK

Who was Thomas Aquinas?

_____

_____

_____

VOCABULARY STRATEGY

What does the word *initiated* mean in the underlined sentence? It comes from a Latin word that means "to begin." Use this word-origins clue to help you figure out the meaning of *initiated*.

READING SKILL

Recognize Multiple Causes
Why did Europe in the High Middle Ages experience a blossoming in education, literature, and the arts?

_____

_____

Note Taking Study Guide

A TIME OF CRISIS

Focus Question: How did the combination of plague, upheaval in the Church, and war affect Europe in the 1300s and 1400s?

A. *As you read "The Black Death: A Global Epidemic," complete the flowchart to recognize causes and effects of the Black Death.*

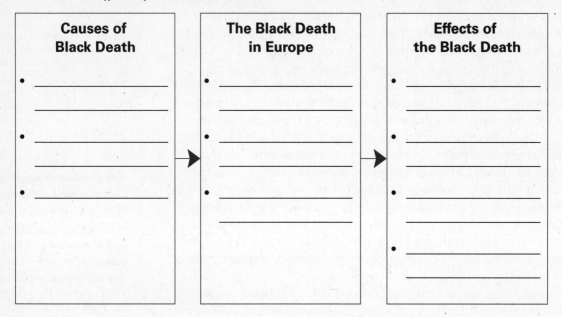

Causes of Black Death	The Black Death in Europe	Effects of the Black Death
• _____ _____	• _____ _____	• _____ _____
• _____ _____	• _____ _____	• _____ _____
• _____ _____	• _____ _____	• _____ _____
		• _____ _____

B. *As you read "The Hundred Years' War," complete the flowchart to record causes and effects of the war.*

Causes	Hundred Years' War	Effects
• _____ _____	• _____ _____	• _____ _____
• _____ _____	• _____ _____	• _____ _____
• _____ _____	• _____ _____	• _____ _____
		• _____

CHAPTER 8
SECTION 5

Section Summary
A TIME OF CRISIS

In the mid-1300s a deadly disease called bubonic plague, or the **Black Death,** reached Europe. It was spread by fleas carried by rats. Eventually, the **epidemic,** or outbreak, killed one-third of all Europeans. People were terrified and normal life broke down. People fled cities or hid in their homes. Without workers, production declined. Survivors demanded higher wages, leading to **inflation,** or rising prices. Landlords tried to limit wages and forced villagers off the land. The plague not only spread death but also social unrest, as bitter, angry peasants revolted.

By the late Middle Ages, the Church, too, was in crisis. Many monks and priests had died during the plague. Survivors asked tough spiritual questions. The Church could not provide the strong leadership that was needed. For 70 years, a luxury-loving papal court ruled in Avignon. Reformers arose within the Church, calling for change. In 1378, they elected their own pope in Rome. French cardinals elected a rival pope. This Church **schism,** or split, finally ended in 1417 when a Church council removed authority from all three popes and elected a compromise candidate.

For most of this time, a destructive war raged. Between 1337 and 1453 England and France fought a series of conflicts known as the Hundred Years' War. Both sides wanted control of lands in France that had once been England's, the English Channel, and regional trade. England won early victories with new technology, the **longbow.** However, led by 17-year-old Joan of Arc, France began to win battles. <u>Joan had told the uncrowned king, Charles VII, that God sent her to save France, so he authorized her to lead an army against the English.</u> In one year, her troops won several victories, but she was captured, tried, and burned at the stake. Her martyrdom rallied French forces, and with their powerful new weapon, the cannon, they drove the English out of most of France. Ultimately, the war helped French kings expand their power. In England, it strengthened Parliament.

As Europe recovered from the plague, its population grew, manufacturing expanded, and trade increased. This set the stage for the Renaissance, Reformation, and Age of Exploration.

Review Questions

1. What caused a schism in the Church in the late 1300s?

_____

_____

2. Why did France and England fight the Hundred Years' War?

_____

_____

READING CHECK

What powerful new weapon did the French develop?

_____

_____

_____

VOCABULARY STRATEGY

What is the meaning of *authorized* in the underlined sentence? The word *authorized* comes from a Latin word that means "power." Use this word-origins clue to help you figure out the meaning of *authorized*.

READING SKILL

Recognize Causes and Effects
What caused the Black Death? What was the effect of the Black Death?

_____

_____

_____

Name_____ Class_____ Date_____

Focus Question: What made the Byzantine empire rich and successful for so long, and why did it finally crumble?

As you read this section in your textbook, complete the table below to keep track of the sequence of events in the Byzantine empire.

The Byzantine Empire

330	Constantinople becomes the capital of the eastern Roman empire.							

Section Summary

THE BYZANTINE EMPIRE

The Roman emperor Constantine rebuilt the city of Byzantium and renamed it **Constantinople.** Constantinople grew wealthy from trade. In 330, Constantine made Constantinople the new capital of the Roman empire. In time, the eastern Roman empire became known as the Byzantine empire.

The Byzantine empire reached its peak under **Justinian.** Byzantine armies reconquered North Africa and parts of southern Europe. However, these victories were only temporary, as Justinian's successors later lost these lands. After a fire in 532, Justinian made Constantinople even grander. One of his most important achievements was rebuilding the church of Hagia Sophia. Justinian also had a commission collect and organize the laws of Rome. This collection became known as **Justinian's Code.** It helped unify the empire, which Justinian ruled as an **autocrat,** or with complete authority. His wife, **Theodora,** served as his advisor and co-ruler.

Christianity was practiced differently in the Byzantine empire than in the West. The Byzantine emperor controlled Church affairs and appointed the **patriarch,** or highest Church official in Constantinople. Byzantine Christians rejected the pope's claim to authority over all Christians. During the Middle Ages, the eastern and western branches of Christianity grew further apart, partly due to a dispute over the use of **icons,** or holy images. In 1054, other controversies caused a complete split known as the **Great Schism.** The Byzantine church became known as the Eastern Orthodox Church. The western branch became known as the Roman Catholic Church.

By this time, the Byzantine empire was in decline. In the 1090s, the Byzantine emperor asked the pope for help in fighting the Muslim Seljuks. This started the First Crusade. In 1204, knights on the Fourth Crusade attacked Constantinople. The Byzantines lost control of trade and much of their wealth. In 1453, Ottoman Turks conquered Constantinople, renamed it Istanbul, and made it the capital of their empire.

The Byzantines left an influential heritage. Their civilization combined Christian beliefs with Greek science, philosophy, and arts. Byzantine artists created unique religious icons and mosaics. Byzantine scholars preserved Greek literature and produced their own great books, especially in the field of history.

Review Questions

1. How did Constantinople become a wealthy city?

_____

_____

2. How did the Crusades help to weaken the Byzantine empire?

_____

_____

READING CHECK

What was the Great Schism?

_____

_____

_____

VOCABULARY STRATEGY

What does the word *temporary* mean in the underlined sentence? Note that the victories were "only *temporary*" because Justinian's successors later lost these lands. Use this context clue to help you understand the meaning of *temporary.*

READING SKILL

Recognize Sequence List in chronological order the three names that Constantinople has had.

_____

_____

_____

Note Taking Study Guide
THE RISE OF RUSSIA

Focus Question: How did geography and the migrations of different peoples influence the rise of Russia?

As you read this section in your textbook, complete the timeline below to sequence the events in the rise of Russia from the 700s to the 1500s.

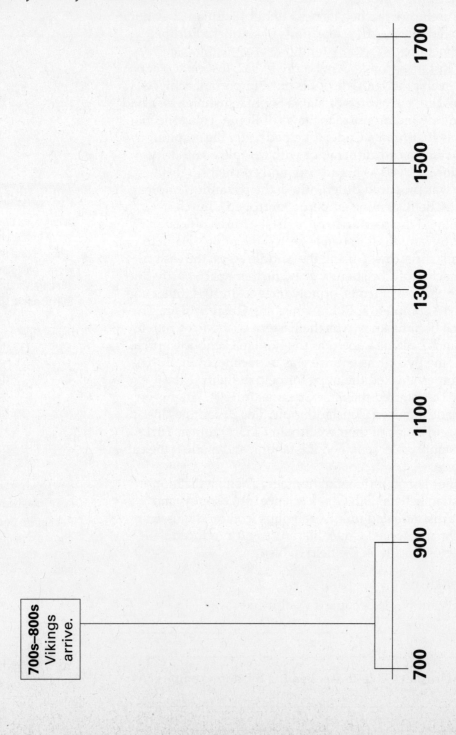

700s–800s
Vikings arrive.

700   900   1100   1300   1500   1700

CHAPTER 9 SECTION 2

Section Summary

THE RISE OF RUSSIA

Russia has three main geographic regions that shaped early life there. The northern forests have poor soil and a cold climate. A band of fertile land farther south attracted farmers. The southern **steppe**—an open, treeless grassland—provided pasture for herds. It allowed nomads to migrate easily from Asia into Europe.

Two peoples came together to form the first Russian state. The Slavs migrated from Asia to southern Russia. Vikings came from Scandinavia. The Vikings traveled south along Russia's rivers, trading with the Slavs and with Constantinople. The city of **Kiev** was at the center of this trade.

Russians date the origins of their country to 862, when a Viking tribe called the Rus began ruling from Novgorod in the north. Rus lands expanded to include Kiev, which became their capital.

In the 800s, Constantinople sent missionaries to Russia. Two Orthodox monks, Cyril and Methodius, developed the **Cyrillic** alphabet, which is still used in Russia. During the reign of the Rus king Vladimir, Orthodox Christianity became the religion of the Rus and they aligned themselves with the Byzantines.

Between 1236 and 1241, Mongols advanced into Russia. They were known as the **Golden Horde.** They burned Kiev and ruled Russia for the next 240 years. <u>However, as long as they received tribute, the Mongols let Russian princes rule and they tolerated the Russian Orthodox Church.</u> Although trade increased under the Mongols, Mongol rule cut Russia off from Western Europe at a time when Europeans were making great advances.

The princes of Moscow gained power under the Mongols, and Moscow became Russia's political and spiritual center. In 1380, these princes led other Russians in defeating the Golden Horde at the battle of Kulikovo. A driving force behind Moscow's successes was Ivan III, or **Ivan the Great.** Between 1462 and 1505, he brought much of northern Russia under his rule. He tried to limit the power of the nobles, and sometimes called himself **tsar**, the Russian word for Caesar. His grandson, Ivan IV, became the first Russian ruler officially crowned tsar. However, Ivan IV became unstable and violent. The ways in which he used his power earned him the title **Ivan the Terrible.**

Review Questions

1. Why do Russians consider 862 as the year when their country began?

_____

_____

2. What Russian ruler first called himself *tsar*?

_____

_____

READING CHECK

What was the Golden Horde?

_____

_____

_____

VOCABULARY STRATEGY

What does the word *tolerated* mean in the underlined sentence? Think about the fact that although the Mongols were not Christians, they *tolerated* the Russian Orthodox Church. Use this context clue to help you understand the meaning of *tolerated.*

READING SKILL

Recognize Sequence Identify the three groups mentioned in the Summary that either migrated into or invaded Russia. Sequence them in the order in which they appeared.

_____

_____

_____

Name_____ Class_____ Date_____

Focus Question: How did geography and ethnic diversity contribute to the turmoil of Eastern European history?

A. *As you read "Geography Shapes Eastern Europe" and "Migrations Contribute to Diversity," complete the concept web to record the conditions and events that led to the diversity of peoples and cultures in Eastern Europe.*

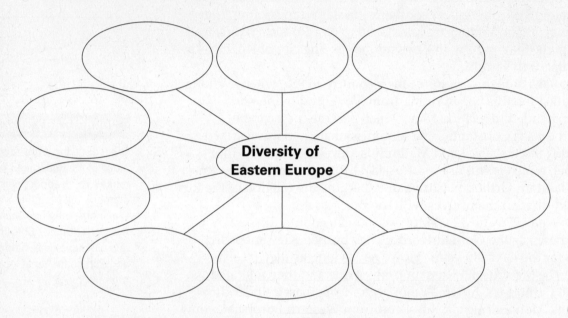

B. *As you read "Three Early Kingdoms Develop," complete the chart below to help you sequence the events in the history of these countries.*

Important Events in Eastern Europe		
Poland	**Hungary**	**Serbia**
• _____	• _____	• _____
_____	_____	_____
• _____	• _____	• _____
_____	_____	_____
• _____	• _____	• _____
_____	_____	_____
• _____	• _____	• _____
_____	_____	_____
• _____	• _____	• _____
_____	_____	_____

CHAPTER 9
SECTION 3

Section Summary
SHAPING EASTERN EUROPE

Eastern Europe lies between Central Europe to the west and Russia to the east. Included in this region is the **Balkan Peninsula.** Both goods and cultural influences traveled along its rivers.

Many ethnic groups settled in Eastern Europe. An **ethnic group** is a large group of people who share the same language and culture. The West Slavs from Russia settled in Poland and other parts of Eastern Europe, while the South Slavs occupied the Balkans. Asian peoples, like the Magyars, as well as Vikings and other Germanic peoples also migrated to Eastern Europe. <u>At times, some groups tried to dominate the region.</u>

Many cultural and religious influences spread to Eastern Europe. Byzantine missionaries brought Eastern Orthodox Christianity and Byzantine culture to the Balkans. German knights and missionaries brought Roman Catholic Christianity to Poland and other areas. In the 1300s, the Ottomans invaded the Balkans and introduced Islam. Jews who were persecuted in Western Europe fled to Eastern Europe, especially to Poland, where their liberties were protected.

During the Middle Ages, Eastern Europe included many kingdoms and small states. The marriage in 1386 of Queen Jadwiga of Poland to Duke Wladyslaw Jagiello of Lithuania made Poland-Lithuania the largest state in Europe. However, power gradually shifted from the monarch to the nobles. The nobles met in a **diet,** or assembly, where a single noble could block passage of a law. Without a strong central government, Poland-Lithuania declined and eventually disappeared from the map.

The Magyars settled in Hungary and became Roman Catholics. The Hungarian king was forced to sign the **Golden Bull of 1222,** which strictly limited royal power. The Mongols overran Hungary in 1241, killing half of its people. Although they soon withdrew, the Ottoman Turks ended Hungarian independence in 1526.

Some of the South Slavs who settled in the Balkans became the ancestors of the Serbs. Most Serbs became Orthodox Christians and set up a state based on a Byzantine model. Serbia reached its height in the 1300s but could not withstand the advance of the Ottoman Turks. It was conquered by the Ottomans in 1389.

Review Questions

1. Why did Poland-Lithuania decline?

_____

_____

2. What group ended Hungarian and Serbian independence?

_____

_____

READING CHECK

What is an ethnic group?

_____

_____

_____

VOCABULARY STRATEGY

What does the word *dominate* mean in the underlined sentence? The word comes from the Latin word *dominus,* which means "master" or "lord." Use this word-origins clue to help you understand what *dominate* means.

READING SKILL

Recognize Multiple Causes
Jews migrated from Western Europe to Poland for two main reasons. List the two reasons below.

_____

_____

_____

Focus Question: What messages, or teachings, did Muhammad spread through Islam?

A. *As you read the section "Muhammad Becomes a Prophet" in your textbook, complete the following timeline to record the sequence of events.*

B. *As you read the section "Teachings of Islam" in your textbook, complete the following concept web to keep track of the teachings of Islam.*

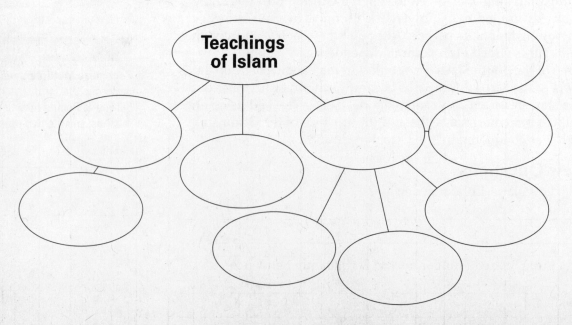

Section Summary

THE RISE OF ISLAM

The religion of Islam, whose followers are called Muslims, emerged in the Arabian Peninsula. There, in A.D. 570, **Muhammad** was born in **Mecca**—a trading and religious center. Muhammad worked among nomadic herders called **Bedouins.** Later, he became a successful merchant and decided to marry at 25. He was known for his honesty in business and devotion to his family.

Muhammad often meditated on the moral ills of Meccan society, including greed. According to Muslim tradition, Muhammad became a prophet at 40 when he was asked by an angel to become God's messenger. When he began teaching, a few listened, but others opposed him with threats. In 622, he and his followers fled Mecca for **Yathrib,** on a journey called the **hijra.** Later Yathrib was called **Medina.** In Medina, thousands adopted Islam and formed strong, peaceful communities. When Meccan leaders grew hostile, Muslims defeated them in battle. Muhammad returned to Mecca in 630, where the **Kaaba,** which Muhammad dedicated to Allah, became the holiest Islamic site. Muhammad died in 632.

The sacred text of Islam is the **Quran,** believed to be the direct word of God as told to Muhammad. All Muslims study it to learn about God's will and living a good life.

<u>Muslims believe that priests are not necessary to mediate between people and God.</u> Muslims gather in **mosques** to pray. They follow the Five Pillars of Islam, which are the following duties: declaring faith, praying five times daily, giving charity to the poor, fasting during their holy month, and making the **hajj,** or pilgrimage to Mecca. Another duty is **jihad,** which means to struggle in God's service.

Because Jews and Christians worship the same God and study what are considered God's earlier revelations, Muslims call them "People of the Book." In most cases, they have been allowed religious freedom in Muslim societies.

The **Sharia,** a body of laws that interprets the Quran and applies religious principles to legal situations, helps Muslim societies govern daily life. According to the Quran, women are spiritually equal to men but have different roles. In different places, Muslims interpret women's roles and rights differently. In some cases, Muslims adopted practices of conquered peoples, such as requiring upper-class women to wear veils.

Review Questions

1. What is the Quran?

_____

_____

2. Why do Muslims call Jews and Christians "People of the Book"?

_____

_____

READING CHECK

What was the hijra?

_____

_____

_____

VOCABULARY STRATEGY

What does the word *mediate* mean in the underlined sentence? What clues to its meaning can you find in the surrounding words or phrases? Circle the context clues you find that help you to figure out what *mediate* means.

READING SKILL

Identify Main Ideas Which of the following would be considered main ideas for this Summary? Circle your answers.

- Muslim holy days are enforced very strictly.

- Muslims believe in making a hajj.

- Muslims believe in one God, the Quran, and the Five Pillars of Islam.

- Islam governs daily life and affects the roles and rights of women.

- Muslims have little religious connection to Jews and Christians.

Note Taking Study Guide
BUILDING A MUSLIM EMPIRE

Focus Question: How did Muhammad's successors extend Muslim rule and spread Islam?

A. *As you read this section in your textbook, complete the following timeline to record the major events in the spread of Islam and the rise and fall of Muslim empires.*

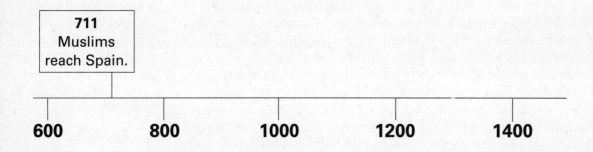

```
711
Muslims
reach Spain.
```

600   800   1000   1200   1400

B. *As you read the section "Divisions Emerge Within Islam" in your textbook, complete the Venn diagram to record points on which Sunni and Shiite Muslims agree and differ.*

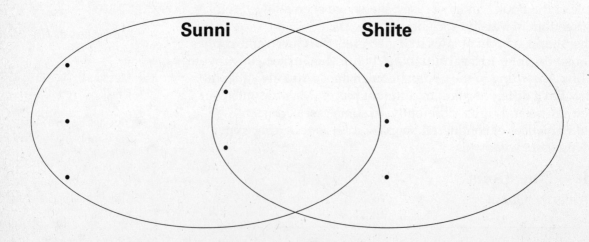

Sunni   Shiite

CHAPTER 10 SECTION 2 — Section Summary
BUILDING A MUSLIM EMPIRE

In 632, **Abu Bakr** became the first **caliph,** or successor to Muhammad. He united all Arab tribes as Muslims. Once united, the Arabs defeated the Persian empire and parts of the Byzantine empire. However, a schism between Sunni and Shiite Muslims occurred after Muhammad's death, and still exists today.

Shiites believe that Muhammad's successors must be descendants of his son-in-law, Ali. They also should be religious leaders and interpret the Quran. **Sunnis** believe that male Muslims from Muhammad's tribe can lead without performing religious functions. Today, about 90 percent of Muslims are Sunni. Both groups believe in the same God, the Quran, and the Five Pillars of Islam, but they differ in religious practices, laws, and rules about daily life. A third group are **Sufis,** who meditate and fast to gain communion with God.

In the 700s, a powerful Meccan clan set up the Sunni **Umayyad** caliphate. They directed conquests that extended Muslim rule from Spain to the Indus River Valley. Their empire lasted until 750. The Muslims brought many people under their rule. Muslim leaders imposed a special tax on non-Muslims, but Jews, Christians, and Zoroastrians could worship and some held important positions. Many people converted to Islam.

However, the Umayyads later faced economic tensions and opposition from those who did not have the same privileges as Muslims. After capturing Damascus in 750, with strong support from Shiites and non-Arabs, Abu al-Abbas founded the **Abbasid** dynasty. The Abbasids ended conquests and supported education and learning. They enjoyed a golden age, with a more efficient government and a beautiful new capital, **Baghdad,** in the former Persian empire. Mosques with **minarets,** or slender towers, graced the cities, and markets sold goods from far-off lands.

In Spain, one of the Umayyads established a separate state. Muslims ruled parts of Spain until 1492. They were tolerant of other religions, supported scholars, and constructed grand buildings.

As the empire declined, independent dynasties took power. Seljuk Turks gained power and their **sultan,** or ruler, controlled Baghdad by 1055, keeping the Abbasid caliph as a figurehead. Beginning in 1216, the Mongols attacked across southwest Asia. In 1258, they burned and looted Baghdad, ending the Abbasid dynasty.

Review Questions

1. What are the differences between Shiite and Sunni beliefs?

_____

_____

2. What two groups took power from the Abbasid dynasty?

_____

_____

READING CHECK
Which dynasty enjoyed a golden age?

_____

_____

_____

VOCABULARY STRATEGY
What does the word *schism* mean in the underlined sentence? Read the nearby words, sentences, and phrases to find clues to its meaning. What do the context clues tell you about the meaning of *schism?*

READING SKILL
Recognize Sequence Number the following events to show their correct sequence:

____ Umayyads take power.

____ Damascus becomes the capital.

____ Abu Bakr becomes the caliph.

____ Muslim empire expands into Persia and Byzantine empire.

Note Taking Study Guide

CHAPTER 10 SECTION 3

MUSLIM CIVILIZATION'S GOLDEN AGE

Focus Question: What achievements did Muslims make in economics, art, literature, and science?

As you read this section in your textbook, complete the following chart to categorize the advances made during the golden age of Muslim civilization.

Muslim Achievements	
Economics	• _____ • _____ • _____ • _____ • _____ • _____
Arts	• _____ • _____ • _____
Literature	• _____ • _____ • _____
Philosophy	• _____ • _____
Sciences	• _____ • _____ • _____ • _____ • _____

CHAPTER 10 SECTION 3 — Section Summary

MUSLIM CIVILIZATION'S GOLDEN AGE

Muslim civilization enjoyed a golden age under the Abbasids. Their empire stretched into Asia, the Middle East, Africa, and Europe. Merchants crossed the Sahara, traveled the Silk Road to China, and sailed to India and Asia. New products and ideas were exchanged, and the religion of Islam was introduced to many regions. All this fueled the Muslim economy, leading to the development of partnerships, the use of credit, and a banking system. Artisans created manufactured goods for trade, and the government helped improve farming through large irrigation systems.

Muslim society allowed some **social mobility,** the ability to move up in social class through religious, scholarly, or military achievements. Most slaves were household servants and some were able to purchase their freedom. The children of some slaves could become free under another system.

The diverse cultures in the empire, as well as Islam, influenced art and literature. Early oral poetry told tales of nomadic life, while later poets developed elaborate rules for poems. Great Muslim poets include **Firdawsi,** who told the history of Persia, and **Omar Khayyám,** who wrote about fate and life in *The Rubáiyát.* Storytellers often used short anecdotes to entertain people. In architecture, buildings reflected Byzantine influences, and mosques included domes and minarets. Muslim artists also used **calligraphy,** the art of beautiful handwriting, for decoration on buildings and in books.

Muslims made great strides in education. Both boys and girls were educated so they could study the Quran. Several cities supported learning centers with vast libraries. There, scholars translated Greek, Hindu, and Buddhist texts. Known in Europe as Averröes, the philosopher **Ibn Rushd** believed that knowledge should meet the standards of reason. Another Muslim thinker, **Ibn Khaldun,** studied history scientifically and advised others in avoiding errors.

In mathematics, **al-Khwarizmi** pioneered the study of algebra. **Muhammad al-Razi,** chief physician in the hospital at Baghdad, wrote books on diseases and medical practices. **Ibn Sina,** a famous Persian physician, compiled an encyclopedia of medical knowledge. Both doctors' works guided medical study in Europe for 500 years. Other physicians improved ways to save eyesight and mix medicines.

Review Questions

1. How did trade affect the Abbasid empire?

_____

_____

2. How did Muslim poetry change during this time?

_____

_____

READING CHECK

Why were children educated?

_____

_____

_____

VOCABULARY STRATEGY

What does the word *anecdotes* mean in the underlined sentence? The word *anecdotes* comes from a Greek word that means "unpublished items." Use this word-origins clue to help you figure out the meaning of *anecdotes.*

READING SKILL

Categorize Categorize the following Muslim advances:

• Mixing medicines

• Elaborate rules for written poems

• Partnerships

• Calligraphy

• A system of credit

• Improvements in treating eye problems

Name_____ Class_____ Date_____

Focus Question: How did Muslim rule affect Indian government and society?

As you read this section in your textbook, complete the following outline to record the supporting details related to Muslim empires in India.

I. **The Delhi Sultanate**
  A. The Sultan of Delhi defeats the Hindus
    1. _____
    2. _____
    3. _____
  B. _____
    1. _____
    2. _____
    3. _____
II. _____
  A. _____
    1. _____
    2. _____
  B. _____
    1. _____
    2. _____
    3. _____
III. _____
  A. _____
    1. _____
    2. _____
  B. _____
    1. _____
    2. _____
    3. _____
  C. _____
    1. _____
    2. _____

CHAPTER 10
SECTION 4
Section Summary
INDIA'S MUSLIM EMPIRES

After 550, rival princes fought for control of India. Around 1000, Muslim armies moved in. <u>Muslim attacks included onslaughts that killed many Hindus and destroyed Buddhist temples.</u> Muslims triumphed due to military superiority, rivalries among Hindu princes, and the many Hindus who converted to Islam. By the 1100s, a **sultan** controlled northern India. From the capital in **Delhi,** the Delhi sultanate ruled from 1206 to 1526.

Muslim rulers reorganized Indian government and increased trade. During the Mongol raids of the 1200s, scholars fled from Baghdad to India, bringing Persian and Greek learning with them. These newcomers helped turn Delhi into a place where art and architecture flourished. However, in 1389, Mongols attacked Delhi, destroying much of its culture.

The Muslim advance brought two very different religious groups—Hindus and Muslims—face to face. Muslims worshiped a single god, while Hindus prayed to many. Hindus accepted the caste system, while Islam promoted equality.

Gradually, the cultures blended. Hindus were allowed to practice their religion and some **rajahs,** or local Hindu rulers, continued governing. Many Hindus converted to Islam because it rejected the caste system. Muslims followed some Hindu customs and ideas. A new language, called Urdu, blended Arabic, Persian, and Hindi. A new religion, **Sikhism,** was a blend of Muslim and Hindu beliefs.

In 1526, **Babur** led Turkish and Mongol armies into northern India to establish the **Mughal** dynasty, which would last until 1857. Babur's grandson, **Akbar,** known as Akbar the Great, ruled from 1556 to 1605. He established a strong central government that had paid officials; he also modernized the army and encouraged international trade. He allowed Hindus to work in government and promoted peace through religious tolerance.

After Akbar's death, his son's wife, **Nur Jahan,** managed the government skillfully, and supported Indian culture. She was the most powerful woman in Indian history until the twentieth century. Akbar's grandson, **Shah Jahan,** ruled when Mughal literature, art, and architecture were at their height. He built the **Taj Mahal,** a tomb for his wife. It is a spectacular building and a great monument of the Mughal empire.

Review Questions

1. What are two differences between Hindu and Muslim beliefs?

_____

_____

2. What were Nur Jahan's contributions to the Mughal empire?

_____

_____

READING CHECK

What religion is a blend of Muslim and Hindu beliefs?

_____

_____

_____

VOCABULARY STRATEGY

What does the word *onslaughts* mean in the underlined sentence? Look for context clues to its meaning in the sentence. Use those clues to help you write a definition of *onslaughts.*

READING SKILL

Identify Supporting Details
Record details that support this statement:

In India, the Hindu and Muslim cultures blended.

_____

_____

_____

CHAPTER 10
SECTION 5

Note Taking Study Guide

THE OTTOMAN AND SAFAVID EMPIRES

Focus Question: What were the main characteristics of the Ottoman and Safavid empires?

As you read this section in your textbook, complete the following chart to record characteristics of the Ottoman and Safavid empires.

Characteristics	Ottomans	Safavids
Capital		
Dates		
Strongest ruler		
Extent of empire		
Type of Islam		
Relationship with Europe		

CHAPTER 10 SECTION 5

Section Summary
THE OTTOMAN AND SAFAVID EMPIRES

The **Ottomans** were Turkish-speaking nomads who had expanded into Asia Minor and the Balkan Peninsula by the 1300s. They were successful in capturing Constantinople in 1453. The city was renamed **Istanbul** and became the capital of the Ottoman empire.

The Ottoman empire enjoyed a golden age under **Suleiman,** who ruled from 1520 to 1566. He expanded the empire into Asia, Africa, and Europe. Although he was defeated at Vienna in 1529, the empire remained the largest and most powerful in Europe and the Middle East for centuries. Suleiman had absolute power, but a council helped him govern. He based the justice system on the Sharia, as well as royal edicts.

The top two social classes in Ottoman society—military men and intellectuals, such as scientists and lawyers—were nearly all Muslims. Below them were men involved in trade and production, and then farmers. All people belonged to religious communities, which provided for education and legal matters. The Jewish community, which had been expelled from Spain, possessed international banking connections that benefited the Ottomans.

Ottomans converted some young Christian boys to Islam and trained them for government service. Some were chosen for the **janizaries,** an elite force of the Ottoman army. The brightest became government officials.

Ottoman culture included great poets, painters, and architects. However, after Suleiman's death, the empire declined. By the 1700s, it had lost control of areas in Europe and Africa.

By the early 1500s, the **Safavids** united an empire in Persia (modern Iran). They were Shiite Muslims who fought with Sunni Ottomans to the west and the Mughals in India to the east. Their greatest king, or **shah**, was **Shah Abbas** who ruled from 1588 to 1629. He created a strong military and developed military alliances with Europeans. Abbas lowered taxes and encouraged industry. He tolerated other religions and built a capital at **Isfahan,** which became a center for silk trading.

After Abbas' death, the empire suffered from religious disputes until its end in 1722. In the late 1700s, a new dynasty, the **Qajars,** won control of Iran, made **Tehran** the capital, and ruled until 1925.

Review Questions

1. What social classes existed in the Ottoman empire?

_____

_____

2. What religious difference existed between the Ottoman and Safavid empires?

_____

_____

READING CHECK

Who were the Safavids?

_____

_____

_____

VOCABULARY STRATEGY

What does *edicts* mean in the underlined sentence? Notice that *edicts* were royal and were related to the justice system. Use this context clue to help you figure out the meaning of the word *edicts.*

READING SKILL

Synthesize Information Briefly describe society under the Ottomans.

_____

_____

_____

CHAPTER
11
SECTION 1

Note Taking Study Guide
EARLY CIVILIZATIONS OF AFRICA

Focus Question: How did geography and natural resources affect the development of early societies throughout Africa?

As you read this section in your textbook, complete the following outline to record the important effects of Africa's geography and natural resources.

I. **The influence of geography**
   A. Geographic patterns
      1. _____
         _____
      2. _____
         _____
      3. _____
   B. Resources spur trade
      1. _____
         _____
      2. _____

II. _____
   A. _____
      1. _____
         _____
      2. _____
         _____
      3. _____
         _____
      4. _____
         _____
      5. _____
         _____
   B. _____
      1. _____
         _____
      2. _____
         _____

(Outline continues on the next page.)

CHAPTER
11
SECTION 1

Note Taking Study Guide

EARLY CIVILIZATIONS OF AFRICA

(Continued from page 98)

III. _____

   A. _____

   B. _____

   C. _____

      1. _____

         _____

      2. _____

         _____

IV. _____

   A. _____

   B. _____

   C. _____

CHAPTER 11 SECTION 1

Section Summary
EARLY CIVILIZATIONS OF AFRICA

What led to Nubia's decline?

_____

_____

_____

What does the word *utilized* mean in the underlined sentence? A related word is *utility,* which means "having a use." Use this information and your prior knowledge to figure out the meaning of *utilized.*

Identify Causes and Effects
Identify the effects mentioned in the Summary of each of these causes:

Rome conquered Carthage.

_____

_____

_____

Muslim Arabs took North Africa.

_____

_____

_____

Africa includes tropical rain forests, grassy plains called **savannas,** and deserts such as the vast **Sahara.** Deserts, rain forests, the interior plateau, and rivers with **cataracts,** or waterfalls, limited travel and trade. On the other hand, an interior valley and the Mediterranean and Red seas provided overseas trade routes to Asia and Europe. By A.D. 200, camel caravans helped transport goods across the Sahara. Valuable minerals also encouraged trade.

Before 2500 B.C., there were forests and rivers in the Sahara. A climate change, however, slowly resulted in the area drying up and becoming desert—a process called **desertification.** As a result, people migrated to find new farmland. Between 1000 B.C. and A.D. 1000, people from West Africa moved south and east. They spoke forms of a root language known as **Bantu.** These Bantu people merged with existing cultures and brought skills in farming and ironworking.

About 2700 B.C., the civilization of **Nubia,** or Kush, developed on the upper Nile. Egypt controlled Nubia for about 500 years beginning in 1500 B.C. Early Nubian culture was influenced by Egyptian architecture and religion.

Forced to move by Assyrian invaders, the Nubians established a new capital in **Meroë** about 500 B.C. Meroë developed into a successful trade center. Nearby areas were rich in iron ore and timber. Using wood to fuel smelting furnaces, the Nubians made iron tools and weapons, improving their defense. The Nubians also established a new religion and a system of writing. In A.D. 350, Nubia was conquered by an invader from the south, King Ezana of Axum.

While Nubia was thriving along the Nile, Carthage emerged along the Mediterranean in North Africa. Founded by Phoenician traders, Carthage forged a huge empire from 800 B.C. to 146 B.C. At the end of the Third Punic War, however, Rome destroyed Carthage. The Romans then utilized North Africa's farmlands to provide grain for their armies. They also built roads and cities, and later brought Christianity to the area.

Muslim Arabs took control of North Africa in the 690s. Islam replaced Christianity, and traders later carried the religion to West Africa. Arabic replaced Latin as North Africa's main language.

Review Questions

1. How did the Bantu migrations affect existing cultures?

_____

_____

2. How did Meroë's resources strengthen Nubia?

_____

_____

Note Taking Study Guide

KINGDOMS OF WEST AFRICA

Focus Question: How did the kingdoms of West Africa develop and prosper?

As you read this section in your textbook, complete the following flowchart to record the causes and effects related to the development of West African kingdoms.

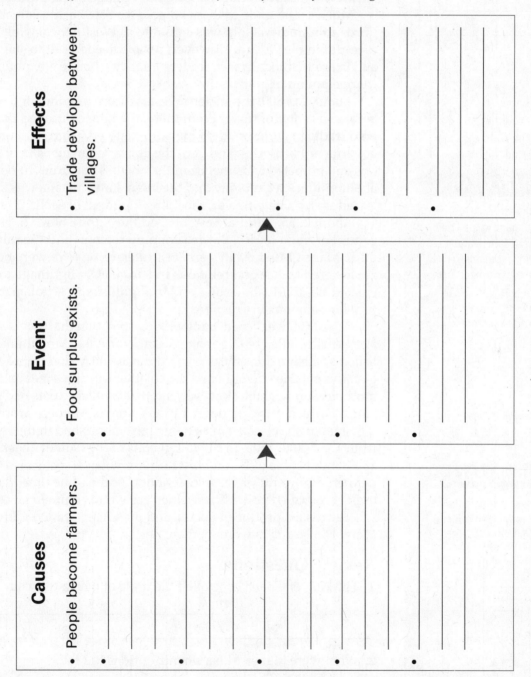

Effects

• Trade develops between villages.

Event

• Food surplus exists.

Causes

• People become farmers.

CHAPTER 11
SECTION 2

Section Summary
KINGDOMS OF WEST AFRICA

READING CHECK

Who were the Hausa?

_____

_____

_____

After early farmers moved from the Sahara to more fertile lands to the south, they began to produce more food than they needed, or a **surplus.** They were then able to trade surplus food for goods from other villages. A trade network developed that eventually connected Africa with Asia and Europe. Cities developed along the trade routes.

Much of the trade exchanged gold for salt, each a valuable product or **commodity.** Gold was common in West Africa, while salt was plentiful in the Sahara. However, people needed salt to stay healthy and preserve food. In fact, traders might exchange one pound of salt for one pound of gold.

About A.D. 800, the ancient West African kingdom of **Ghana** became a center of trade. From there, the king controlled the salt and gold trade. <u>In addition, the king administered justice and other government activities, and kept the peace.</u> Ghana was very prosperous and attracted Muslims from the north. They brought new ideas about military technology and business. Later, Ghana was swallowed up by a new power, the rising kingdom of Mali.

VOCABULARY STRATEGY

What does the word *administered* mean in the underlined sentence? It is related to the word *administration*. Think of where you may have heard either word used before. Use this prior knowledge to help you write a definition of *administered*.

About 1235, **Sundiata** established the empire of **Mali.** He gained control of trade routes, the gold mining regions, and the salt supplies. **Mansa Musa,** Mali's greatest ruler, came to power about 1312. He fostered justice and religious freedom. His pilgrimage to Mecca created ties to Muslim states and brought Islamic scholars to Mali to provide religious instruction.

After Mali weakened, another kingdom, **Songhai,** developed in West Africa. After 1492, Songhai's emperor Askia Muhammad established a Muslim dynasty, expanded the territory, and improved the government. He strengthened ties to other Muslim states and built mosques and schools. However, internal conflicts weakened the empire, which was conquered by the sultan of Morocco around 1591.

Smaller societies, such as Benin, also flourished in the region from A.D. 500 to 1500. In the rain forests of the Guinea coast in the 1300s, the people of Benin built farming villages. They also traded pepper, ivory, and slaves to neighbors. At the same time, the Hausa built clay-walled cities. These cities grew into commercial centers, where artisans produced goods, and merchants traded with Arabs. Many Hausa rulers were women.

READING SKILL

Identify Causes and Effects
Identify the cause and effect of Songhai's decline.

_____

_____

_____

Review Questions

1. The king of Ghana controlled the trade of which two commodities?

_____

_____

2. What were Mansa Musa's contributions to Mali?

_____

_____

Name_____ Class_____ Date_____

Note Taking Study Guide

KINGDOMS AND TRADING STATES OF EAST AFRICA

Focus Question: What influence did religion and trade have on the development of East Africa?

As you read this section in your textbook, complete the following flowchart to record the effects of trade on the societies of East Africa.

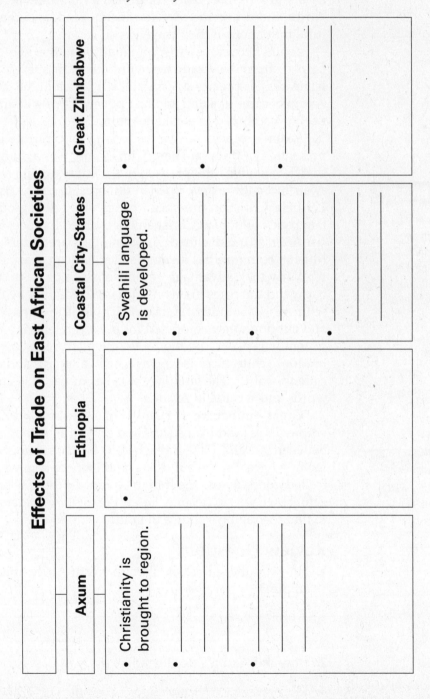

Effects of Trade on East African Societies

Great Zimbabwe

Coastal City-States
- Swahili language is developed.

Ethiopia

Axum
- Christianity is brought to region.

CHAPTER 11 — SECTION 3

Section Summary

KINGDOMS AND TRADING STATES OF EAST AFRICA

The kingdom of **Axum** conquered Nubia about A.D. 350. Axum included two main cities—the upland capital city of Axum and the port of **Adulis** on the Red Sea. The peoples of Axum were descended from African farmers and people from the Middle East. By about A.D. 400, Axum controlled a rich trade network connecting Africa, India, and the Mediterranean. Traders exchanged many cultural influences in their travels.

Axum became a Christian kingdom in the 300s. At first, this helped strengthen trade ties with other Christian countries. When Islam began spreading across North Africa in the 600s, however, Axum became isolated and lost power. Civil war and economic decline combined to weaken Axum.

Axum's legacy, however, survived for centuries in a portion of present-day **Ethiopia**. There, Christianity was a unifying influence that helped give Ethiopia a unique identity among Muslim neighbors. A distinct culture developed in Ethiopia. In the 1200s, under **King Lalibela,** Christian churches were carved below ground into mountain rocks. Ethiopian Christianity absorbed local customs.

After Axum declined, Arab and Persian traders established Muslim communities along the East African coast. By the 600s, ships regularly took advantage of monsoon winds to sail to India and back, and the cities in East Africa grew wealthy by trading goods with Africa, Southeast Asia, and China. The cities were independent, and although they competed for power, relations among them were generally peaceful. By the 1000s, the mixture of cultures created unique architecture, as well as a new language and culture, both called **Swahili.** The language was Bantu-based, using some Arabic words and written in Arabic.

Great Zimbabwe, the capital of a great inland Zimbabwe empire, was built by a succession of Bantu-speaking peoples between 900 and 1500. It reached its height around 1300. The city included great stone buildings, and its people mined gold and traded goods across the Indian Ocean. By the 1500s, the empire of Zimbabwe was in decline. Later, Portuguese traders tried, but failed, to find the region's source of gold.

Review Questions

1. How did the spread of Islam in North Africa affect the Axum empire?

_____

_____

2. How did Axum's decline affect trade in East Africa?

_____

_____

CHAPTER 11 SECTION 4	# Note Taking Study Guide
	SOCIETIES IN MEDIEVAL AFRICA

Focus Question: What factors influenced the development of societies in Africa?

As you read this section in your textbook, complete the following concept web to record the factors that influenced the development of African societies.

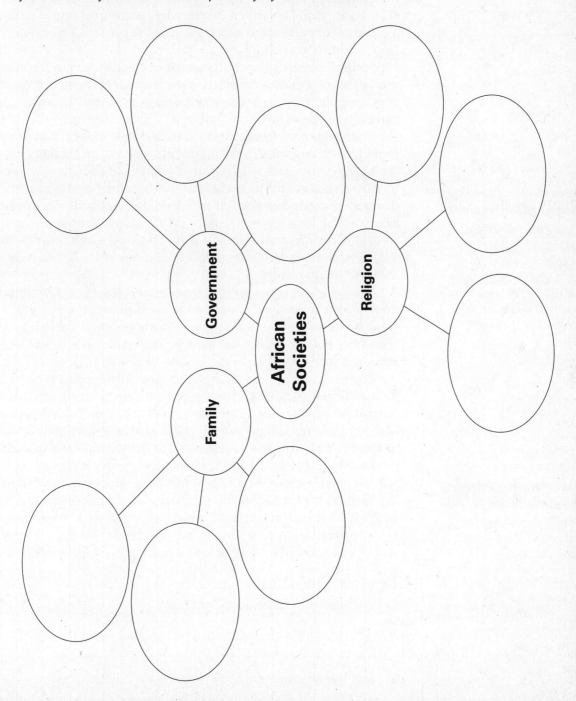

CHAPTER 11

SECTION 4

Section Summary

SOCIETIES IN MEDIEVAL AFRICA

In small societies in medieval Africa, the **nuclear family,** or one set of parents and their children, lived and worked together. In other societies, the family included several generations. **Patrilineal** families passed inheritances through the father's side of the family, while **matrilineal** families passed property down through the mother's side. Each family belonged to a **lineage,** a group of households with a common ancestor, and a clan included several lineages descended from a common ancestor.

Political patterns depended on the size and culture of a community. In small societies, political power was often shared among a number of people. Village decisions were often made by **consensus,** or general agreement, after open discussions. Because elders had experience, their opinions usually carried the greatest weight. Women sometimes took strong roles in the marketplace or as peacemakers.

Large empires usually required villages to obey decisions made by distant rulers and their courts. Another form of government that developed grouped many villages into districts and provinces governed by the king's officials. Around A.D. 1500, Kongo, a kingdom in central Africa, governed in this way. The king had limited powers. Villagers were governed by appointed royal officials, but each village had its own chief.

Early African religions were varied and complex. They involved many gods, goddesses, rituals, and ceremonies. Many people believed in one supreme being, and some honored the spirits of ancestors. By A.D. 1000, Christianity and Islam had spread and absorbed many local practices and beliefs.

The tradition of African arts includes the Egyptian pyramids, built 4,000 years ago. Much art served decorative, religious, or ceremonial purposes, such as cloths, pottery, and jewelry. Objects often had symbolic meanings, such as the bright blue-and-gold kente cloth of West Africa, which was reserved for the wealthy and powerful.

Medieval written histories from Africa provide records of laws, religion, and society. Arabic provided a common written language in Muslim areas, and Muslim scholars gathered in important cities. In West Africa, **griots,** or professional storytellers, kept traditions alive by reciting ancient stories and histories. Folktales and other stories encouraged a sense of community and common values.

Review Questions

1. What are a lineage and a clan?

_____

_____

2. How did the rulers of the Kongo control their lands?

_____

_____

CHAPTER
12
SECTION 1

Note Taking Study Guide
TWO GOLDEN AGES OF CHINA

Focus Question: Describe the political, economic, and cultural achievements of the Tang and Song dynasties.

As you read this section, complete the Venn diagram below to compare and contrast the Tang and Song dynasties. Use the overlapping portion of the circles for information that applies to both dynasties.

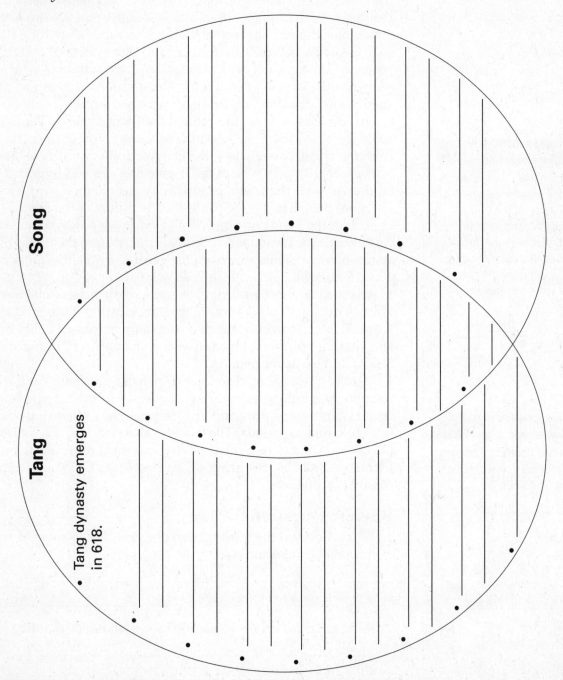

Song

Tang

• Tang dynasty emerges in 618.

Name_____ Class_____ Date_____

READING CHECK

What are tributary states?

_____

_____

_____

VOCABULARY STRATEGY

What does the word *compelled* mean in the underlined sentence? Note that Li Shimin *compelled* his father to step down and then took the throne himself. Use this context clue to help you understand the meaning of the word *compelled*.

READING SKILL

Compare and Contrast Compare and contrast the social classes in Tang and Song China.

_____

_____

_____

_____

_____

After the Han dynasty collapsed, China broke apart. During the Sui dynasty (589–618), the emperor Sui Wendi reunited north and south. In 618, the general Li Yuan and his son Li Shimin led a revolt and established the **Tang dynasty.** Eight years later, Li Shimin compelled his aging father to step down. Li Shimin then took the throne under the name **Tang Taizong.** Later Tang rulers conquered many territories and forced Vietnam, Tibet, and Korea to become **tributary states,** or self-governing states that sent tribute. Other Tang rulers, such as Empress Wu Zhao, restored the Han system of uniform government. Tang emperors also undertook **land reform** in which they redistributed land to peasants. However, the Tang eventually weakened. In 907, the last Tang emperor was overthrown.

In 960, Zhao Kuangyin founded the **Song dynasty.** The Song ruled for 319 years. They faced the constant threat of invaders from the north. Nonetheless, the Song period was a time of great achievement. A new type of faster-growing rice was imported from Southeast Asia. The rise in productivity created food surpluses, freeing more people to pursue commerce, learning, or the arts.

Under the Tang and Song, China was a well-ordered society. At its head was the emperor. Scholar-officials had the highest social status. Most of them came from the **gentry,** or wealthy, landowning class. The vast majority of Chinese were poor peasant farmers. Merchants had the lowest status because their riches came from the labor of others. Women had higher status during this period than they did later. However, when a woman married, she could not keep her **dowry,** the payment that a woman brings to a marriage. She could also never remarry.

The Tang and Song developed a rich culture. Song landscape painting was influenced by Daoist beliefs. Buddhist themes influenced Chinese sculpture and architecture. The Indian stupa evolved into the Chinese **pagoda.** The Chinese also perfected the making of porcelain. Among the gentry, poetry was the most respected form of literature. Probably the greatest Tang poet was Li Bo, who wrote some 2,000 poems.

Review Questions

1. What effect did the introduction of a new, faster-growing rice have on Chinese society?

_____

_____

2. What religious beliefs influenced Song landscape painting?

_____

_____

Name_____ Class_____ Date_____

Focus Question: What were the effects on China of the Mongol invasion and the rise of the Ming dynasty?

As you read this section, complete the timeline below to record important events during the Mongol and Ming empires.

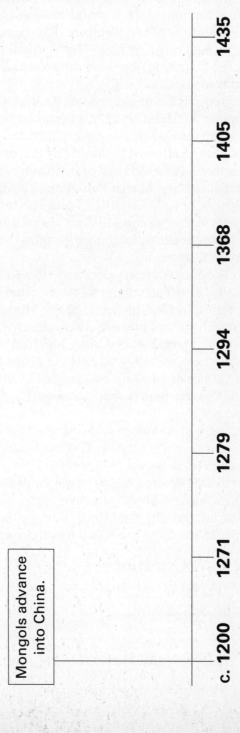

1435

1405

1368

1294

1279

1271

Mongols advance into China.

c. 1200

CHAPTER 12 SECTION 2 — Section Summary
THE MONGOL AND MING EMPIRES

The Mongols were nomads who grazed their animals on the **steppes,** or treeless plains, of Central Asia. Mongol clans spent much of their time warring with one another. In the early 1200s, however, a Mongol chieftain united these clans. He took the name **Genghis Khan,** meaning "Universal Ruler." Under his leadership, Mongol forces conquered a vast empire. After his death, his heirs continued to expand the Mongol empire. For the next 150 years, they dominated much of Asia. The Mongols established peace and order within their domains. They controlled and protected the Silk Road, and trade flourished.

Genghis Khan's grandson, **Kublai Khan,** toppled the last Song emperor in China, in 1279. He named his dynasty the **Yuan.** Only Mongols could serve in his military and in the highest government jobs, but he allowed Chinese officials to continue to rule in the provinces. He welcomed many foreigners to his court, including Ibn Battuta and **Marco Polo.** Polo's writings about the wealth and splendor of China sparked European interest in Asia. The pope sent priests to China, and Muslims also set up communities there. Chinese products, including gunpowder and porcelain, made their way to Europe.

The Yuan dynasty declined after Kublai Khan's death in 1294. Finally, Zhu Yuanzhang formed a rebel army that toppled the Mongols. In 1368, he founded the **Ming,** or "brilliant," dynasty. Ming China was immensely productive. Better methods of fertilizing improved farming. The Ming repaired the canal system, which made trade easier and allowed cities to grow. Ming artists developed their own styles of painting and created beautiful blue-and-white porcelain. Ming writers composed novels and the world's first detective stories.

Early Ming rulers sent Chinese fleets into distant waters to show the glory of their empire. The most famous voyages were those of **Zheng He.** Between 1405 and 1433, he commanded seven expeditions that explored the coasts of Southeast Asia, India, the Persian Gulf, and East Africa. However, after Zheng He died in 1435, the Ming emperor banned the building of seagoing ships, and overseas expeditions came to a halt. Historians are not sure why.

Review Questions
1. Why did trade flourish under the Mongols?

_____

_____

2. What effect did Marco Polo's writings have in Europe?

_____

_____

Name_____ Class_____ Date_____

Focus Question: How are Korea's history and culture linked to those of China and Japan?

As you read this section, complete the concept web below to record important information about Korea.

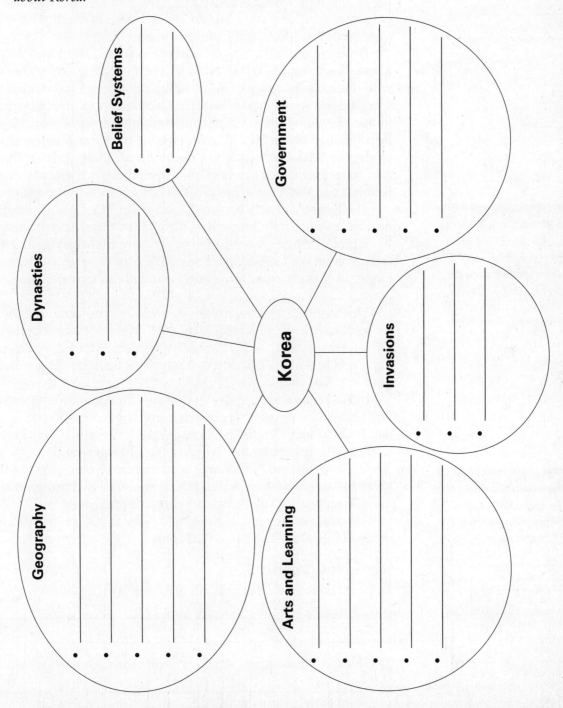

CHAPTER 12 SECTION 3	Section Summary
	KOREA AND ITS TRADITIONS

Korea is located on a peninsula that juts south from the Chinese mainland. Because of its location, Korea has been strongly influenced by China. The earliest Koreans probably migrated from Siberia and northern Manchuria. They evolved their own ways of life before they were influenced by China. In 108 B.C., the Han emperor, Wudi, invaded Korea. The invasion brought with it Confucian traditions and Chinese ideas.

Between A.D. 300 and 600, local rulers forged three kingdoms in Korea: Koguryo, Paekche, and Silla. The three kingdoms often warred with one another or with China. Still, Chinese ideas continued to spread there. Missionaries brought Buddhism to Korea. Korean monks then traveled to China and brought home Chinese arts and learning. In 668, the Silla kingdom united the Korean peninsula. Under the **Silla dynasty,** Korea became a tributary state of China. As Chinese influence increased, Confucian views took root. However, Koreans adapted Confucian ideas to fit their own traditions.

The **Koryo dynasty** replaced the Silla in 935. Confucianism and Buddhism were both influential during this time. Koreans used woodblock printing from China to produce Buddhist texts. They learned to make Chinese porcelain. They then perfected the technique for making **celadon,** a porcelain with an unusual blue-green glaze.

The Mongols first invaded Korea in 1231 and occupied the country until the 1350s. When their rule collapsed, the Koryo returned to power. However, in 1392, the Korean general Yi Song-gye overthrew them and set up the **Choson dynasty.** This was the longest-lasting, but final, Korean dynasty.

In 1443, **King Sejong** decided to replace complex Chinese writing. Sejong had experts develop **hangul,** the Korean phonetic alphabet. Hangul spread quickly because it was easier to use than written Chinese. Its use led to an extremely high **literacy rate.**

In the 1590s, the Japanese armies invaded Korea. To stop the invaders at sea, Korean Admiral Yi Sun-shin sailed armored ships into the Japanese fleet. After six years, the Japanese armies withdrew from Korea. As they left, they carried off many Korean artisans in order to introduce their skills to Japan.

Review Questions

1. How did Korea's location affect its cultural development?

_____

_____

2. Why did Japanese invaders carry off many Korean artisans?

_____

_____

Note Taking Study Guide

CHAPTER 12 SECTION 4

THE EMERGENCE OF JAPAN AND THE FEUDAL AGE

Focus Question: What internal and external factors shaped Japan's civilization, and what characterized Japan's feudal age?

As you read this section, complete the table below with examples of internal and external factors that shaped Japan's civilization.

Influences on Japan	
Internal Factors	**External Factors**
• Geography both protected and isolated Japan.	• _____
• _____	• _____
• _____	• _____
• _____	• _____
• _____	• _____
• _____	• _____
• _____	• _____
• _____	• _____
• _____	• _____
• _____	• _____

CHAPTER 12 SECTION 4

Section Summary

THE EMERGENCE OF JAPAN AND THE FEUDAL AGE

READING CHECK

What is bushido?

_____

_____

_____

VOCABULARY STRATEGY

What does the word *stressed* mean in the underlined sentence? When you put *stress* on a syllable, do you say it with more or less emphasis? Use this clue to help you understand what *stressed* means in this sentence.

READING SKILL

Categorize List the levels in Japanese feudal society and give details about each level.

_____

_____

_____

Japan sits on an **archipelago,** or chain of islands. In early times, surrounding seas both protected and isolated Japan. This region has many volcanoes, earthquakes, and tidal waves called **tsunamis.**

Early Japanese society was divided into clans. The clans honored kami, or powers that were natural or divine. The worship of these forces of nature became known as **Shinto.** Missionaries from Korea introduced Buddhism to Japan in the 500s. They also brought knowledge of Chinese culture. In the 600s, Prince Shotoku sent nobles to study in China. The visitors brought back Chinese technology and arts. In 710, the Japanese emperor built a new capital at Nara, modeled after the Chinese capital.

The Japanese kept some Chinese ways but discarded others. This process is known as **selective borrowing.** The Japanese revised the Chinese writing system and added **kana,** symbols representing syllables. From 794 to 1185, Heian was the Japanese capital. Heian women, such as Murasaki Shikibu, produced some of the most important works of Japanese literature.

Japan evolved into a feudal society. Theoretically, the emperor was the head of this society, but really he was powerless. The shogun, or supreme military commander, had the real power. Minamoto Yoritomo was appointed shogun in 1192. He set up the Kamakura shogunate. The shogun distributed land to lords, called daimyo, who agreed to support him with their armies. They, in turn, granted land to lesser warriors called **samurai.** Samurai developed a code of values, known as **bushido.** The code emphasized honor, bravery, and loyalty to one's lord.

Kublai Khan tried to invade Japan in 1274 and 1281, but typhoons wrecked the Mongol ships during both invasions. However, after the attempted invasions, the Kamakura shogunate crumbled. By 1590, Toyotomi Hideyoshi had brought most of Japan under his control. In 1600, Tokugawa Ieyasu defeated his rivals to become master of Japan. The Tokugawa shoguns created an orderly society. With peace restored to the countryside, agriculture improved and trade flourished.

During Japan's feudal age, a Buddhist sect known as **Zen** won widespread acceptance. Zen monks were great scholars, yet they stressed the importance of reaching a moment of "non-knowing."

Review Questions

1. How did the surrounding seas affect Japan's development?

_____

_____

2. How did the shogun gain the support of the daimyo?

_____

_____

CHAPTER 12 SECTION 5

Note Taking Study Guide

DIVERSE CULTURES OF SOUTHEAST ASIA

Focus Question: How was Southeast Asia affected by the cultures of both China and India?

As you read this section, complete the outline below to summarize the diverse characteristics of Southeast Asia.

I. Geography of Southeast Asia

   A. Location

      1. Mainland set apart by mountains and plateaus.

      2. _____

   B. Trade routes in the southern seas

      1. _____

      2. _____

      3. _____

   C. _____

      1. _____

      2. _____

      3. _____

      4. _____

         a. _____

         b. _____

II. _____

   A. _____

      1. _____

      2. _____

      3. _____

      4. _____

   B. _____

      1. _____

      2. _____

(Outline continues on the next page.)

(Continued from page 115)

III. _____
  A. _____
    1. _____
    2. _____
    3. _____
    4. _____
  B. _____
    1. _____
    2. _____
    3. _____
  C. _____
    1. _____
    2. _____
    3. _____
IV. _____
  A. _____
    1. _____
    2. _____
  B. _____
    1. _____
    2. _____
    3. _____
  C. _____
    1. _____
    2. _____

CHAPTER 12 SECTION 5

Section Summary

DIVERSE CULTURES OF SOUTHEAST ASIA

Southeast Asia is made up of two regions: mainland Southeast Asia, which includes present-day Myanmar, Thailand, Cambodia, Laos, Vietnam, and Malaysia; and island Southeast Asia, which consists of more than 20,000 islands. These islands include the present-day nations of Indonesia, Singapore, Brunei, and the Philippines. Historically, sea trade between China and India had to pass through the Malacca or Sunda straits, so the islands that controlled these straits were strategically important. Women took part in the spice trade and had greater equality there than they did elsewhere in Asia. **Matrilineal** descent, or inheritance through the mother, was an accepted custom in this region.

In the early centuries A.D., Indian merchants and Hindu priests slowly spread their culture through Southeast Asia. Later, monks introduced Theravada Buddhism. Indian traders eventually carried Islam to Indonesia, and as far east as the Philippines. Trade with India brought prosperity. Merchants exchanged cotton cloth, jewels, and perfume for timber, spices, and gold.

A series of kingdoms and empires developed in Southeast Asia. The kingdom of Pagan arose in present-day Myanmar. In 1044, King Anawrahta united the region and brought Buddhism to his people. He filled his capital city with magnificent **stupas,** or dome-shaped shrines. Indian influences also shaped the Khmer empire, which reached its peak between 800 and 1350. Its greatest rulers controlled much of present-day Cambodia, Thailand, and Malaysia. Khmer rulers became Hindus, but most people were Buddhists. In Indonesia, the trading empire of Srivijaya flourished from the 600s to the 1200s. Both Hinduism and Buddhism reached Srivijaya.

The heart of northern Vietnam was the Red River delta. There, the river irrigated fertile rice **paddies.** In 111 B.C., Han armies conquered the region, and China remained in control for the next 1,000 years. During that time, the Vietnamese absorbed Confucian ideas. Unlike the rest of Southeast Asia, where Theravada Buddhism had the strongest impact, Vietnam adopted Mahayana Buddhism from China. In A.D. 39, two noble sisters, Trung Trac and Trung Nhi, led an uprising that briefly drove out the Chinese. Finally, in 939, Vietnam was able to break free from China.

Review Questions

1. Why were the islands of Southeast Asia strategically important?

_____

_____

2. Why was Vietnam influenced more by Confucian and Mahayana beliefs than by Hindu and Theravada beliefs?

_____

_____

READING CHECK

What is matrilineal descent?

_____

_____

_____

VOCABULARY STRATEGY

What does the word *impact* mean in the underlined sentence? The sentence contrasts the power of Buddhist beliefs in Vietnam with the power of Buddhist beliefs in the rest of Southeast Asia. Use this context clue to help you understand the meaning of the word *impact.*

READING SKILL

Summarize Summarize the influence of India on Southeast Asia.

_____

_____

_____

CHAPTER 13 SECTION 1

Note Taking Study Guide
THE RENAISSANCE IN ITALY

Focus Question: What were the ideals of the Renaissance, and how did Italian artists and writers reflect these ideals?

As you read this section in your textbook, complete the following outline to identify main ideas and supporting details about the Italian Renaissance.

I. What was the Renaissance?

    A. A changing worldview

        1. _____

        2. _____

    B. A spirit of adventure

        1. _____

        2. _____

    C. _____

        1. _____

        2. _____

II. _____

    A. _____

        1. _____

        2. _____

        3. _____

    B. _____

        1. _____

        2. _____

III. _____

    A. _____

        1. _____

        2. _____

    B. _____

        1. _____

        2. _____

(Outline continues on the next page.)

CHAPTER
13
SECTION 1

Note Taking Study Guide

THE RENAISSANCE IN ITALY

(Continued from page 118)

C. _____
   1. _____
   2. _____
D. _____
   1. _____
   2. _____
E. _____
   1. _____
   2. _____
F. _____
   1. _____
   2. _____
IV. _____
   A. _____
      1. _____
      2. _____
   B. _____
      1. _____
      2. _____

CHAPTER 13 SECTION 1

Section Summary

THE RENAISSANCE IN ITALY

A new age called the Renaissance, meaning "rebirth," marked a great change in culture, politics, society, and economics. In Italy, it began in the 1300s and reached its peak around 1500. Instead of focusing on religion, as in the Middle Ages, the Renaissance explored the human experience. At the same time, there was a new emphasis on individual achievement. At the heart of the Renaissance was an intellectual movement called **humanism.** Renaissance humanists studied the classical culture of Greece and Rome to try to comprehend their own times. They wanted to broaden their understanding. They emphasized the **humanities**—subjects such as rhetoric, poetry, and history. Poet Francesco **Petrarch** was an early Renaissance humanist. He gathered a library of Greek and Roman manuscripts. This opened the works of Cicero, Homer, and Virgil to Western Europeans.

Italy was the birthplace of the Renaissance for many reasons. It had been the center of the Roman empire; remains of that ancient culture were all around. Rome was also the seat of the Roman Catholic Church, an important **patron** of the arts. Furthermore, Italy's location encouraged trade with markets on the Mediterranean, in Africa, and in Europe. Trade provided the wealth that fueled the Renaissance. In Italy's city-states, powerful merchant families, such as the Medici family of **Florence,** lent political and economic leadership and supported the arts.

Renaissance art reflected humanism. Renaissance painters returned to the realism of classical times by developing improved ways to represent humans and landscapes. For example, the discovery of **perspective** allowed artists to create realistic art and to paint scenes that appeared three-dimensional. The greatest of the Renaissance artists were **Leonardo** da Vinci, **Michelangelo,** and **Raphael.**

Some Italian writers wrote guidebooks to help ambitious people who wanted to rise in the Renaissance world. The most widely read of these was *The Book of the Courtier*, by **Baldassare Castiglione.** His ideal courtier was a well-educated, well-mannered aristocrat who mastered many fields. **Niccolò Machiavelli** wrote a guide for rulers, titled *The Prince*, on how to gain and maintain power.

Review Questions

1. How did the focus of study change between the Middle Ages and the Renaissance?

_____

_____

2. Identify two reasons why the Renaissance began in Italy.

_____

_____

CHAPTER 13
SECTION 2

Note Taking Study Guide
THE RENAISSANCE IN THE NORTH

Focus Question: How did the Renaissance develop in northern Europe?

As you read this section in your textbook, complete the following chart to record the main ideas about the Renaissance in the North.

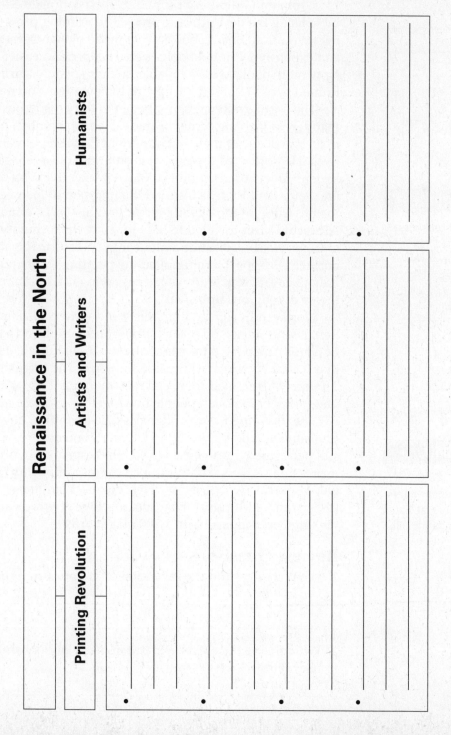

CHAPTER 13 SECTION 2

Section Summary
THE RENAISSANCE IN THE NORTH

By the 1400s, northern Europe began to enjoy the economic growth needed to develop its own Renaissance. An astounding invention—the printing press—helped to spread Renaissance ideas. In about 1455, **Johann Gutenberg** printed the first complete edition of the Bible using the new printing press. The printing press caused a printing revolution. Before, books were made by hand. They were rare and expensive. Printed books were cheaper and easier to produce. Now more books were available, so more people learned to read. Printed books exposed Europeans to new ideas and new places.

The northern Renaissance began in the prosperous cities of Flanders, a thriving center of trade. Flemish painters pursued realism in their art. One of the most important Flemish painters was Jan van Eyck. He portrayed townspeople and religious scenes in rich detail. Pieter Bruegel used vibrant color to portray lively scenes of peasant life. Peter Paul Rubens blended the tradition of Flemish realism with themes from mythology, the Bible, and history. German painter **Albrecht Dürer** traveled to Italy to study the techniques of the Italian masters. He soon became a pioneer in spreading Renaissance ideas to northern Europe. Dürer applied the painting techniques he learned in Italy to **engraving.** Many of his engravings and paintings portray the theme of religious upheaval.

Northern European humanists and writers also helped spread Renaissance ideas. The Dutch priest and humanist Desiderius **Erasmus** called for a translation of the Bible into the **vernacular** so that it could be read by a wider audience. The English humanist **Sir Thomas More** called for social reform in the form of a **utopian,** or ideal, society in which people live together in peace and harmony.

The towering figure of Renaissance literature, however, was the English poet and playwright William **Shakespeare.** His 37 plays are still performed around the world. Shakespeare's genius was in expressing universal themes, such as the complexity of the individual, in everyday, realistic settings. He used language that people understand and enjoy. Shakespeare's love of words also enriched the English language with 1,700 new words.

Review Questions

1. What changes did the invention of the printing press bring about?

_____

_____

2. What theme did Dürer explore in many of his paintings and engravings?

_____

_____

CHAPTER 13 SECTION 3

Note Taking Study Guide

THE PROTESTANT REFORMATION

Focus Question: How did revolts against the Roman Catholic Church affect northern European society?

As you read this section in your textbook, complete the following concept web to identify main ideas about the Protestant Reformation.

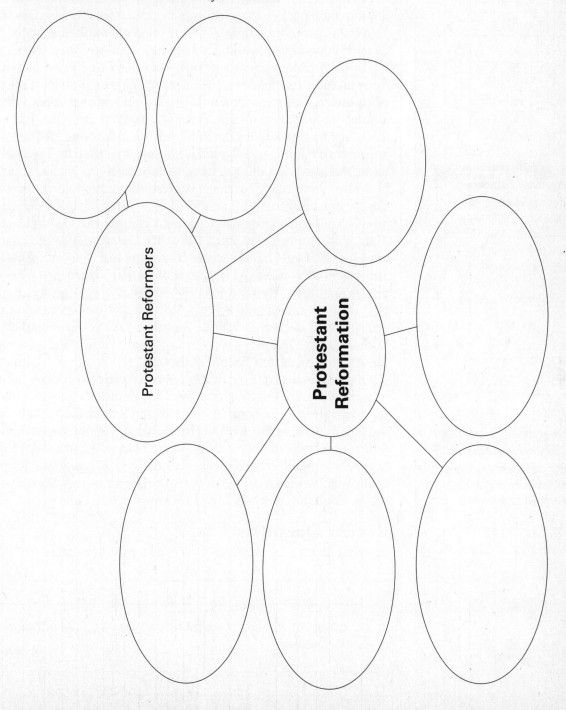

CHAPTER 13 SECTION 3

Section Summary
THE PROTESTANT REFORMATION

In the 1500s, the Renaissance in northern Europe sparked a religious upheaval that affected Christians at all levels of society. This movement is known as the Protestant Reformation. In the late Middle Ages, the Catholic Church had become caught up in worldly affairs. Popes led lavish lives and hired artists to enhance churches. To finance such projects, the Church increased fees for services. Many Christians protested such acts. They also questioned why the Church in distant Rome should have power over their lives.

In 1517, protests against Church abuses turned into a revolt. A German monk named **Martin Luther** triggered it over an event in **Wittenberg,** Germany. There, a priest sold **indulgences** to Christians to raise money to rebuild St. Peter's Cathedral in Rome. To Luther, the priest's actions were the final outrage. He wrote 95 Theses, or arguments, against indulgences. He said that they had no biblical basis, that the pope did not have the authority to release souls from purgatory, and that Christians could be saved only through faith. Throughout Europe, Luther's 95 Theses stirred furious debate. The new Holy Roman emperor, **Charles V,** summoned Luther to the **diet,** or assembly, at the city of Worms. Luther refused to change his views. Thousands hailed Luther as a hero and renounced the authority of the pope. <u>At the heart of Luther's doctrines were several beliefs, including the idea that all Christians have equal access to God through faith and the Bible.</u> Printing presses spread Luther's writings and ideas throughout Germany and Scandinavia. By 1530, Luther's many followers were using a new name, "Protestants," for those who "protested" papal authority.

In Switzerland, the reformer **John Calvin** also challenged the Catholic Church. Calvin shared many of Luther's beliefs, but also preached **predestination.** Protestants in **Geneva** asked Calvin to lead them. In keeping with his teachings, Calvin set up a **theocracy.** Reformers from all over Europe visited Geneva and then returned home to spread Calvin's ideas. This new challenge to the Roman Catholic Church set off fierce wars of religion across Europe. In the 1600s, English Calvinists sailed to America to escape persecution.

VOCABULARY STRATEGY

What does the word *doctrine* mean in the underlined sentence? The word comes from a Latin word that means "teaching" or "instruction." Use the word's origin to help you figure out what *doctrine* means.

READING SKILL

Identify Main Ideas What was one of the main beliefs at the heart of Luther's doctrines?

_____

_____

_____

Review Questions

1. What factors encouraged the Protestant Reformation?

_____

_____

2. What arguments did Martin Luther make against indulgences in the 95 Theses?

_____

_____

Note Taking Study Guide
REFORMATION IDEAS SPREAD

Focus Question: How did the Reformation bring about two different religious paths in Europe?

As you read this section in your textbook, complete the following flowchart to identify main ideas about the spread of the Protestant Reformation in Europe.

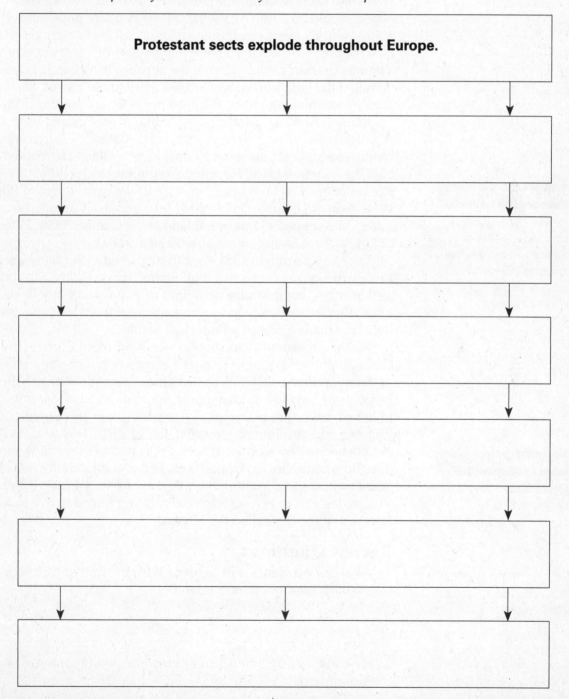

Protestant sects explode throughout Europe.

Section Summary
REFORMATION IDEAS SPREAD

READING CHECK

What happened at the Council of Trent?

_____

_____

_____

VOCABULARY STRATEGY

What does the word *rigorous* mean in the underlined sentence? What clues can you find in nearby words? Circle the words in the sentence that could help you figure out what *rigorous* means.

READING SKILL

Identify Main Ideas How did Elizabeth restore unity to England?

_____

_____

_____

As the Reformation continued, hundreds of new Protestant **sects** arose, influencing Protestant thinking in many countries. In England, the break with the Catholic Church came from **Henry VIII.** He and his wife, Catherine of Aragon, had one child, **Mary Tudor.** Henry wanted to divorce Catherine and marry another woman whom he hoped would bear him a male heir. However, the pope refused to annul Henry's marriage. Furious, Henry had Parliament pass laws to take the English church from the pope's control. Henry appointed **Thomas Cranmer** archbishop of the new English church. Cranmer annulled the king's marriage. In 1534, Parliament passed the Act of Supremacy, making Henry the head of the Church of England.

Many Catholics, including Sir Thomas More, refused to accept the Act of Supremacy and were executed. The Catholic Church later **canonized** More for his stand against Henry. When Henry died in 1547, his son Edward VI inherited the throne. Under Edward, Parliament passed laws bringing more Protestant reforms to England. When Edward died, his half-sister Mary Tudor, a Catholic, became queen. She wanted to return England to the Catholic faith. Hundreds of English Protestants were burned at the stake.

On Mary's death in 1558, the throne passed to her half-sister, **Elizabeth.** She made reforms that became known as the Elizabethan settlement—a **compromise** between Protestant and Catholic practices. Elizabeth restored unity to England; she kept many Catholic traditions, but made England a Protestant nation.

As the Protestant Reformation swept northern Europe, the Catholic Church began a Counter Reformation. The pope's **Council of Trent** reaffirmed Catholic beliefs that Protestants had challenged. **Ignatius of Loyola** founded a new religious order, the Jesuits. They followed a rigorous program of strict discipline, thorough religious training, and absolute obedience to the Church. **Teresa of Avila** established her own order of nuns dedicated to prayer and meditation. Both Catholics and Protestants fostered intolerance, and persecuted radical sects. Innocent people were executed for witchcraft. In Venice, Jews were pressured to convert and forced to live in a separate part of the city called the **ghetto.**

Review Questions

1. What caused Henry VIII to break with the Catholic Church and establish the Church of England?

_____

_____

2. How did many Catholics in England respond to the Act of Supremacy?

_____

_____

Note Taking Study Guide
THE SCIENTIFIC REVOLUTION

Focus Question: How did discoveries in science lead to a new way of thinking for Europeans?

As you read this section in your textbook, complete the following to identify main ideas about the Scientific Revolution in Europe.

Thinkers of the Scientific Revolution												
Nicolaus Copernicus	Developed sun-centered universe theory											

CHAPTER 13 SECTION 5

Section Summary
THE SCIENTIFIC REVOLUTION

READING CHECK

What did Isaac Newton call the force that keeps planets in their orbits around the sun?

_____

_____

_____

In the mid-1500s, a big shift in scientific thinking caused the Scientific Revolution. At the heart of this movement was the idea that mathematical laws governed nature and the universe. Before the Renaissance, Europeans thought that Earth was the center of everything in the heavens. In 1543, Polish scholar **Nicolaus Copernicus** proposed a **heliocentric,** or sun-centered, model of the solar system. In the late 1500s, the Danish astronomer **Tycho Brahe** provided evidence that supported Copernicus's theory. The German astronomer and mathematician **Johannes Kepler** used Brahe's data to calculate the orbits of the planets revolving around the sun. His calculations also supported Copernicus's heliocentric view.

Scientists from different lands built on the foundations laid by Copernicus and Kepler. In Italy, **Galileo** assembled a telescope and observed that the four moons of Jupiter move slowly around that planet. He realized that these moons moved the same way that Copernicus had said that Earth moves around the sun. Galileo's findings caused an uproar. Other scholars attacked him because his observations contradicted ancient views about the world. The Church condemned him because his ideas challenged the Christian teaching that the heavenly bodies were fixed in relation to Earth, and perfect.

VOCABULARY STRATEGY

What does the word *contradicted* mean in the underlined sentence? The prefix *contra-* means "against." Use the meaning of the word's prefix to help you figure out what *contradict* means.

Despite the opposition of the Church, a new approach to science had emerged, based upon observation and experimentation. To explain their data, scientists used reasoning to propose a logical **hypothesis,** or possible explanation. This process became known as the **scientific method.** The new scientific method was a revolution in thought. Two giants of this revolution were the Englishman **Francis Bacon** and the Frenchman **René Descartes.** Both were devoted to understanding how truth is determined, but they differed in their approaches. Bacon stressed experimentation and observation. Descartes focused on reasoning.

The 1500s and 1600s saw dramatic changes in many branches of science. English chemist **Robert Boyle** explained that matter is composed of particles that behave in knowable ways. **Isaac Newton** used mathematics to show that a single force keeps the planets in their orbits around the sun. He called this force **gravity.** To help explain his laws, Newton developed a branch of mathematics called **calculus.**

READING SKILL

Identify Main Ideas How did Copernicus's proposed model of the solar system differ from earlier beliefs?

_____

_____

_____

Review Questions

1. What assumption was at the heart of the Scientific Revolution?

_____

_____

2. Why did the Church condemn Galileo?

_____

_____

CHAPTER 14
SECTION 1

Note Taking Study Guide
THE SEARCH FOR SPICES

Focus Question: How did the search for spices lead to global exploration?

As you read this section in your textbook, complete the following flowchart to identify causes and effects of European exploration.

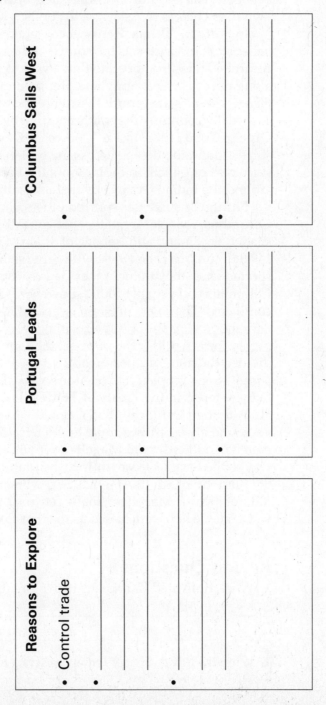

Columbus Sails West

•   •   •

Portugal Leads

•   •   •

Reasons to Explore

• Control trade

•   •   •

Section Summary
THE SEARCH FOR SPICES

What was the Line of Demarcation?

_____

_____

_____

What does the word *authority* mean in the underlined sentence? What context clues can you find in the surrounding words? Circle the words in the same sentence that could help you learn what *authority* means.

Identify Causes and Effects

Identify one cause of European exploration.

_____

_____

Identify two effects of Prince Henry's encouragement of sea exploration.

_____

_____

_____

By the 1400s, Europe's population and its demand for trade goods from Asia were growing. Especially desirable were spices. The chief source of spices was the **Moluccas,** an island chain in present-day Indonesia. Arab and Italian merchants controlled most trade between Asia and Europe. Europeans outside Italy wanted their own direct access to Asia's trade goods.

In Portugal, **Prince Henry** encouraged sea exploration. He believed that Africa was the source of the riches the Muslim traders controlled. He also hoped to find a way to reach Asia by sailing along the coast. **Cartographers** prepared maps for the voyages. Henry's ships sailed south to explore the western coast of Africa, eventually rounding the southern tip, which became known as the Cape of Good Hope. In 1497, **Vasco da Gama** led four Portuguese ships around the tip and across the Indian Ocean to reach the great spice port of Calicut in India. Soon, the Portuguese seized ports around the Indian Ocean, creating a vast trading empire.

Portugal's successes spurred others, including **Christopher Columbus,** to look for another sea route to Asia. Columbus persuaded Ferdinand and Isabella of Spain to finance his voyage. In 1492, Columbus sailed west with three small ships. When the crew spotted land, they thought they had reached the Indies. What Columbus had actually found, however, were previously unknown continents. The rulers of Spain appealed to the Spanish-born Pope Alexander VI to support their authority, or power, to claim the lands of this "new world." The pope set the **Line of Demarcation,** which divided the non-European world into two trading and exploration zones—one for Spain and one for Portugal. The two nations agreed to these terms in the **Treaty of Tordesillas.**

Although Europeans had claimed vast territories, they had not yet found a western sea route to Asia. In 1519, a Portuguese nobleman named **Ferdinand Magellan** set out west from Spain to find a way to the Pacific Ocean. In 1520, he found a passageway at the Southern tip of South America. Survivors of the long voyage, who did not include Magellan, finally returned to Spain nearly three years later. They were hailed as the first to **circumnavigate** the world.

Review Questions
1. What motivated Europeans to explore the seas?

_____

_____

2. Why did Prince Henry focus on Africa for his explorers' voyages?

_____

_____

CHAPTER 14 · SECTION 2
Note Taking Study Guide
TURBULENT CENTURIES IN AFRICA

Focus Question: What effects did European exploration have on the people of Africa?

As you read this section in your textbook, complete the following chart to identify the effects of European exploration on Africa.

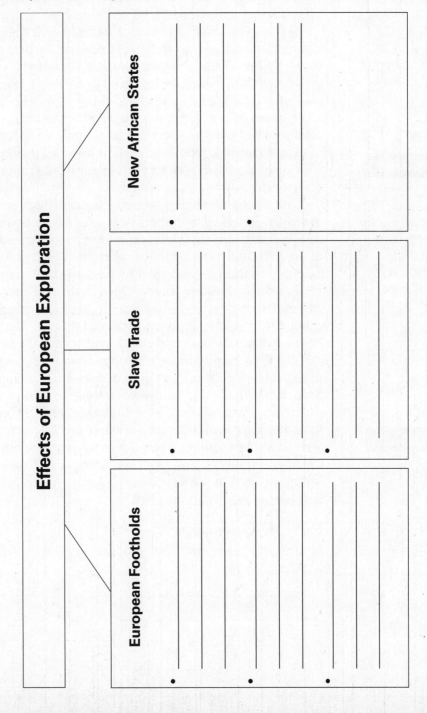

Effects of European Exploration

New African States
-
-

Slave Trade
-
-
-

European Footholds
-
-
-

Section Summary
TURBULENT CENTURIES IN AFRICA

Why did the Portuguese and other Europeans want slaves?

_____

_____

_____

VOCABULARY STRATEGY

What does the word *unified* mean in the underlined sentence? What clue can you find in the word's prefix, *uni-?* Think of other words you may know that start with *uni-*. Use what you may know about related words to help you figure out what *unified* means.

READING SKILL

Identify Effects Identify two effects the slave trade had on African states.

_____

_____

_____

The Portuguese established footholds on the coast of West Africa, building small forts and trading posts. From West Africa, they sailed around the continent. They continued to establish forts and trading posts, but they also attacked coastal cities of East Africa, such as **Mombasa** and **Malindi,** which were hubs of international trade. They also took over the Arabs' thriving East African trade network.

Slavery had existed in Africa since ancient times. Europeans began to view slaves as the most important aspect of the African trade. By the 1500s, European participation had encouraged a much broader Atlantic slave trade, and it grew into a huge and profitable business to fill the need for cheap labor. They especially needed workers on their **plantations** in the Americas. Some African leaders tried to slow down or stop the transatlantic slave trade. The ruler of Kongo, **Affonso I,** who had been tutored by Portuguese **missionaries,** wanted to maintain contact with Europe but end the slave trade. The slave trade, however, continued.

The slave trade had major effects on African states. Because of the loss of countless numbers of young Africans, some small states disappeared forever. At the same time, new states arose, with ways of life that depended on the slave trade. The **Asante kingdom** emerged in the area occupied by present-day Ghana. In the late 1600s, an able military leader, **Osei Tutu,** won control of the trading city of Kumasi. <u>From there, he conquered neighboring peoples and unified the Asante kingdom.</u> Under Osei Tutu, the Asante kingdom held a **monopoly** over both gold mining and the slave trade.

The **Oyo empire** arose from successive waves of settlement by the Yoruba people in the region of present-day Nigeria. Its leaders used wealth gained from the slave trade to build a strong army.

By the 1600s, several other European powers had established forts along the west coast of Africa. In 1652, Dutch immigrants arrived at the southern tip of the continent. They built **Cape Town,** the first permanent European settlement in Africa, to supply ships sailing to or from the East Indies. Dutch farmers, called **Boers,** settled the lands around the port.

Review Questions

1. How did the Portuguese establish footholds on the coasts of Africa?

_____

_____

2. Who created the first permanent European settlement in Africa?

_____

_____

CHAPTER 14 SECTION 3

Note Taking Study Guide

EUROPEAN FOOTHOLDS IN SOUTH AND SOUTHEAST ASIA

Focus Question: How did European nations build empires in South and Southeast Asia?

As you read this section in your textbook, complete the flowchart below to identify causes and effects of European exploration in South and Southeast Asia.

Britain

Spain

Netherlands

Portugal

CHAPTER
14
SECTION 3

Section Summary
EUROPEAN FOOTHOLDS IN SOUTH AND SOUTHEAST ASIA

READING CHECK

What was the Dutch East India Company?

_____

_____

_____

VOCABULARY STRATEGY

What does the word *strategic* mean in the underlined sentence? Note that *strategic* is an adjective describing the settlement of Cape Town. The sentence following the underlined sentence gives you more information about Cape Town. Based on these context clues, what do you think *strategic* means?

READING SKILL

Identify Causes and Effects Identify one cause and one effect of the Mughal emperors' decision to grant trading rights to Europeans.

_____

_____

_____

After Vasco da Gama's voyage to India, the Portuguese, under the command of **Afonso de Albuquerque,** burst into the Indian Ocean. By then, Muslim rulers had established the **Mughal empire** throughout much of India. The Portuguese gained footholds in southern India, however, by promising local princes aid against other European rulers. In 1510, the Portuguese seized the island of **Goa** off the coast of India. Then, they took **Malacca.** In less than 50 years, the Portuguese built a trading empire with military and merchant **outposts.** For most of the 1500s, they controlled the spice trade between Europe and Asia.

The Dutch challenged Portuguese domination of Asian trade. In 1599, a Dutch fleet from Asia returned with a cargo of spices. Soon after, Dutch warships and trading vessels made the Netherlands a leader in European commerce. The Dutch set up colonies and trading posts around the world, including their strategic settlement at Cape Town. Cape Town's location gave the Dutch a secure presence in the region. In 1602, a group of wealthy Dutch merchants formed the **Dutch East India Company,** which had full **sovereign** powers. With its power to build armies, wage war, negotiate peace treaties, and govern overseas territory, the Dutch East India Company dominated Southeast Asia. Meanwhile, Spain took over the **Philippines,** which became a key link in Spain's colonial empire.

India was the center of the valuable spice trade. The Mughal empire was larger, richer, and more powerful than any kingdom in Europe. When Europeans sought trading rights, Mughal emperors saw no threat in granting them. The Portuguese—and later the Dutch, British, and French—were permitted to build forts and warehouses in coastal towns. Over time, the Mughal empire weakened, and French and British traders fought for power. Like the Dutch, both the British and the French had established East India companies. Each nation's trading company organized its own army of **sepoys,** or Indian troops. By the late 1700s, however, the British East India Company controlled most of India.

Review Questions

1. How did Portugal build a trading empire in South and Southeast Asia?

_____

_____

2. How did the Dutch come to dominate trade in Southeast Asia?

_____

_____

Note Taking Study Guide
ENCOUNTERS IN EAST ASIA

Focus Question: How were European encounters in East Asia shaped by the worldviews of both Europeans and Asians?

As you read this section in your textbook, complete the following chart to understand the effects of European contacts in East Asia.

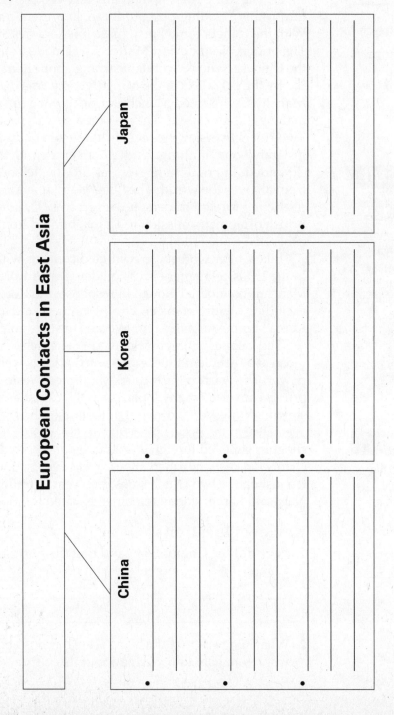

CHAPTER
14
SECTION 4

Section Summary
ENCOUNTERS IN EAST ASIA

READING CHECK

Who conquered the Ming dynasty in 1644?

_____

_____

_____

When Portuguese traders reached China in 1514, they wanted Chinese silks and porcelains. The European textiles and metalwork they had to offer in exchange, however, were inferior to Chinese products. The Chinese, therefore, demanded payment in gold or silver. The Ming rulers eventually allowed the Portuguese and other Europeans a trading post at **Macao,** in present-day **Guangzhou.** With the traders came Portuguese missionaries and, later, the Jesuits. The brilliant Jesuit priest **Matteo Ricci** made a strong impression on the Chinese, who welcomed learning about Renaissance Europe.

By the early 1600s, the Ming dynasty was decaying. In 1644, the **Manchus,** who ruled Manchuria, succeeded in seizing Beijing and making it their capital. They set up a new dynasty called the **Qing.** Two rulers oversaw the most brilliant age of the Qing—Kangxi and his grandson **Qianlong.** Under both emperors, the Chinese economy expanded. Internal trade grew, as did the demand for Chinese goods from all over the world. The Qing maintained the Ming policy of restricting foreign traders, however. In 1793, **Lord Macartney** led a British diplomatic mission to China, but his attempt to negotiate for expanded trade failed.

VOCABULARY STRATEGY

What does the word *allegiance* mean in the underlined sentence? Think about your prior knowledge of this word. Ask yourself: To what do I owe my allegiance? Use your prior knowledge to help you figure out what *allegiance* means.

Like China, Korea also restricted contacts with the outside world. In the 1590s, a Japanese invasion devastated Korea. Then in 1636, the Manchus conquered Korea. In response, the Koreans chose isolation, excluding all foreigners except the Chinese and a few Japanese. Korea became known in the West as the "Hermit Kingdom."

The Japanese at first welcomed Westerners. Traders arrived in Japan at a turbulent time, when warrior lords were struggling for power. The warrior lords quickly adopted Western firearms. Jesuit priests converted many Japanese to the Christian faith. <u>The Tokugawa shoguns, however, worried that Japanese Christians owed their allegiance to the pope rather than to Japanese leaders.</u> In response, the shoguns expelled foreign missionaries and barred all European merchants. To keep informed about world events, however, they permitted just one or two Dutch ships each year to trade at a small island in **Nagasaki** harbor. Japan remained isolated for more than 200 years.

READING SKILL

Identify Effects Describe the effect of the Japanese and Manchu invasions on Korea.

_____

_____

_____

Review Questions

1. Why did the Chinese demand that the Portuguese traders pay for Chinese silks and porcelain with gold or silver?

_____

_____

2. What suggests that the Ming were curious about Europe and wanted to gain knowledge about its culture?

_____

_____

CHAPTER 15	Note Taking Study Guide
SECTION 1	CONQUEST IN THE AMERICAS

Focus Question: How did a small number of Spanish conquistadors conquer huge Native American empires?

As you read this section of your textbook, fill in the chart below to help you record the sequence of events that led to European empires in the Americas.

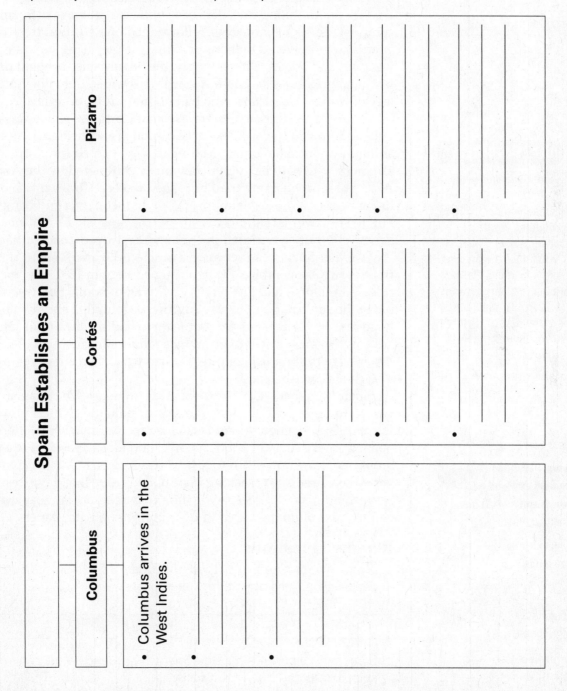

Spain Establishes an Empire

Pizarro

Cortés

Columbus
- Columbus arrives in the West Indies.

CHAPTER **15** SECTION 1	**Section Summary**
	CONQUEST IN THE AMERICAS

READING CHECK

How did Malinche aid Cortés?

_____

_____

_____

VOCABULARY STRATEGY

Find the word *compelled* in the underlined sentence. What clues to its meaning can you find in the surrounding words, phrases, or sentences? For example, what does the phrase "relations grew strained" suggest about the relations between the two men? Circle other context clues in the paragraph that could help you figure out what *compelled* means.

READING SKILL

Recognize Sequence Sequence the following events:

____ Spanish forces take over Inca lands.

____ Pizarro arrives in Peru.

____ Columbus takes the Taínos as prisoners.

____ Cortés captures Tenochtitlán.

In 1492, Christopher Columbus reached the Caribbean islands now called the West Indies. Columbus' first meeting with Native Americans there began a recurring cycle of encounter, conquest, and death across the Western Hemisphere.

Columbus first encountered the Taíno people and claimed their land for Spain, taking prisoners back with him. A wave of Spanish **conquistadors,** or conquerors, followed. Ultimately, hundreds of Spanish overpowered millions of native people, using superior weapons and horses. Unknowingly, the Spanish also brought diseases like smallpox, measles, and influenza. This wiped out village after village of Native Americans, who had no **immunity,** or resistance.

One of the earliest explorers, **Hernán Cortés,** reached Mexico in 1519 and moved toward the Aztec capital, **Tenochtitlán.** Cortés was aided by an Indian woman, **Malinche,** who helped him form **alliances** with native peoples previously conquered by the Aztecs. Aztec ruler **Moctezuma** tried but failed to keep Cortés from coming to Tenochtitlán. <u>Cortés later imprisoned Moctezuma and compelled him to sign over lands and treasure to the Spanish.</u> Cortés was driven out, but he returned in 1521 and destroyed Tenochtitlán.

Another Spanish adventurer, **Francisco Pizarro,** sought riches from Peru's Inca empire. Pizarro reached Peru in 1532. The Inca ruler, Atahualpa, had just won a **civil war,** or conflict between people of the same nation. Pizarro captured Atahualpa and demanded a huge ransom. This was paid, but Pizarro had the Inca ruler killed anyway. Spanish forces overran Inca lands, adding much of South America to the Spanish empire. Pizarro was killed a few years later by a rival Spanish group.

Spain's impact on the Americas was immense. The Spanish took vast fortunes in gold and silver, making Spain the greatest power of Europe. They opened sea routes that connected two hemispheres and opened an exchange of goods, people, and ideas. However, they also brought disease and death to Native Americans. Many survivors converted to Christianity, seeking hope. Others, like the Maya, resisted Spanish influence by preserving their own religion, language, and culture, and ultimately leaving their imprint on Latin America.

Review Questions

1. Name two factors that helped hundreds of Spanish soldiers conquer millions of Native Americans.

_____

_____

2. Some native peoples resisted Spanish influence. What was one such group and how did it resist?

_____

_____

CHAPTER
15
SECTION 2.

Note Taking Study Guide

SPANISH AND PORTUGUESE COLONIES IN THE AMERICAS

Focus Question: How did Spain and Portugal build colonies in the Americas?

A. *As you read "Ruling the Spanish Empire," fill in the chart below to record the steps the Spanish took to establish an empire in America.*

Governing the empire	Catholic Church	Trade	Labor
• Viceroys	• _____	• _____	• _____
• _____ _____ _____	_____ _____ • _____ _____ • _____ _____	_____ _____ • _____ _____	_____ _____ • _____ _____

B. *As you read "Colonial Society and Culture" and "Beyond the Spanish Empire," fill in the Venn diagram below to compare and contrast the Spanish and Portuguese empires.*

Spanish empire   **Portuguese empire**

- _____
  _____
- _____
  _____

- _____
  _____
- _____
  _____
- _____
  _____

- _____
  _____
- _____
  _____

CHAPTER 15 SECTION 2 — Section Summary

SPANISH AND PORTUGUESE COLONIES IN THE AMERICAS

READING CHECK

What was the name of the priest who pleaded with the Spanish king to end the abuse of Native Americans?

_____

_____

_____

VOCABULARY STRATEGY

In the underlined sentence, what do you think the word *drastic* means? Try to determine the meaning based on the context, or how and where it is used. Circle any nearby words or phrases that help you figure out the meaning of *drastic*.

READING SKILL

Recognize Sequence Circle the event that happened first.

• Spanish colonies are closely monitored.

• The king of Spain appoints viceroys.

• Laws are passed banning enslavement of workers.

Spanish settlers and missionaries followed conquerors into the Americas. They built colonies and created a culture that blended European, Native American, and African traditions. By the mid-1500s, Spain's empire reached from modern California to South America.

The Spanish monarch appointed **viceroys,** or representatives who ruled in his name. They closely monitored Spanish colonies and managed their valuable raw materials. Conquistadors received **encomiendas,** or rights to demand work from Native Americans. Under this system, Native Americans were forced to work under brutal conditions. Disease, starvation, and cruel treatment caused a drastic decline in the Native American population. A priest, **Bartolomé de Las Casas,** begged the Spanish king to end the abuse, and laws were passed in 1542, banning enslavement and mistreatment. But Spain was too far away to enforce the laws. Some landlords forced people to become **peons,** paid workers who labored to repay impossibly high debts created by the landlord. To fill a labor shortage, colonists also brought in millions of Africans as slaves.

Blending of diverse cultures resulted. Native Americans contributed building styles, foods, and arts. The Spanish introduced Christianity and the use of animals, especially horses. Africans contributed farming methods, crops, and arts.

However, society in the colonies was strictly structured. **Peninsulares,** or people born in Spain, filled the highest positions. Next were **creoles,** or American-born descendants of Spanish settlers. Lower groups included **mestizos,** people of Native American and European descent, and **mulattoes,** people of African and European descent. At the bottom were Native Americans and African slaves.

Portugal, too, had an empire in South America, with colonies in Brazil. Portugal granted land to nobles, who sent settlers to develop the area. As in Spanish colonies, Native Americans in Brazil were nearly wiped out from disease. Brazil's rulers also used African slaves and forced Native American labor. A new culture emerged, blending European, Native American, and African traditions.

In the 1500s, wealth from the Americas made Spain and Portugal Europe's most wealthy and powerful countries. Pirates often attacked treasure ships from the colonies. Some pirates, called **privateers,** even did so with the support of their nations' monarchs.

Review Questions

1. What were encomiendas?

_____

_____

2. How were the Spanish and Portuguese colonies similar?

_____

_____

Note Taking Study Guide

THE ATLANTIC SLAVE TRADE

Focus Question: How did the Atlantic slave trade shape the lives and economies of Africans and Europeans?

As you read this section in your textbook, complete the following flowchart to record the sequence of events that led to millions of Africans being brought to the Americas.

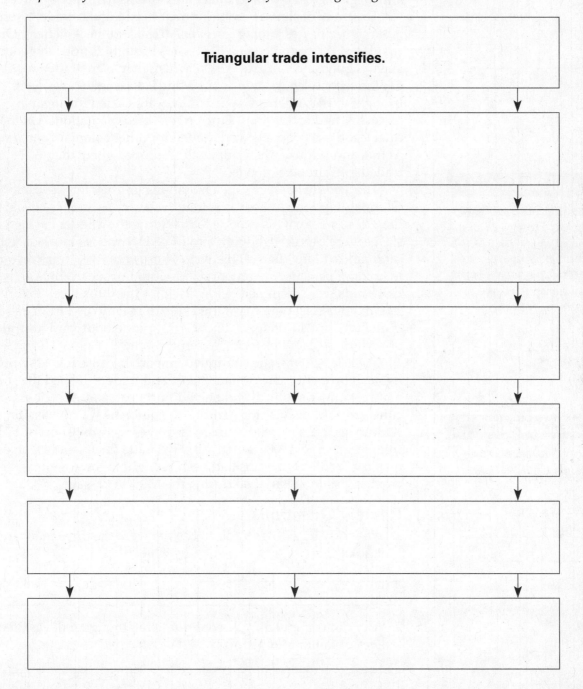

Triangular trade intensifies.

CHAPTER 15 SECTION 4

Section Summary
THE ATLANTIC SLAVE TRADE

Empires grew in the 1500s, and trade increased between the Americas and other parts of the world. Spain was the first major power to import slaves into its South American colonies, but slave trade grew as other European powers established colonies. Slave labor became a way to gain greater profits, but at the expense of millions of lives.

The trade of slaves became known as **triangular trade,** a series of Atlantic sea routes joining Europe, Africa, and the Americas. On the first leg of the triangle, merchant ships brought European goods, such as guns and cloth, to Africa, where they were traded for slaves. On the second leg, known as the **Middle Passage,** slaves were brought to the Americas, where they were traded for sugar, molasses, and cotton from European-owned plantations. On the final leg, these products were traded for other colonial goods, such as furs and salt fish, then shipped to Europe, where they were traded for European goods.

The Middle Passage was a horrifying journey for Africans. **Olaudah Equiano,** who was sold into slavery as an 11-year-old in the 1750s, wrote of his experiences. During the Middle Passage, slaves were captured, bound, and forced to walk as much as a thousand miles. Many died on the way. Those who lived were restrained in holding pens in African port cities until European ships arrived. Hundreds were crammed below deck for the three-week to three-month voyages. Some committed suicide. Many died from disease, brutality, or other dangers, like storms, pirate raids, and **mutinies,** or revolts, by captives trying to return home.

The triangular trade continued, in part, because it was so profitable. It brought riches to merchants and traders, helped the colonial economies succeed, and helped European and American port cities grow. However, for Africans the outcome was devastating. African societies were torn apart, and lives were cut short or brutalized. By the mid-1800s, when the slave trade finally ended, an estimated 11 million Africans had been brought to the Americas, and another 2 million had died during the Middle Passage.

Review Questions

1. What was triangular trade, and what were the three main areas it linked?

_____

_____

2. Why did triangular trade continue, even though it devastated the lives of millions of people?

_____

_____

CHAPTER 15 SECTION 5

Note Taking Study Guide

EFFECTS OF GLOBAL CONTACT

Focus Question: How did the voyages of European explorers lead to new economic systems in Europe and its colonies?

A. *As you read "The Columbian Exchange," complete the following flowchart to record the sequence of events that led to the Columbian Exchange, as well as the effects.*

Causes	Columbian Exchange	Effects
• _____ _____	• _____ _____	• _____ _____
• _____ _____	• _____ _____	• _____ _____
• _____ _____	• _____ _____	• _____
		• _____
		• _____
		• _____

B. *As you read "A Commercial Revolution," complete the following flowchart to record the sequence of events that led to new global economic systems, as well as the effects.*

Causes	New Economic Systems	Effects
• _____ _____	• Capitalism	• _____ _____
• _____ _____	• _____	• _____ _____
• _____ _____	• _____	• _____
		• _____ _____ _____

CHAPTER **15** SECTION 5	**Section Summary** EFFECTS OF GLOBAL CONTACT

What is the name for the vast global interchange begun by Columbus' first voyage?

_____

_____

_____

VOCABULARY STRATEGY

In the underlined sentence, what does the word *dispersal* mean? Study the surrounding words, phrases, or sentences. Circle any context clues that help you decide on the meaning of *dispersal.*

READING SKILL

Recognize Sequence What happened in the 1500s that led to inflation in Europe?

_____

_____

_____

Exploration in the 1500s and 1600s led to European domination of the globe. By the 1700s, worldwide contact brought major changes to people in Europe, the Americas, Asia, and Africa.

When Columbus returned to Europe in 1493, he brought back American plants and animals. Later, he carried European plants, animals, and settlers back to the Americas. This began a vast global interchange named for Columbus, the **Columbian Exchange.** Sharing different foodstuffs and livestock helped people around the world. The dispersal of new crops from the Americas also contributed to worldwide population growth by the 1700s. Additionally, the Columbian Exchange started a migration to the Americas, the forcible transfer of millions of slaves, and brought death to millions of Native Americans from European diseases.

Another effect of global contact was great economic change. In the 1500s, the pace of **inflation** increased in Europe, fueled by silver and gold flowing in from the Americas. Inflation is a rise in prices linked to sharp increases in the money supply. This period of rapid inflation in Europe is known as the **price revolution.** Out of this change came **capitalism,** an economic system of private business ownership. The key to capitalism was **entrepreneurs,** or people who take financial risks for profits. European entrepreneurs hired workers, paid production costs, joined investors in overseas ventures, and ultimately helped convert local economies into international trading economies. Fierce competition for trade and empires led to a new economic system called **mercantilism,** which measured wealth by a nation's gold and silver. Mercantilists believed the nation must export more than it imports. They also pushed governments to impose **tariffs,** or taxes on foreign goods, giving an advantage to local goods over now costlier imports.

Economic changes, however, took centuries to affect most Europeans, who were still peasants. But by the 1700s, many social changes had taken place, too. Nobles, whose wealth was in land, were hurt by the price revolution. Merchants who invested in overseas ventures grew wealthy, and skilled workers in Europe's growing cities thrived. A thriving middle class developed.

Review Questions

1. Why did mercantilists push governments to impose tariffs?

_____

_____

2. By the 1700s, what groups were benefiting most from economic change?

_____

_____

CHAPTER 16
SECTION 1

Note Taking Study Guide
SPANISH POWER GROWS

Focus Questions: How did Philip II extend Spain's power and help establish a golden age?

As you read this section in your textbook, use the outline to identify main ideas and supporting details about Spain's power.

I. **Charles V Inherits Two Crowns**
  A. Ruling the Hapsburg empire
    1. Spain
    2. Holy Roman Empire and Netherlands
  B. Charles V abdicates
    1. _____
    2. _____
    3. _____
II. _____
  A. _____
    1. _____
    2. _____
  B. _____
    1. _____
    2. _____
  C. _____
    1. _____
    2. _____
  D. _____
    1. _____
    2. _____
    3. _____
    4. _____
    5. _____

(Outline continues on next page.)

Note Taking Study Guide
SPANISH POWER GROWS

(Continued from page 147)

III. _____

    A. _____

        _____

    B. _____

        _____

    C. _____

        _____

    D. _____

        _____

    E. _____

        _____

Name_____ Class_____ Date_____

In 1519, **Charles V,** the king of Spain and ruler of the Spanish colonies in the Americas, inherited the **Hapsburg empire.** This included the Holy Roman Empire and the Netherlands. Ruling two empires involved Charles in constant religious warfare. <u>Additionally, the empire's vast territory became too cumbersome for Charles to rule effectively.</u> His demanding responsibilities led him to abdicate the throne and divide his kingdom between his brother Ferdinand and his son Philip.

Under **Philip II,** Spanish power increased. He was successful in expanding Spanish influence, strengthening the Catholic Church, and making his own power absolute. Philip reigned as an **absolute monarch**—a ruler with complete authority over the government and the lives of the people. He also declared that he ruled by **divine right.** This meant he believed that his authority to rule came directly from God. Philip was determined to defend the Catholic Church against the Protestant Reformation in Europe. He fought many battles in the Mediterranean and the Netherlands to advance or preserve Spanish Catholic power.

To expand his empire, Philip II needed to eliminate his rivals. He saw Elizabeth I of England as his chief Protestant enemy. Philip prepared a huge **armada,** or fleet, to carry an invasion force to England. However, the English ships were faster and easier to maneuver than Spanish ships. Several disasters led to the defeat of this powerful Spanish fleet.

This defeat marked the beginning of a decline in Spanish power. Wars were costly and contributed to Spain's economic problems. However, while Spain's strength and wealth decreased, art and learning took on new importance. Philip was a supporter of the arts and founded academies of science and mathematics. The arts flourished between 1550 and 1650, a time known as Spain's *Siglo de Oro,* or "golden century." Among the outstanding artists of this period was a painter called **El Greco.** Famous for his religious paintings and portraits of Spanish nobles, his use of vibrant color influenced many other artists. This period also produced several remarkable writers. One of the most significant was **Miguel de Cervantes.** His *Don Quixote,* which mocks medieval tales of chivalry, is considered Europe's first modern novel.

Review Questions

1. What territories were included in the Hapsburg empire?

_____

_____

2. In what ways was Philip II an absolute monarch?

_____

_____

READING CHECK

Who wrote Europe's first modern novel?

_____

_____

VOCABULARY STRATEGY

What does the word *cumbersome* mean in the underlined sentence? Circle context clues in the nearby words and phrases to help you figure out the meaning of *cumbersome.*

READING SKILL

Identify Main Ideas and Supporting Details What details support the main idea that the period from 1550 to 1650 was a "golden century" in Spain?

_____

_____

_____

Name_____ Class_____ Date_____

Focus Question: How did France become the leading power of Europe under the absolute rule of Louis XIV?

As you read this section in your textbook, complete the concept web to identify supporting details about the rule of Louis XIV.

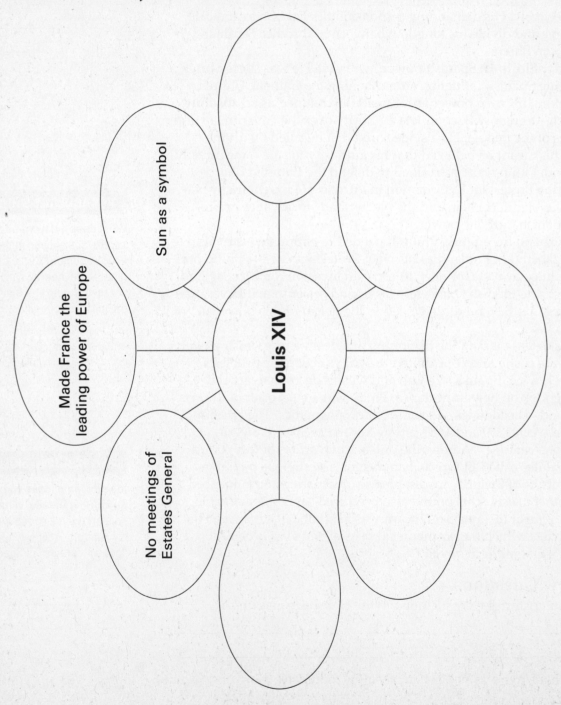

CHAPTER 16 SECTION 2

Section Summary

FRANCE UNDER LOUIS XIV

In the late 1500s, France was torn apart by religious conflict between French Protestants, called **Huguenots,** and Catholics. In an event called the St. Bartholomew's Day Massacre, thousands of Huguenots were slaughtered. In 1598, King **Henry IV** issued the **Edict of Nantes** to protect Protestants. This granted the Huguenots religious toleration and other freedoms.

After Henry's assassination in 1610, his nine-year-old son, Louis XIII, inherited the throne. Louis appointed **Cardinal Richelieu** as his chief minister. Richelieu sought to strengthen royal power by crushing any groups that did not bow to royal authority. In 1643, five-year-old **Louis XIV** inherited the French throne. When his chief minister died, Louis XIV resolved to take complete control of the government. He believed in his divine right to rule and even called himself the Sun King to symbolize his vital role within the nation.

Louis XIV expanded the royal government and appointed **intendants**—royal officials who collected taxes, recruited soldiers, and carried out his policies in the provinces. To fuel the country's economy, Louis's finance minister, **Jean Baptiste Colbert,** expanded commerce and trade. Taxes helped finance the king's extravagant lifestyle.

Outside Paris, Louis XIV transformed a royal hunting lodge into the grand palace of **Versailles.** The palace represented the king's great power and wealth. Elaborate court ceremonies were held to emphasize the king's importance. For example, during the ritual known as the *levée,* or rising, high-ranking nobles would compete for the honor of handing the king his shoes. The purpose was to keep the nobles in Versailles to gain their support and prevent them from getting too powerful.

Under Louis XIV, France became the strongest state in Europe. <u>However, the country's prosperity began to erode.</u> This loss of wealth was caused by some of Louis's decisions. He fought costly wars to extend French borders, but rival rulers resisted in order to maintain the **balance of power.** Louis also revoked the Edict of Nantes, driving over 100,000 hard-working and prosperous Huguenots out of France.

Review Questions

1. How did Henry IV end religious conflict?

_____

_____

2. What was the purpose of intendants?

_____

_____

READING CHECK

What were the main reasons why France lost economic strength?

_____

_____

_____

VOCABULARY STRATEGY

What does the word *erode* mean in the underlined sentence? Do you know what *erosion* is? Use any prior knowledge you might have about the word *erosion* to help you figure out the meaning of *erode.*

READING SKILL

Identify Supporting Details How did Louis XIV strengthen the French monarchy? Identify key details that contributed to France's becoming the leading power of Europe.

_____

_____

_____

CHAPTER
16
SECTION 3

Note Taking Study Guide

PARLIAMENT TRIUMPHS IN ENGLAND

Focus Question: How did the British Parliament assert its rights against royal claims to absolute power in the 1600s?

As you read this section in your textbook, complete the flowchart to identify supporting details about the evolution of Parliament.

Tudors consult with and control Parliament.

CHAPTER 16 SECTION 3 — Section Summary
PARLIAMENT TRIUMPHS IN ENGLAND

From 1485 to 1603, England was ruled by the Tudors. While believing in divine right, the Tudors also recognized the value of good relations with Parliament.

This was not the view of the first Stuart king, **James I.** He inherited the throne after Elizabeth I died childless in 1603. He claimed absolute power. Parliament, however, resisted the king's claim. James clashed often with Parliament over money. James was also at odds with **dissenters**—Protestants who disagreed with the Church of England. One such group, the **Puritans,** wanted simpler services and a more democratic church with no bishops.

In 1625, **Charles I** inherited the throne. He too behaved like an absolute monarch. Tensions between Charles and Parliament escalated into civil war. The English Civil War lasted from 1642 to 1651. Supporters of Charles were called Cavaliers. The supporters of Parliament were known as Roundheads. **Oliver Cromwell,** the leader of the Parliament forces, guided them to victory. In January 1649, Charles I was beheaded.

The House of Commons abolished the monarchy and declared England a republic under Cromwell, called the Commonwealth. Many new laws reflected Puritan beliefs. <u>Cromwell did not tolerate open worship for Catholics; however, he did respect the beliefs of other Protestants and welcomed Jews back to England.</u> Eventually people tired of the strict Puritan ways. Cromwell died in 1658. Two years later, Parliament invited Charles II to return to England as king.

Charles II's successor, James II, was forced from the English throne in 1688. Protestants feared that he planned to restore the Roman Catholic Church to power in England. Parliament offered the crown to James's Protestant daughter Mary and her husband William. However, William and Mary had to accept the **English Bill of Rights.** This helped establish a **limited monarchy.** This bloodless overthrow of James II was known as the Glorious Revolution.

During the next century, Britain's government became a **constitutional government,** whose power was defined and limited by law. A **cabinet,** or group of parliamentary advisors who set policies, developed. In essence, British government was now an **oligarchy**—a government that was run by a powerful few.

Review Questions

1. How did the English government change under Cromwell's leadership?

_____

_____

2. Why was James II forced from the throne?

_____

_____

READING CHECK

What was the Glorious Revolution?

_____

_____

_____

VOCABULARY STRATEGY

What does the word *tolerate* mean in the underlined sentence? Look for an alternative meaning of *tolerate* later in the same sentence. Use this context clue to figure out what *tolerate* means.

READING SKILL

Identify Supporting Details
Find two details in this Summary that support the statement, "Parliament triumphs in England."

_____

_____

_____

Name_____ Class_____ Date_____

Note Taking Study Guide
RISE OF AUSTRIA AND PRUSSIA

Focus Question: How did the two great empires of Austria and Prussia emerge from the Thirty Years' War and subsequent events?

As you read this section in your textbook, use the table to identify supporting details about the emergence of Austria and Prussia as European powers.

Rise of Prussia

- Hohenzollern rulers take over German states.
  -
  -

Rise of Austria

- Austrian ruler keeps title of Holy Roman Emperor.
  -
  -
  -

CHAPTER 16 SECTION 4

Section Summary

RISE OF AUSTRIA AND PRUSSIA

By the seventeenth century, the Holy Roman Empire had become a mix of several hundred small, separate states. Theoretically, the Holy Roman emperor, who was chosen by seven leading German princes called **electors,** ruled these states. Yet, the emperor had little power over the numerous princes. This power vacuum led to a series of brutal wars that are together called the Thirty Years' War. It began when **Ferdinand,** the Catholic Hapsburg king of Bohemia, wanted to suppress Protestants and declare royal power over nobles. This led to several revolts and then a widespread European war.

The war devastated the German states. **Mercenaries,** or soldiers for hire, burned villages, destroyed crops, and murdered and tortured villagers. This led to famine and disease, which caused severe **depopulation,** or reduction in population.

It was not until 1648 that a series of treaties known as the **Peace of Westphalia** were established. <u>These treaties aspired to bring peace to Europe and also settle other international problems.</u>

While Austria was becoming a strong Catholic state, a region within the German states called **Prussia** emerged as a new Protestant power. The Prussian ruler **Frederick William I** came to power in 1713. He created a new bureaucracy and placed great emphasis on military values.

In Austria, **Maria Theresa** became empress after her father's death in 1740. That same year, **Frederick II** of Prussia seized the Hapsburg province of Silesia. This action sparked the eight-year **War of the Austrian Succession.** Despite tireless efforts, Maria Theresa did not succeed in forcing Frederick out of Silesia. However, she did preserve her empire and won the support of most of her people. She also strengthened Hapsburg power by reorganizing the bureaucracy and improving tax collection.

At his father's insistence, Frederick II endured harsh military training at a early age. After becoming king, he used his military education brilliantly, making Prussia a leading power. By 1750, the great European powers included Austria, Prussia, France, Britain, and Russia. These nations formed various alliances to maintain the balance of power. Often, Austria and Prussia were rivals.

Review Questions

1. What started the Thirty Years' War?

_____

_____

2. What caused the depopulation in the German states?

_____

_____

_____

READING CHECK

What was the Peace of Westphalia supposed to accomplish?

_____

_____

_____

VOCABULARY STRATEGY

What does the word *aspired* mean in the underlined sentence? The word *strived* is a synonym for *aspired.* Apply what you already know about *strived* to help you understand the meaning of *aspired.*

READING SKILL

Identify Supporting Details List details to support the statement: The Thirty Years' War had a terrible effect on German states.

_____

_____

_____

Note Taking Study Guide

CHAPTER 16 SECTION 5

ABSOLUTE MONARCHY IN RUSSIA

Focus Questions: How did Peter the Great and Catherine the Great strengthen Russia and expand its territory?

As you read this section in your textbook, complete the Venn diagram to identify the main ideas about the reigns of Peter the Great and Catherine the Great.

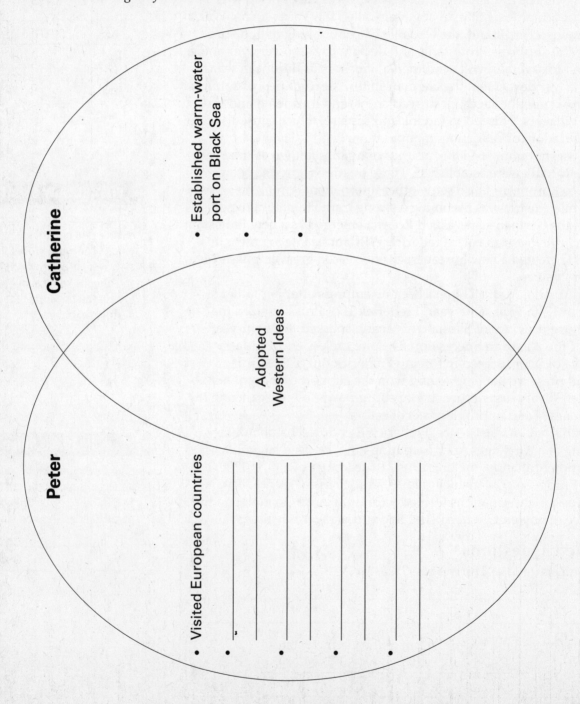

Catherine

• Established warm-water port on Black Sea

Adopted Western Ideas

Peter

• Visited European countries

Name_____ Class_____ Date_____

CHAPTER 16 SECTION 5

Section Summary

ABSOLUTE MONARCHY IN RUSSIA

In the early 1600s, Russia was isolated from Western Europe and had remained a medieval state. It was not until the end of that century that a new tsar, **Peter the Great,** transformed Russia into a leading power.

To modernize Russia, Peter began a new policy of **westernization**—the adoption of Western ideas, technologies, and culture. Many resisted change. To enforce his new policy, Peter became an **autocratic** monarch—one who ruled with unlimited authority.

All Russian institutions were under Peter the Great's control. He executed anyone who resisted the new order. He forced the **boyars**—landowning nobles—to serve the state in civilian or military positions. Peter also stipulated that they shave their beards and wear Western-style clothes.

Peter pushed through social and economic reforms. He also increased Russia's military power and extended its borders. However, Russia still needed a **warm-water port.** This would increase Russia's trade with the West. The nearest port of this kind to Russia was on the Black Sea, but Peter could not defeat the Ottoman empire, which controlled the region.

Determined to expand Russia's territory, Peter also waged a long war against Sweden to win territory along the Baltic Sea. On this territory, he built a new capital city, **St. Petersburg.** It became the symbol of modern Russia. When Peter died in 1725, he left a mixed legacy. Although he had modernized Russia, he had used terror to enforce his absolute power.

In 1762, **Catherine the Great** ruled as an absolute monarch. She followed Peter's lead in embracing Western ideas and expanding Russia's borders. She was an efficient and energetic empress. Under her rule, laws were codified and state-supported education began for both boys and girls. After waging war, she defeated the Ottoman empire and finally won the warm-water port on the Black Sea.

In the 1770s, Russia, Prussia, and Austria each wanted Poland as part of their territory. In order to avoid war, the three kingdoms agreed to **partition,** or divide up, Poland. In 1772, Russia gained part of eastern Poland, while Prussia and Austria took over the West. Poland vanished from the map.

Review Questions

1. What did Peter the Great do to modernize Russia?

_____

_____

2. What were two achievements of Catherine the Great?

_____

_____

READING CHECK

Where was St. Petersburg built?

_____

_____

_____

VOCABULARY STRATEGY

What does *stipulated* mean in the underlined sentence? It comes from a Latin word that means "to bargain." Use this word-origins clue to help you figure out the meaning of *stipulated.*

READING SKILL

Identify Main Ideas Write a new title for this Summary that identifies its main idea.

_____

_____

_____

Note Taking Study Guide

PHILOSOPHY IN THE AGE OF REASON

Focus Question: What effects did Enlightenment philosophers have on government and society?

As you read this section in your textbook, complete the following table to summarize each thinker's works and ideas.

Thinkers' Works and Ideas	
Hobbes	• *Leviathan* • _____
Locke	• _____ • _____ • _____
Montesquieu	• _____ • _____ • _____
	• _____ • _____ • _____
	• _____ • _____ • _____ • _____
	• _____ • _____
	• _____ • _____ • _____

Section Summary

PHILOSOPHY IN THE AGE OF REASON

In the 1500s and 1600s, the Scientific Revolution introduced reason and scientific method as the basis of knowledge, changing the way people looked at the world. In the 1700s, scientific successes, such as a vaccine against smallpox, convinced educated Europeans of the power of human reason. **Natural law**—rules discovered by reason—could be used to study human behavior and solve society's problems. In this way, the Scientific Revolution sparked another revolution in thinking, known as the Enlightenment.

The ideas of **Thomas Hobbes** and **John Locke,** two seventeenth-century English thinkers, were key to the Enlightenment. Hobbes argued that people are "brutish" by nature, and therefore need to be controlled by an absolute monarchy. According to Hobbes, people enter into a **social contract** with their government, giving up their freedom in exchange for an organized society. In contrast, Locke thought that people are basically reasonable and moral. He also believed that people have certain **natural rights,** including the right to life, liberty, and property. Locke rejected absolute monarchy, believing that the best kind of government had limited power. In fact, Locke felt that people could overthrow a government if it violated their natural rights.

In France, Enlightenment thinkers called *philosophes* believed that the use of reason could lead to reforms in government, law, and society. Baron de **Montesquieu** proposed the ideas of separation of powers and of checks and balances as a way to protect liberty. His ideas would deeply affect the Framers of the United States Constitution. With his biting wit, **Voltaire** exposed abuses of power and defended the principle of freedom of speech. Denis **Diderot** edited a 28-volume *Encyclopedia.* This work included articles on human knowledge, explaining new ideas on topics such as government, philosophy, and religion. **Jean-Jacques Rousseau** believed that the good of the community should be placed above individual interests. However, the Enlightenment slogan "free and equal" did not apply to women.

Other thinkers, including **Adam Smith,** focused on using natural laws for economic reform. They rejected government regulation of the economy and instead urged the policy of **laissez faire.**

Review Questions

1. How did the Scientific Revolution lead to the Enlightenment?

_____

_____

2. Identify three major ideas developed by Enlightenment thinkers.

_____

_____

READING CHECK

Who were the *philosophes* and what did they believe?

_____

_____

_____

VOCABULARY STRATEGY

What does the word *philosophy* mean in the underlined sentence? It comes from a Greek word that means "love of wisdom." Use this word-orgins clue to help you figure out what *philosophy* means.

READING SKILL

Summarize What ideas did Thomas Hobbes and John Locke have about human nature and the role of government?

_____

_____

Note Taking Study Guide
ENLIGHTENMENT IDEAS SPREAD

Focus Question: As Enlightenment ideas spread across Europe, what cultural and political changes took place?

A. *As you read "New Ideas Challenge Society" and "Arts and Literature Reflect New Ideas," complete the following concept web to categorize how Enlightenment ideas spread.*

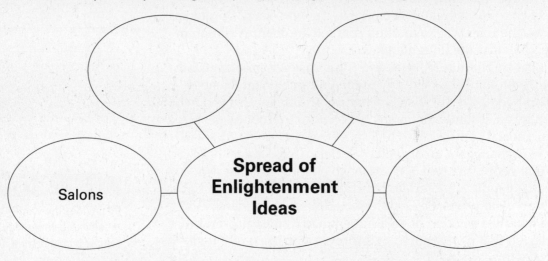

B. *As you read "Enlightened Despots Embrace New Ideas" and "Lives of the Majority Change Slowly," complete the following concept web to summarize information about enlightened despots and their contributions.*

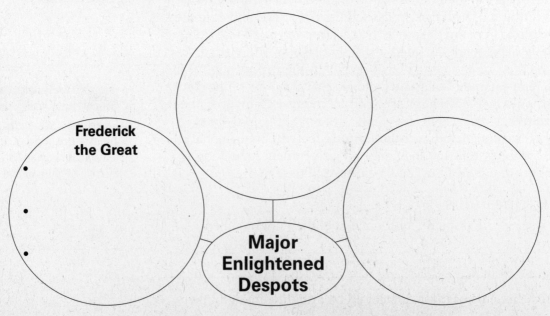

CHAPTER 17 SECTION 2

Section Summary
ENLIGHTENMENT IDEAS SPREAD

Enlightenment ideas flowed from France, across Europe and beyond. Before the Enlightenment, most Europeans had accepted a society based on divine-right rule, a strict class system, and a belief in a heavenly reward for earthly suffering. The ideas of the Enlightenment, found in books such as Diderot's *Encyclopedia*, challenged those traditional beliefs and customs. In response, most government and church authorities waged a war of **censorship.** They banned and burned books, and imprisoned writers. Censorship, however, did not stop the spread of ideas. *Philosophes* and others disguised their ideas in works of fiction. Ideas continued to spread in **salons,** where people gathered to discuss new concepts in literature, the arts, science, and philosophy.

In the 1600s and 1700s, the arts evolved to meet changing tastes and reflect new Enlightenment ideals. In visual art and in music there was a transition from the heavier splendor of the **baroque** style to the lighter, more charming style of **rococo.** Ballets and operas—plays set to music—were performed at royal courts. Opera houses sprang up in Europe. Composers later created elegant works in a style known as classical. A growing audience of middle-class readers also led to the rise of a new type of literature—a prose form called the novel. Daniel Defoe's *Robinson Crusoe* was written at this time.

The courts of Europe were also affected by the Enlightenment as *philosophes* tried to persuade European rulers to make reforms. A few European monarchs did accept Enlightenment ideas, but retained their absolute control. These **enlightened despots** used their power to bring about some political and social changes. In Prussia, **Frederick the Great** kept tight control over his subjects yet allowed a free press and religious tolerance. **Catherine the Great** of Russia abolished torture and criticized the institution of serfdom. In Austria, **Joseph II** traveled in disguise among his subjects to learn of their problems. Despite the spread of Enlightenment ideas, however, the lives of most regular Europeans changed slowly.

Review Questions

1. How did most government and church authorities try to stop the spread of Enlightenment ideas?

_____

_____

2. What effect did Enlightenment ideas have on art, music, and literature?

_____

_____

READING CHECK

What traditional beliefs and customs did the ideas of the Enlightenment challenge?

_____

_____

_____

VOCABULARY STRATEGY

What does the word *evolved* mean in the underlined sentence? What clues can you find in the surrounding words, phrases, or sentences? Circle the context clues in the paragraph that could help you learn what *evolved* means.

READING SKILL

Summarize How did enlightened despots contribute to the Enlightenment?

_____

_____

_____

Note Taking Study Guide

BIRTH OF THE AMERICAN REPUBLIC

Focus Question: How did ideas of the Enlightenment lead to the independence and founding of the United States of America?

As you read this section in your textbook, complete the following timeline with the dates of important events that led to the formation of the United States.

French and Indian War ends.

1763

1760

CHAPTER 17 SECTION 3

Section Summary
BIRTH OF THE AMERICAN REPUBLIC

In the mid-1700s, Britain was a formidable global power. Key reasons for this status included its location, support of commerce, and huge gains in territory around the world. <u>Furthermore, the new king, **George III**, began to assert his leadership and royal power.</u>

Britain's growing empire included 13 prosperous colonies on the east coast of North America. The colonists shared many values. These included an increasing sense of their own destiny separate from Britain. In some cases, Britain neglected to enforce laws dealing with colonial trade and manufacturing.

Tensions between the colonists and Britain grew as Parliament passed laws, such as the **Stamp Act,** that increased colonists' taxes. The colonists protested what they saw as "taxation without representation." A series of violent clashes with British soldiers intensified the colonists' anger. Finally, representatives from each colony, including **George Washington** of Virginia, met in the Continental Congress to decide what to do. Then in April 1775, colonists fought British soldiers at Lexington and Concord, and the American Revolution began.

On July 4, 1776, the Second Continental Congress adopted the Declaration of Independence. Written primarily by **Thomas Jefferson,** it reflects John Locke's ideas about the rights to "life, liberty, and property." It also details the colonists' grievances and emphasizes the Enlightenment idea of **popular sovereignty.**

At first, chances for American success looked bleak. The colonists struggled against Britain's trained soldiers, huge fleet, and greater resources. When the colonists won the Battle of Saratoga, other European nations, such as France, joined the American side. With the help of the French fleet, Washington forced the British to surrender at **Yorktown, Virginia,** in 1781. Two years later American, British, and French diplomats signed the **Treaty of Paris**, ending the war.

By 1789, leaders of the new United States, such as **James Madison** and **Benjamin Franklin,** had established a **federal republic** under the Constitution. The new government was based on the separation of powers, an idea borrowed directly from Montesquieu. The Bill of Rights, the first ten amendments to the Constitution, protected basic rights. The United States Constitution put Enlightenment ideas into practice and has become an important symbol of freedom.

Review Questions

1. What first caused tensions to rise between the colonists and Britain?

_____

_____

2. What are some Enlightenment ideas found in the Declaration of Independence?

_____

_____

READING CHECK

How did France help the Americans win the Revolution?

_____

_____

_____

VOCABULARY STRATEGY

What does the word *assert* mean in the underlined sentence? What context clues can you find in the surrounding words, phrases, or sentences that hint at its meaning? Circle the word below that is a synonym for *assert*.

1. declare

2. deny

READING SKILL

Recognize Sequence Place the events leading to the American Revolution in the correct order.

_____

_____

_____

CHAPTER **18** SECTION 1	**Note Taking Study Guide**
	ON THE EVE OF REVOLUTION

Focus Question: What led to the storming of the Bastille, and therefore, to the start of the French Revolution?

As you read this section in your textbook, complete the following chart by identifying the multiple causes of the French Revolution.

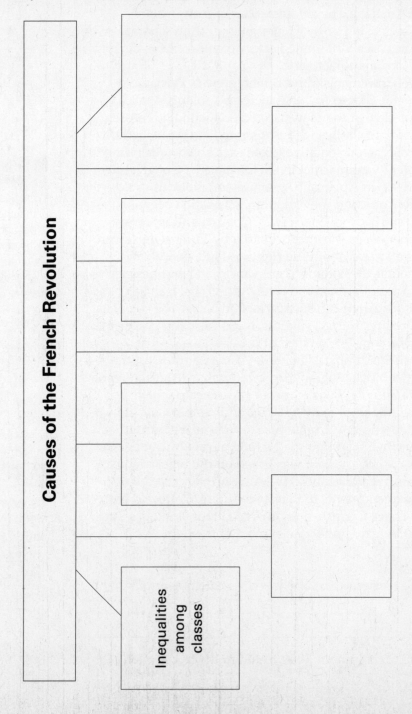

CHAPTER 18
SECTION 1

Section Summary
ON THE EVE OF REVOLUTION

Under France's **ancien régime**, there were three social classes, or **estates**. The First Estate was the clergy, who enjoyed great wealth and privilege. The Second Estate was the titled nobility. They held top jobs in government, the army, and the courts. The vast majority of the population, including the **bourgeoisie,** or middle class, formed the Third Estate. The bulk of the Third Estate consisted of rural peasants. The poorest members of the Third Estate were urban workers.

Members of the Third Estate resented the privileges enjoyed by their social "betters." The First and Second Estates, for example, were exempt from most taxes, while peasants paid taxes on many things, including necessities. Then Enlightenment ideas led people to question the inequalities of the old social structure. The Third Estate demanded that the privileged classes pay their share.

Economic troubles added to the social unrest. **Deficit spending** had left France deeply in debt. In the 1780s, bad harvests sent food prices soaring. **Louis XVI** chose **Jacques Necker** as an economic advisor. Later, the king was forced to dismiss Necker for proposing to tax the First and Second Estates. The crisis deepened. Powerful nobles and clergy called for a meeting of the **Estates-General** to try to control reform. Louis XVI finally set a meeting at Versailles. Beforehand, the king asked all three estates to prepare **cahiers** listing their grievances. Some lists demonstrated the high level of resentment among the classes.

The Estates-General met in May 1789. After weeks of stalemate, delegates of the Third Estate abandoned the Estates-General and formed the National Assembly. Later, when they were locked out of their meeting place, the members of the new legislature took their famous **Tennis Court Oath.** They swore never to separate until they had established a just constitution.

On July 14, 1789, the streets of Paris buzzed with rumors that royal troops were going to occupy the city. More than 800 Parisians assembled outside the **Bastille,** demanding weaponry stored there. When the commander refused, the enraged mob stormed the Bastille, sparking the French Revolution.

Review Questions

1. How was society structured under France's *ancien régime?*

_____

_____

2. What economic troubles did France face in the 1780s?

_____

_____

READING CHECK

Which group paid the most taxes?

_____

_____

_____

VOCABULARY STRATEGY

What does the word *urban* mean in the underlined sentence? Notice that the word *rural* appears in the previous sentence. *Rural* is an antonym of *urban.* Use the meaning of the antonym to help you figure out what *urban* means.

READING SKILL

Recognize Multiple Causes Identify three causes of the French Revolution.

_____

_____

Name_____ Class_____ Date_____

Focus Question: What political and social reforms did the National Assembly institute in the first stage of the French Revolution?

As you read this section in your textbook, complete the following outline by identifying the main ideas and supporting details in this section.

I. Political crisis leads to revolt
   A. The Great Fear
      1. Inflamed by famine and rumors
      2. _____
   B. _____
      1. _____
      2. _____

II. _____
   A. _____
      1. _____
      2. _____
   B. _____
      1. _____
      2. _____
   C. _____
      1. _____
      2. _____

III. _____
   A. _____
      1. _____
      2. _____
   B. _____
      1. _____
      2. _____
   C. _____
      1. _____
      2. _____

(Outline continues on the next page.)

CHAPTER
18
SECTION 2

Note Taking Study Guide

THE FRENCH REVOLUTION UNFOLDS

(Continued from page 166)

IV. _____
    A. _____
        1. _____
        2. _____
    B. _____
        1. _____
        2. _____
    C. _____
        1. _____
        2. _____
    D. _____
        1. _____
        2. _____

CHAPTER 18
SECTION 2

Section Summary
THE FRENCH REVOLUTION UNFOLDS

READING CHECK

Who were the sans-culottes?

_____

_____

_____

In France, the political crisis of 1789 coincided with a terrible famine. Peasants were starving and unemployed. In such desperate times, rumors ran wild. Inflamed by famine and fear, peasants unleashed their fury on the nobles. Meanwhile, a variety of **factions** in Paris competed to gain power. Moderates looked to the **Marquis de Lafayette** for leadership. However, a more radical group, the Paris Commune, replaced the city's royalist government.

The storming of the Bastille and the peasant uprisings pushed the National Assembly into action. In late August, the Assembly issued the Declaration of the Rights of Man and the Citizen. <u>It proclaimed that all male citizens were equal before the law.</u> Upset that women did not have equal rights, journalist **Olympe de Gouges** wrote a declaration that provided for this. The Assembly did not adopt it, however. Nor was King Louis XVI willing to accept reforms. Much anger was directed at the queen, **Marie Antoinette,** who lived a life of great extravagance.

VOCABULARY STRATEGY

What do you think the word *proclaimed* means in the underlined sentence? The words *proclamation, declaration,* and *announcement* are all synonyms for *proclaimed.* Use what you know about these synonyms to figure out the meaning of *proclaimed.*

The National Assembly produced the Constitution of 1791. This document reflected Enlightenment goals, set up a limited monarchy, ensured equality before the law for all male citizens, and ended Church interference in government.

Events in France stirred debate all over Europe. Some applauded the reforms of the National Assembly. Rulers of other nations, however, denounced the French Revolution. Horror stories were told by **émigrés** who had fled France. Rulers of neighboring monarchies increased border patrols to stop the spread of the "French plague" of revolution.

READING SKILL

Identify Supporting Details
Identify two aspects of the Constitution of 1791 that reflect Enlightenment goals.

_____

_____

_____

In October 1791, the newly elected Legislative Assembly took office, but falling currency values, rising prices, and food shortages renewed turmoil. Working-class men and women, called **sans-culottes,** pushed the revolution in a more radical direction, and demanded a **republic.** The sans-culottes found support among other radicals, especially the **Jacobins.** The radicals soon held the upper hand in the Legislative Assembly. Eager to spread the revolution, they declared war against Austria and other European monarchies.

Review Questions

1. What was the Declaration of the Rights of Man and the Citizen? Why were some people dissatisfied with it?

_____

_____

2. How did rulers of European monarchies react to the French Revolution?

_____

_____

CHAPTER
18
SECTION 3

Note Taking Study Guide
RADICAL DAYS OF THE REVOLUTION

Focus Question: What events occurred during the radical phase of the French Revolution?

As you read this section in your textbook, complete the following timeline to show the sequence of events that took place during the radical phase of the French Revolution.

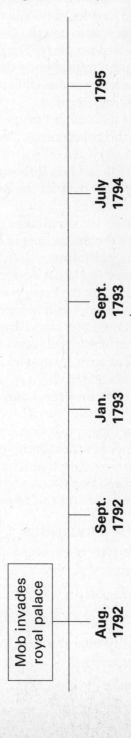

Name_____ Class_____ Date_____

READING CHECK

Who was Robespierre?

_____

_____

_____

VOCABULARY STRATEGY

What do you think *radical* means in the underlined sentence? Notice that the word *more* appears before *radical*. Use the word *more* and your prior knowledge to help you figure out what *radical* means.

READING SKILL

Recognize Sequence What occurred after the radicals took control of the Assembly in 1792?

_____

_____

_____

In 1793, the revolution entered a frightening and bloody phase. The war with Austria was not going well for France. Some felt the king was in league with France's enemies. Others wanted to restore the king's power. On August 10, 1792, a mob stormed the royal palace. Radicals then took control of the Assembly and called for the election of a new legislative body called the National Convention. **Suffrage** was to be extended to all male citizens, not just to those who owned property. The Convention that met in September 1792 was a more radical body than earlier assemblies. It voted to abolish the monarchy and establish the French Republic. Louis XVI and his queen were executed.

War with other European nations and internal rebellions concerned the government. The Convention created the Committee of Public Safety to deal with these issues. It had almost absolute power. Jacobin Maximilien **Robespierre** led the Committee. He was one of the chief architects of the **Reign of Terror,** which lasted from September 1793 to July 1794. During that time, courts conducted hasty trials for those suspected of resisting the revolution. Many people were the victims of false accusations. About 17,000 were executed by **guillotine.**

In reaction to the Terror, the revolution entered a third stage, dominated by the bourgeoisie. It moved away from the excesses of the Convention, and moderates created the Constitution of 1795. This set up a five-man Directory to rule, and a two-house legislature. However, discontent grew because of corrupt leaders. Also, war continued with Austria and Britain. Politicians planned to use **Napoleon** Bonaparte, a popular military hero, to advance their goals.

By 1799, the French Revolution had dramatically changed France. It had dislodged the old social order, overthrown the monarchy, and brought the Church under state control. **Nationalism** spread throughout France. From the city of **Marseilles,** troops marched to a rousing new song that would become the French national anthem. Revolutionaries also made social reforms. They set up systems to help the poor and abolished slavery in France's Caribbean colonies.

Review Questions

1. What type of government did the National Convention establish in September 1792?

_____

_____

2. Identify three changes that the French Revolution brought to France.

_____

_____

Note Taking Study Guide
THE AGE OF NAPOLEON

Focus Question: Explain Napoleon's rise to power in Europe, his subsequent defeat, and how the outcome still affects Europe today.

As you read this section in your textbook, complete the flowchart to list the main ideas about Napoleon's rise to power and his defeat.

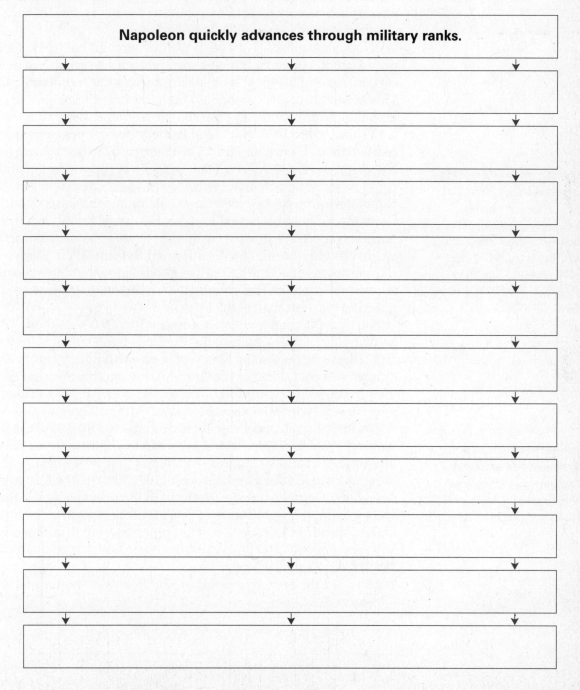

Napoleon quickly advances through military ranks.

CHAPTER 18 SECTION 4

Section Summary
THE AGE OF NAPOLEON

What was the Napoleonic Code?

_____

_____

_____

The final phase of the revolution is known as the Age of Napoleon. When the revolution first broke out, Napoleon Bonaparte was a young lieutenant. Battle victories fueled his ambitions and his rise through army ranks. By 1804, Napoleon had acquired enough power to assume the title Emperor of the French. At each step on his rise to power, Napoleon had held a **plebiscite.** However, he still had absolute power, although he was elected.

Napoleon consolidated his power by strengthening the central government. His economic and social reforms won support across classes. Among his most lasting reforms was the **Napoleonic Code.** This new code of laws embodied Enlightenment principles of equality, religious tolerance, and the abolition of feudalism.

From 1804 to 1812, Napoleon battled the European powers and created a vast French empire. A brilliant general, before each battle Napoleon developed a new plan. <u>In this way, opposing generals could never anticipate what he would do next.</u> He rarely lost. Napoleon **annexed** the Netherlands, Belgium, and parts of Italy and Germany to build his Grand Empire. However, Britain remained outside Napoleon's grasp. His attempt to wage economic warfare against Britain through the **Continental System** failed. Many Europeans resented the scarcity of goods. Growing nationalism led to resistance against French influence. In Spain, patriots waged **guerrilla warfare** against the French.

In 1812, Napoleon invaded Russia with 600,000 soldiers. To avoid battles with Napoleon, the Russians retreated, burning crops and villages as they went. This **scorched-earth policy** left the French hungry and cold. Most of the Grand Army was destroyed. Fewer than 20,000 soldiers survived. The retreat from Moscow through the long Russian winter shattered Napoleon's reputation for success.

In 1815, British and Prussian forces crushed the French at the Battle of Waterloo. Napoleon was forced to **abdicate.** After Waterloo, diplomats met at the **Congress of Vienna** to restore stability and order in Europe after years of revolution and war. The Congress strived to create a lasting peace through the principle of **legitimacy** and by maintaining a balance of power. Leaders also met periodically in the **Concert of Europe** to discuss problems that threatened peace.

VOCABULARY STRATEGY

What do you think the word *anticipate* means in the underlined sentence? What clues can you find in the surrounding words and phrases? Use these context clues to figure out the meaning of *anticipate.*

READING SKILL

Identify Main Ideas Write a new title for this section Summary to express the main idea in another way.

_____

_____

_____

Review Questions

1. How did the French respond to Napoleon's economic and social reforms?

_____

_____

2. Why did Napoleon's invasion of Russia fail?

_____

_____

CHAPTER 19
SECTION 1

Note Taking Study Guide
DAWN OF THE INDUSTRIAL AGE

Focus Question: What events helped bring about the Industrial Revolution?

As you read this section in your textbook, complete the following flowchart to list multiple causes of the Industrial Revolution.

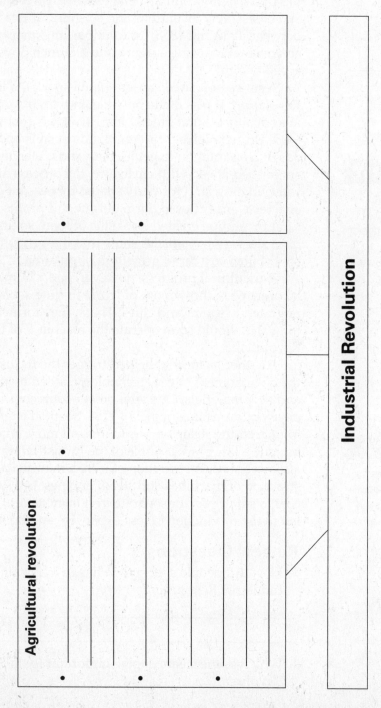

CHAPTER 19 · SECTION 1

Section Summary

DAWN OF THE INDUSTRIAL AGE

_____

_____

_____

What does the word *statistics* mean in the underlined sentence? What prior knowledge do you have of this word? For example, think of where you may have seen statistics before. Use your prior knowledge and context clues in the sentence to help you learn what *statistics* means.

Recognize Multiple Causes Identify three events in the agricultural revolution that caused population and industry to grow.

_____

_____

_____

The Industrial Revolution started in Britain. In 1750, most people worked the land, using handmade tools. They made their own clothing and grew their own food. With the onset of the Industrial Revolution, the rural way of life in Britain began to disappear. By the 1850s, many country villages had grown into industrial towns and cities. New inventions and scientific "firsts" appeared each year. Between 1830 and 1855, for example, an American dentist first used an **anesthetic** during surgery and a French physicist measured the speed of light.

A series of related causes helped spark the Industrial Revolution. It was made possible, in part, by another revolution—in agriculture—that greatly improved the quality and quantity of food. Farmers mixed different kinds of soils and tried out new methods of crop rotation to get higher yields. Meanwhile, rich landowners pushed ahead with **enclosure,** the process of taking over and consolidating land formerly shared by peasant farmers. As millions of acres were enclosed, farm output and profits rose. The agricultural revolution created a surplus of food, so fewer people died from starvation. Statistics show that the agricultural revolution contributed to a rapid growth in population.

Agricultural progress, however, had a human cost. Many farm laborers were thrown out of work. In time, jobless farm workers migrated to towns and cities. There, they formed a growing labor force that would soon operate the machines of the Industrial Revolution.

Another factor that helped trigger the Industrial Revolution was the development of new technology, aided by new sources of energy and new materials. One vital power source was coal, used to develop the steam engine. In 1764, Scottish engineer **James Watt** improved the steam engine to make it more efficient. Watt's engine became a key power source of the Industrial Revolution. Coal was also used in the production of iron, a material needed for the construction of machines and steam engines. In 1709, Adam Darby used coal to **smelt** iron, or separate iron from its ore. Darby's experiments led to the production of less-expensive and better-quality iron.

Review Questions

1. How did people's lifestyles change in Britain with the start of the Industrial Revolution?

_____

_____

2. Why was the steam engine important to the Industrial Revolution?

_____

_____

Name_____ Class_____ Date_____

Note Taking Study Guide

CHAPTER 19
SECTION 2

BRITAIN LEADS THE WAY

Focus Question: What key factors allowed Britain to lead the way in the Industrial Revolution?

As you read this section in your textbook, complete the following concept webs to identify causes and effects of Britain's early lead in industrialization. Fill in the first concept web with causes. Fill in the second concept web with effects.

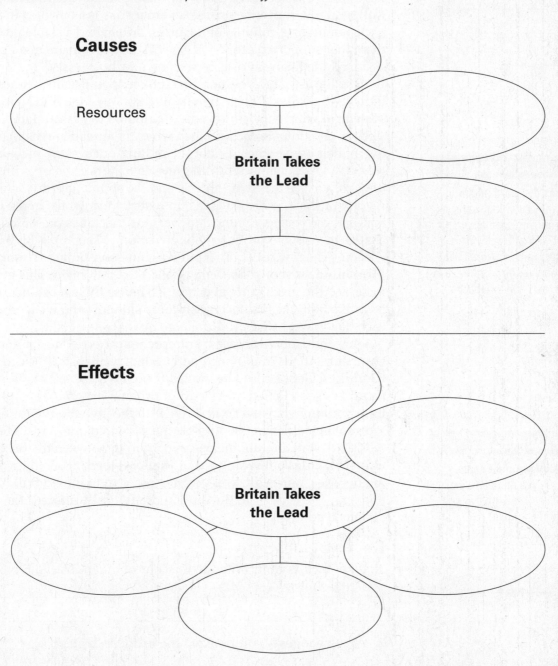

Causes

Resources

Britain Takes the Lead

Effects

Britain Takes the Lead

CHAPTER 19 SECTION 2

Section Summary
BRITAIN LEADS THE WAY

READING CHECK

READING CHECK

What machine did Eli Whitney invent?

_____

_____

_____

VOCABULARY STRATEGY

What does the word *decades* mean in the underlined sentence? The word *decades* comes from the Greek word *deka,* which means "ten." Use the meaning of the word *deka* to help you learn what *decades* means.

READING SKILL

Identify Causes and Effects Identify causes and effects of the great revolution in transportation in England.

_____

_____

_____

The start of the Industrial Revolution in Britain can be attributed to many factors, including population growth and plentiful natural resources. The growing population and ready workforce boosted demand for goods. To increase production to meet the demand, however, another key ingredient was needed—money to start businesses. Beginning with the slave trade, the business class accumulated **capital** to invest in enterprises. An **enterprise** is a business in areas such as shipping, mining, or factories. Britain had a stable government that supported economic growth. **Entrepreneurs** managed and assumed the financial risks of starting new businesses.

The Industrial Revolution first took hold in Britain's largest industry—textiles. British merchants developed the **putting-out system,** in which raw cotton was distributed to peasant families. They spun it into thread and then wove the thread into cloth, working in their own homes. Under the putting-out system, production was slow. As demand for cloth grew, inventors came up with new devices, such as the flying shuttle and the spinning jenny, which revolutionized the British textile industry. Meanwhile, in the United States, these faster spinning and weaving machines presented a challenge—how to produce enough cotton to keep up with Britain. Cleaning the raw cotton by hand was time-consuming. To solve this, **Eli Whitney** invented a machine called the cotton gin. This greatly increased the production of cotton. To house these machines, manufacturers built the first factories, where spinners and weavers came each day to work and produce large quantities of goods.

As production increased, entrepreneurs needed faster and cheaper methods of moving goods. Some capitalists invested in **turnpikes.** Goods could be moved faster on these toll roads, and turnpikes soon linked every part of Britain. The great revolution in transportation, however, occurred with the invention of the steam locomotive, which made possible the growth of railroads. The world's first major rail line began operating between the British industrial cities of **Liverpool** and **Manchester** in 1830. In the following decades, railroad travel became faster and railroad building boomed. The Industrial Revolution dramatically affected the way people lived.

Review Questions

1. What factors contributed to the start of the Industrial Revolution?

_____

_____

2. What changes revolutionized the textile industry?

_____

_____

Note Taking Study Guide

SOCIAL IMPACT OF THE INDUSTRIAL REVOLUTION

Focus Question: What were the social effects of the Industrial Revolution?

As you read this section in your textbook, complete the following table to understand the effects of industrialization.

Industrialization

Challenges
- Crowded cities
-
-
-

Benefits
- Created jobs
-
-
-

Section Summary
SOCIAL IMPACT OF THE INDUSTRIAL REVOLUTION

READING CHECK

Who made up the new middle class that emerged during the Industrial Revolution?

_____

_____

_____

VOCABULARY STRATEGY

What does the word *contaminated* mean in the underlined sentence? What clues can you find in the surrounding words, phrases, or sentences? Circle the words in the paragraph that could help you figure out what *contaminated* means.

READING SKILL

Understand Effects How did the Industrial Revolution affect the lives of the working class?

_____

_____

_____

The Industrial Revolution brought rapid **urbanization,** or the movement of people to cities. Changes in farming, soaring population growth, and a demand for workers led masses of people to migrate from farms to cities. Almost overnight, small towns that were located around coal or iron mines grew into cities. Other cities developed around the factories in once-quiet market towns.

Those who benefited most from the Industrial Revolution were the entrepreneurs who set it in motion. The Industrial Revolution created this new middle class, whose members came from a variety of backgrounds. While the wealthy and the middle class lived in pleasant neighborhoods, vast numbers of poor struggled to survive in slums. They packed into tiny rooms in **tenements** that had no running water and no sewage or sanitation system. Sewage rotted in the streets or was dumped into rivers, which created an overwhelming stench and contaminated drinking water. This led to the spread of diseases such as cholera.

The heart of the new industrial city was the factory. Working in a factory differed greatly from working on a farm. In rural villages, people worked hard, but the work varied according to the season. Some seasons were easier than others. The factory system imposed a harsh new way of life on workers. Working hours were long, with shifts lasting from twelve to sixteen hours, six or seven days a week. Exhausted workers were injured by machines that had no safety devices. Working conditions in the mines were even worse than in the factories. Factories and mines also hired many boys and girls. These children often started working at age seven or eight; a few were as young as five.

The early industrial age brought terrible hardships. In time, however, reformers pressed for laws to improve working conditions. **Labor unions** won the right to bargain with employers for better wages, hours, and working conditions. Despite the social problems created by the Industrial Revolution—low pay, dismal living conditions—the industrial age did have some positive effects. Wages rose. Also as the cost of railroad travel fell, more people could afford to travel further and faster than ever before.

Review Questions

1. What caused rapid urbanization to occur during the Industrial Revolution?

_____

_____

2. How did the factory system change the way people worked?

_____

_____

CHAPTER 19
SECTION 4

Note Taking Study Guide
NEW WAYS OF THINKING

Focus Question: What new ideas about economics and society were fostered as a result of the Industrial Revolution?

As you read this section in your textbook, complete the following outline to identify main ideas about the new economic and social theories.

I. Laissez-faire economics

    A. Adam Smith and free enterprise

        1. _____

        2. _____

II. Malthus on population

    A. _____

        1. _____

        2. _____

        3. _____

    B. _____

        1. _____

        2. _____

III. _____

    A. _____

        1. _____

        2. _____

IV. _____

    A. _____

        1. _____

        2. _____

    B. _____

        1. _____

        2. _____

(Outline continues on the next page.)

CHAPTER
19
SECTION 4

Note Taking Study Guide

NEW WAYS OF THINKING

(Continued from page 179)

V. _____
    A. _____
        1. _____
        2. _____

VI. _____
    A. _____
        1. _____
        2. _____
        3. _____
    B. _____
        1. _____
        2. _____

CHAPTER **19** SECTION 4	**Section Summary** NEW WAYS OF THINKING

Many thinkers tried to understand the staggering changes taking place in the early Industrial Age. These thinkers looked for natural laws that governed the world of business and economics. Middle-class business leaders embraced the laissez-faire, or "hands-off" approach, believing that a free market would eventually help every-one, not just the rich. However, one British laissez-faire economist, **Thomas Malthus,** felt that the population would grow faster than the food supply. As long as the population kept growing the poor would suffer. He opposed any government help including charity and vaccinations. He urged families to have fewer children.

Other thinkers sought to modify laissez-faire ideas to justify some government intervention. The British philosopher and econo-mist **Jeremy Bentham** advocated **utilitarianism,** or the idea that the goal of society should be the "greatest happiness for the greatest number" of citizens. Bentham's ideas influenced the British philoso-pher and economist John Stuart Mill. Although he strongly believed in individual freedom, Mill wanted the government to step in to improve the hard lives of the working class.

To end poverty and injustice, others offered a radical solution—**socialism.** Under socialism, the people, as a whole rather than as individuals, would own and operate the **means of production—**the farms, factories, railways, and other businesses that produced and distributed goods. A number of early socialists, such as **Robert Owen,** established communities where all work was shared and all property was owned in common. These early socialists were called Utopians.

Karl Marx, a German philosopher, formulated a new theory— a form of socialism called **communism,** in which the struggle between social classes would lead to the creation of a classless society. According to Marx, the modern class struggle pitted the bourgeoisie against the **proletariat,** or working class. In a classless, communist society, people's struggles would end because wealth and power would be equally shared. In the 1860s, Germany adapted Marx's beliefs to form a **social democracy** in which there was a grad-ual transition from capitalism to socialism.

Review Questions

1. Why did middle-class business leaders support laissez-faire eco-nomics?

_____

_____

2. How did utilitarians seek to modify laissez-faire ideas?

_____

_____

READING CHECK

Who were the Utopians?

_____

_____

_____

VOCABULARY STRATEGY

What does the word *formulated* mean in the underlined sen-tence? What clue can you find in the base word, *form*? Use the meaning of *form* to help you fig-ure out what *formulated* means.

READING SKILL

Identify Main Ideas Explain the main ideas of Karl Marx's theory.

_____

_____

_____

Note Taking Study Guide

CHAPTER 20 SECTION 1

AN AGE OF IDEOLOGIES

Focus Question: What events proved that Metternich was correct in his fears?

A. *As you read "Conservatives Prefer the Old Order," and "Liberals and Nationalists Seek Change," fill in the table to identify main ideas about conservatism, liberalism, and nationalism.*

Conservatism	Liberalism	Nationalism
• _____	• _____	• _____
• _____	• _____	_____
• _____	• _____	_____
• _____	• _____	
• _____	• _____	
• _____	• _____	
• _____		

B. *As you read "Central Europe Challenges the Old Order," use the table to identify supporting details about revolts in Serbia, Greece, and other countries.*

Serbia	Greece	Other Revolts
• _____	• _____	• _____
• _____	• _____	• _____
• _____	• _____	• _____
• _____	• _____	

CHAPTER 20 SECTION 1

Section Summary

AN AGE OF IDEOLOGIES

After the Congress of Vienna, people with opposing **ideologies** plunged Europe into decades of turmoil. Conservatives, including monarchs, nobles, and church leaders, favored a return to the social order that had existed before 1789. They decided to work together in an agreement called the Concert of Europe. They wanted to restore the royal families that Napoleon had deposed. They supported a social hierarchy in which lower classes respected and obeyed their social superiors. They also backed established churches and opposed constitutional governments. Conservative leaders such as Prince Metternich of Austria sought to suppress revolutionary ideas.

Inspired by the Enlightenment and the French Revolution, liberals and nationalists challenged conservatives. Liberals included business owners, bankers, lawyers, politicians, and writers. They wanted governments based on written constitutions. They opposed established churches and divine-right monarchies. They believed that liberty, equality, and property were natural rights. They saw government's role as limited to protecting basic rights, such as freedom of thought, speech, and religion. Only later in the century did liberals come to support **universal manhood suffrage,** giving all men the right to vote. Liberals also strongly supported laissez-faire economics.

Nationalism gave people with a common heritage a sense of identity and the goal of creating their own homeland. In the 1800s, national groups within the Austrian and Ottoman empires set out to create their own states. Rebellions erupted in the Balkans, where there were people of various religions and ethnic groups. The Serbs were the first to revolt. By 1830, Russian support helped the Serbs win **autonomy,** or self-rule, within the Ottoman empire. In 1821, the Greeks revolted, and by 1830, Greece was independent from the Ottomans. Revolts spread to Spain, Portugal, and Italy. Metternich urged conservative rulers to crush the uprisings. In response, French and Austrian troops smashed rebellions in Spain and Italy.

In the next decades, sparks of rebellion would flare anew. Added to liberal and nationalist demands were the goals of the new industrial working class. <u>By the mid-1800s, social reformers and agitators were urging workers to support socialism or other ways of reorganizing property ownership.</u>

Review Questions

1. How did government views of conservatives and liberals differ?

_____

_____

2. Why did French and Austrian troops stop revolts in Spain and Italy?

_____

_____

READING CHECK

What is universal manhood suffrage?

_____

_____

_____

VOCABULARY STRATEGY

What does the word *agitators* mean in the underlined sentence? Review the surrounding words and phrases to look for clues to its meaning. Use these context clues to help you understand what an *agitator* is.

READING SKILL

Identify Main Ideas What two groups generally struggled for political control during the early nineteenth century?

_____

_____

_____

CHAPTER 20 SECTION 2

Note Taking Study Guide

REVOLUTIONS OF 1830 AND 1848

Focus Question: What were the causes and effects of the revolutions in Europe in 1830 and 1848?

As you read this section, fill in the table below with a country, date, and main idea for each revolution of 1830 and 1848.

Revolutions of 1830 and 1848	Radicals force king to abdicate.								
	1830								
	France								

Section Summary
REVOLUTIONS OF 1830 AND 1848

When Louis XVIII died in 1824, Charles X inherited the French throne. In 1830, Charles suspended the legislature, limited the right to vote, and restricted the press. Angry citizens, led by liberals and **radicals,** rebelled and soon controlled Paris. Charles X abdicated. Radicals hoped to set up a republic, but liberals insisted on a constitutional monarchy. **Louis Philippe** was chosen king. As the "citizen king," Louis favored the bourgeoisie, or middle class, over the workers.

The Paris revolts inspired uprisings elsewhere in Europe. Most failed, but the revolutions frightened rulers and encouraged reforms. One notable success was in Belgium, which achieved its independence from Holland in 1831. Nationalists also revolted in Poland in 1830, but they failed to win widespread support. Russian forces crushed the rebels.

In the 1840s, discontent began to grow again in France. <u>Radicals, socialists, and liberals denounced Louis Philippe's government.</u> Discontent was heightened by a **recession.** People lost their jobs, and poor harvests caused bread prices to rise. When the government tried to silence critics, angry crowds took to the streets in February 1848. The turmoil spread, and Louis Philippe abdicated. A group of liberals, radicals, and socialists proclaimed the Second Republic. By June, the upper and middle classes had won control of the government. Workers again took to the streets of Paris. At least 1,500 people were killed before the government crushed the rebellion. By the end of 1848, the National Assembly issued a constitution for the Second Republic, giving the right to vote to all adult men. When the election for president was held, Louis Napoleon, the nephew of Napoleon Bonaparte, won. However, by 1852 he had proclaimed himself Emperor **Napoleon III.** This ended the Second Republic.

The revolts in Paris in 1848 again led to revolutions across Europe, especially in the Austrian empire. Revolts broke out in Vienna, and Metternich resigned. In Budapest, Hungarian nationalists led by **Louis Kossuth** demanded an independent government. In Prague, the Czechs made similar demands. The Italian states also revolted, and the German states demanded national unity. While the rebellions had some short-term success, most of them had failed by 1850.

Review Questions

1. What caused the rebellion in France in 1830?

_____

_____

2. In what parts of Europe did revolts take place following the Paris revolts of 1848?

_____

_____

READING CHECK

What brought the Second Republic to an end?

_____

_____

_____

VOCABULARY STRATEGY

What does the word *denounced* mean in the underlined sentence? Reread the sentences before and after the underlined sentence. Were the French people happy or unhappy with Louis Philippe's government? Note that the government "tried to silence critics." Use these context clues to help you understand the meaning of *denounce.*

READING SKILL

Identify Main Ideas What is the main idea of the last paragraph in the Summary?

_____

_____

_____

CHAPTER 20
SECTION 3

Note Taking Study Guide
REVOLTS IN LATIN AMERICA

Focus Question: Who were the key revolutionaries to lead the movements for independence in Latin America, and what were their accomplishments?

As you read this section, fill in the table below with a country, a date, and a main idea for each of the revolts in Latin America.

Revolts in Latin America										
Haiti	1791	Toussaint L'Ouverture leads an army of former slaves and ends slavery there.								

CHAPTER 20 SECTION 3

Section Summary

REVOLTS IN LATIN AMERICA

By the late 1700s, revolutionary fever had spread to Latin America, where the social system had led to discontent. Spanish-born *peninsulares,* the highest social class, dominated the government and the Church. Many **creoles**—Latin Americans of European descent who owned the haciendas, ranches, and mines—resented their second-class status. **Mestizos,** people of Native American and European descent, and **mulattoes,** people of African and European descent, were angry at being denied the status, wealth, and power that the other groups enjoyed. The Enlightenment and the French and American revolutions inspired creoles, but they were reluctant to act. However, when Napoleon invaded Spain in 1808, Latin American leaders decided to demand independence from Spain.

Revolution had already erupted in Hispaniola in 1791 when **Toussaint L'Ouverture** led a slave rebellion there. The fighting cost many lives, but the rebels achieved their goal of abolishing slavery and taking control of the island. Napoleon's army tried to reconquer the island but failed. In 1804, the island declared itself independent under the name Haiti.

In 1810, a creole priest, **Father Miguel Hidalgo,** called Mexicans to fight for independence. After some successes, he was captured and executed. **Father José Morelos** tried to carry the revolution forward, but he too was captured and killed. Success finally came in 1821 when revolutionaries led by Agustín de Iturbide overthrew the Spanish viceroy and declared independence. Central American colonies soon declared independence, too.

In the early 1800s, discontent spread across South America. **Simón Bolívar** led an uprising in Venezuela. Conservative forces toppled his new republic, but Bolívar did not give up. In a grueling campaign, he marched his army across the Andes, swooping down into Bogotá and taking the city from the surprised Spanish. Then he moved south to free Ecuador, Peru, and Bolivia. There, he joined forces with another great leader, **José de San Martín.** San Martín helped Argentina and Chile win freedom from Spain. The wars of independence ended in 1824, but power struggles among South American leaders led to destructive civil wars. In Brazil, **Dom Pedro,** the son of the Portuguese king, became emperor and proclaimed independence for Brazil in 1822.

Review Questions

1. Why were creoles ready to revolt by 1808?

_____

_____

2. How did Brazil gain its independence?

_____

_____

READING CHECK

What two leaders helped free much of South America?

_____

_____

_____

VOCABULARY STRATEGY

What does the word *proclaimed* mean in the underlined sentence? *Proclaim* comes from the Latin word *proclamare.* The prefix *pro-* means "before," and *clamare* means "to cry out" or "shout." Use these word-origin clues to help you to figure out the meaning of *proclaimed.*

READING SKILL

Identify Main Ideas In the first paragraph of the Summary, most of the sentences are supporting details. Which sentence states the main idea of that paragraph?

_____

_____

_____

CHAPTER
21
SECTION 1

Note Taking Study Guide

THE INDUSTRIAL REVOLUTION SPREADS

Focus Question: How did science, technology, and big business promote industrial growth?

As you read this section in your textbook, complete the following chart to identify main ideas about the major developments of the Industrial Revolution.

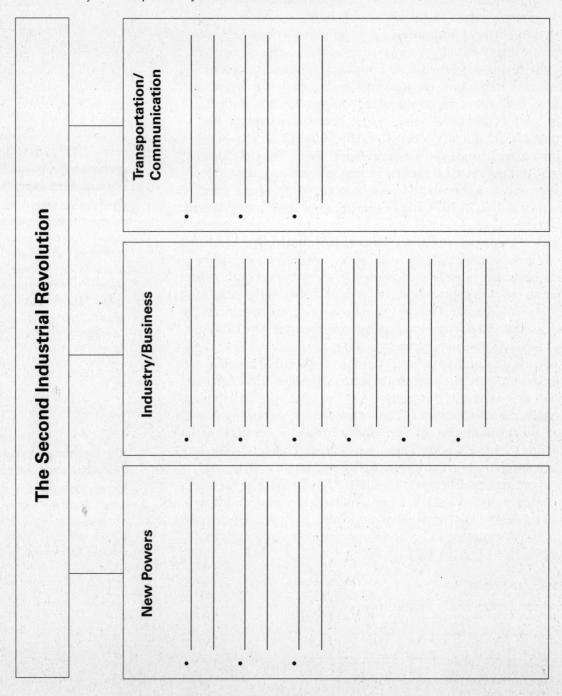

The Second Industrial Revolution

Transportation/Communication
-
-
-

Industry/Business
-
-
-
-
-
-

New Powers
-
-
-

CHAPTER 21 SECTION 1

Section Summary
THE INDUSTRIAL REVOLUTION SPREADS

During the early Industrial Revolution, Britain was the world's industrial giant. Later, two new industrial powers emerged—Germany and the United States. These nations had more abundant supplies of coal, iron, and other resources than Britain. This helped them become the new industrial leaders. These nations also had the advantage of being able to follow Britain's lead, borrowing its experts and technology. The demands of an industrial society brought about many social, economic, and political changes.

Technology sparked industrial and economic growth. **Henry Bessemer** patented the process for making steel from iron. Steel became so important that industrialized countries measured their success in steel output. **Alfred Nobel** earned enough money from his invention of dynamite to fund today's Nobel prizes. Electricity replaced steam as the dominant industrial energy source. **Michael Faraday** created the first simple electric motor, as well as the first **dynamo.** In the 1870s, **Thomas Edison** made the first electric light bulb. Soon, electricity lit entire cities, the pace of city life quickened, and factories continued to operate after dark. **Interchangeable parts** and the **assembly line** made production faster and cheaper.

Technology also transformed transportation and communication. Steamships replaced sailing ships. Railroads connected cities, seaports, and industrial centers. The invention of the internal combustion engine sparked the automobile age. In the early 1900s, Henry Ford developed an assembly line to produce cars, making the United States a leader in the automobile industry. The air age began when **Orville and Wilbur Wright** flew their plane for a few seconds in 1904. Communication advances included the telegraph and telephone. **Guglielmo Marconi's** radio became the cornerstone of today's global communication network.

New technologies needed investments of large amounts of money. To get the money, owners sold **stock** to investors, growing businesses into giant **corporations.** By the late 1800s, what we call "big business" came to dominate industry. Corporations formed **cartels** to control markets.

Review Questions

1. What advantages did the new industrial powers have?

_____

_____

2. How did the development of electricity change life in cities?

_____

_____

READING CHECK

What two new industrial powers emerged in the mid-1800s?

_____

_____

_____

VOCABULARY STRATEGY

What does the word *dominate* mean in the underlined sentence? It comes from a Latin word that means "lord" or "master." Use this information about the word's origin to help you figure out what *dominate* means.

READING SKILL

Identify Main Ideas How was transportation transformed during the Industrial Revolution?

_____

_____

_____

CHAPTER 21
SECTION 2

Note Taking Study Guide
THE RISE OF THE CITIES

Focus Question: How did the Industrial Revolution change life in the cities?

As you read this section in your textbook, complete the following outline to identify main ideas and supporting details about how the Industrial Revolution changed life in the cities.

I. Medicine and the population explosion

   A. The fight against disease

      1. _____

      2. _____

   B. _____

      1. _____

      2. _____

II. _____

   A. _____

      1. _____

      2. _____

   B. _____

      1. _____

      2. _____

   C. _____

      1. _____

      2. _____

   D. _____

      1. _____

      2. _____

III. _____

   A. _____

      1. _____

      2. _____

   B. _____

      1. _____

      2. _____

CHAPTER 21 SECTION 2

Section Summary
THE RISE OF THE CITIES

Between 1800 and 1900, the population of Europe more than doubled. Advances in medicine slowed death rates and caused a population explosion. In the fight against disease, scientists speculated about a **germ theory**. They believed that certain germs might cause specific diseases. In 1870, French chemist **Louis Pasteur** showed that this link is real. Ten years later, German doctor **Robert Koch** identified the bacteria that causes tuberculosis, a deadly respiratory disease. As people began to understand how germs cause diseases, they practiced better hygiene. This helped decrease the number of deaths from disease. Better hygiene also led to improvements in hospital care. British nurse and reformer **Florence Nightingale** introduced sanitary measures in hospitals. The English surgeon **Joseph Lister** discovered how antiseptics prevent infection.

As industrialization progressed, city life underwent dramatic changes in Europe and the United States. The most extensive **urban renewal** took place in Paris in the 1850s. Wide boulevards, paved streets, and splendid public buildings replaced old streets full of tenement housing. Architects used steel to build soaring buildings called skyscrapers. Electric streetlights illuminated the night, increasing safety. Massive new sewage systems in London and Paris provided cleaner water and better sanitation, sharply cutting death rates from disease.

Despite these efforts, urban life remained difficult for the poor. In the worst tenements, whole families were often crammed into a single room. Slums remained a fact of city life. Still, millions of people were attracted to cities because of the promise of work, entertainment, and educational opportunities.

However, industrialization and urban improvements did not improve conditions for workers. Most experienced low wages, long hours, unsafe environments, and the constant threat of unemployment. Workers protested these terrible conditions. They formed **mutual-aid societies** and organized unions. Pressured by unions, reformers, and working-class voters, governments passed laws to regulate working conditions. Wages varied, but overall, the **standard of living** for most workers did rise.

Review Questions

1. How did advances in medicine cause a population explosion?

_____

_____

2. What two changes in the 1800s made city life safer and healthier?

_____

_____

READING CHECK

What did Louis Pasteur do in 1870?

_____

_____

_____

VOCABULARY STRATEGY

What does the word *illuminated* mean in the underlined sentence? The root of this word is from *lumen*, which is Latin for "light." How can you use the root of *illuminated* to help you figure out its meaning?

READING SKILL

Identify Supporting Details In what ways were working conditions difficult for most industrial workers?

_____

_____

_____

Note Taking Study Guide

CHANGING ATTITUDES AND VALUES

Focus Question: How did the Industrial Revolution change the old social order and long-held traditions in the Western world?

As you read this section in your textbook, complete the following table. List new issues that caused change in the first column and identify two supporting details for each in the second column.

Changes in Social Order and Values	
Issue	**Change**
• New social order	• Upper class: old nobility, new industrialists, business families • •
• Rights for women	• •
•	• •
•	• •
•	• •

CHAPTER 21 SECTION 3

Section Summary
CHANGING ATTITUDES AND VALUES

In the late 1800s, the social order in the Western world slowly changed. Instead of nobles and peasants, a more complex social structure emerged, made up of three classes. The new upper class included very rich business families. Below this tiny elite were a growing middle class and a struggling lower middle class. Workers and peasants were at the bottom of the social ladder.

The middle class developed its own values and way of life, which included a strict code of rules that dictated behavior for every occasion. A **cult of domesticity** also emerged that idealized women and the home.

Demands for women's rights also challenged the traditional social order. Across Europe and the United States, many women campaigned for fairness in marriage, divorce, and property laws. Many women's groups also supported the **temperance movement.** In the United States, reformers such as **Elizabeth Cady Stanton** and **Sojourner Truth** were dedicated to achieving **women's suffrage.**

Industrialized societies recognized the need for a literate work-force. Reformers persuaded many governments to require basic education for all children and to set up public schools. More and more children attended school, and public education improved.

At the same time, new ideas in science challenged long-held beliefs. **John Dalton** developed the modern atomic theory. <u>The most controversial new idea, however, came from the British naturalist</u> <u>**Charles Darwin.**</u> His ideas upset those who debated the validity of his conclusions. Darwin argued that all forms of life had evolved over millions of years. His theory of natural selection explained the long, slow process of evolution. In natural selection, members of each species compete to survive. Unfortunately, some people applied Darwin's theory of natural selection to encourage **racism.** Others applied his ideas to economic competition.

Religion continued to be a major force in Western society. The grim realities of industrial life stirred feelings of compassion and charity. For example, the **social gospel** urged Christians to push for reforms in housing, healthcare, and education.

Review Questions

1. How did the social structure change in the late 1800s?

_____

_____

2. For what rights did women in Europe and the United States campaign?

_____

_____

READING CHECK

What new scientific theory did Charles Darwin promote to explain evolution?

_____

_____

_____

VOCABULARY STRATEGY

What does the word *controversial* mean in the underlined sentence? Use context clues, or surrounding words and sentences, to figure out what *controversial* means.

READING SKILL

Identify Supporting Details
What changes in education were brought about by the Industrial Revolution?

_____

_____

_____

Name_____ Class_____ Date_____

Focus Question: What artistic movements emerged in reaction to the Industrial Revolution?

As you read this section in your textbook, complete the following table. Identify supporting details about the major features of the artistic movements of the 1800s.

Major Artistic Movements of the 1800s		
Movement	**Goals/Characteristics**	**Major Figures**
Romanticism	• Rebellion against reason • • • • •	• William Wordsworth • • • • • • •
Realism	• • • • •	• • • •
Impressionism	• •	• •
	• 	• • •

CHAPTER 21 SECTION 4

Section Summary
ARTS IN THE INDUSTRIAL AGE

From about 1750 to 1850, a cultural movement called **romanticism** emerged in Western art and literature. The movement was a reaction against the rationality and restraint of the Enlightenment. Romanticism emphasized imagination, freedom, and emotion. In contrast to Enlightenment literature, the works of romantic writers included direct language, intense feelings, and a glorification of nature.

Poets **William Wordsworth, William Blake,** and **Lord Byron** were among the major figures of the romantic movement. Romantic novelists, such as **Victor Hugo,** were inspired by history, legend, and folklore. Romantic composers also tried to stir deep emotions. The passionate music of **Ludwig van Beethoven** combined classical forms with a stirring range of sound. Painters, too, broke free from the formal styles of the Enlightenment. They sought to capture the beauty and power of nature with bold brush strokes and colors.

By the mid-1800s, another new artistic movement, **realism,** took hold in the West. Realists sought to represent the world as it was, without romantic sentiment. Their works made people aware of the grim conditions of the Industrial Age. Many realists wanted to improve the lives of those they depicted. **Charles Dickens,** for example, vividly portrayed in his novels the lives of slum dwellers and factory workers. Some of his novels shocked middle-class readers with images of poverty, mistreatment of children, and urban crime. Painters such as **Gustave Courbet** also portrayed the realities of the time.

By the 1840s, a new art form, photography, emerged. **Louis Daguerre** produced some of the first successful photographs. Some artists questioned the effectiveness of realism when a camera could make such exact images. By the 1870s, one group had started a new art movement, **impressionism.** Impressionists, such as **Claude Monet,** sought to capture the first fleeting impression made by a scene or object on the viewer's eye. By concentrating on visual impressions, rather than realism, artists created a fresh view of familiar subjects. Later painters, called postimpressionists, developed a variety of styles. **Vincent van Gogh,** for example, experimented with sharp brush lines and bright colors.

Review Questions

1. How did the romantic movement differ from the Enlightenment?

_____

_____

2. What was the goal of the impressionist artists?

_____

_____

READING CHECK

Against what was the romantic movement a reaction?

_____

_____

_____

VOCABULARY STRATEGY

What does the word *intense* mean in the underlined sentence? What clues can you find in the surrounding words, phrases, or sentences that might have a similar meaning? Use these context clues to help you learn what *intense* means.

READING SKILL

Identify Supporting Details
Identify two supporting details for the following main idea: The artists of the realism movement made people more aware of the harsh conditions of life in the Industrial Age.

_____

_____

_____

CHAPTER 22
SECTION 1

Note Taking Study Guide
BUILDING A GERMAN NATION

Focus Question: How did Otto von Bismarck, the chancellor of Prussia, lead the drive for German unity?

As you read this section in your textbook, complete the following chart to record the sequence of events that led to German unification.

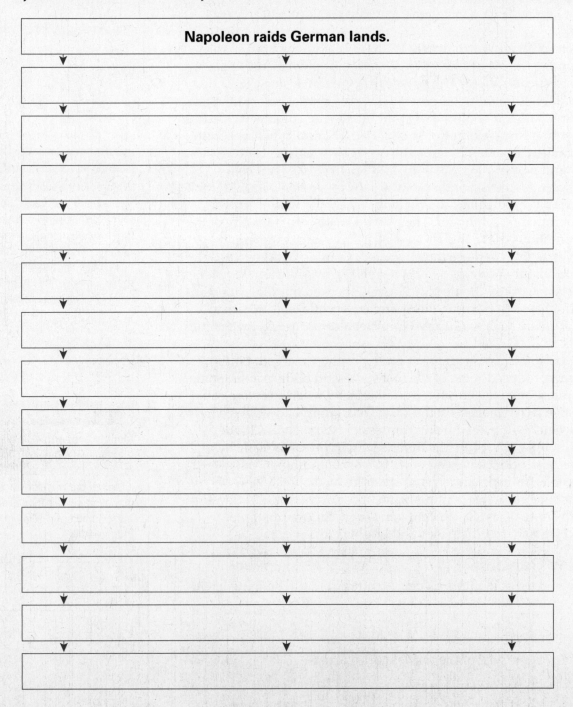

Napoleon raids German lands.

CHAPTER 22 SECTION 1

Section Summary

BUILDING A GERMAN NATION

In the early 1800s, German-speaking people lived in a number of German states. Many also lived in Prussia and the Austrian empire. There was no unified German nation. However, events unfolded in the mid-nineteenth century that eventually led to the formation of one Germany. Between 1806 and 1812, Napoleon invaded these lands. He organized a number of German states into the Rhine Confederation. After Napoleon's defeat, the Congress of Vienna created the German Confederation. This was a weak alliance of German states headed by Austria. In the 1830s, Prussia created an economic union called the *Zollverein*. This union removed tariff barriers between many German states, yet they remained politically fragmented.

Otto von Bismarck, the **chancellor** of Prussia, led the drive to unite the German states—but under Prussian rule. Bismarck was a master of **Realpolitik,** or realistic politics based on the needs of the state. After creating a powerful military, he was ready to pursue an aggressive foreign policy. Over the next decade, Bismarck led Prussia into three wars. Each war increased Prussian power and paved the way for German unity.

In 1866, Bismarck created an excuse to attack Austria. The Austro-Prussian War lasted only seven weeks. Afterwards, Prussia **annexed** several north German states. In France, the Prussian victory angered Napoleon III. A growing rivalry between the two nations led to the Franco-Prussian War of 1870. Bismarck worsened the crisis by rewriting and releasing to the press a telegram that reported on a meeting between William I of Prussia and the French ambassador. <u>Bismarck's editing of the telegram made it seem that William I had insulted the Frenchman.</u> Furious, Napoleon III declared war on Prussia, as Bismarck had hoped. The Prussian army quickly defeated the French.

Delighted by the victory, German princes persuaded William I to take the title **kaiser** of Germany. In January 1871, German nationalists celebrated the birth of the Second **Reich.** Bismarck drafted a constitution that created a two-house legislature. Even so, the real power was in the hands of the kaiser and Bismarck.

Review Questions

1. What events occurred in the early 1800s that helped promote German unity?

_____

_____

2. How did Bismarck use war to create a united Germany under Prussian rule?

_____

_____

READING CHECK

What was Realpolitik?

_____

_____

_____

VOCABULARY STRATEGY

What does the word *editing* mean in the underlined sentence? Circle the context clues in the paragraph that could help you figure out what *editing* means.

READING SKILL

Recognize Sequence What events led Napoleon III to declare war on Prussia?

_____

_____

_____

Name_____ Class_____ Date_____

Focus Question: How did Germany increase its power after unifying in 1871?

As you read this section in your textbook, complete the following chart to record the causes and effects of a strong German nation.

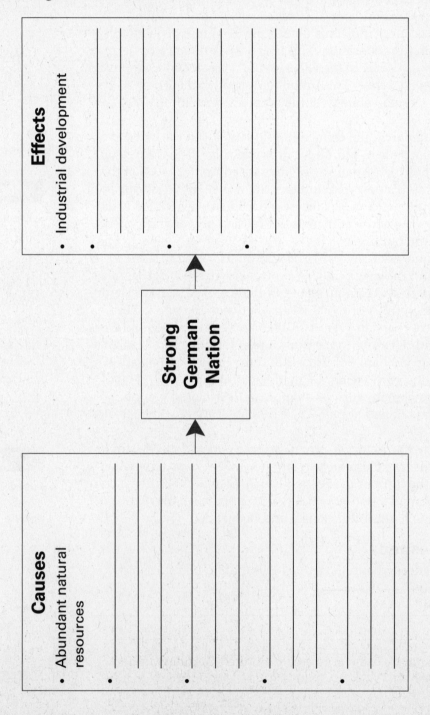

Effects
- Industrial development

Strong German Nation

Causes
- Abundant natural resources

CHAPTER 22 SECTION 2

Section Summary
GERMANY STRENGTHENS

After unification in 1871, the new German empire emerged as an industrial giant. Several factors made industrialization in Germany possible, such as ample iron and coal resources. These are the basic ingredients for industrial development. A disciplined and educated workforce also helped the economy grow. The German middle class created a productive and efficient society that prided itself on its sense of responsibility. Additionally, a growing population provided a huge home market for goods and a large supply of industrial workers.

German industrialists recognized the value of applied science in developing new products, such as synthetic chemicals and dyes. Both industrialists and the government supported scientific research and development. The government also promoted economic development. It issued a single form of currency for Germany and reorganized the banking system. The leaders of the new empire were determined to maintain economic strength as well as military power.

Bismarck pursued several foreign-policy goals. He wanted to keep France weak and build strong links with Austria and Russia. On the domestic front, Bismarck, called "the Iron Chancellor," targeted the Catholic Church and the Socialists. He believed these groups posed a threat to the new German state. He thought Catholics would be more loyal to the Church than to Germany. He also worried that Socialists would undermine the loyalty of workers and turn them toward revolution. Bismarck tried to repress both groups, but his efforts failed. For example, the *Kulturkampf* was a set of laws intended to weaken the role of the Church. Instead, the faithful rallied to support the Church. When repressing the Socialists failed to work, Bismarck changed course and pioneered social reform.

In 1888, **William II** became the kaiser. He believed that his right to rule came from God, and he shocked Europe by asking Bismarck to resign. Not surprisingly, William II resisted efforts to introduce democratic reforms. However, his government provided many **social welfare** programs to help certain groups of people. The government also provided services such as cheap transportation and electricity.

Review Questions

1. What did the German government do to promote economic development?

_____

_____

2. Why did Bismarck believe Catholics posed a threat to the new German state?

_____

_____

READING CHECK

What two ingredients are basic for industrial development?

_____

_____

_____

VOCABULARY STRATEGY

What does the word *synthetic* mean in the underlined sentence? Notice that these chemicals and dyes did not appear in nature, but were developed. Using this clue, write a definition for *synthetic*.

READING SKILL

Recognize Sequence Correctly number the following events:

____ William II becomes Kaiser.

____ Germany unifies in 1871.

____ Government reorganizes the banking system.

____ Bismarck is asked to resign.

CHAPTER
22
SECTION 3

Note Taking Study Guide

UNIFYING ITALY

Focus Question: How did influential leaders help create a unified Italy?

As you read this section in your textbook, complete the following timeline to show the sequence of events that led to Italian unification.

1870

1850

1831
Mazzini founds
Young Italy.

1830

CHAPTER 22 SECTION 3

Section Summary

UNIFYING ITALY

The peoples of the Italian peninsula had not been unified since
Roman times. By the early 1800s, however, patriots were determined
to build a new, united Italy. As in Germany, Napoleon's invasions
had sparked dreams of nationalism.

In the 1830s, the nationalist leader Giuseppe Mazzini founded
Young Italy. The goal of this secret society was "to constitute Italy,
one, free, independent, republican nation." To nationalists like
Mazzini, establishing a unified Italy made sense because of geography and a common language and history. It also made economic
sense because it would end trade barriers among Italian states. Unification would stimulate industry, too.

Victor Emmanuel II, the constitutional monarch of Sardinia,
hoped to join other states with his own and increase his power. In
1852, he made Count **Camillo Cavour** his prime minister. Cavour's
long-term goal was to end Austrian power in Italy. With help from
France, Sardinia defeated Austria and annexed Lombardy. Meanwhile, nationalist groups overthrew Austrian-backed leaders in
other northern Italian states. In the south, **Giuseppe Garibaldi** had
recruited a force of 1,000 red-shirted volunteers. He and his "Red
Shirts" quickly won control of Sicily. Then they crossed to the mainland and marched triumphantly to Naples. Garibaldi turned over
both regions to Victor Emmanuel. In 1861, Victor Emmanuel II was
crowned king of Italy. Only Rome and Venetia remained outside the
nation. During the Franco-Prussian War, however, France was
forced to withdraw its troops from Rome. Additionally, Italy
acquired Venetia in a deal with Bismarck after the Austro-Prussian
War. For the first time since the fall of the Roman empire, Italy was a
united land.

However, Italy faced many problems as **anarchists** and radicals
struggled against the conservative government. Tensions grew
between the north and south. The north was richer and had more
cities. The south was poor and rural. Still, Italy developed economically and the population grew. For many, however, **emigration**
offered a chance to improve their lives. Large numbers of Italians left
for the United States, Canada, and Latin America.

Review Questions

1. Why did nationalists feel that a unified Italy made sense?

_____

_____

2. Why did tensions between the north and south grow after
unification?

_____

_____

READING CHECK

What was Camillo Cavour's long-
term goal as prime minister?

_____

_____

_____

VOCABULARY STRATEGY

What does the word *constitute*
mean in the first underlined sentence? Note that the word is a
verb, which means it describes
an action. Read the second
underlined sentence to find out
what action the nationalists
wanted to take. Use this information to help you figure out
what *constitute* means.

READING SKILL

Recognize Sequence What
events took place between
Garibaldi's recruitment of the
"Red Shirts" and Victor
Emmanuel II's crowning as king
of Italy?

_____

_____

_____

Note Taking Study Guide

CHAPTER 22 SECTION 4

NATIONALISM THREATENS OLD EMPIRES

Focus Question: How did the desire for national independence among ethnic groups weaken and ultimately destroy the Austrian and Ottoman empires?

As you read this section in your textbook, complete the following table to record some major events in Austrian history during the 1800s.

Events in Austrian History					
	1840	1848	1859	1866	1867

Name_____ Class_____ Date_____

In 1800, the Hapsburgs of Austria, the oldest ruling house in Europe, presided over a multinational empire. The emperor, Francis I, upheld conservative goals against growing liberal forces. He could not, however, hold back the changes that were happening throughout Europe. By the 1840s, Austria was facing the problems of industrial life, including growth of cities, worker discontent, and socialism. Nationalists were threatening the old order. The Hapsburgs ignored these demands for change and crushed revolts. Amid the turmoil, 18-year-old **Francis Joseph** inherited the Hapsburg throne. He granted some limited reforms, such as adopting a constitution. The reforms, however, satisfied only the German-speaking Austrians, but none of the other ethnic groups.

Austria's defeat in the 1866 war with Prussia brought even more pressure for change, especially from Hungarians within the empire. **Ferenc Deák** helped work out a compromise known as the **Dual Monarchy** of Austria-Hungary. Under this agreement, Austria and Hungary became separate states. Each had its own constitution, but Francis Joseph ruled both—as emperor of Austria and king of Hungary. However, other groups within the empire resented this arrangement. Restlessness increased among various Slavic groups. Some nationalist leaders called on Slavs to unite in "fraternal solidarity." By the early 1900s, nationalist unrest left the government paralyzed in the face of pressing political and social problems.

Like the Hapsburgs, the Ottomans ruled a multinational empire. It stretched from Eastern Europe and the Balkans to the Middle East and North Africa. As in Austria, nationalist demands tore at the fabric of the Ottoman empire. During the 1800s, various peoples revolted, hoping to set up their own independent states. With the empire weakened, European powers scrambled to divide up Ottoman lands. A complex web of competing interests led to a series of crises and wars in the Balkans. Russia fought several wars against the Ottomans. France and Britain sometimes joined the Russians, and sometimes the Ottomans. By the early 1900s, observers were referring to the region as the "Balkan powder keg." The "explosion" came in 1914 and helped set off World War I.

Review Questions

1. What problems threatened the Hapsburg empire in the 1840s?

_____

_____

2. What effect did nationalist unrest have on the Ottoman empire?

_____

_____

READING CHECK

What new political entity did Ferenc Deák help create?

_____

_____

_____

VOCABULARY STRATEGY

What does the word *fraternal* mean in the underlined sentence? The word derives from the Latin word *frater*, which means "brother." Use this information about the word's origin to help you figure out what *fraternal* means.

READING SKILL

Recognize Sequence What are two events that led to the decline of the Austrian empire in the late 1800s?

1. _____

_____

2. _____

_____

CHAPTER
22
SECTION 5

Note Taking Study Guide

RUSSIA: REFORM AND REACTION

Focus Question: Why did industrialization and reform come more slowly to Russia than to Western Europe?

As you read this section in your textbook, complete the following timeline to show the sequence of events in Russia during the late 1800s and early 1900s.

CHAPTER 22
SECTION 5

Section Summary
RUSSIA: REFORM AND REACTION

By 1815, Russia was the largest, most populous nation in Europe. The Russian **colossus** had immense natural resources. Reformers hoped to free Russia from autocratic rule, economic backwardness, and social injustice. One of the obstacles to progress was the rigid social structure. Another was that, for centuries, tsars had ruled with absolute power, while the majority of Russians were poor serfs.

Alexander II became tsar in 1855 during the **Crimean War.** Events in his reign represent the pattern of reform and repression of previous tsars. The war, which ended in a Russian defeat, revealed the country's backwardness and inefficient bureaucracy. People demanded changes, so Alexander II agreed to some reforms. He ordered the **emancipation** of the serfs. He also set up a system of local, elected assemblies called **zemstvos.** Then he introduced legal reforms, such as trial by jury. These reforms, however, failed to satisfy many Russians. <u>Radicals pressed for even greater changes and more reforms.</u> The tsar then backed away from reform and moved toward repression. This sparked anger among radicals and, in 1881, terrorists assassinated Alexander II. In response to his father's death, Alexander III revived harsh, repressive policies. He also suppressed the cultures of non-Russian peoples, which led to their persecution. Official persecution encouraged **pogroms,** or violent mob attacks on Jewish people. Many left Russia and became **refugees.**

Russia began to industrialize under Alexander III and his son Nicholas II. However, this just increased political and social problems because nobles and peasants feared the changes industrialization brought. News of military disasters added to the unrest. On Sunday, January 22, 1905, a peaceful protest calling for reforms turned deadly when the tsar's troops killed and wounded hundreds of people. In the months that followed this "Bloody Sunday," discontent exploded across Russia. Nicholas was forced to make sweeping reforms. He agreed to summon a **Duma.** He then appointed a new prime minister, **Peter Stolypin.** Stolypin soon realized Russia needed reform, not just repression. Unfortunately, the changes he introduced were too limited. By 1914, Russia was still an autocracy, but the nation was simmering with discontent.

Review Questions

1. What effect did the Crimean War have on Russia?

_____

_____

2. What happened on January 22, 1905?

_____

_____

READING CHECK

What were zemstvos?

_____

_____

_____

VOCABULARY STRATEGY

What does the word *radicals* mean in the underlined sentence? Think about why these people were dissatisfied with Alexander II's reforms. Circle the words in the underlined sentence that help you figure out what *radical* means.

READING SKILL

Recognize Sequence What happened between Alexander II's becoming tsar and his assassination in 1881?

_____

_____

_____

CHAPTER 23 SECTION 1

Note Taking Study Guide

DEMOCRATIC REFORM IN BRITAIN

Focus Question: How did political reform gradually expand suffrage and make the British Parliament more democratic during the 1800s?

As you read this section in your textbook, complete the outline below to identify the main ideas in the section.

I. Reforming Parliament

    A. Reformers press for change.

        1. _____

        2. _____

    B. _____

        1. _____

        2. _____

        3. _____

    C. _____

        1. _____

        2. _____

II. _____

    A. _____

        1. _____

        2. _____

    B. _____

        1. _____

        2. _____

III. _____

    A. _____

        1. _____

        2. _____

        3. _____

    B. _____

        1. _____

        2. _____

CHAPTER 23 SECTION 1

Section Summary

DEMOCRATIC REFORM IN BRITAIN

In 1815, Britain was governed by a constitutional monarchy with a Parliament and two political parties. However, it was far from democratic. The House of Commons, although elected, was controlled by wealthy nobles and squires. The House of Lords could veto any bill passed by the House of Commons. Catholics and non-Church of England Protestants could not vote. **Rotten boroughs,** rural towns that had lost most of their voters during the Industrial Revolution, still sent members to Parliament. At the same time, new industrial cities had no seats allocated in Parliament.

The Great Reform Act of 1832 redistributed seats in the House of Commons, giving representation to new cities and eliminating rotten boroughs. It enlarged the **electorate** but kept a property requirement for voting. Protesters known as the Chartists demanded universal male suffrage, annual parliamentary elections, salaries for members of Parliament, and a **secret ballot.** In time, most of the reforms they proposed were passed by Parliament.

From 1837 to 1901, the great symbol in British life was **Queen Victoria.** She set the tone for the Victorian age that was named for her. She embodied the values of duty, thrift, honesty, hard work, and respectability. Under Victoria, the middle class felt confident. That confidence grew as the British empire expanded.

In the 1860s, a new era dawned in British politics. **Benjamin Disraeli** forged the Tories into the modern Conservative Party. The Whigs, led by **William Gladstone,** evolved into the Liberal Party. Disraeli and Gladstone alternated as prime minister and fought for important reforms. The Conservative Party pushed through the Reform Bill of 1867, which gave the vote to many working-class men. In the 1880s, the Liberals got the vote extended to farm workers and most other men.

By century's end, Britain had truly transformed from a constitutional monarchy to a **parliamentary democracy.** In this form of government, executive leaders are chosen by and responsible to the parliament, and they are members of it. In 1911, measures were passed that restricted the power of the House of Lords, and it eventually became a largely ceremonial body.

Review Questions

1. What was the result of the Great Reform Act of 1832?

_____

_____

2. How is a parliamentary democracy organized?

_____

_____

READING CHECK

What are rotten boroughs?

_____

_____

_____

VOCABULARY STRATEGY

What does the word *allocated* mean in the underlined sentence? Note that the Great Reform Act of 1832 corrected the problem described in this sentence by "redistributing" seats in the House of Commons. Use this context clue to help you understand the meaning of the word *allocated*.

READING SKILL

Identify Main Ideas What is the main idea in the first paragraph of the Summary?

_____

_____

_____

CHAPTER 23
SECTION 2

Note Taking Study Guide
SOCIAL AND ECONOMIC REFORM IN BRITAIN

Focus Question: What social and economic reforms were passed by the British Parliament during the 1800s and early 1900s?

As you read this section in your textbook, complete the chart below by listing reforms in Britain during the 1800s and early 1900s.

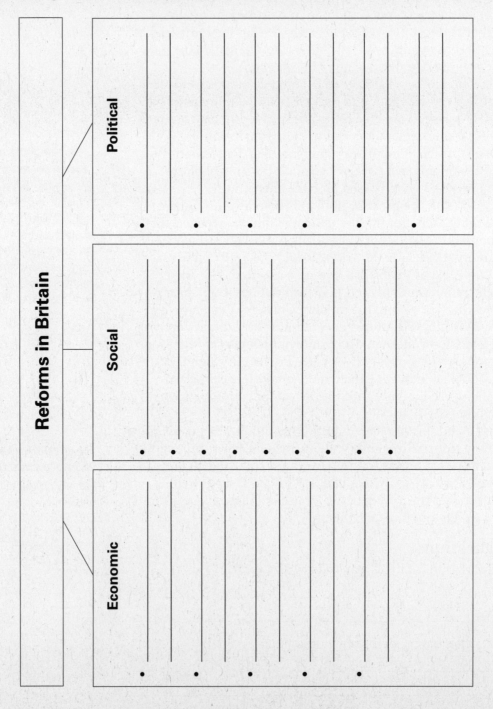

CHAPTER 23 SECTION 2

Section Summary

SOCIAL AND ECONOMIC REFORM IN BRITAIN

During the 1800s, the British Parliament passed important laws. One issue was **free trade,** or trade without restrictions between countries. The Corn Laws caused fierce debate. These laws imposed high tariffs on imported grain. Farmers and landowners benefited, but the tariffs made bread more expensive. In 1846, Parliament **repealed** the Corn Laws. Another important reform, brought about by the **abolition movement,** was the end of the slave trade in 1807. By 1833, Parliament had banned slavery in all British colonies. Other reforms reduced the number of **capital offenses,** or crimes punishable by death. Instead of being put to death, many petty criminals were transported to **penal colonies** in Australia and New Zealand.

Working conditions in the industrial age were grim and often dangerous. Gradually, Parliament passed laws to regulate conditions in factories and mines. Other laws set minimum wages and maximum hours of work. Trade unions became legal in 1825 and worked to improve the lives of their members. Both the Liberal and Conservative parties enacted reforms to benefit workers, including free elementary education. The Labour Party, formed in 1900, soon became one of Britain's major parties. In the early 1900s, Parliament passed laws to protect workers with old-age pensions and accident, health, and unemployment insurance.

During this time, women struggled for the right to vote. When mass meetings and other peaceful efforts brought no results, Emmeline Pankhurst and other suffragists turned to more drastic, violent protest. They smashed windows, burned buildings, and went on hunger strikes. Not until 1918 did Parliament finally grant suffrage to women over 30.

Throughout the 1800s, Britain faced the "Irish Question." The Irish resented British rule. Many Irish peasants lived in poverty while paying high rents to **absentee landlords** living in England. Irish Catholics also had to pay tithes to the Church of England. The potato famine made problems worse. Charles Stewart Parnell and other Irish leaders argued for **home rule,** or self-government, but this was debated for decades. Under Gladstone, the government finally ended the use of Irish tithes to support the Church of England and passed laws to protect the rights of Irish tenant farmers.

Review Questions

1. Why did the Corn Laws cause fierce debate in Britain?

_____

_____

2. How did the government under Gladstone help improve conditions in Ireland?

_____

_____

READING CHECK

What are capital offenses?

_____

_____

_____

VOCABULARY STRATEGY

What does the word *drastic* mean in the underlined sentence? Note that the suffragists first tried "peaceful efforts" before turning to "more *drastic,* violent protest." The next sentence describes this. Use these context clues to help you understand what *drastic* means.

READING SKILL

Categorize Sort the laws that were passed to help workers into three categories.

_____

_____

_____

CHAPTER
23
SECTION 3

Note Taking Study Guide
DIVISION AND DEMOCRACY IN FRANCE

Focus Question: What democratic reforms were made in France during the Third Republic?

As you read this section in your textbook, complete the timeline below by labeling the main events described in this section.

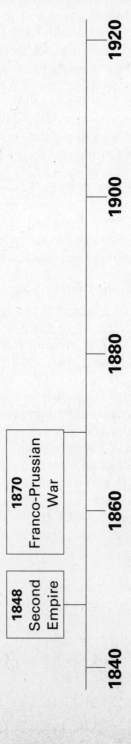

1920

1900

1880

1870
Franco-Prussian War

1860

1848
Second Empire

1840

CHAPTER 23 SECTION 3

Section Summary

DIVISION AND DEMOCRACY IN FRANCE

After the revolution of 1848, **Napoleon III** established the Second Empire in France. At first, he ruled like a dictator. In the 1860s, however, he lifted some censorship and gave the legislature more power. He promoted investment in industry and ventures such as railroad building. During this period, a French entrepreneur organized the building of the **Suez Canal** in Egypt.

However, Napoleon III had major failures in foreign affairs. He tried to put the Austrian archduke Maximilian on the throne of Mexico, but Maximilian was overthrown and killed. France and Britain won the Crimean War, but France suffered terrible losses and few gains. The Franco-Prussian War was a disaster, and the Prussians captured Napoleon. He died a few years later in England.

Following Napoleon's capture, republicans established a **provisional,** or temporary, government. In 1871, an uprising broke out in Paris, and rebels set up the Paris Commune. Its goal was to save the Republic from royalists. When the rebels did not disband, the government sent troops and 20, 000 rebels were killed.

The provisional government soon became the Third Republic. Although the legislature elected a president, the **premier** had the real power. There were many political parties, and none could take control. Because of this, parties had to form **coalitions,** or alliances, to rule. Coalition governments are often unstable, and France had 50 different coalition governments in the first 10 years of the Third Republic.

A series of political scandals in the 1880s and 1890s shook public trust in the government. The most divisive scandal was the **Dreyfus affair.** Alfred Dreyfus was a Jewish army officer wrongly accused of spying for Germany. Author Émile Zola was convicted of **libel** when he charged the army and government with suppressing the truth. The affair revealed strong anti-Semitic feelings in France and led Theodor Herzl to launch modern **Zionism.**

France achieved serious reforms in the early 1900s, however. It passed labor laws regulating wages, hours, and safety conditions. Free public elementary schools were established. France tried to repress Church involvement in government. In 1905, it passed a law to separate church and state. Women made some gains, but they did not win the right to vote until after World War II.

Review Questions

1. What failures in foreign affairs took place under Napoleon III?

_____

_____

2. Why did French governments have to form coalitions to rule?

_____

_____

READING CHECK

What did the Dreyfus affair reveal about France?

_____

_____

_____

VOCABULARY STRATEGY

What does the word *repress* mean in the underlined sentence? Reread the sentence after the underlined sentence. What did France do to *repress* Church involvement in government? Use this context clue to help you understand the meaning of *repress.*

READING SKILL

Recognize Sequence List, in chronological order, the three French governments described in this section.

_____

_____

_____

Note Taking Study Guide

EXPANSION OF THE UNITED STATES

Focus Question: How did the United States develop during the 1800s?

As you read this section in your textbook, complete the chart below by listing key events under the appropriate headings.

Civil War	
Before	**After**
• Western expansion	• Fifteenth Amendment extends voting rights to all adult male citizens.
• _____ _____	• _____ _____
• _____ _____	• _____ _____
• _____ _____	• _____
	• _____
	• _____ _____
	• _____ _____

Name_____ Class_____ Date_____

In the 1800s, the United States followed a policy of **expansionism,** or extending the nation's boundaries. In 1803, the **Louisiana Purchase** nearly doubled the size of the country. More territory was soon added in the West and South. Americans believed in **Manifest Destiny,** or the idea that their nation was destined to spread across the entire continent.

Voting, slavery, and women's rights were important issues at this time. In 1800, only white men who owned property could vote. By the 1830s, most white men had the right to vote. William Lloyd Garrison, Frederick Douglass, and other abolitionists called for an end to slavery. Lucretia Mott, Elizabeth Cady Stanton, Susan B. Anthony, and others began to seek equality.

Economic differences, as well as slavery, divided the country into the North and the South. When Abraham Lincoln was elected in 1860, most Southern states **seceded,** or withdrew, from the Union. The American Civil War soon began. Southerners fought fiercely, but the North had more people, more industry, and more resources. The South finally surrendered in 1865.

During the war, Lincoln issued the Emancipation Proclamation, which declared that the slaves in the South were free. After the war, slavery was banned throughout the nation, and African Americans were granted some political rights. However, African Americans still faced restrictions, including **segregation,** or legal separation, in public places. Some state laws prevented African Americans from voting.

After the Civil War, the United States became the world leader in industrial and agricultural production. By 1900, giant monopolies controlled whole industries. <u>For example, John D. Rockefeller's Standard Oil Company dominated the world's petroleum industry.</u> Big business enjoyed huge profits, but not everyone shared in the prosperity. Reformers tried to address this problem. Unions sought better wages and working conditions for factory workers. Farmers and city workers formed the Populist Party to seek changes. Progressives sought to ban child labor, limit working hours, regulate monopolies, and give voters more power. Progressives also worked to get women the right to vote, which they did in 1920.

Review Questions
1. Why did the North win the Civil War?

_____

_____

2. How were African Americans deprived of equality after the Civil War?

_____

_____

READING CHECK

What is Manifest Destiny?

_____

_____

_____

VOCABULARY STRATEGY

What does the word *dominated* mean in the underlined sentence? Reread the sentence that precedes the underlined sentence. The Standard Oil Company was an example of the giant monopolies that "controlled" whole industries. Use this context clue to help you understand the meaning of the word *dominated.*

READING SKILL

Categorize Categorize the reforms discussed in this Summary by the group that did or would benefit from them.

_____

_____

_____

Name_____ Class_____ Date_____

Focus Question: How did Western nations come to dominate much of the world in the late 1800s?

As you read this section in your textbook, complete the chart below with the multiple causes of imperialism in the 1800s.

Event

The New Imperialism

Causes

Need for natural resources

- • • • • • • • • • • •

CHAPTER 24 SECTION 1

Section Summary

BUILDING OVERSEAS EMPIRES

Many western countries built overseas empires in the late 1800s. This expansion, referred to as **imperialism,** is the domination by one country of the political, economic, or cultural life of another country or region. In the 1800s, Europeans embarked on a path of aggressive expansion called the "new imperialism." There were several causes. The Industrial Revolution was one. Manufacturers wanted access to natural resources, as well as markets for their goods. Colonies also were an outlet for Europe's growing population. Leaders claimed that colonies were needed for national security. Industrial nations seized overseas islands and harbors as bases to supply their ships.

Nationalism played an important role, too. When one European country claimed an area, rival nations would move in and claim nearby areas. <u>Europeans felt that ruling a global empire increased a nation's prestige</u>. Missionaries, doctors, and colonial officials believed that they had a duty to spread Western civilization. Behind the idea of the West's civilizing mission was a growing sense of racial superiority. Many Westerners used Social Darwinism to justify their domination of non-Western societies. As a result, millions of non-Westerners were robbed of their cultural heritage.

Europeans had the advantages of strong economies, well-organized governments, and powerful armies and navies. Superior technology, such as riverboats, the telegraph, and the Maxim machine gun enhanced European power. Africans and Asians tried to resist Western expansion. Some people fought the invaders. Others tried to strengthen their societies by reforming their traditions. Many organized nationalist movements to expel the imperialists.

The leading imperial powers developed several systems to control colonies. The French practiced direct rule. They sent officials and soldiers from France to run the colony. Their goal was to impose French culture on the natives. The British, by contrast, relied on indirect rule. To govern their colonies, they used local rulers. In a **protectorate,** local rulers were left in place but were expected to follow the advice of European advisors on issues such as trade or missionary activity. In a **sphere of influence,** an outside power claimed exclusive investment or trading privileges, but did not rule the area.

Review Questions

1. Which aspect of the new imperialism led to non-Westerners being robbed of their cultural heritage?

   _____

   _____

2. What is the difference between a protectorate and a sphere of influence?

   _____

   _____

READING CHECK

How did Africans and Asians resist Western expansion?

_____

_____

_____

VOCABULARY STRATEGY

What does the word *prestige* mean in the underlined sentence? Notice that the word *increased* appears in the same sentence. What would ruling a global empire *increase* for a European nation? Use this context clue to help you figure out the meaning of *prestige*.

READING SKILL

Multiple Causes List the multiple causes of imperialism mentioned in this summary.

_____

_____

_____

Name_____ Class_____ Date_____

Focus Question: How did imperialist European powers claim control over most of Africa by the end of the 1800s?

As you read this section in your textbook, complete the chart below by identifying the causes and effects of the partition of Africa by European nations.

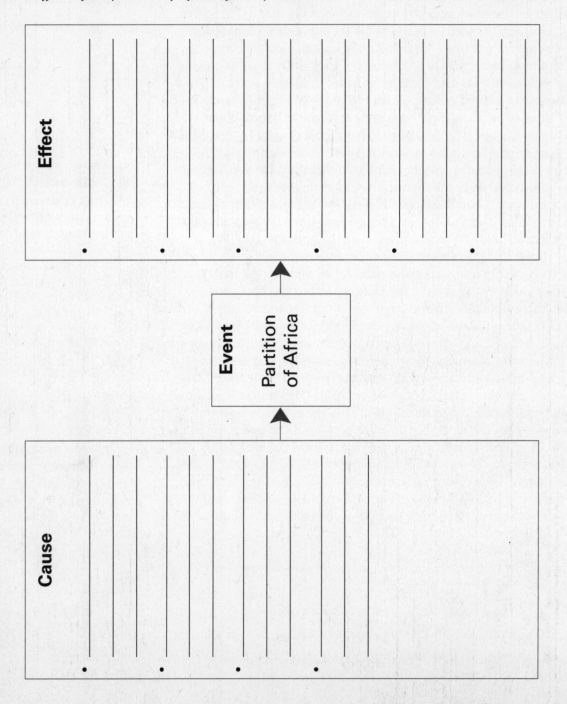

CHAPTER 24

SECTION 2

Section Summary
THE PARTITION OF AFRICA

Before the scramble for colonies began in the 1800s, North Africa was under the rule of the declining Ottoman empire. West Africa experienced an Islamic revival inspired by **Usman dan Fodio.** In East Africa, port cities carried on a profitable trade. Zulus were a major force in southern Africa. A brilliant Zulu leader, **Shaka,** conquered nearby peoples. Groups driven from their homelands by the Zulus migrated north, conquering other peoples and creating powerful states.

For many years, Europeans had been trading along the African coasts. In the 1800s, contact increased as European explorers began pushing into the interior of Africa. One of the best-known was the missionary explorer **Dr. David Livingstone.** In 1869, the journalist **Henry Stanley** trekked into Africa to find Livingstone, who had not been heard from for years. Other missionaries followed explorers such as Livingstone. They built schools, churches, and medical clinics, often taking a **paternalistic** view of Africans.

About 1871, **King Leopold II** of Belgium hired Stanley to arrange trade treaties with African leaders. Leopold's action prompted Britain, France, and Germany to join in a scramble for African land. Eventually, without consulting any Africans, European leaders met in Berlin to divide the continent of Africa among themselves. In the following years, Europeans expanded further into Africa, often exploiting African people and resources. In southern Africa, the **Boer War** began when Britain wanted to claim Boer land. The Boers were descendants of Dutch farmers. The British wanted the land because gold and diamonds had been discovered there.

Africans fought back against European imperialism. In West Africa, **Samori Touré** fought French forces. **Yaa Asantewaa** was an Asante queen who led the fight against the British in West Africa. Another female leader was **Nehanda** of the Shona in Zimbabwe. In most cases resistance was not successful. However, Ethiopia was able to keep its independence. Earlier, Ethiopia had been divided up among a number of rival princes who then ruled their own domains. **Menelik II** modernized his country and trained an army, successfully resisting Italian invaders.

The Age of Imperialism caused a Western-educated African **elite** to emerge. Some admired Western ways. Others sought independence through nationalist movements.

Review Questions

1. Who ruled North Africa before the 1800s?

_____

_____

2. What set off a European scramble for African territories?

_____

_____

READING CHECK

Which African country was able to resist European conquest and maintain its independence?

_____

_____

_____

VOCABULARY STRATEGY

What does the word *domains* mean in the underlined sentence? Use context clues. Think about what a prince rules. What would have been divided? Use these context clues to help you figure out the meaning of *domains.*

READING SKILL

Cause and Effect What caused groups of Africans in southern Africa to migrate north? What was the effect of this?

_____

_____

CHAPTER
24
SECTION 3

Note Taking Study Guide
EUROPEAN CLAIMS IN MUSLIM REGIONS

Focus Question: How did European nations extend their power into Muslim regions of the world?

As you read this section in your textbook, complete the concept web below to understand the effects of European imperialism on Muslim regions of the world.

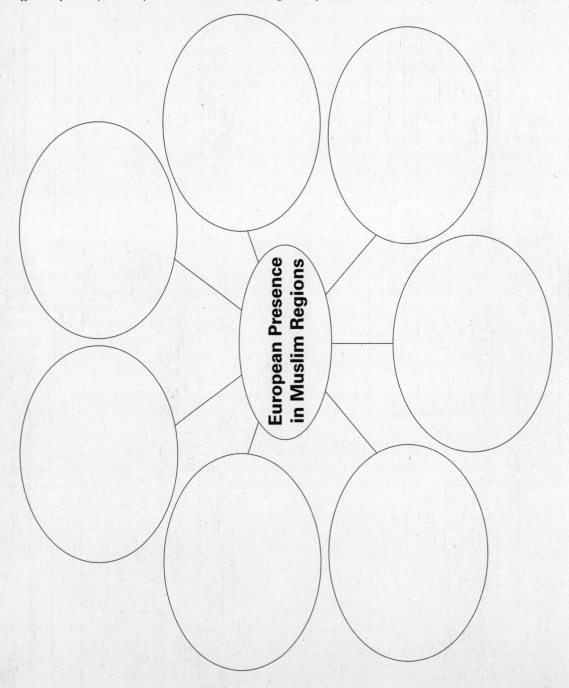

CHAPTER 24 SECTION 3

Section Summary

EUROPEAN CLAIMS IN MUSLIM REGIONS

In the 1500s, three giant Muslim empires ruled large areas of the world—the Ottomans in the Middle East, the Safavids in Persia, and the Mughals in India. By the 1700s, all three Muslim empires were in decline, in part because of corruption and discontent. Reform movements arose, stressing religious piety and strict rules of behavior. For example, in the Sudan, **Muhammad Ahmad** announced that he was the **Mahdi,** the long-awaited savior of the faith. The Mahdi and his followers fiercely resisted British expansion into the region.

At its height, the Ottoman empire extended across North Africa, Southeastern Europe, and parts of the Middle East. Ambitious **pashas** and economic problems added to the Ottoman decline. As ideas of nationalism spread from Western Europe, internal revolts by subject peoples weakened the empire. European states took advantage of this weakness to grab Ottoman territory. Some Ottoman leaders saw the need for reform. They looked to the West for ideas on reorganizing the government and its rigid rules. <u>In the early 1700s, they reorganized the bureaucracy and system of tax collection.</u> However, **sultans** usually rejected reform, adding to the tension. Tension between Ottoman Turkish nationalists and minority groups led to a brutal **genocide** of Christian Armenians. Turks accused Christian Armenians of supporting Russia against the Ottoman empire.

In the early 1800s, Egypt was a semi-independent province of the Ottoman empire. **Muhammad Ali** is sometimes called the "father of modern Egypt" because he introduced a number of political and economic reforms. He also conquered the neighboring lands of Arabia, Syria, and Sudan. Before he died in 1849, he had set Egypt on the road to becoming a major Middle Eastern power. His successors were less skilled, however, and in 1882 Egypt became a protectorate of Britain.

Like the Ottoman empire, Persia—now Iran—faced major challenges. The Qajar shahs exercised absolute power. Foreign nations, especially Russia and Britain, wanted to control Iran's oil fields. They were granted **concessions** and sent troops to protect their interests. These actions outraged Iranian nationalists.

Review Questions

1. What was the extent of the Ottoman empire?

_____

_____

2. Why is Muhammad Ali sometimes called the "father of modern Egypt"?

_____

_____

READING CHECK

What were the three great Muslim empires in the 1500s?

_____

_____

_____

VOCABULARY STRATEGY

What does the word *bureaucracy* mean in the underlined sentence? *Bureau* is a French word that means "office." The suffix *-cracy* means "type of government." Use these word-origin clues to help you figure out what *bureaucracy* means.

READING SKILL

Understanding Effects What was the effect of the concessions granted to Britain and Russia in Iran?

_____

_____

_____

CHAPTER
24
SECTION 4

Note Taking Study Guide
THE BRITISH TAKE OVER INDIA

Focus Question: How did Britain gradually extend its control over most of India despite opposition?

As you read this section in your textbook, complete the flowchart below to identify the causes and effects of British colonial rule in India.

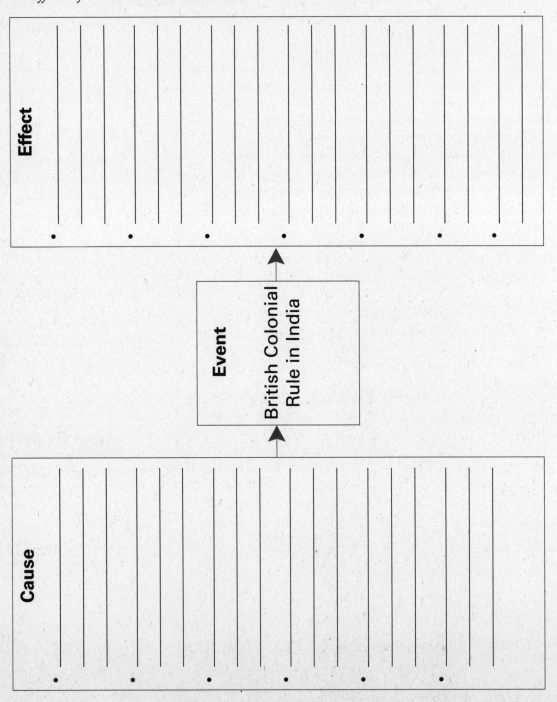

Effect

Event

British Colonial Rule in India

Cause

CHAPTER 24 SECTION 4

Section Summary

THE BRITISH TAKE OVER INDIA

Mughal rulers governed a powerful Muslim empire in India. The British East India Company had trading rights on the fringes of the Mughal empire. The main goal of the East India Company was to make money. As Mughal power declined, the East India Company extended its power. By the mid-1800s, it controlled three-fifths of India. The British were able to conquer India by exploiting its diversity, and by encouraging competition and disunity among rival princes. When necessary, the British also used force. However, British officials worked to end slavery and the caste system. They banned **sati,** a custom that called for a widow to throw herself on her husband's funeral fire. In the 1850s, the East India Company made several unpopular moves. The most serious brought about the Sepoy Rebellion. Indian soldiers, or **sepoys,** were told to bite off the tips of their rifle cartridges. This order caused a rebellion because the cartridges were greased with animal fat, violating local religious beliefs. The British crushed the revolt, killing thousands of unarmed Indians. The rebellion left a legacy of mistrust on both sides.

After the rebellion, Parliament ended the rule of the East India Company. Instead, a British **viceroy** governed India in the name of the monarch. <u>In this way, all of Britain could benefit from trade with India as Britain incorporated India into the overall British economy.</u> However, it remained an unequal partnership, favoring the British. Although the British built railroads and telegraph lines, they destroyed India's hand-weaving industry. Encouraging Indian farmers to grow cash crops led to massive **deforestation** and famines.

Some educated Indians urged India to follow a Western model of progress. Others felt they should keep to their own Hindu or Muslim cultures. In the early 1800s, **Ram Mohun Roy** combined both views. Roy condemned rigid caste distinctions, child marriage, sati, and **purdah,** or the isolation of women in separate quarters. He also set up educational societies to help revive pride in Indian culture. Most British disdained Indian culture and felt that Western-educated Indians would support British rule. Instead, Indians dreamed of ending British control. In 1885, Indian nationalists formed the Indian National Congress and began pressing for self-rule.

Review Questions

1. How were the British able to conquer India?

_____

_____

2. How did India benefit from Western technology?

_____

_____

READING CHECK

What was sati?

_____

_____

_____

VOCABULARY STRATEGY

What does the word *overall* mean in the underlined sentence? Notice that it is a compound word. A compound word is made from two separate words. Use the two words that make up *overall* to help you figure out what it means.

READING SKILL

Identify Causes and Effects
What caused the sepoys to rebel? What were two effects of the rebellion?

_____

_____

Name_____ Class_____ Date_____

Focus Question: How did Western powers use diplomacy and war to gain power in Qing China?

As you read this section in your textbook, complete the chart below by listing the multiple causes that led to the decline of Qing China.

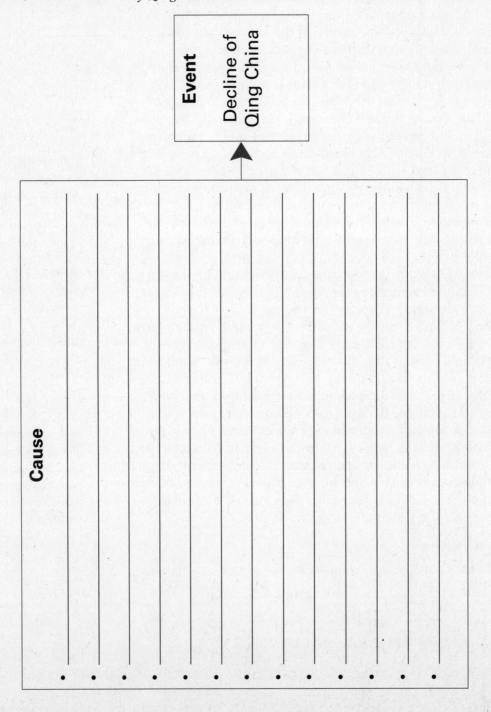

Event

Decline of Qing China

Cause

CHAPTER 24 SECTION 5

Section Summary
CHINA AND THE NEW IMPERIALISM

For centuries, China had a favorable **balance of trade,** because of a **trade surplus.** Westerners had a **trade deficit** with China, buying more from the Chinese than they sold to them. This changed in the late 1700s when the British began trading opium grown in India in exchange for Chinese tea. The Chinese government outlawed opium and called on Britain to stop this drug trade. The British refused, leading to the **Opium War** in 1839. With outdated weapons and fighting methods, the Chinese were easily defeated. Under the Treaty of Nanjing, which ended the war, Britain received a huge **indemnity** and British citizens gained the right of **extraterritoriality.** About a decade later China lost another war. France, Russia, and the United States then each made specific demands on China. <u>China was pressured to sign treaties stipulating the opening of more ports and allowing Christian missionaries in China.</u>

China also faced internal problems. Peasants hated the Qing government because of corruption. The resulting **Taiping Rebellion** against this government led to an estimated 20 million to 30 million deaths. However, the Qing government survived. In addition, the Chinese were divided over the need to adopt Western ways. Some felt Western ideas and technology threatened Confucianism. Reformers who wanted to adopt Western ways in the "self-strengthening movement" did not have government support.

Meanwhile, China's defeat in the **Sino-Japanese War** of 1894 encouraged European nations to carve out spheres of influence in China. The United States feared that American merchants might be shut out. Eventually, without consulting the Chinese, the United States insisted that Chinese trade should be open to everyone on an equal basis as part of an **Open Door Policy.** Chinese reformers blamed conservatives for not modernizing China. In 1898, the emperor, **Guang Xu,** launched the Hundred Days of Reform. Conservatives opposed this reform effort and the emperor was imprisoned.

Many Chinese, including a secret society known to Westerners as the Boxers, were angry about the presence of foreigners. Antiforeign feeling exploded in the **Boxer Uprising** in 1900. Although the Boxers failed, nationalism increased. Reformers called for a republic. One of them, **Sun Yixian,** became president of the new Chinese republic when the Qing dynasty fell in 1911.

Review Questions

1. What were the results of the Opium War?

_____

_____

2. Why was the Qing government so hated?

_____

_____

READING CHECK

Who was the Chinese reformer who became president of China in 1911?

_____

_____

_____

VOCABULARY STRATEGY

What does the word *stipulating* mean in the underlined sentence? What clues can you find in the surrounding words, phrases, or sentences? Use these context clues to help you figure out what *stipulating* means.

READING SKILL

Recognize Multiple Causes
What brought about the Open Door Policy in China?

_____

_____

_____

CHAPTER
25
SECTION 1

Note Taking Study Guide
JAPAN MODERNIZES

Focus Question: How did Japan become a modern industrial power, and what did it do with its new strength?

As you read this section in your textbook, complete the chart below to identify causes and effects of the Meiji Restoration.

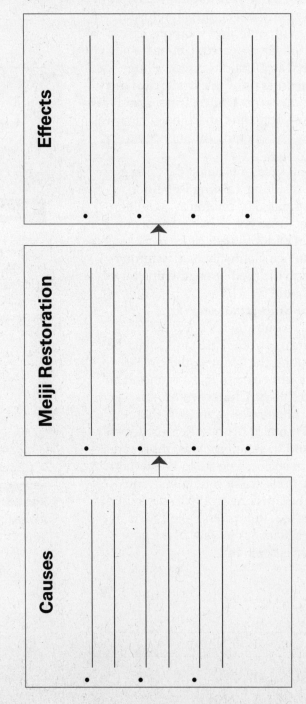

CHAPTER 25 SECTION 1 — Section Summary

JAPAN MODERNIZES

In 1603, the Tokugawa shoguns seized power in Japan and closed it to foreigners. For more than 200 years, Japan was isolated from other nations. Over time, unrest grew among many Japanese as they suffered financial hardship and lack of political power. <u>The government responded by trying to revive old ways, emphasizing farming over commerce.</u> These efforts had little success, and the shoguns' power weakened.

Then, in 1853, a fleet of well-armed U.S. ships led by Commodore **Matthew Perry** arrived. He demanded that Japan open its ports. Unable to defend itself, Japan was forced to sign treaties giving the United States trading and other rights. Humiliated by the terms of these unequal treaties, discontented daimyo and samurai led a revolt that unseated the shogun and placed the emperor Mutsuhito in power. Mutsuhito moved to the shogun's palace in the city of Edo, which was renamed **Tokyo,** and began a long reign known as the **Meiji Restoration.** This was a turning point in Japan's history.

The Meiji reformers wanted to create a new political and social system and build a modern industrial economy. The Meiji constitution gave all citizens equality before the law. A legislature, or **Diet,** was formed, but the emperor held absolute power. With government support, powerful banking and industrial families, known as **zaibatsu,** soon ruled over industrial empires. By the 1890s, industry was booming. Japan, a **homogeneous society,** modernized with amazing speed, partly due to its strong sense of identity.

As a small island nation, Japan lacked many resources essential for industry. Spurred by the need for natural resources and a strong ambition to equal the western imperial nations, Japan sought to build an empire. In 1876, Japan forced Korea to open its ports to Japanese trade. In 1894, competition between Japan and China in Korea led to the **First Sino-Japanese War,** which Japan easily won. Japan gained ports in China, won control over Taiwan, and joined the West in the race for empire. Ten years later, Japan successfully fought Russia in the **Russo-Japanese War.** By the early 1900s, Japan was the strongest power in Asia.

Review Questions

1. How did the Japanese respond to the unequal treaties signed with the United States?

_____

_____

2. How did the Meiji reformers try to modernize Japan?

_____

_____

READING CHECK

What helped to create a strong sense of identity in Japanese society?

_____

_____

_____

VOCABULARY STRATEGY

What does the word *emphasizing* mean in the underlined sentence? Look for context clues to its meaning in the surrounding words. Use the context clues to help you figure out what *emphasizing* means.

READING SKILL

Identify Causes and Effects
What were the causes and effects of the Meiji Restoration?

_____

_____

_____

Name_____ Class_____ Date_____

Focus Question: How did industrialized powers divide up Southeast Asia, and how did the colonized peoples react?

As you read this section, complete the flowchart below to identify causes, events, and effects of imperialism in Southeast Asia and the Pacific.

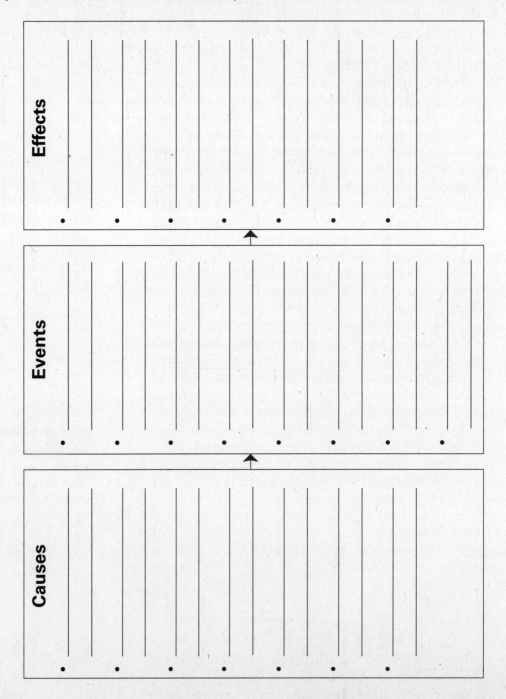

Effects

Events

Causes

CHAPTER 25 SECTION 2

Section Summary
IMPERIALISM IN SOUTHEAST ASIA AND THE PACIFIC

By the 1700s, European merchants had gained footholds in Southeast Asia, but most of the area was still independent. In the 1800s, however, Westerners colonized much of Southeast Asia. The Dutch, for example, expanded to dominate the Dutch East Indies (now Indonesia). The British expanded from India into Burma and Malaya.

The Burmese resisted British rule and annexation but suffered disastrous defeats. The French invaded Vietnam, seeking more influence and trade markets. The Vietnamese fought fiercely but lost to superior European firepower. The French eventually took over all of Vietnam, Laos, and Cambodia and referred to these holdings as **French Indochina.** Meanwhile, the king of Siam, **Mongkut,** accepted some unequal treaties to keep Siam from becoming a European colony. By the 1890s, Europeans controlled most of Southeast Asia, where they introduced modern technology and expanded commerce and industry.

The Philippines had been under Spanish rule since the 1500s. In 1898, the **Spanish-American War** broke out. During the war, U.S. battleships destroyed the Spanish fleet stationed in the Philippines. Filipino rebel leaders declared independence and joined the Americans against Spain. In return for their help, the Filipino rebels expected the United States to recognize their independence. Instead, in the treaty that ended the war, the United States gave Spain $20 million in exchange for control of the Philippines. Bitterly disappointed, Filipinos renewed their struggle for independence, but the United States crushed the rebellion. The United States, however, did promise Filipinos a gradual transition to self-rule sometime in the future.

In the 1800s, the industrialized powers also began to take an interest in the Pacific islands. American sugar growers, for example, pressed for power in the Hawaiian Islands. When the Hawaiian queen **Liliuokalani** tried to reduce foreign influence, American planters overthrew her. In 1898, the United States annexed Hawaii. Supporters of annexation argued that if the United States did not take Hawaii, Britain or Japan might. By 1900, the United States, Britain, France, or Germany had claimed nearly every island in the Pacific.

Review Questions

1. How did the people of Burma and Vietnam respond to European attempts to colonize them?

_____

_____

2. Why did Filipino rebels renew their struggle for independence after the Spanish-American War?

_____

_____

READING CHECK

Which countries made up French Indochina?

_____

_____

_____

VOCABULARY STRATEGY

What does the word *transition* mean in the underlined sentence? Note that the word begins with the prefix *trans-*, which means "across or through." Use this knowledge to help you learn what the word *transition* means.

READING SKILL

Identify Causes and Effects
Identify the causes and effects of Liliuokalani's attempts to reduce foreign influence in Hawaii.

_____

_____

_____

Note Taking Study Guide

CHAPTER 25 SECTION 3

SELF-RULE FOR CANADA, AUSTRALIA, AND NEW ZEALAND

Focus Question: How were the British colonies of Canada, Australia, and New Zealand settled, and how did they win self-rule?

As you read this section, complete the chart below to identify the causes and effects of events in the British colonies of Canada, Australia, and New Zealand.

Cause	Event	Effect					
Loyalist Americans flee to Canada.	Up to 30,000 loyalists settle in Canada.	Ethnic tensions arise between English- and French-speaking Canadians.					

Section Summary
SELF-RULE FOR CANADA, AUSTRALIA, AND NEW ZEALAND

In Canada, Britain created two provinces: English-speaking Upper Canada and French-speaking Lower Canada. <u>When unrest grew in both colonies, the British sent Lord Durham to compile a report on the causes of the unrest.</u> In response to his report, Parliament joined the two Canadas into one colony in 1840.

As the country grew, Canadian leaders urged **confederation** of Britain's North American colonies. They felt that confederation would strengthen the new nation against the United States' ambitions and help Canada's economic development. Britain finally agreed, and Parliament passed a law that created the Dominion of Canada. As a **dominion,** Canada had its own parliament. As the growing country expanded westward, the way of life of Native Americans was destroyed. People of French and Native American descent, called **métis,** resisted in two revolts. However, government troops put down both uprisings.

In 1770, Captain James Cook claimed Australia for Britain. Like most regions claimed by imperialist powers, Australia had already long been inhabited. The **indigenous** people there are called Aborigines. When white settlers arrived in Australia, the Aborigines suffered. Britain made Australia into a **penal colony** to fill a need for prisons. Then, Britain encouraged free citizens to emigrate to Australia by offering them land and tools. As the newcomers settled in, they thrust aside or killed the Aborigines. Like Canada, Australia was made up of separate colonies scattered around the continent. To counter possible interference from other European powers and to boost development, Britain agreed to Australian demands for self-rule. In 1901, the colonies united into the independent Commonwealth of Australia.

Captain James Cook also claimed New Zealand for Britain. The indigenous people of New Zealand are the **Maori.** The Maori were determined to defend their land. In 1840, Britain annexed New Zealand. As colonists poured in, they took more and more land, leading to fierce wars with the Maori. Many Maori died in the struggle. By the 1870s, resistance crumbled. Like settlers in Australia and Canada, white New Zealanders sought self-rule. In 1907, New Zealand won independence.

Review Questions

1. Why did Britain agree to create the Dominion of Canada?

_____

_____

2. Why did Britain agree to demands for self-rule in Australia?

_____

_____

READING CHECK

What happened to the Aborigines when white settlers arrived in Australia?

_____

_____

_____

VOCABULARY STRATEGY

What does the word *compile* mean in the underlined sentence? Think about research reports you have written for school. What process did you go through to create a report? Use your prior knowledge to help you learn what *compile* means.

READING SKILL

Identify Causes and Effects
Identify the causes and effects of the Maori fight against New Zealand colonists.

_____

_____

_____

Note Taking Study Guide

ECONOMIC IMPERIALISM IN LATIN AMERICA

Focus Question: How did Latin American nations struggle for stability, and how did industrialized nations affect them?

A. *As you read this section, complete the chart below to identify multiple causes of instability in Latin America. Then, give an example of how each cause affected Mexico.*

Instability in Latin America	
Causes	**Mexican Example**

B. *As you read "The Economics of Dependence" and "The Influence of the United States," complete the chart below to identify effects of foreign influence on Latin America.*

Effects of Foreign Influence		

CHAPTER 25 SECTION 4

Section Summary

ECONOMIC IMPERIALISM IN LATIN AMERICA

Many factors undermined democracy in the newly independent nations of Latin America. Constitutions in these nations guaranteed equality before the law, but inequalities remained. With no tradition of unity, **regionalism** also weakened the new nations. Local strongmen, called *caudillos,* assembled private armies to resist the central government. Power remained in the hands of a privileged few.

Mexico is an example of the challenges faced by many Latin American nations. Large landowners, army leaders, and the Catholic Church dominated Mexican politics. The ruling elite was divided between conservatives and liberals. Conservatives defended the traditional social order. <u>Liberals saw themselves as enlightened supporters of progress.</u> Bitter battles between these two groups led to revolts and the rise of dictators. When **Benito Juárez** and other liberals gained power, they began an era of reform known as **La Reforma.** Juárez offered hope to the oppressed people of Mexico. After Juárez died, however, General Porfirio Díaz ruled as a harsh dictator. Many Indians and mestizos fell into **peonage** to their employers.

Under colonial rule, Latin America was economically dependent on Spain and Portugal, which had prevented the colonies from developing their own economies. After independence, the new Latin American republics did adopt free trade, but Britain and the United States replaced Spain as Latin America's chief trading partners.

As nations like Mexico tried to build stable governments, the United States expanded across North America. To discourage any new European colonization of the Americas, the United States issued the **Monroe Doctrine.** The United States then issued a series of policies claiming "international police power" in the Western Hemisphere. Under these policies, U.S. companies continued to invest in the countries of Latin America. To protect these investments, the United States sent troops to many of these countries, which made the United States a target of increasing resentment and rebellion. When the United States built the **Panama Canal** across Central America, it was an engineering marvel that boosted trade and shipping worldwide. To people in Latin America, however, the canal was another example of "Yankee imperialism."

Review Questions

1. What limited democracy in the independent nations of Latin America?

_____

_____

2. Why did the new Latin American republics remain economically dependent after independence?

_____

_____

READING CHECK

Which Mexican leader offered hope to the oppressed people of Mexico?

_____

_____

_____

VOCABULARY STRATEGY

What does the word *enlightened* mean in the underlined sentence? Break the word into its word parts. Circle the root word, or the word part without the prefix and suffixes. Use the meaning of the root word to help you figure out what *enlightened* means.

READING SKILL

Identify Causes and Effects Identify what caused the United States to issue the Monroe Doctrine and what its effects were on Latin America.

_____

_____

CHAPTER 26 SECTION 1

Note Taking Study Guide
THE GREAT WAR BEGINS

Focus Question: Why and how did World War I begin in 1914?

As you read this section in your textbook, complete the following chart to summarize the events that led to the outbreak of World War I.

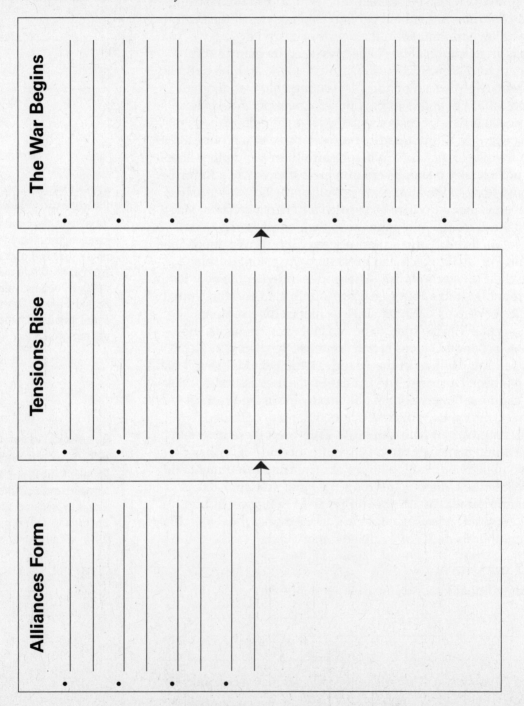

The War Begins

Tensions Rise

Alliances Form

CHAPTER 26 SECTION 1
Section Summary
THE GREAT WAR BEGINS

Although powerful forces were pushing Europe towards war, the great powers had formed alliances signing non-binding agreements, called **ententes,** to try to keep the peace. The Triple Alliance included Germany, Austria-Hungary, and Italy. Russia and France, and later Britain, formed the Triple Entente. During World War I, Germany and Austria fought together as the Central Powers. At that time, Russia, France, and Britain became known as the Allies.

In the decades before 1914, European powers competed to protect their status. <u>Overseas rivalries divided them, as they fought for new colonies in Africa and elsewhere.</u> They began to build up their armies and navies. The rise of **militarism** helped to feed this arms race. At the same time, sensational journalism stirred the public against rival nations.

Nationalism also increased tensions. Germans were proud of their military and economic might. The French yearned for the return of **Alsace and Lorraine.** Russia supported a powerful form of nationalism called Pan-Slavism. This led Russia to support nationalists in Serbia. Austria-Hungary worried that nationalism might lead to rebellions within its empire, while Ottoman Turkey felt threatened by nearby new nations in the Balkans, such as Serbia and Greece. Serbia's dreams of a South Slav state could take land away from both Austria-Hungary and Turkey. Soon, unrest made the Balkans a "powder keg." Then, in 1914, a Serbian nationalist assassinated the heir to the Austrian throne at Sarajevo, Bosnia.

Some Austrian leaders saw this as an opportunity to crush Serbian nationalism. They sent Serbia an **ultimatum,** which Serbia refused to meet completely. Austria, with the full support of Germany, declared war on Serbia in July 1914.

Soon, the network of alliances drew other great powers into the conflict. Russia, in support of Serbia, began to **mobilize** its army. Germany declared war on Russia. France claimed it would honor its treaty with Russia, so Germany declared war on France, too. When the Germans violated Belgian **neutrality** to reach France, Britain declared war on Germany. World War I had begun.

Review Questions

1. How did the network of European alliances cause World War I to develop?

_____

_____

2. What act caused Britain to declare war?

_____

_____

READING CHECK

Which countries made up the Central Powers?

_____

_____

_____

VOCABULARY STRATEGY

What does the word *overseas* mean in the underlined sentence? What clues can you find in the surrounding words, phrases, or sentences? Circle the words in the paragraph that could help you learn what *overseas* means.

READING SKILL

Summarize Describe the events that led Austria to declare war on Serbia.

_____

_____

_____

Name_____ Class_____ Date_____

Focus Question: How and where was World War I fought?

A. As you read "Stalemate on the Western Front," "Battle on Other European Fronts," and "War Around the World," complete the following flowchart with important details about each battlefront of World War I.

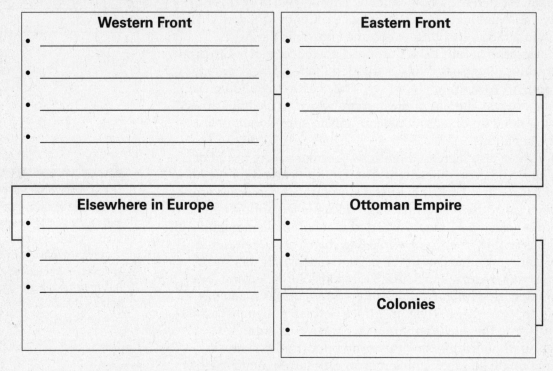

Western Front
- _____
- _____
- _____
- _____

Eastern Front
- _____
- _____
- _____

Elsewhere in Europe
- _____
- _____
- _____

Ottoman Empire
- _____
- _____

Colonies
- _____

B. As you read "Technology of Modern Warfare," complete the following concept web to summarize information about the technology of World War I. Add ovals as needed.

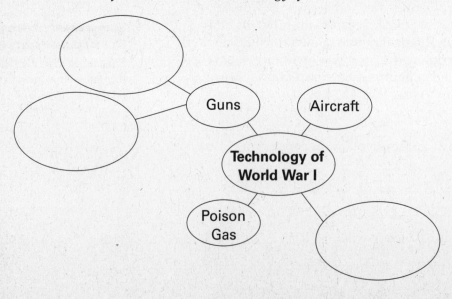

Guns

Aircraft

Technology of World War I

Poison Gas

CHAPTER 26 SECTION 2

Section Summary

A NEW KIND OF WAR

The Great War was the largest conflict in history up to that time. Millions of French, British, Russian, and German soldiers mobilized for battle. German forces fought their way toward France, but Belgian resistance foiled Germany's plans for a quick victory. Both sides dug deep trenches along the battlefront to protect their armies from enemy fire. The fighting on this Western Front turned into a long, deadly **stalemate,** a deadlock that neither side could break.

Technology made World War I different from earlier wars. Modern weapons caused high casualties. In 1915, first Germany then the Allies began using poison gas. Advances in technology brought about the introduction of tanks, airplanes, and modern submarines. Germany used **zeppelins** to bomb the English coast. Both sides equipped airplanes with machine guns. <u>Pilots known as "flying aces" confronted each other in the skies, but these "dog fights" had little effect on the ground war.</u> German submarines, called **U-boats,** did tremendous damage to the Allied shipping. To defend against them, the Allies organized **convoys,** or groups of merchant ships protected by warships.

On Europe's Eastern Front, battle lines shifted back and forth, sometimes over large areas. Casualties rose higher than on the Western Front. Russia was ill-prepared and suffered a disastrous defeat when pushing into eastern Germany. In 1915, Italy declared war on Austria-Hungary and Germany. In 1917, the Austrians and Germans launched a major offensive against the Italians.

Although most of the fighting took place in Europe, World War I was a global conflict. Japan used the war to seize German outposts in China and islands in the Pacific. The Ottoman empire joined the Central Powers. Its strategic location enabled it to cut off Allied supply lines to Russia through the **Dardanelles,** a vital strait.. The Ottoman Turks were hard hit in the Middle East, however. Arab nationalists revolted against Ottoman rule. The British sent **T.E. Lawrence,** or Lawrence of Arabia, to aid the Arabs. European colonies in Africa and Asia were also drawn into the war.

Review Questions

1. Why did a stalemate develop on the Western Front?

_____

_____

2. How did technology make World War I different from earlier wars?

_____

_____

READING CHECK

What were the two battlefronts in Europe called?

_____

_____

_____

VOCABULARY STRATEGY

What does the word *confronted* mean in the underlined sentence? What clues or examples can you find in the surrounding words that hint at its meaning? Think about what the goal of these pilots was. Circle the words in the underlined sentence that could help you learn what *confronted* means.

READING SKILL

Identify Supporting Details
Identify important details that show the differences between the course of the war on the Western Front and on the Eastern Front.

_____

_____

_____

CHAPTER
26
SECTION 3

Note Taking Study Guide
WINNING THE WAR

Focus Question: How did the Allies win World War I?

As you read this section in your textbook, complete the following outline to summarize the content of this section.

I. Waging total war
  A. Economies committed to war production.
    1. Conscription
    2. Rationing
    3. Price controls
  B. Economic warfare
    1. _____
    2. _____
    3. _____
  C. _____
    1. _____
    2. _____
    3. _____
  D. _____
    1. _____
    2. _____
    3. _____
II. _____
  A. _____
    1. _____
    2. _____
    3. _____
  B. _____
    1. _____
    2. _____
    3. _____

(Outline continues on the next page.)

CHAPTER
26
SECTION 3

Note Taking Study Guide
WINNING THE WAR

(Continued from page 236)

III. _____

   A. _____

      1. _____

      2. _____

      3. _____

   B. _____

      1. _____

      2. _____

      3. _____

   C. _____

      1. _____

      2. _____

      3. _____

IV. _____

   A. _____

   B. _____

   C. _____

CHAPTER 26 SECTION 3

Note Taking Study Guide

WINNING THE WAR

World War I was a **total war,** in which the participants channeled all their resources into the war effort. Both sides set up systems to recruit, arm, transport, and supply their armies. Nations imposed universal military **conscription,** or "the draft," requiring all young men to be ready to fight. Women also played a critical role. As millions of men left to fight, women took over their jobs and kept national economies going.

International law allowed wartime blockades to confiscate **contraband,** but British blockades kept ships from carrying other supplies, such as food, in and out of Germany. In retaliation, German U-boats torpedoed the British passenger liner *Lusitania.* Both sides used **propaganda** to control public opinion, circulating tales of **atrocities,** some true and others completely made up.

As time passed, war fatigue set in. Long casualty lists, food shortages, and the failure to win led to calls for peace. The morale of both troops and civilians plunged. <u>In Russia, stories of incompetent generals and corruption eroded public confidence and led to revolution.</u>

Until 1917, the United States had been neutral, but in that year it declared war on Germany. Many factors contributed to this decision, including Germany's unrestricted submarine warfare. Also, many Americans supported the Allies because of cultural ties with Britain and sympathy for its fellow democracy, France. By 1918, about two million fresh American soldiers had joined the war-weary Allied troops on the Western Front. In that year, President Wilson also issued his **Fourteen Points,** his terms for resolving this and future wars. Among the most important was **self-determination** for peoples in Eastern Europe.

A final showdown on the Western Front began in March 1918. With American troops, the Allies drove back German forces. In September, German generals told the kaiser that the war could not be won. The kaiser stepped down and the new German government sought an **armistice** with the Allies. At 11 A.M. on November 11, 1918, the Great War at last came to an end.

VOCABULARY STRATEGY

What does the word *eroded* mean in the underlined sentence? What clues or examples can you find in the surrounding words, phrases, or sentences that hint at its meaning? Circle the words in the paragraph that could help you learn what *eroded* means.

Review Questions

1. What caused the morale of troops and civilians to plunge?

_____

_____

2. What are two factors that caused the United States to enter the war?

_____

_____

Name_____ Class_____ Date_____

CHAPTER 26 SECTION 4
Note Taking Study Guide
MAKING THE PEACE

Focus Question: What factors influenced the peace treaties that ended World War I, and how did people react to the treaties?

A. *As you read "The Costs of War," complete this concept web to summarize the costs of World War I.*

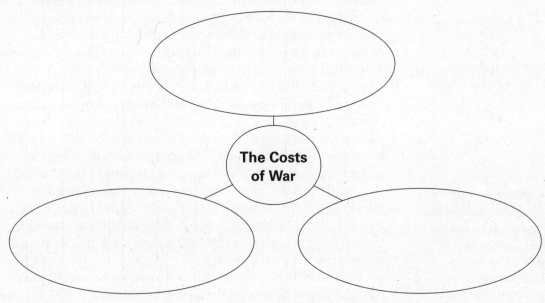

The Costs of War

B. *As you read "The Paris Peace Conference," "The Treaty of Versailles," and "Outcome of the Peace Settlements," complete this table to categorize issues and problems that resulted from agreements made after the war.*

Issue	Treaty Settlement	Problems
War Debt		
Fear of German Strength		
Nationalism		
Colonies and Other Non-European Territories		
League of Nations		

CHAPTER 26 SECTION 4

Section Summary

MAKING THE PEACE

Which three main Allied leaders negotiated the terms of the Treaty of Versailles?

_____

_____

_____

VOCABULARY STRATEGY

What does the word *widespread* mean in the underlined sentence? Look at the two words that form this compound word, and think about their meanings. Use what you know about the parts of this compound word to figure out its meaning.

READING SKILL

Summarize How did the goals of the three main leaders at the Paris Peace Conference differ?

_____

_____

_____

The human, material, and political costs of World War I were staggering. The huge loss of life was made even worse in 1918 by a deadly **pandemic** of influenza. From France to Russia, homes, farms, factories, and roads had been bombed into rubble. Reconstruction costs and war debts would burden an already battered world. The Allies blamed the war on their defeated foes and insisted that they make **reparations.** Governments had collapsed in Russia, Germany, Austria-Hungary, and the Ottoman empire. Out of the chaos, political **radicals** dreamed of building a new social order.

The victorious Allies met at the Paris Peace Conference to discuss the fate of Europe, the former Ottoman empire, and various colonies around the world. The Central Powers and Russia were not allowed to participate. This would lead to problems regarding the issue of self-determination. The three main Allied leaders had conflicting goals. British Prime Minister David Lloyd George focused on rebuilding Britain. French leader Georges Clemenceau wanted to punish Germany severely. American President Wilson insisted on the creation of an international League of Nations, based on the idea of **collective security.** In this system, a group of nations acts as one to preserve the peace of all.

In June 1919, the Allies ordered representatives of the new German Republic to sign the Treaty of Versailles. The German delegates were horrified. The treaty forced Germany to assume full blame for the war. The treaty also imposed huge reparations that would burden an already damaged German economy and limited the size of Germany's military.

The Allies drew up treaties with the other Central Powers. <u>Like the Treaty of Versailles, these treaties left widespread dissatisfaction, especially among many colonies that had hoped for an end to imperial rule.</u> Many nations felt betrayed by the peacemakers. As a result of these treaties, new nations emerged where the German, Austrian, and Russian empires had once ruled. Outside Europe, the Allies added to their overseas empires. The treaties also created a system of **mandates.** The one ray of hope was the establishment of the League of Nations. The failure of the United States to support the League, however, weakened the League's power.

Review Questions

1. What were some of the human, material, and political costs of the war?

_____

_____

2. Why were German representatives at Versailles horrified?

_____

_____

Focus Question: How did two revolutions and a civil war bring about Communist control of Russia?

As you read the section, fill in the following timeline with dates and facts about the series of events that led to Communist control of Russia. Then write two sentences summarizing the information in the timeline.

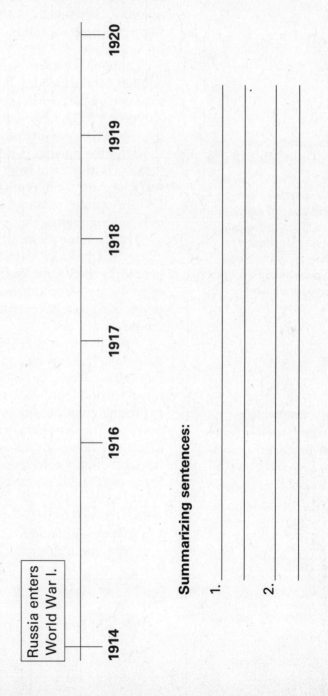

1914

Russia enters World War I.

1916

1917

1918

1919

1920

Summarizing sentences:

1.

2.

CHAPTER 26 SECTION 5

Section Summary
REVOLUTION AND CIVIL WAR IN RUSSIA

At the beginning of the 1900s, Russia had many political, economic, and social problems. Tsar Nicholas II resisted change. Marxists tried to ignite revolution among the **proletariat.** World War I quickly strained Russian resources. By March 1917, disasters on the battle-field and shortages at home brought the monarchy to collapse, and the tsar abdicated. While politicians set up a temporary government, revolutionary socialists set up **soviets,** or councils of workers and soldiers. These radical socialists were called Bolsheviks and were led by V. I. Lenin.

Lenin believed revolution could bring change. Leon Trotsky, another Marxist leader, helped Lenin lead the fight. To the weary Russian people, Lenin promised "Peace, Land, and Bread." In November 1917, Lenin and the Bolsheviks, renamed Communists, overthrew the government and seized power.

After the Bolshevik Revolution, events in Russia led to the nation's withdrawal from World War I. After the withdrawal, civil war raged for three years between the Communist "Reds" and the "White" armies of tsarist imperial officers. The Russians now fought only among themselves.

The Communists shot the former tsar and his family. They orga-nized the **Cheka,** a brutal secret police force, to control their own people. Trotsky kept Red Army officers under the close watch of **commissars**—Communist Party officials. The Reds' position in the center of Russia gave them a strategic advantage, and they defeated the White armies.

After the civil war, Lenin had to rebuild a shattered state and economy. The new nation was called the Union of Soviet Socialist Republics (USSR), or Soviet Union. The Communist constitution set up an elected legislature. All political power, resources, and means of production would now belong to workers and peasants. In reality, however, the Communist Party, not the people, had all the power. Lenin did, however, allow some capitalist ventures that helped the Soviet economy recover. After Lenin's death, party leader Joseph Stalin took ruthless steps to win total control of the nation.

Review Questions

1. What brought about the tsar's abdication and the end of the monarchy in Russia?

_____

_____

2. Why did Lenin want revolution?

_____

_____

CHAPTER
27
SECTION 1

Note Taking Study Guide

STRUGGLE IN LATIN AMERICA

Focus Question: How did Latin Americans struggle for change in the early 1900s?

A. *As you read the "The Mexican Revolution" and "Revolution Leads to Change," complete the chart by listing the causes and effects of the Mexican Revolution.*

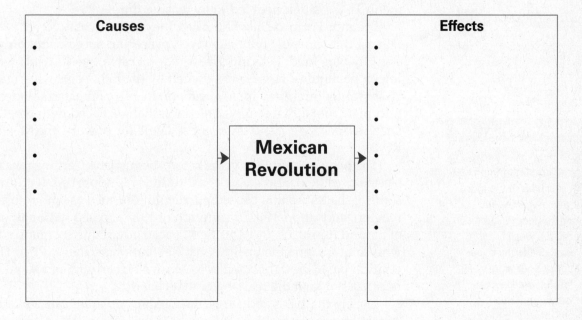

Causes
-
-
-
-
-

Mexican Revolution

Effects
-
-
-
-
-
-

B. *As you read "Nationalism at Work in Latin America," complete the following chart as you list the effects of nationalism in Latin America.*

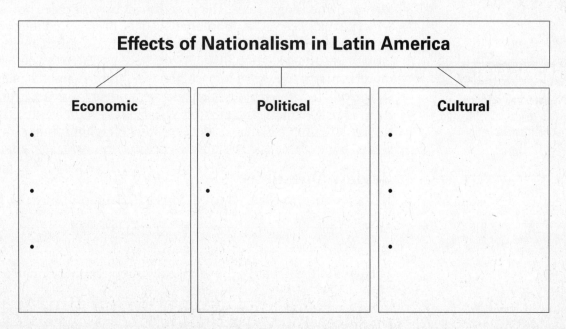

Effects of Nationalism in Latin America

Economic
-
-
-

Political
-
-

Cultural
-
-
-

CHAPTER 27 SECTION 1

Section Summary
STRUGGLE IN LATIN AMERICA

READING CHECK

What was the PRI, and what was its impact on Mexico?

_____

_____

_____

In the early 1900s, exports kept Latin America's economy booming. Even though foreign investors controlled much of the natural resources, stable governments helped keep economies strong. Yet turmoil brewed because military leaders and wealthy landowners held most of the power. Workers and peasants had no say in government. These differences led to increasing unrest.

Dictator Porfirio Díaz had ruled Mexico for nearly 35 years. During this time, the nation enjoyed peace and success, but only the wealthy benefited. Peasants lived in desperate poverty while working on **haciendas,** large farms owned by the rich. A growing middle class wanted more say in government. In 1910, Francisco Madero, a reformer from a rich family, called for change. Faced with rebellion, Díaz stepped down and a violent struggle for power—the Mexican Revolution—began.

The people fought for years before Venustiano Carranza was elected president, and a new constitution was approved. It addressed some of the issues that caused the revolution, such as land reform, religion, and labor. The Constitution of 1917 allowed **nationalization** of natural resources. In 1929, the Mexican government organized what later became the Institutional Revolutionary Party (PRI). This political party brought stability to Mexico by carrying out some reforms, but kept the real power in its hands.

VOCABULARY STRATEGY

What does the word *intervening* mean in the first underlined sentence? It is similar to the word *interference* in the second underlined sentence. You may have heard the word *interference* used when you watch sports. Both words begin with the prefix *inter-*, which means "between." Use the meaning of *inter-* and the context clues to help you figure out what *intervening* means.

During the 1920s and 1930s, the Great Depression caused Latin American exports to drop and import prices to rise. As a result, **economic nationalism** became popular. Latin Americans wanted to develop their own industries. Some Latin American nations took over foreign-owned companies. The government became more powerful when people accepted authoritarian leaders, hoping that they could improve the economy. Along with economic nationalism, there was a growth in **cultural nationalism.** Artists such as Diego Rivera painted murals or large images of Mexico's history, culture, and the people's struggles. The United States also became more involved in Latin America, often intervening to protect U.S. interests or troops. This led to anti-American feelings. Under the **Good Neighbor Policy,** the United States promised less interference in Latin American affairs.

READING SKILL

Identify Causes and Effects
What were two effects of United States involvement in Latin America?

_____

_____

_____

Review Questions

1. Under Porfirio Díaz, which groups had the most power?

_____

_____

2. How did the Great Depression lead to economic nationalism?

_____

_____

CHAPTER 27
SECTION 2

Note Taking Study Guide
NATIONALISM IN AFRICA AND THE MIDDLE EAST

Focus Question: How did nationalism contribute to changes in Africa and the Middle East following World War I?

As you read this section in your textbook, complete the following table to identify the causes and effects of the rise of nationalism.

Rise of Nationalism

Region	Reasons for Rise	Effects
Africa	• • •	• • •
Turkey and Persia	• • •	• • • •
Middle East	• • • •	• •

Section Summary
NATIONALISM IN AFRICA AND THE MIDDLE EAST

What was the négritude movement?

_____

_____

_____

What does the word *advocated* mean in the underlined sentence? What clues can you find in the surrounding sentences? Think about why Britain issued the Balfour Declaration. Use this information to help you understand the meaning of *advocated*.

Identify Causes and Effects
What was one effect of the Balfour Declaration?

_____

_____

_____

Europe ruled over most of Africa during the early 1900s. Improved farming methods meant more exports; however, this mostly benefited colonial rulers. Europeans kept the best lands, and African farmers were forced to grow cash crops instead of food. They also were forced to work in mines and then pay taxes to the colonial governments. Many Africans began criticizing imperial rule, but their freedoms only eroded further. An example was the system of **apartheid** in South Africa. Under this policy, black Africans were denied many of their previous rights, such as the right to vote.

During the 1920s, the **Pan-Africanism** movement called for the unity of Africans and people of African descent around the world. During the first Pan-African Congress, delegates asked world leaders at the Paris Peace Conference to approve a charter of rights for Africans. Their request was ignored. The members of the **négritude movement** in West Africa and the Caribbean protested colonial rule while expressing pride in African culture. These movements, however, brought about little real change.

In **Asia Minor,** Mustafa Kemal overthrew the Ottoman ruler and established the republic of Turkey. Also referred to as Atatürk (father of the Turks), his government promoted industrial expansion by building factories and railroads. Inspired by Atatürk's successes, Reza Khan overthrew the shah of Persia. Khan sought to turn Persia into a modern country. He, too, built factories and railroads. Khan also demanded a bigger portion of profits for Persia from British-controlled oil companies. Both leaders pushed aside Islamic traditions, replacing them with Western alternatives.

Pan-Arabism was a movement based on a shared history of Arabs living from the Arabian Peninsula to North Africa. Leaders of Arab nations and territories had hoped to gain independence after World War I, but felt betrayed when France and Britain were given control over their lands. In Palestine, Arab nationalists faced Zionists, or Jewish nationalists. To win the support of European Jews, Britain issued the **Balfour Declaration.** In it, the British advocated for a "national home for the Jewish people" in Palestine. Arabs felt the declaration favored the Jews. As a result, an ongoing conflict developed in the Middle East.

Review Questions

1. How did colonial rule hurt Africans?

_____

_____

2. How did Reza Khan change Persia?

_____

_____

CHAPTER
27
SECTION 3

Note Taking Study Guide
INDIA SEEKS SELF-RULE

Focus Question: How did Gandhi and the Congress party work for independence in India?

As you read this section in your textbook, complete the following chart by recording the causes and effects of Gandhi's leadership on India's independence movement.

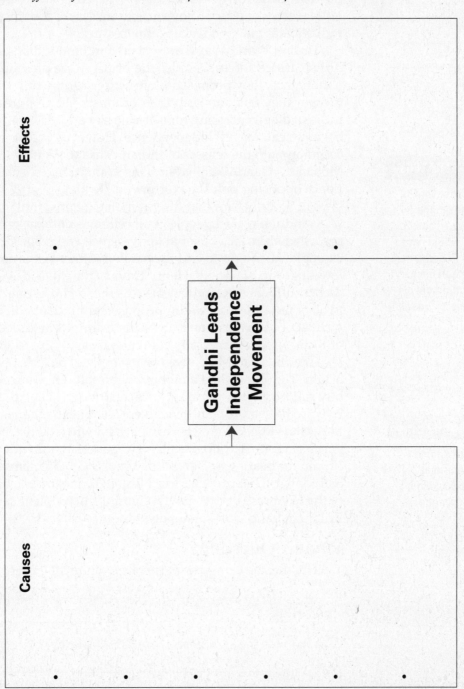

Effects

-
-
-
-
-

Gandhi Leads Independence Movement

Causes

-
-
-
-
-
-

CHAPTER 27 SECTION 3

Section Summary

INDIA SEEKS SELF-RULE

READING CHECK

READING CHECK

What had Gandhi done before becoming a leader for Indian independence?

_____

_____

_____

VOCABULARY STRATEGY

What do you think the word *discriminated* means in the underlined sentence? Think about why Gandhi would have been fighting laws in South Africa. Note what the Summary says about the government of South Africa in the previous sentence.

READING SKILL

Identify Causes and Effects What caused the Amritsar massacre? What effect did it have on the independence movement?

Cause:_____

_____

Effect:_____

_____

In 1919, Indian protests against colonial rule led to riots and attacks on British residents. The British then banned public meetings. On April 13, 1919, a peaceful crowd of Indians gathered in an enclosed field in Amritsar. As Indian leaders spoke, British soldiers fired on the unarmed crowd. Nearly 400 people were killed and more than 1,100 were wounded. The **Amritsar massacre** convinced many Indians that independence was necessary.

During World War I, more than a million Indians served in the British armed forces. Because the British were pressured by Indian nationalists, they promised more self-government for India. After the war they failed to keep their promise. The Congress Party of India had been pressing for self-rule since 1885. After Amritsar it began to call for full independence. However, the party had little in common with the masses of Indian peasants. A new leader, Mohandas Gandhi, united Indians. Gandhi had a great deal of experience opposing unjust government. He had spent 20 years fighting laws in South Africa that discriminated against Indians.

Gandhi inspired people of all religions and backgrounds. He preached **ahimsa,** a belief in nonviolence and respect for all life. For example, he fought to end the harsh treatment of **untouchables,** the lowest group of society. Henry David Thoreau's idea of civil disobedience influenced Gandhi. This was the idea that one should refuse to obey unfair laws. Gandhi proposed **civil disobedience** and nonviolent actions against the British. For example, he called for a **boycott** of British goods, especially cotton textiles.

Gandhi's Salt March was an example of civil disobedience in action. The British had a monopoly on salt. They forced Indians to buy salt from British producers even though salt was available naturally in the sea. As Gandhi walked 240 miles to the sea to collect salt, thousands joined him. He was arrested when he reached the water and picked up a lump of salt. Newspapers worldwide criticized Britain for beating and arresting thousands of Indians during the Salt March. That protest forced Britain to meet some of the demands of the Congress Party. Slowly, Gandhi's nonviolent campaign forced Britain to hand over some power to Indians.

Review Questions

1. Why did the Congress party fail to unite all Indians?

_____

_____

2. What was the significance of the Salt March?

_____

_____

CHAPTER
27
SECTION 4

Note Taking Study Guide
UPHEAVALS IN CHINA

Focus Question: How did China cope with internal division and foreign invasion in the early 1900s?

A. *As you read "The Chinese Republic in Trouble," complete the following chart by listing the multiple causes of upheaval in the Chinese Republic.*

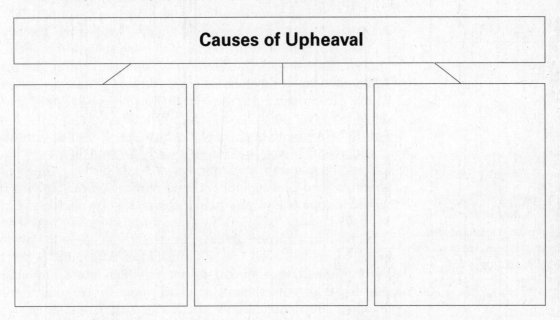

Causes of Upheaval

B. *As you read "Struggle for a New China" and "Japanese Invasion," complete the chart to sequence the fighting among the Guomindang, the warlords, the Chinese Communists, and the Japanese.*

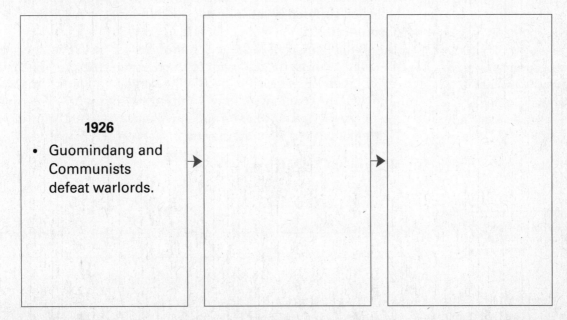

1926
• Guomindang and Communists defeat warlords.

Section Summary
UPHEAVALS IN CHINA

What group of people spear-
headed the May Fourth
Movement?

_____

_____

_____

VOCABULARY STRATEGY

What does the word *intellectual*
mean in the first underlined sentence? Circle the words in the
second underlined sentence that
could help you figure out what
intellectual means.

READING SKILL

Recognize Multiple Causes
Why did Chinese peasants support the Communists?

_____

_____

_____

When the Qing dynasty collapsed in 1911, Sun Yixian became president of China's new republic. He hoped to rebuild China, but he
made little progress. The country fell into chaos when local warlords
seized power and the economy fell apart. Millions of peasants suffered severe hardships. Sun Yixian stepped down as president in 1912.

Amid the upheaval, foreign imperialism increased in China. During World War I, Japan presented Chinese leaders the **Twenty-One
Demands.** These were intended to give Japan control over China,
and the Chinese gave into some of the demands. After the war, the
Allies gave Japan control over some former German possessions in
China. This infuriated Chinese nationalists. As protests spread, stu-
dents led a cultural and intellectual rebellion known as the **May
Fourth Movement.** Leaders of this movement rejected Confucian
tradition and looked to Western knowledge and learning. Other
Chinese people embraced Marxism. Also at this time, the Soviet
Union trained Chinese students and military officers, hoping they
would become the **vanguard** of a communist revolution in China.

In 1921, Sun Yixian led the **Guomindang,** or Nationalist party, as
it established a government in south China. To defeat the warlords he
joined forces with the Chinese communists. After Sun's death, Jiang
Jieshi assumed leadership of the party. Jiang felt the Communists
threatened his power. He ordered his troops to slaughter Communists
and their supporters. Led by Mao Zedong, the Communist army
escaped north in what became known as the **Long March.** During the
March, Mao's soldiers fought back using guerrilla tactics. Along the
way, Mao's soldiers treated the peasants kindly. They paid for the
goods they needed and were careful not to destroy crops. Many peasants had suffered because of the Guomindang, so they supported the
Communists.

While Jiang pursued the Communists across China, the Japanese
invaded Manchuria, adding it to their growing empire. Then, in
1937, Japanese planes bombed Chinese cities and Japanese soldiers
marched into Nanjing, killing hundreds of thousands of people. In
response, Jiang and Mao formed an alliance to fight the invaders.
The alliance held up until the end of the war with Japan.

Review Questions

1. How did Japan gain territory and control of areas of China during
   World War I?

   _____

   _____

2. Why did Jiang and Mao form an alliance?

   _____

   _____

CHAPTER 27 SECTION 5

Note Taking Study Guide

CONFLICTING FORCES IN JAPAN

Focus Question: How did Japan change in the 1920s and 1930s?

As you read this section in your textbook, complete the table by listing the effects of liberalism and militarism in Japan during the 1920s and 1930s.

Conflicting Forces in Japan	
Liberalism in the 1920s	**Militarism in the 1930s**
•	•
•	•
•	•
•	•

CHAPTER 27 SECTION 5

Section Summary

CONFLICTING FORCES IN JAPAN

The Japanese economy grew during World War I, based on the export of goods to the Allies and increased production. At this time, Japan also expanded its influence throughout East Asia and sought further rights in China. Additionally, Japan gained control of some former German possessions in China after the war. **Hirohito** became emperor of Japan in 1926, and during his reign, the country experienced both success and tragedy

In the 1920s, the Japanese government moved toward greater democracy. All adult men gained the right to vote, regardless of social class. Despite greater democratic freedoms, however, the zaibatsu, a group of powerful business leaders, manipulated politicians. By donating to political parties, the zaibatsu were able to push for policies that favored their interests.

Peasants and factory workers did not share in the nation's prosperity. Young Japanese rejected tradition and family authority. There was tension between the government and the military. The Great Depression fed the discontent of the military and the extreme nationalists, or **ultranationalists.** They resented Western limits on the expansion of Japan's empire. As the economic crisis worsened, the ultranationalists set their sights on **Manchuria** in northern China. In 1931, a group of Japanese army officers set explosives to blow up railroad tracks in Manchuria. They blamed it on the Chinese and used it as an excuse to invade. Without consulting government leaders, the military conquered Manchuria. Politicians objected to the army's actions, but the people sided with the military. When the League of Nations condemned the invasion, Japan withdrew from the organization.

Militarists and ultranationalists increased their power in the 1930s. Extremists killed some politicians and business leaders who opposed expansion. To please the ultranationalists, the government suppressed most democratic freedoms. Japan planned to take advantage of China's civil war and conquer the country. In 1939, however, World War II broke out in Europe. The fighting quickly spread to Asia. Earlier, Japan had formed an alliance with Germany and Italy. In September 1940, Japan's leaders signed the Tripartite Pact linking the three nations. Together, the three nations formed the Axis Powers.

Review Questions

1. Describe the economic success of Japan in the 1920s.

_____

_____

2. How did militarists and ultranationalists increase their power in the 1930s?

_____

_____

Note Taking Study Guide
POSTWAR SOCIAL CHANGES

Focus Question: What changes did Western society and culture experience after World War I?

As you read this section in your textbook, complete the concept web below to identify supporting details related to "Changes to Society" and "Cultural Changes."

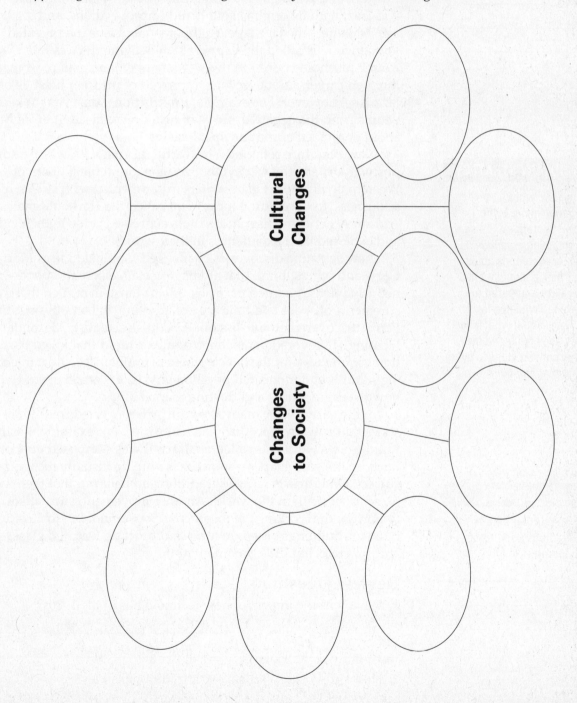

Name_____ Class_____ Date_____

Section Summary
POSTWAR SOCIAL CHANGES

READING CHECK

What were two symbols of American culture in the 1920s?

_____

_____

_____

VOCABULARY STRATEGY

What does the word *emancipation* mean in the underlined sentence? The sentence containing *emancipation* follows two sentences about women. Think about what flappers were like compared to young women who had lived before. Think about what labor-saving devices did for women. Use these context clues to figure out what *emancipation* means.

READING SKILL

Identify Supporting Details
What were three aspects of postwar literature?

_____

_____

_____

In reaction to World War I, society and culture in the United States and elsewhere underwent rapid changes. During the 1920s, new technologies helped create a mass culture, and to connect people around the world. American culture was characterized by a greater freedom and willingness to experiment. One symbol of this new age was jazz, with its original sound and improvisations, and it gave the age its name—the Jazz Age. Another symbol was the liberated young woman called the **flapper.** Labor-saving devices freed women from household chores. In this new era of emancipation, women pursued careers. Not everyone approved of the freer lifestyle of the Jazz Age, however. For example, **Prohibition** was meant to keep people from the negative effects of drinking. Instead, it brought about organized crime and **speakeasies.**

New literature reflected a powerful disgust with war. To some postwar writers, the war symbolized the moral breakdown of Western civilization. Other writers experimented with stream of consciousness. In the cultural movement called the **Harlem Renaissance,** African American artists and writers expressed pride in their culture and explored their experiences in their work.

New scientific discoveries challenged long-held ideas. Marie Curie and others found that atoms of certain elements spontaneously release charged particles. Albert Einstein argued that measurements of space and time are not absolute. Italian physicist Enrico Fermi discovered atomic fission. A Scottish scientist, Alexander Fleming, discovered penicillin, a nontoxic mold that killed bacteria. It paved the way for the development of antibiotics to treat infections. Sigmund Freud pioneered **psychoanalysis,** a method of studying how the mind works and treating mental illness.

In the early 1900s, many Western artists rejected traditional styles that tried to reproduce the real world. For example, Vasily Kandinsky's work was called **abstract.** It was composed only of lines, colors, and shapes—sometimes with no visually recognizable subject. **Dada** artists rejected tradition and believed that there was no sense or truth in the world. Another movement, **surrealism,** tried to portray the workings of the unconscious mind. In architecture, Bauhaus buildings based on form and function featured glass, steel, and concrete, but little ornamentation.

Review Questions

1. What was the impact of new technologies in the 1920s?

_____

_____

2. How did Western artists reject traditional styles?

_____

_____

CHAPTER
28
SECTION 2

Note Taking Study Guide

THE WESTERN DEMOCRACIES STUMBLE

Focus Question: What political and economic challenges did the leading democracies face in the 1920s and 1930s?

A. *As you read "Politics in the Postwar World," "Postwar Foreign Policy," and "Postwar Economics," complete the chart below to identify the main ideas under each heading.*

Postwar Issues			
Country	**Politics**	**Foreign Policy**	**Economics**

B. *As you read "The Great Depression," and "The Democracies React to the Depression," complete the chart below to identify the main ideas on the causes, effects, and reactions related to the Great Depression.*

The Great Depression

Causes	Effects	Reactions
•	•	•
•	•	•
•	•	•
•		
•		

CHAPTER 28 SECTION 2

Section Summary
THE WESTERN DEMOCRACIES STUMBLE

In 1919, after World War I, Britain, France, and the United States appeared powerful. However, postwar Europe faced grave problems. The most pressing issues were finding jobs for veterans and rebuilding war-ravaged lands. These problems made radical ideas more popular. Britain had to deal with growing socialism and the "Irish question." Fear of radicals set off a "Red Scare" in the United States.

The three democracies also faced international issues. Concern about a strong Germany led France to build the **Maginot Line** and insist on strict enforcement of the Versailles treaty. Many nations signed the **Kellogg-Briand Pact** promising to "renounce war as an instrument of national policy." In this optimistic spirit, the great powers pursued **disarmament.** Unfortunately, neither the Kellogg-Briand Pact nor the League of Nations had the power to stop aggression. Ambitious dictators in Europe noted this weakness.

The war affected economies all over the world. Both Britain and France owed huge war debts to the United States and relied on reparation payments from Germany to pay their loans. Britain was deeply in debt, with high unemployment and low wages. In 1926, a **general strike** lasted nine days and involved three million workers. On the other hand, the French economy recovered fairly quickly, and the United States emerged as the world's top economic power. In the affluent 1920s, middle-class Americans enjoyed the benefits of capitalism, buying cars, radios, and refrigerators.

However, better technologies allowed factories to make more products faster, leading to **overproduction** in the United States. Factories then cut back, and many workers lost their jobs. A crisis in **finance** led the **Federal Reserve** to raise interest rates. This made people even more nervous about the economy. In the autumn of 1929, financial panic set in. Stock prices crashed. The United States economy entered the **Great Depression,** which soon spread around the world.

Governments searched for solutions. In the United States, President **Franklin D. Roosevelt** introduced the programs of the **New Deal.** Although the New Deal failed to end the Depression, it did ease much suffering. However, as the Depression wore on, it created fertile ground for extremists.

Review Questions

1. After the war, what international agreement was intended to ensure peace?

_____

_____

2. What economic problems did Britain face after the war?

_____

_____

Focus Question: How and why did fascism rise in Italy?

A. *As you read "Mussolini's Rise to Power" and Mussolini's Rule," complete the flowchart below as you identify the main ideas under each heading.*

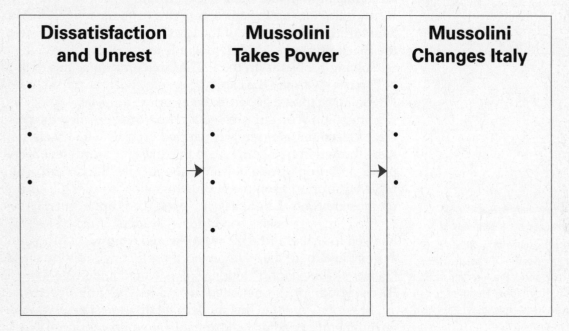

Dissatisfaction and Unrest	**Mussolini Takes Power**	**Mussolini Changes Italy**
•	•	•
•	•	•
•	•	•
	•	

B. *As you read "The Nature of Fascism," use the table below to identify the main ideas for each heading.*

What Is Fascism?	
Values	
Characteristics	
Differences from Communism	
Similarities to Communism	

Name_____ Class_____ Date_____

CHAPTER 28 SECTION 3

Section Summary
FASCISM IN ITALY

READING CHECK

Who were the Black Shirts?

_____

_____

_____

After World War I, Italian nationalists were outraged when Italy received just some of the territories promised by the Allies. Chaos ensued as peasants seized land, workers went on strike, veterans faced unemployment, trade declined, and taxes rose. The government could not end the crisis. Into this turmoil stepped **Benito Mussolini,** the organizer of the Fascist party. Mussolini's supporters, the **Black Shirts,** rejected democratic methods and favored violence for solving problems. In the 1922 **March on Rome,** tens of thousands of Fascists swarmed the capital. Fearing civil war, the king asked Mussolini to form a government as prime minister.

Mussolini soon suppressed rival parties, muzzled the press, rigged elections, and replaced elected officials with Fascists. Critics were thrown into prison, forced into exile, or murdered. Secret police and propaganda bolstered the regime. In 1929, Mussolini also received support from the pope. Mussolini brought the economy under state control, but basically preserved capitalism. His system favored the upper class and industry leaders. Workers were not allowed to strike, and their wages were kept low. In Mussolini's new system, loyalty to the state replaced conflicting individual goals. "Believe! Obey! Fight!" loudspeakers blared and posters proclaimed. Fascist youth groups marched in parades chanting slogans.

VOCABULARY STRATEGY

What does the word *proclaimed* mean in the underlined sentence? Think about the function of a poster. How does the purpose of a poster help explain the meaning of *proclaimed*?

Mussolini built the first modern **totalitarian state.** In this form of government, a one-party dictatorship attempts to control every aspect of the lives of its citizens. Today, we usually use the term **fascism** to describe the underlying ideology of any centralized, authoritarian governmental system that is not communist. Fascism is rooted in extreme nationalism. Fascists believe in action, violence, discipline, and blind loyalty to the state. They praise warfare. They are anti-democratic, rejecting equality and liberty. Fascists oppose communists on important issues. Communists favor international action and the creation of a classless society. Fascists are nationalists who support a society with defined classes. Both base their power on blind devotion to a leader or the state. Both flourish during economic hard times.

Fascism appealed to Italians because it restored national pride, provided stability, and ended the political feuding that had paralyzed democracy in Italy.

READING SKILL

Identify Main Ideas How did Mussolini's Fascists take over Italy?

_____

_____

_____

Review Questions

1. What was the result of the March on Rome?

_____

_____

2. How are communism and fascism similar?

_____

_____

CHAPTER
28
SECTION 4

Note Taking Study Guide
THE SOVIET UNION UNDER STALIN

Focus Question: How did Stalin transform the Soviet Union into a totalitarian state?

As you read this section in your textbook, complete the chart below by identifying the main ideas about the Soviet Union under Stalin for each heading.

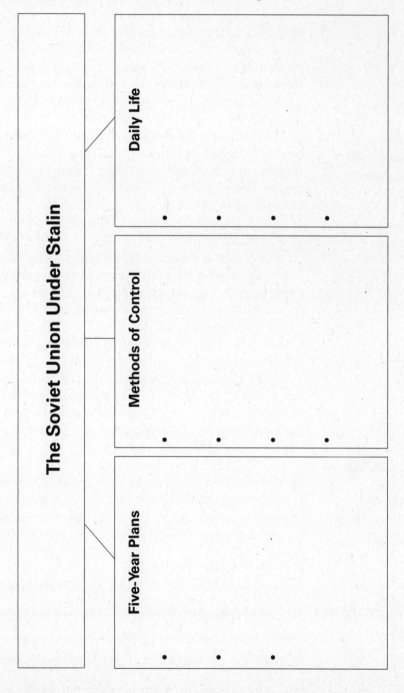

Section Summary
THE SOVIET UNION UNDER STALIN

What is a command economy?

_____

_____

_____

What does the word *conform* mean in the underlined sentence? Circle the letter of the word set below that contains words you could substitute for *to conform.* Use the correct word set and context clues to help you figure out what *conform* means.

a. to go along with

b. to disagree with

Identify Main Ideas Reread the last paragraph in the Summary. Write a sentence that expresses the main idea of that paragraph.

_____

_____

_____

Under Joseph Stalin, the Soviet Union grew into a totalitarian state, controlling all aspects of life, including agriculture, culture, art, and religion. The state also developed a **command economy,** in which it made all economic decisions. Stalin's five-year plans set high production goals. Despite great progress in some sectors, products such as clothing, cars, and refrigerators were scarce. Stalin forced changes in agriculture, too. He wanted peasants to farm on either state-owned farms or **collectives,** large farms owned and operated by groups of peasants. Some peasants balked. Stalin believed that the **kulaks** were behind the resistance. He took their land and sent them to labor camps, where many died. In 1932, Stalin's policies led to a famine that caused millions to starve.

The ruling Communist party used secret police, torture, and bloody purges to force people to obey. Those who opposed Stalin were rounded up and sent to the **Gulag,** a system of brutal labor camps. Fearing that rival party leaders were plotting against him, Stalin launched the Great Purge in 1934. Among the victims of this and other purges were some of the brightest and most talented people in the country.

Stalin demanded that artists and writers create works in a style called **socialist realism.** If they refused to conform to government expectations, they faced persecution. Another way Stalin controlled cultural life was to promote **russification.** The goal was to force people of non-Russian nationalities to become more Russian. The official Communist party belief in **atheism** led to the cruel treatment of religious leaders.

The Communists destroyed the old social order. Instead of creating a society of equals, Communist party members became the heads of society. Still, under communism most people enjoyed free medical care, day care for children, cheaper housing, and public recreation. Women had equal rights by law.

Soviet leaders had two foreign policy goals. They hoped to spread world revolution through the **Comintern,** or Communist International. At the same time, they wanted to ensure their nation's security by winning the support of other countries. These contradictory goals caused Western powers to mistrust the Soviet Union.

Review Questions

1. How did Stalin's changes in agriculture lead to a famine?

_____

_____

2. How did the Communist party and Stalin force people to obey?

_____

_____

Name_____ Class_____ Date_____

Focus Question: How did Hitler and the Nazi Party establish and maintain a totalitarian government in Germany?

As you read this section in your textbook, complete the flowchart below to identify the main ideas about Hitler and the rise of Nazi Germany for each heading.

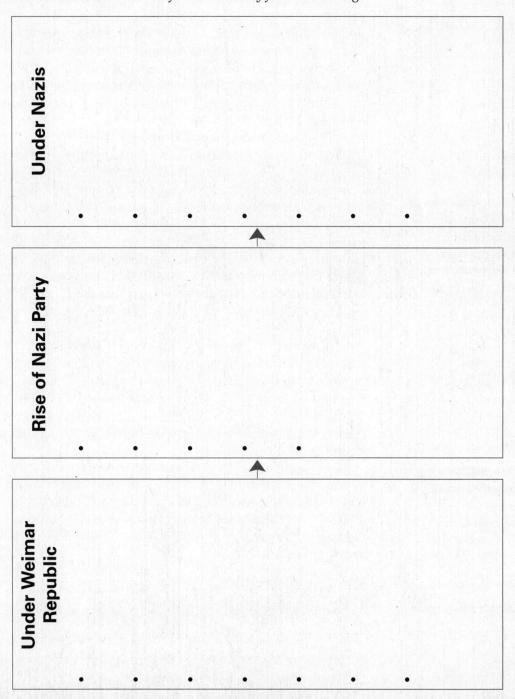

Section Summary
HITLER AND THE RISE OF NAZI GERMANY

After World War I, German leaders set up a democratic government
known as the Weimar Republic. The Weimar constitution established
a parliamentary system led by a **chancellor.** It gave women the right
to vote and included a bill of rights. However, the new republic faced
severe problems. When Germany could not make its war reparations
France seized the coal-rich **Ruhr Valley.** Government actions led to
inflation and skyrocketing prices. The German mark was almost
worthless. Many middle-class families lost their savings.

Many Germans believed that energetic leader Adolf Hitler
would solve Germany's problems. As head of the Nazi party, Hitler
promised to end reparations, create jobs, and rearm Germany. He
was elected chancellor in 1933, and within a year he was dictator
over the new fascist state in Germany.

To appeal to nationalism and recall Germany's glorious past,
Hitler called his government the **Third Reich.** To combat the
Depression, Hitler launched public works programs. In violation of
the Versailles treaty, he rearmed Germany. Hitler relied on his secret
police, the **Gestapo,** to root out opposition. He organized a brutal system of terror, repression, and totalitarian rule. A fanatical anti-Semite,
Hitler set out to drive the Jews from Germany. In 1935, the Nazis
passed the **Nuremberg Laws,** which deprived Jews of German citizenship and placed severe restrictions on them. The Nazis indoctrinated
German youth and rewrote textbooks to reflect Nazi racial views.

VOCABULARY STRATEGY

What does the word *regime*
mean in the underlined sentence? Circle the words in the
sentence that refer to the phrase
"the new *regime.*" What do you
think is the meaning of *regime?*

Hitler also limited women's roles and encouraged "pure-blooded
Aryan" women to bear many children. He sought to purge German
culture of what he believed were corrupt influences. Nazis denounced
modern art and jazz, but glorified German artists and myths. Hitler
despised Christianity as "weak." He combined all Protestant sects into
a single state church. <u>Although many clergy either supported the new
regime or remained silent, some courageously spoke out against
Hitler's government.</u>

Like Germany, most new nations in Eastern Europe slid from
systems of democratic to authoritarian rule. Economic problems and
ethnic tensions contributed to instability and helped fascist rulers to
gain power. The new dictators promised to keep order, and won the
backing of the military and the wealthy. They also supported the
growth of anti-Semitism.

READING SKILL

Identify Main Ideas Reread the
last paragraph in the Summary.
Write the main idea of that
paragraph on the lines below.

_____

_____

_____

Review Questions

1. What were the basic features of the Weimar constitution?

_____

_____

2. Why did many Germans support Hitler?

_____

_____

CHAPTER 29
SECTION 1

Note Taking Study Guide
FROM APPEASEMENT TO WAR

Focus Question: What events unfolded between Chamberlain's declaration of "peace in our time" and the outbreak of a world war?

A. *As you read "Aggression Goes Unchecked" and "Spain Collapses into Civil War," complete the chart below to record the sequence of events that led to the outbreak of World War II.*

Acts of Aggression	
Japan	• _____ • _____
Italy	• _____
Germany	• _____ • _____
Spain	• _____

B. *As you read "German Aggression Continues" and "Europe Plunges Toward War," complete the timetable below to recognize the sequence of German aggression.*

German Aggression	
March 1938	
September 1938	
March 1939	
September 1939	

CHAPTER 29 SECTION 1 — Section Summary

FROM APPEASEMENT TO WAR

Throughout the 1930s, dictators took aggressive action. Yet, they met only verbal protests and pleas for peace from Western powers. For example, when the League of Nations condemned Japan's invasion of Manchuria in 1931, Japan simply withdrew from the League. A few years later, Japanese armies invaded China, starting the Second Sino-Japanese War. Meanwhile, Mussolini invaded Ethiopia in 1935. The League of Nations voted sanctions against Italy, but the League had no power to enforce its punishment of Mussolini. Hitler, too, defied the Western democracies by building up the German military and sending troops into the "demilitarized" Rhineland. This went against the Treaty of Versailles. The Western democracies denounced Hitler but adopted a policy of **appeasement.** Appeasement developed for a number of reasons, including widespread **pacifism.** The United States responded with a series of **Neutrality Acts.** The goal was to avoid involvement in a war, rather than to prevent one. While the Western democracies sought to avoid war, Germany, Italy, and Japan formed an alliance. It became known as the **Axis powers.**

In Spain, a new, more liberal government passed reforms that upset conservatives. General **Francisco Franco,** who was opposed to the new government, started a civil war. Hitler and Mussolini supported Franco, their fellow fascist. The Soviet Union sent troops to support the anti-Fascists, or Loyalists. The governments of Britain, France, and the United States remained neutral, although individuals from these countries fought with the Loyalists. By 1939, Franco had triumphed.

German aggression continued. In 1938, Hitler forced the **Anschluss,** or union with Austria. Next, Hitler set his sights on the **Sudentenland.** This was a part of Czechoslovakia where three million Germans lived. At the Munich Conference, which was held to discuss the situation, British and French leaders chose appeasement and allowed Hitler to annex the territory.

In March 1939, Hitler took over the rest of Czechoslovakia. Months later, Hitler and Stalin signed the **Nazi-Soviet Pact.** They agreed not to fight if the other went to war. This paved the way for Germany's invasion of Poland in September of 1939, which set off World War II.

Review Questions

1. How did the United States respond to the aggressive action of dictators in the 1930s?

_____

_____

2. What was the result of the Munich Conference?

_____

_____

Name_____ Class_____ Date_____

Focus Question: Which regions were attacked and occupied by the Axis powers, and what was life like under their occupation?

A. *As you read "The Axis Attacks," "Germany Invades the Soviet Union," and "Japan Attacks the United States," use the chart below to record the sequence of events.*

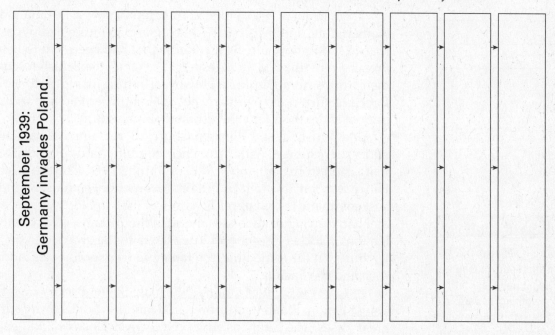

September 1939: Germany invades Poland.

B. *As you read "Life Under Nazi and Japanese Occupation," use the concept web to identify supporting details about the occupations.*

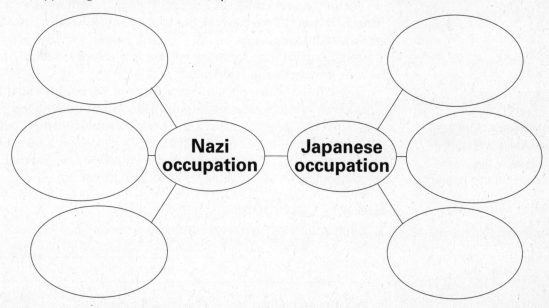

Nazi occupation

Japanese occupation

CHAPTER 29 SECTION 2

Section Summary
THE AXIS ADVANCES

READING CHECK

What was the name of the German government in southern France?

_____

_____

_____

VOCABULARY STRATEGY

Find the word *nullified* in the underlined sentence. In math class you might have learned that there is nothing, or zero, in the null set. Use this clue about related words to help you figure out the meaning of *nullified.*

In September 1939, Nazi forces launched a **blitzkrieg** against Poland. First the **Luftwaffe,** the German air force, bombed. Then, tanks and troops pushed their way in. At the same time, Stalin invaded from the east, grabbing land. Within a month, Poland ceased to exist.

Then, in early 1940, Hitler conquered Norway, Denmark, the Netherlands, and Belgium. By May, German forces had bypassed France's Maginot Line. British forces that had been sent to help the French were trapped. In a desperate scheme, the British rescued their troops from **Dunkirk.** However, in June, the French were forced to surrender. Germany occupied northern France and set up a puppet state, the **Vichy** government, in the south.

The British, led by Winston Churchill, remained defiant against Hitler. In response, Hitler launched bombing raids over British cities that lasted from September 1940 until June 1941. Despite this blitz, Hitler was not able to take Britain. Meanwhile, Hitler sent one of his best commanders, **General Erwin Rommel,** to North Africa. Rommel had a string of successes there. In the Balkans, German and Italian forces added Greece and Yugoslavia to the growing Axis territory. At the same time, the Japanese were occupying lands in Asia and the Pacific.

In June 1941, Hitler nullified the Nazi-Soviet Pact by invading the Soviet Union. Stalin was unprepared, and the Soviet army suffered great losses. The Germans advanced toward Moscow and Leningrad. During a lengthy siege of Leningrad, more than a million Russians died. The severe Russian winter finally slowed the German army.

As they marched across Europe, the Nazis sent millions to **concentration camps** to work as slave laborers. Even worse, Hitler established death camps to kill those he judged racially inferior. Among many others, some six million Jews were killed in what became known as the **Holocaust.**

The United States declared neutrality at the beginning of the war. Yet many Americans sympathized with those who fought the Axis powers. Congress passed the **Lend-Lease Act** of 1941, allowing the United States to sell or lend war goods to foes of the Axis. On December 7, 1941, the Japanese bombed the U.S. fleet at Pearl Harbor. Four days later, Congress declared war on Japan.

Review Questions

1. What countries were conquered by Germany in 1939 and 1940?

_____

_____

2. What was the purpose of the Lend-Lease Act?

_____

_____

Note Taking Study Guide
THE ALLIES TURN THE TIDE

Focus Question: How did the Allies begin to push back the Axis powers?

As you read this section in your textbook, complete the chart below to record the sequence of events that turned the tide of the war in favor of the Allies.

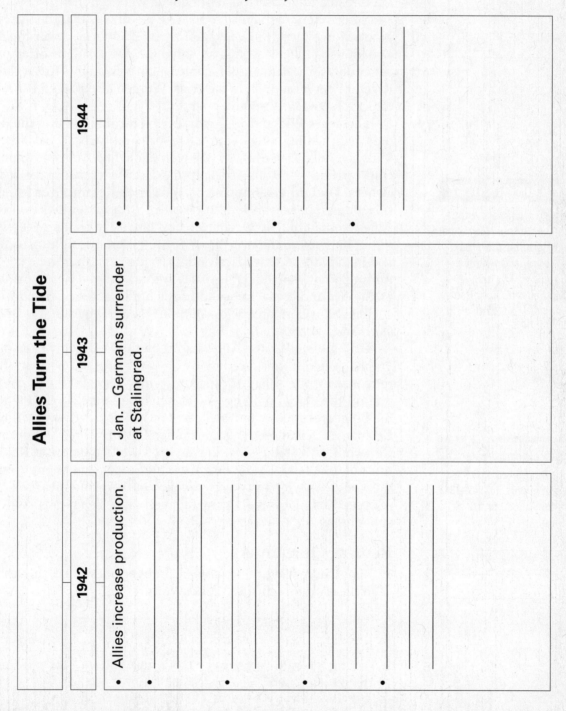

Allies Turn the Tide

1944

•
•
•
•

1943

• Jan.—Germans surrender at Stalingrad.
•
•
•

1942

• Allies increase production.
•
•
•
•

CHAPTER 29 SECTION 3

Section Summary
THE ALLIES TURN THE TIDE

Who were the "Big Three"?

_____

_____

_____

Find the word *incessant* in the underlined sentence. Notice that the phrase "around-the-clock" follows *incessant*. They have similar meanings. Use this context clue to help you figure out the meaning of *incessant*.

Recognize Sequence List the sequence of events in 1942–1943 that gave the Allies control of North Africa.

_____

_____

_____

To defeat the Axis powers in World War II, the Allies devoted all their resources to the war effort. Governments took a greater role in the economy. For example, governments ordered factories to make tanks instead of cars. Consumer goods were rationed, and wages and prices were regulated. A positive result was that the increase in production ended the Great Depression. However, governments also limited citizens' rights, censored the press, and resorted to propaganda. At the same time, women, symbolized by **"Rosie the Riveter,"** replaced men in factories. Women also played a more direct role in some military operations.

The years 1942 and 1943 marked the turning point of the war. In the Pacific, Allied forces won the battles of the Coral Sea and Midway. In both battles, attacks were launched from enormous **aircraft carriers.** In North Africa, British and American forces, led by General **Dwight Eisenhower,** soon trapped Rommel's army, and he surrendered in May 1943. With North Africa under their control, the Allies crossed the Mediterranean and landed in Sicily. Allied victories in Italy led to the overthrow of Mussolini, but fighting continued in Italy for another 18 months. On the Eastern front, a key turning point was the Battle of **Stalingrad.** After a German advance on the city and brutal house-to-house fighting, the Soviet army encircled the German troops. Without food or ammunition, the Germans surrendered.

On June 6, 1944, the Allies launched the **D-Day** invasion of France. Allied troops faced many obstacles, but the Germans finally retreated. <u>As the Allies advanced, Germany reeled from incessant, around-the-clock bombing.</u> A German counterattack, the Battle of the Bulge, resulted in terrible losses on both sides. However, with Germany's defeat seeming inevitable, the "Big Three"—Roosevelt, Churchill, and Stalin—met to plan for the end of the war. Key features of this **Yalta Conference** were the Soviet agreement to enter the war against Japan and the division of Germany into four zones of occupation. However, growing mistrust at Yalta foreshadowed a split among the Allies.

Review Questions

1. Name three ways in which Allied governments took a greater role in the economy during World War II.

_____

_____

2. During the battles of the Coral Sea and Midway, from where were attacks launched?

_____

_____

CHAPTER 29
SECTION 4

Note Taking Study Guide

VICTORY IN EUROPE AND THE PACIFIC

Focus Question: How did the Allies finally defeat the Axis powers?

As you read this section in your textbook, complete the timeline below to sequence the events that led to the defeat of the Axis powers.

Oct.
1945

June
1945

Feb.
1945

Oct.
1944

CHAPTER 29 SECTION 4

Section Summary

VICTORY IN EUROPE AND THE PACIFIC

In Europe, World War II officially ended on May 8, 1945, or **V-E Day.** The Allies were able to defeat the Axis powers for many reasons. Because of their location, the Axis powers had to fight on several fronts at the same time. Hitler also made some poor military decisions. For example, he underestimated the Soviet Union's ability to fight. The huge productive capacity of the United States was another factor. At the same time, Allied bombing hindered German production and caused oil to become scarce. This nearly grounded the Luftwaffe.

Although Germany was defeated, the Allies still had to defeat the Japanese in the Pacific. By May 1942, the Japanese had gained control of the Philippines, killing thousands during the **Bataan Death March.** However, after the battles of Midway and the Coral Sea, the United States took the offensive. General **Douglas MacArthur** began an **"island-hopping"** campaign to recapture islands from the Japanese. The captured islands served as stepping-stones to the next objective—Japan. The Americans gradually moved north and were able to blockade Japan. Bombers pounded Japanese cities and industries. At the same time, the British pushed Japanese forces back into the jungles of Burma and Malaya.

In early 1945, bloody battles on Iwo Jima and Okinawa showed that the Japanese would fight to the death rather than surrender. Some young Japanese became **kamikaze** pilots who flew their planes purposefully into U.S. ships. While Allied military leaders planned to invade, scientists offered another way to end the war. They had conducted research, code-named the **Manhattan Project,** that led to the building of an atomic bomb for the United States. The new U.S. president, Harry Truman, decided that dropping the bomb would save American lives. The Allies first issued a warning to the Japanese to surrender or face "utter and complete destruction," but the warning was ignored. On August 6, 1945, a U.S. plane dropped an atomic bomb on the city of **Hiroshima,** instantly killing more than 70,000 people. Many more died from radiation sickness. When the Japanese did not surrender, another bomb was dropped on **Nagasaki** on August 9. The next day, Japan finally surrendered, ending World War II.

Review Questions

1. What were two reasons why the Allies were able to defeat the Axis powers?

_____

_____

2. Why did Truman decide to drop the atomic bomb on Japan?

_____

_____

CHAPTER
29
SECTION 5

Note Taking Study Guide
THE END OF WORLD WAR II

Focus Question: What issues arose in the aftermath of World War II and how did new tensions develop?

As you read this section in your textbook, sequence the events following World War II by completing the outline below.

I. The War's Aftermath
  A. Devastation
    1. As many as 50 million are dead.
    2. _____
  B. _____
    1. _____
    2. _____
    3. _____
  C. _____
    1. _____
    2. _____
II. _____
  A. _____
    1. _____
  B. _____
    1. _____
    2. _____
  C. _____
    1. _____
    2. _____
III. _____
  A. _____
    1. _____
    2. _____
  B. _____
    1. _____
    2. _____

(Outline continues on the next page.)

CHAPTER
29
SECTION 5

Note Taking Study Guide

THE END OF WORLD WAR II

(Continued from page 271)

3. _____

IV. _____

  A. _____

    1. _____

    2. _____

    3. _____

  B. _____

    1. _____

    2. _____

    3. _____

  C. _____

    1. _____

    2. _____

    3. _____

    4. _____

  D. _____

    1. _____

    2. _____

    3. _____

  E. _____

    1. _____

    2. _____

  F. _____

    1. _____

    2. _____

Section Summary
THE END OF WORLD WAR II

While the Allies enjoyed their victory, the huge costs of World War II began to emerge. As many as 50 million people had been killed. The Allies also learned the full extent of the horrors of the Holocaust. War crimes trials, such as those at **Nuremberg** in Germany, held leaders accountable for their wartime actions. To ensure tolerance and peace, the Western Allies set up democratic governments in Japan and Germany.

In 1945, delegates from 50 nations convened to form the **United Nations.** Under the UN Charter, each member nation has one vote in the General Assembly. A smaller Security Council has greater power. It has five permanent members: the United States, the Soviet Union (today Russia), Britain, France, and China. Each has the right to veto any council decision. UN agencies have tackled many world problems, from disease to helping refugees.

However, conflicting ideologies soon led to a **Cold War.** This refers to the state of tension and hostility between the United States and the Soviet Union from 1946 to 1990. Soviet leader Stalin wanted to spread communism into Eastern Europe. He also wanted to create a buffer zone of friendly countries as a defense against Germany. By 1948, pro-Soviet communist governments were in place throughout Eastern Europe.

When Stalin began to threaten Greece and Turkey, the United States outlined a policy called the **Truman Doctrine.** This policy meant that the United States would resist the spread of communism throughout the world. To strengthen democracies in Europe, the United States offered a massive aid package, called the **Marshall Plan.** Western attempts to rebuild Germany triggered a crisis over the city of Berlin. The Soviets controlled East Germany, which surrounded Berlin. To force the Western Allies out of Berlin, the Soviets blockaded West Berlin, but a yearlong airlift forced them to end the blockade.

However, tensions continued to mount. In 1949, the United States and nine other nations formed a new military alliance called the **North Atlantic Treaty Organization (NATO).** The Soviets responded by forming the **Warsaw Pact,** which included the Soviet Union and seven Eastern European nations.

Review Questions

1. What was the purpose of the post-World War II war crimes trials?

_____

_____

2. Why did the United States offer aid under the Marshall Plan to European countries?

_____

_____

READING CHECK

What was the Cold War?

_____

_____

_____

VOCABULARY STRATEGY

What does the word *convened* mean in the underlined sentence? The word *convene* comes from the Latin *convenire.* In Latin, *con-* means "together" and *venire* means "to come." Use this word-origins clue to help you figure out the meaning of *convened.*

READING SKILL

Recognize Sequence List the sequence of events that led to the Berlin airlift.

_____

_____

_____

Name_____ Class_____ Date_____

Focus Question: What were the military and political consequences of the Cold War in the Soviet Union, Europe, and the United States?

As you read this section in your textbook, complete the following chart to summarize the consequences of the Cold War in the Soviet Union, Europe, and the United States.

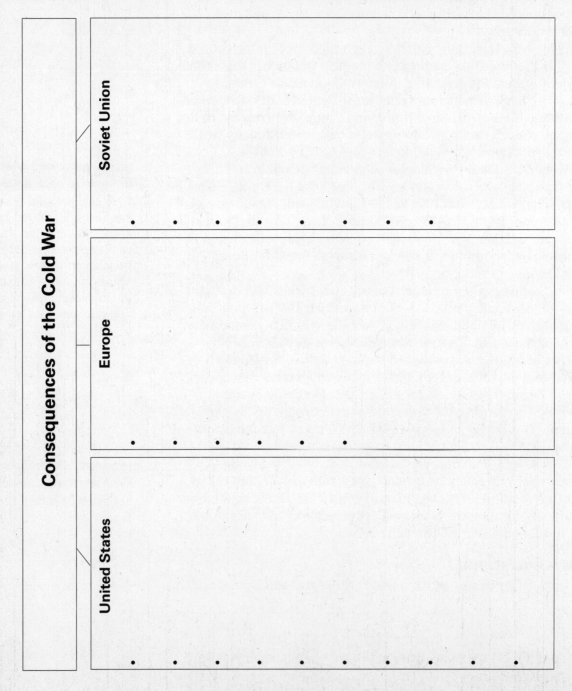

CHAPTER 30
SECTION 1
Section Summary
THE COLD WAR UNFOLDS

After World War II, the United States and the Soviet Union emerged as **superpowers.** They each created military alliances made up of nations they protected or occupied. <u>The United States helped form the North Atlantic Treaty Organization (NATO), which comprised Western European allies.</u> The Soviet Union signed the Warsaw Pact with Eastern European countries. The line between the democratic West and communist East was called the Iron Curtain. Many revolts challenging Soviet domination were extinguished with military force.

The superpowers also engaged in a weapons race—both developed nuclear weapons. To reduce the threat of war, the two sides held several disarmament talks. One agreement was intended to limit the use of **anti-ballistic missiles (ABMs).** These weapons were designed to shoot down missiles launched by hostile nations. The ABMs were considered a threat because they could give one side more protection, which might encourage it to attack. Then during the 1980s, President **Ronald Reagan** proposed a missile defense program called "Star Wars." Other agreements limited the number of nuclear weapons that nations could maintain, which eased Cold War tensions. This period was called the era of **détente.** It ended, however, when the Soviet Union invaded Afghanistan in 1979.

During the 1950s, **Fidel Castro** led a revolution in Cuba and became its leader. To bring down Castro's communist regime, U.S. President **John F. Kennedy** supported an invasion of Cuba, but the attempt failed. One year later, the Soviets sent nuclear missiles to Cuba. Many feared a nuclear war. After the United States blockaded Cuba, Soviet leader **Nikita Khrushchev** agreed to remove the missiles.

The Soviets wanted to spread communist **ideology** around the globe. When Khrushchev came to power, he eased censorship and increased tolerance. However, repression returned under **Leonid Brezhnev.** American leaders followed a policy of **containment.** This was a strategy of keeping communism from spreading to other nations. In addition, a "red scare" in the United States resulted in Senator Joseph McCarthy leading an internal hunt for communists in the government and military. The House Un-American Activities Committee (HUAC) also sought out communist sympathizers.

Review Questions

1. What did the two superpowers do to reduce the threat of war during the Cold War?

_____

_____

2. What ended the period of détente between the United States and the Soviet Union?

_____

_____

READING CHECK

Who were the two superpowers during the Cold War?

_____

_____

_____

VOCABULARY STRATEGY

What does the word *comprised* mean in the underlined sentence? What clues can you find in the surrounding words, phrases, or sentences? Use these context clues to help you figure out what *comprised* means.

READING SKILL

Summarize What was the United States policy known as containment?

_____

_____

_____

CHAPTER 30

SECTION 2

Note Taking Study Guide

THE INDUSTRIALIZED DEMOCRACIES

Focus Question: How did the United States, Western Europe, and Japan achieve economic prosperity and strengthen democracy during the Cold War years?

As you read this section in your textbook, use the chart below to categorize economic and political changes in the industrialized democracies.

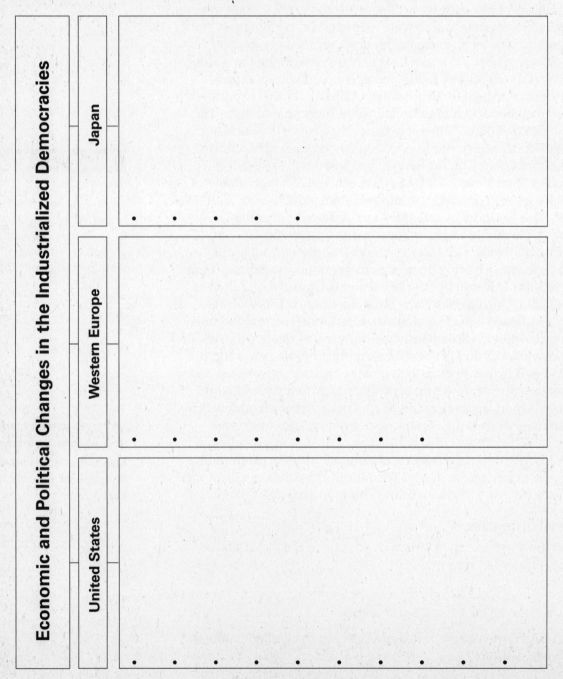

Economic and Political Changes in the Industrialized Democracies

Japan
  • • • • •

Western Europe
  • • • • • • • • •

United States
  • • • • • • • • • •

CHAPTER 30 SECTION 2

Section Summary

THE INDUSTRIALIZED DEMOCRACIES

During the postwar period, U.S. businesses expanded into the global marketplace. Other nations needed goods and services to rebuild. This led to a period of economic success that changed life in the United States. During the 1950s and 1960s, **recessions** were brief and mild. <u>As Americans prospered, they left the cities to live in the suburbs.</u> This trend is called **suburbanization.** Also, job opportunities in the Sunbelt attracted many people to that region. By the 1970s, however, a political crisis in the Middle East made Americans aware of their dependence on imported oil. The price of oil and gas rose substantially, which meant that people had less money to buy other products. The decades of prosperity ended in 1974 with a serious recession.

During the period of prosperity, African Americans and other minorities faced **segregation** in housing and education. They suffered from **discrimination** in jobs and voting. **Dr. Martin Luther King, Jr.,** emerged as the main civil rights leader in the 1960s. The U.S. Congress passed some civil rights legislation. Other minority groups were inspired by the movement's successes. For example, the women's rights movement helped to end much gender-based discrimination.

Western Europe rebuilt after World War II. The Marshall Plan helped restore European economies by providing U.S. aid. After the war, Germany was divided between the communist East and the democratic West, but reunited at the end of the Cold War in 1990. Under **Konrad Adenauer,** West Germany's chancellor from 1949 to 1963, Germany built modern cities and re-established trade. European governments also developed programs that increased government responsibility for the needs of people. These **welfare states** required high taxes to pay for their programs. During the 1980s, some leaders, such as Britain's Margaret Thatcher, reduced the role of the government in the economy. Western Europe also moved closer to economic unity with the **European Community**, an organization dedicated to establishing free trade among its members.

Japan also prospered after World War II. Its **gross domestic product (GDP)** soared. Like Germany, Japan built factories. The government protected industries by raising tariffs on imported goods. This helped create a trade surplus for Japan.

Review Questions

1. What caused a U.S. recession in 1974?

_____

_____

2. Explain how Germany rebuilt its economy after World War II.

_____

_____

READING CHECK

What is suburbanization?

_____

_____

_____

VOCABULARY STRATEGY

What does the word *prospered* mean in the underlined sentence? The word *decline* is an antonym of *prosper*. It means to "sink," "descend," or "deteriorate." Use these meanings of *decline* to figure out the meaning of *prospered*.

READING SKILL

Categorize In what ways were minorities denied equality and opportunity?

_____

_____

_____

Name_____ Class_____ Date_____

Focus Question: What did the Communist victory mean for China and the rest of East Asia?

As you read this section in your textbook, complete the flowchart below to help you summarize the effects of the Communist Revolution on China and the impact of the Cold War on China and Korea.

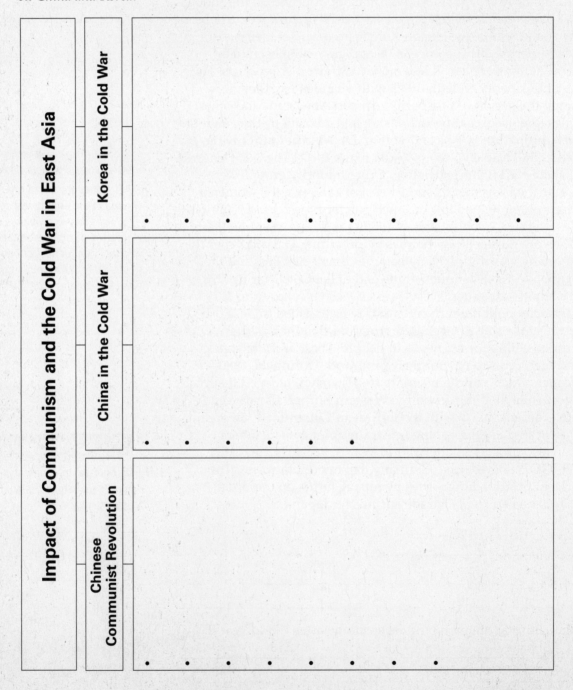

Impact of Communism and the Cold War in East Asia

Korea in the Cold War

China in the Cold War

Chinese Communist Revolution

CHAPTER 30 SECTION 3

Section Summary
COMMUNISM SPREADS IN EAST ASIA

After World War II, Mao Zedong led communist forces to victory over Jiang Jieshi's Nationalists, who fled to Taiwan. Then Mao began to reshape China's economy. First, he gave land to peasants, but then called for **collectivization.** Under this system, <u>Mao moved people from their small villages and individual farms into communes of thousands of people on thousands of acres.</u> Known as the **Great Leap Forward,** the program was intended to increase farm and industrial production. Instead, it produced low quality, useless goods and less food. Bad weather also affected crops, and many people starved.

To remove "bourgeois" tendencies from China, Mao began the **Cultural Revolution.** Skilled workers and managers were removed from factories and forced to work on farms or in labor camps. This resulted in a slowed economy and a threat of civil war.

At first, the United States supported the Nationalist government in Taiwan. The West was concerned that the Soviet Union and China would become allies, but border clashes led the Soviets to withdraw aid and advisors from China. U.S. leaders thought that by "playing the China card," or improving relations with the Chinese, they would further isolate the Soviets. In 1979, the United States established diplomatic relations with China.

Korea was an independent nation until Japan invaded it in World War II. After the war, American and Soviet forces agreed to divide the Korean peninsula at the **38th parallel**. **Kim Il Sung**, a communist, ruled the North; and **Syngman Rhee,** allied with the United States, controlled the South. In 1950, North Korean troops attacked South Korea. The United Nations forces stopped them along a line known as the **Pusan Perimeter,** then began advancing north. Mao sent troops to help the North Koreans. UN forces were pushed back south of the 38th parallel.

In 1953, both sides signed an armistice to end the fighting, but troops remained on both sides of the **demilitarized zone (DMZ).** Over time, South Korea enjoyed an economic boom and a rise in living standards, while communist North Korea's economy declined. Kim Il Sung's emphasis on self-reliance kept North Korea isolated and poor.

Review Questions

1. What was the effect of the Cultural Revolution?

_____

_____

2. How did the North Korean economy differ from the South Korean economy?

_____

_____

READING CHECK

What is the significance of the 38th parallel?

_____

_____

_____

VOCABULARY STRATEGY

What does the word *commune* mean in the underlined sentence? The terms *group home*, *community*, and *collective farm* are all synonyms of *commune*. Use the synonyms to help you figure out the meaning of *commune*.

READING SKILL

Summarize Summarize the effects of the Great Leap Forward on the Chinese people.

_____

_____

_____

CHAPTER 30 SECTION 4

Note Taking Study Guide

WAR IN SOUTHEAST ASIA

Focus Question: What were the causes and effects of war in Southeast Asia, and what was the American role in this region?

As you read this section in your textbook, complete the flowchart below to summarize the events in Southeast Asia after World War II.

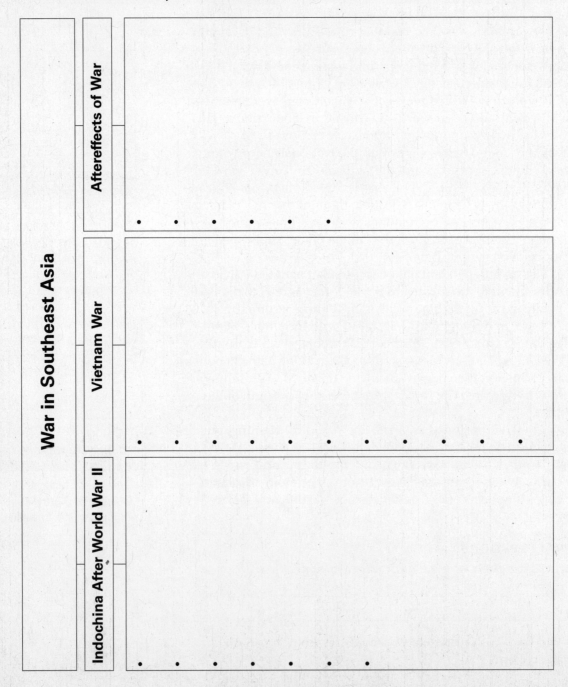

War in Southeast Asia

Aftereffects of War

Vietnam War

Indochina After World War II

CHAPTER 30 SECTION 4

Section Summary
WAR IN SOUTHEAST ASIA

In the 1800s, the French ruled the area in Southeast Asia called French Indochina. During World War II, Japan invaded that region, but faced resistance from **guerrillas.** After the war, the French tried to reestablish authority in Vietnam. However, forces led by communist leader **Ho Chi Minh** fought the colonialists. The French left Vietnam in 1954, after a Vietnamese victory at **Dienbienphu.** After that, Ho controlled the northern part of Vietnam while the United States supported the noncommunist government in the south.

Ho wanted to unite Vietnam. He provided aid to the National Liberation Front, or **Viet Cong,** a communist guerrilla organization in the south. American leaders saw Vietnam as an extension of the Cold War and developed the **domino theory.** This was the belief that if communists won in South Vietnam, then communism could spread to other governments in Southeast Asia. After a North Vietnamese attack on a U.S. Navy destroyer, Congress authorized the president to take military measures to prevent further communist aggression in Southeast Asia.

Despite massive American support, the South Vietnamese failed to defeat the Viet Cong and their North Vietnamese allies. During the **Tet Offensive,** the North Vietnamese attacked cities all over the south. Even though the communists were not able to hold any cities, it marked a turning point in U.S. public opinion. Upset by civilian deaths from the U.S. bombing of North Vietnam as well as growing American casualties, many Americans began to oppose the war. President Nixon came under increasing pressure to terminate the conflict. The Paris Peace Accord of 1973 established a ceasefire and American troops began to withdraw. Two years later communist North Vietnam conquered South Vietnam.

Neighboring Cambodia and Laos also ended up with communist governments. In Cambodia, guerrillas called the **Khmer Rouge** came to power. Led by the brutal dictator **Pol Pot,** their policies led to a genocide that killed about one third of the population. When Vietnam invaded Cambodia, the genocide ended. Pol Pot and the Khmer Rouge were forced to retreat. Communism did not spread any farther in Southeast Asia.

Review Questions
1. What was the domino theory?

_____

_____

2. Who were the Khmer Rouge and what role did they play in Cambodia?

_____

_____

READING CHECK

What was significant about the Tet Offensive?

_____

_____

_____

VOCABULARY STRATEGY

What does the word *terminate* mean in the underlined sentence? Note that the word is a verb. Ask yourself what action President Nixon was being pressured to take. Use this strategy to help you figure out what *terminate* means.

READING SKILL

Summarize Summarize U.S. involvement in Vietnam.

_____

_____

_____

Name_____ Class_____ Date_____

Focus Question: What were the causes and effects of the end of the Cold War?

As you read this section in your textbook, complete this flowchart to help you categorize events connected to the end of the Cold War. Some events have been completed for you.

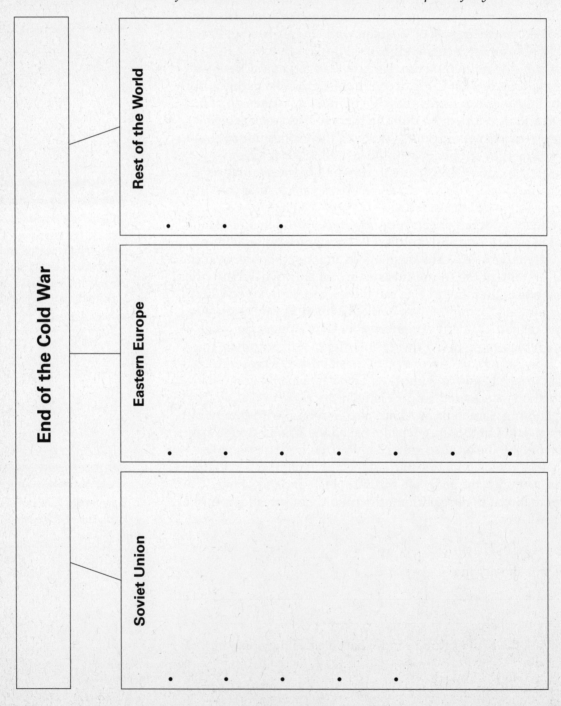

End of the Cold War

Rest of the World

•   •   •

Eastern Europe

•   •   •   •   •   •   •

Soviet Union

•   •   •   •   •

CHAPTER
30
SECTION 5

Section Summary
THE END OF THE COLD WAR

The Soviet Union emerged from World War II as a superpower, with control over many Eastern European countries. For many people, the country's superpower status brought few rewards. Consumer goods were inferior and workers were poorly paid. <u>Because workers had lifetime job security, there was little incentive to produce high-quality goods.</u> Still, there were some important technological successes. One example was *Sputnik I,* the first artificial satellite. Keeping up with the United States in an arms race also strained the economy. Then in 1979, Soviet forces invaded Afghanistan and became involved in a long war. The Soviets had few successes battling the **mujahedin,** or Muslim religious warriors, creating a crisis in morale in the USSR.

Then, new Soviet leader **Mikhail Gorbachev** urged reforms. He called for **glasnost.** He ended censorship and encouraged people to discuss the country's problems. Gorbachev also called for **perestroika,** or a restructuring of the government and economy. His policies, however, fed unrest across the Soviet empire.

Eastern Europeans demanded an end to Soviet rule. Previous attempts to defy the Soviets had failed. When Hungarians and Czechs challenged the communist rulers, military force subdued them. By the end of the 1980s, a powerful democracy movement was sweeping the region. In Poland, **Lech Walesa** led **Solidarity,** an independent, unlawful labor union demanding economic and political changes. When Gorbachev declared he would not interfere in Eastern European reforms, Solidarity was legalized. A year later, Walesa was elected president of Poland.

Meanwhile, East German leaders resisted reform, and thousands of East Germans fled to the West. In Czechoslovakia, **Václav Havel,** a dissident writer, was elected president. One by one, communist governments fell. Most changes happened peacefully, but Romanian dictator **Nicolae Ceausescu** refused to step down and he was executed. The Baltic States regained independence. By the end of 1991, the remaining Soviet republics had all formed independent nations. The Soviet Union ceased to exist after 69 years of communist rule.

In 1992, Czechoslovakia was divided into Slovakia and the Czech Republic. Additionally, some communist governments in Asia, such as China, instituted economic reforms.

Review Questions

1. What kinds of reforms did Gorbachev make?

_____

_____

2. What happened to the Soviet Union by the end of 1991?

_____

_____

READING CHECK

How did the arms race affect the Soviet economy?

_____

_____

_____

VOCABULARY STRATEGY

What does the word *incentive* mean in the underlined sentence? The words *motivation* and *reason* are synonyms of *incentive.* Use these synonyms to help you figure out the meaning of *incentive.*

READING SKILL

Categorize Which leaders mentioned in the summary supported reform and which leaders opposed reform?

_____

_____

_____

Note Taking Study Guide

INDEPENDENT NATIONS OF SOUTH ASIA

Focus Question: What were the consequences of independence in South Asia for the region and for the world?

As you read this section in your textbook, fill in the concept web below to identify causes and effects of events in South Asia.

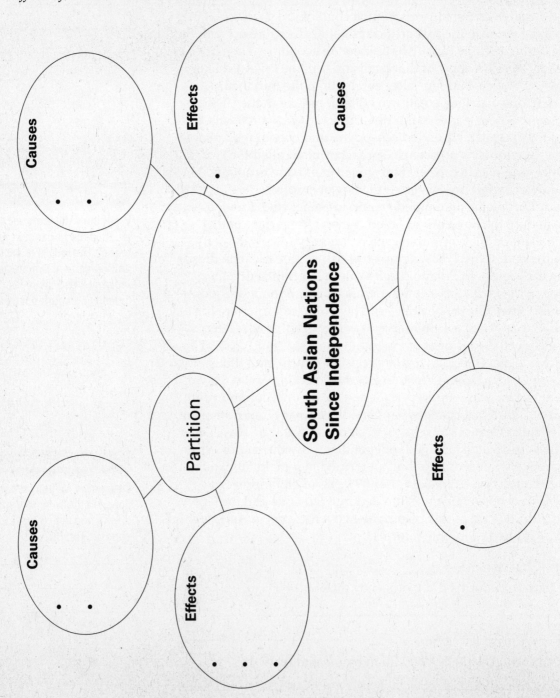

CHAPTER 31 SECTION 1

Section Summary

INDEPENDENT NATIONS OF SOUTH ASIA

In the 1940s, tensions between Hindus and Muslims in India led to violence. The ruling British decided that the only solution was a **partition,** or division, into a Muslim-majority Pakistan and a Hindu-majority India. After Pakistan and India gained their independence in 1947, Hindus in Pakistan fled to India, while Muslims in India fled to Pakistan. As they fled, Muslims, Hindus, and another religious group called **Sikhs** slaughtered one another.

Tensions have continued in the region. India and Pakistan have fought wars over **Kashmir,** a state with Muslim and Hindu populations. When India developed nuclear weapons, Pakistan began its own nuclear weapons program. In the island country of Sri Lanka, a majority are Buddhists. A Tamil-speaking Hindu minority on the island has fought for years for a separate Tamil nation.

In 1947, **Jawaharlal Nehru** became India's first prime minister. He tried to improve living conditions and end discrimination against **dalits,** or outcastes. Nehru's daughter, **Indira Gandhi,** became prime minister in 1966. While she was in office, Sikhs pressed for independence for the state of **Punjab.** In 1984, Sikh separatists occupied the **Golden Temple,** the holiest Sikh shrine. Gandhi sent troops to the temple, and thousands of Sikhs were killed. A few months later, Gandhi's Sikh bodyguards assassinated her.

In 1947, Pakistan was a divided country. A thousand miles separated West Pakistan from East Pakistan. West Pakistan dominated the nation's government. Most people in East Pakistan were Bengalis. They felt their government neglected their region. In 1971, Bengalis declared independence for East Pakistan under the name of **Bangladesh.** Pakistan tried to crush the rebels but was eventually compelled to recognize the independence of Bangladesh.

Pakistan has long lacked political stability. Islamic fundamentalists disagree with those who want a greater separation between religion and government. During the 1980s, the war in Afghanistan drove over a million Afghan refugees into Pakistan. Pakistan's Islamic fundamentalists gained power by forming ties with Afghan refugees.

Despite their differences, India and Pakistan helped organize a conference of newly independent states in 1955. This marked the birth of **nonalignment,** or political and diplomatic independence from the United States or the Soviet Union.

Review Questions

1. Why was Indira Gandhi assassinated?

_____

_____

2. Why did Bengalis want East Pakistan to be independent?

_____

_____

READING CHECK

What is nonalignment?

_____

_____

_____

VOCABULARY STRATEGY

What does the word *compelled* mean in the underlined sentence? *Compel* comes from a Latin word that means "to drive." If you substitute the word "driven" for *compelled* in the underlined sentence, it will help you figure out what *compelled* means.

READING SKILL

Identify Causes and Effects
What caused the British to partition India? What were some of the effects the partition had on Muslims and Hindus?

_____

_____

_____

Focus Question: What challenges did Southeast Asian nations face after winning independence?

As you read this section in your textbook, fill in the concept web below to understand the effects of recent historical processes in Southeast Asia.

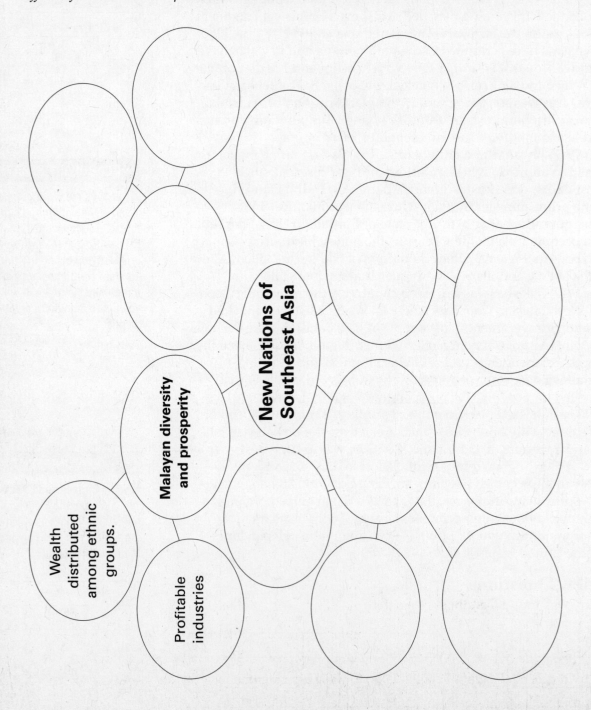

New Nations of Southeast Asia

Malayan diversity and prosperity

Wealth distributed among ethnic groups.

Profitable industries

Section Summary
NEW NATIONS OF SOUTHEAST ASIA

Mainland Southeast Asia is a region of contrasts. Thailand and Malaysia have prospered as market economies. In Malaysia, people of Chinese and Indian descent have made the nation a leader in profitable industries. However, the government has also tried to include the Malay majority in the country's prosperity. By contrast, Myanmar, or Burma, has suffered under an **autocratic** government—a government that has unlimited power. The government has limited foreign trade, and living standards remain low. In 1990, elections were held in Myanmar, and a party that opposed military rule won. It was led by **Aung San Suu Kyi.** However, the military rejected the election results, and Suu Kyi was put under house arrest.

After World War II, Indonesia, formerly the Dutch East Indies, achieved its independence. Indonesia faced many obstacles to its unity. It consists of more than 13,000 islands. Javanese make up almost half of the population, but there are hundreds of ethnic groups. About 90 percent of Indonesians are Muslims, but the population includes Christians, Buddhists, and Hindus. After independence, Indonesia formed a democratic, parliamentary government under its first president, **Sukarno.** In 1966, an army general, **Suharto,** seized power and ruled as a dictator until he was forced to resign in 1998. Religious and ethnic tensions have fueled violence in parts of Indonesia. In 1975, Indonesia seized **East Timor,** a former Portuguese colony. The mostly Catholic East Timorese fought for independence, which they finally achieved in 2002.

In the Philippines, Catholics are the predominant religious group, but there is a Muslim minority in the south. In 1946, the Philippines gained freedom from United States control. Although the Filipino constitution established a democratic government, a wealthy elite controlled politics and the economy. **Ferdinand Marcos,** elected president in 1965, became a dictator and cracked down on basic freedoms. He even had **Benigno Aquino,** a popular rival, murdered. When **Corazon Aquino** was elected in 1986, Marcos tried to deny the results, but the people forced him to resign. Since then, democracy has struggled to survive in the Philippines. Communist and Muslim rebels continue to fight across the country.

Review Questions

1. What happened when Aung San Suu Kyi's party won the 1990 elections in Myanmar?

_____

_____

2. What are some obstacles to Indonesia's unity?

_____

_____

READING CHECK

What are the features of the autocratic government in Myanmar?

_____

_____

_____

VOCABULARY STRATEGY

What does *predominant* mean in the underlined sentence? Note that the second part of the sentence mentions another group that is a minority, or a smaller group. Use this context clue to help you figure out the meaning of *predominant.*

READING SKILL

Understand Effects What was the effect of Ferdinand Marcos' denial of the results of the 1986 election?

_____

_____

_____

Name_____ Class_____ Date_____

Focus Question: What challenges did new African nations face?

As you read this section in your textbook, fill in the concept web below to keep track of the causes and effects of independence in Africa.

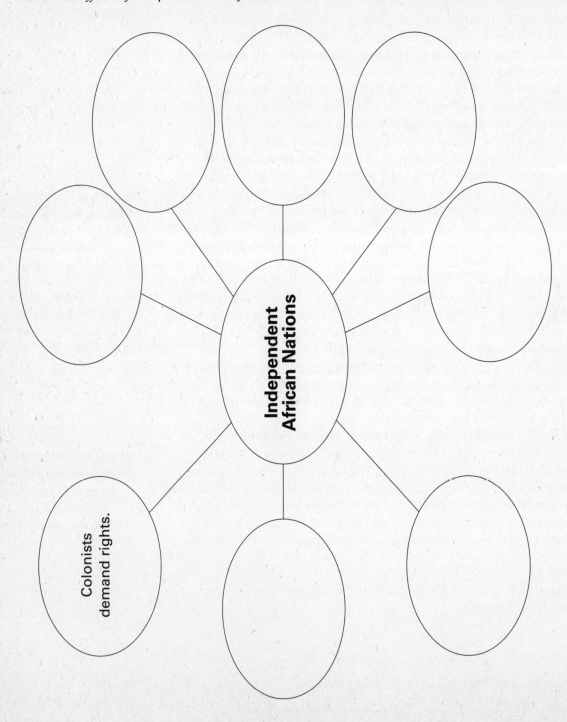

Independent African Nations

Colonists demand rights.

CHAPTER 31 SECTION 3

Section Summary

AFRICAN NATIONS GAIN INDEPENDENCE

Africa is a diverse continent. Vast **savannas,** or grasslands, cover much of it, but there are also rain forests and deserts. Diversity is reflected in the continent's history, people, languages, and traditions.

After World War II, many Africans demanded freedom from European powers. After gaining independence, some African nations enjoyed peace and democracy. Others faced civil wars, military rule, or corrupt dictators. European powers had drawn colonial boundaries without regard for Africa's ethnic groups. This led to ethnic conflict in many new nations once colonial powers withdrew.

In 1957, Gold Coast gained its freedom from Britain and took the name Ghana. The government of its first president, **Kwame Nkrumah,** eventually became corrupt, and Nkrumah was overthrown in a military **coup d'etat.** Other coups followed, but today Ghana is a democracy.

In Kenya, white settlers had passed laws to ensure their domination of the country. In the 1950s, rebels turned to guerrilla warfare, but the British crushed the rebellion. Kenya finally gained its independence in 1963. **Jomo Kenyatta,** a prominent independence leader, became the first president of the new country. In 2002, Kenya's first fair election removed the ruling party from office.

In Algeria, independence from France came only after a long war but was finally achieved in 1962. A coup in 1965 began a long period of military rule. When the government allowed free elections in 1992, an **Islamist** party won. The military rejected the results, and seven years of civil war followed. Although the fighting has ended, the country remains tense.

After the Congo became independent from Belgium, the copper-rich province of **Katanga** rebelled. The United Nations ended the rebellion in 1963. **Mobutu Sese Seko** ruled as a harsh military dictator from 1965 to 1997. Seven years of civil war ended with a cease-fire in 2003.

Nigeria won its independence in 1960, but regional, ethnic, and religious differences soon led to conflict. In 1966, the Ibo people in the southeast declared independence as the Republic of **Biafra.** After three years of fighting, Nigeria's military ended Biafra's independence. A series of dictators then ruled, but Nigeria returned to democracy in 1999.

Review Questions

1. Why was the first president of Ghana overthrown?

_____

_____

2. What country did the Ibo people of Nigeria try to establish?

_____

_____

READING CHECK

What is a coup d'etat?

_____

_____

_____

VOCABULARY STRATEGY

What does the word *ensure* mean in the underlined sentence? The prefix *en-* means to "make" or "cause to be." Think about what the root word, *sure,* means. Use these clues about word parts to help you understand the meaning of *ensure.*

READING SKILL

Identify Causes and Effects
How did past decisions made by European powers cause ethnic conflict in many new African nations?

_____

_____

_____

Name_____ Class_____ Date_____

Focus Question: What are the main similarities and differences among Middle Eastern nations?

As you read this section in your textbook, fill in the concept web below to identify causes and effects of events in the Middle East since 1945.

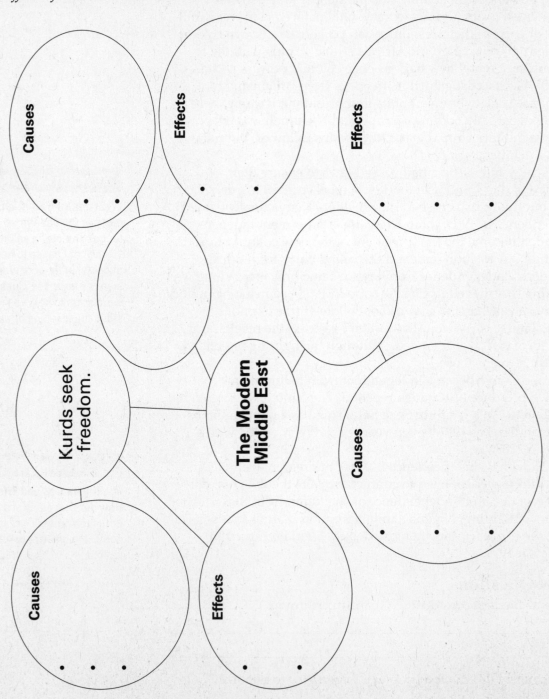

CHAPTER 31 SECTION 4

Section Summary

THE MODERN MIDDLE EAST

Most of the people in the Middle East are Muslims, but there are also Christian communities and the predominantly Jewish nation of Israel. Most countries also have large ethnic or religious minorities. The Kurds are an example of an ethnic minority. They live in Iran, Iraq, Syria, and Turkey and have faced discrimination in each country.

The Holocaust created support for a Jewish homeland after World War II. In 1947, the UN drew up a plan to divide Palestine into an Arab and a Jewish state. In 1948, Jews proclaimed the independent state of Israel. This led to Arab-Israeli conflicts that forced 700,000 Palestinians from their homes. Despite the conflicts, Israel has developed rapidly due to a skilled workforce. Kibbutzim work on what is called a **kibbutz,** or collective farm.

Resources and religion have led to conflicts in the Middle East. The region has the world's largest oil and gas reserves. As a result, it has strategic importance. Some Middle Eastern countries have adopted **secular,** or non-religious, government and laws. However, many Muslim leaders argue that a renewed commitment to Islamic doctrine is needed. In Iran and Saudi Arabia, women are required to wear **hejab,** the traditional Muslim garments.

Egypt, the most populous Arab country, is important because it controls the **Suez Canal.** Under **Gamal Abdel Nasser,** Egypt fought two unsuccessful wars against Israel. His successor, **Anwar Sadat,** made peace with Israel. Islamists were angry about government corruption and the failure to end poverty. In 1981, Sadat was assassinated by Muslim fundamentalists.

In Iran, Shah Mohammad Reza Pahlavi ruled with the support of the United States, which helped oust one of his opponents, **Mohammad Mosaddeq.** The shah's secret police terrorized critics. In the 1970s, the shah's enemies rallied behind Ayatollah **Ruhollah Khomeini.** Protests forced the shah into exile, and Khomeini established an Islamic **theocracy,** or government ruled by religious leaders.

Saudi Arabia has the world's largest oil reserves and is the location of Islam's holy land. Kings from the Sa'ud family have ruled Saudi Arabia since the 1920s. Fundamentalists have criticized the kingdom's close ties to Western nations, and some opponents have adopted violent tactics that threaten to disrupt the Saudi oil industry.

Review Questions

1. What makes the Middle East of strategic importance?

_____

_____

2. Why have some Islamic fundamentalists criticized the Saudis?

_____

_____

READING CHECK

What is a theocracy?

_____

_____

_____

VOCABULARY STRATEGY

What does the word *doctrine* mean in the underlined sentence? The words *policy, dogma,* and *tenet* are all synonyms of doctrine. Use what you may know about these synonyms to help you figure out the meaning of the word *doctrine.*

READING SKILL

Identify Causes and Effects
What effect did the proclamation of an independent state of Israel have on Palestinians?

_____

_____

_____

Name_____ Class_____ Date_____

Focus Question: Why have ethnic and religious conflicts divided some nations?

As you read this section in your textbook, fill in the flowchart below to help you recognize the sequence of events that took place in Northern Ireland, Chechnya, and Yugoslavia.

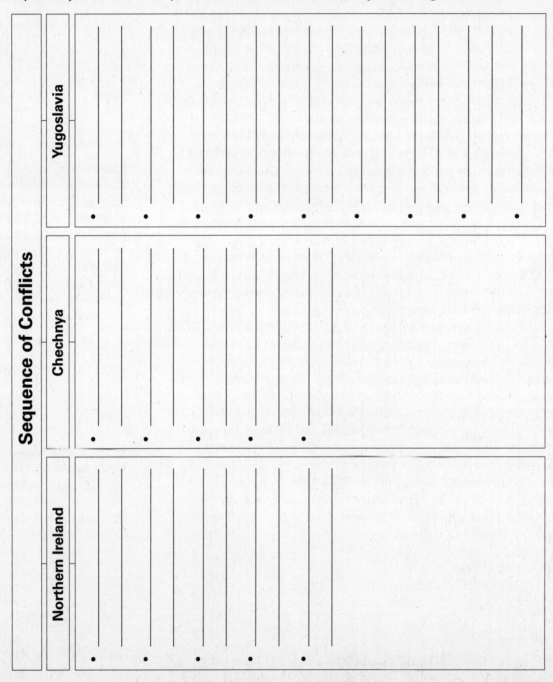

Sequence of Conflicts

Yugoslavia

Chechnya

Northern Ireland

CHAPTER 32 SECTION 1

Section Summary

CONFLICTS DIVIDE NATIONS

In recent decades, many wars and conflicts have arisen over ethnic differences. For example, in Sri Lanka, Sinhalese Buddhists are the majority. Sinhalese nationalists forbade the use of the Tamil language and made Sinhalese the official language. This and other policies led to a civil war between the Buddhists and Tamils. Tamils agreed to a ceasefire when the government agreed to negotiations over a separate Tamil government.

In some countries, however, conflicts have been peacefully resolved. In Canada the democratic government helped prevent French-speaking Quebec from seeking independence.

Northern Ireland was the scene of another long-term conflict. In 1922 the Protestant majority in six northern counties voted to remain part of Britain when Ireland became independent. However, many Catholics in those counties wanted to join with Ireland, which has a Catholic majority. Beginning in the 1960s, extremists on both sides turned to violence. Peace talks dragged on for years. Finally, in 1998, Protestants and Catholics signed the **Good Friday Agreement,** a peace accord.

After the fall of the Soviet Union, many minorities in several former republics wanted independence. For example, ethnic Armenians fought for freedom against Azerbaijanis. The fiercest struggle occurred in **Chechnya,** where Muslim Chechen nationalists fought to free Chechnya from Russian control. Russia crushed a Chechen revolt in the mid-1990s. As a result, many civilians were killed. When a 1997 peace treaty failed, some Chechens turned to terrorism.

Ethnic tensions also tore Yugoslavia apart during the 1990s. Before 1991, Yugoslavia was a **multiethnic,** communist country. The Serbs dominated Yugoslavia, which was controlled by the Communist Party. The fall of communism resulted in nationalist unrest and fighting between Serbs and Croats in Croatia. Soon the fighting spread to neighboring Bosnia. During the war, all sides committed atrocities. In Bosnia, the Serbs conducted a vicious campaign of **ethnic cleansing.** In 1995, the war in Bosnia ended. Then, however, another crisis broke out in the Serbian province of **Kosovo.** In 1989 Serbian president **Slobodan Milosevic** began oppressing Kosovar Albanians. Ten years later, NATO launched air strikes against Serbia. UN and NATO forces eventually restored peace.

Review Questions

1. What two groups are in conflict in Sri Lanka?

_____

_____

2. Why did Chechnya become an area of conflict in Russia?

_____

_____

READING CHECK

In which country did ethnic tensions not lead to war?

_____

_____

_____

VOCABULARY STRATEGY

What does *dominated* mean in the underlined sentence? What clues can you find in the surrounding words, phrases, or sentences? Use these context clues to help you figure out what *dominated* means.

READING SKILL

Recognize Sequence What happened in Ireland after independence to cause conflict?

_____

_____

Name_____ Class_____ Date_____

Note Taking Study Guide

STRUGGLES IN AFRICA

Focus Question: Why have conflicts plagued some African countries?

A. *As you read "South Africa Struggles for Freedom," "South Africa's Neighbors Face Long Conflicts," and "Ethnic Conflicts Kill Millions," record the sequence of events in the conflicts in South Africa and its neighbors.*

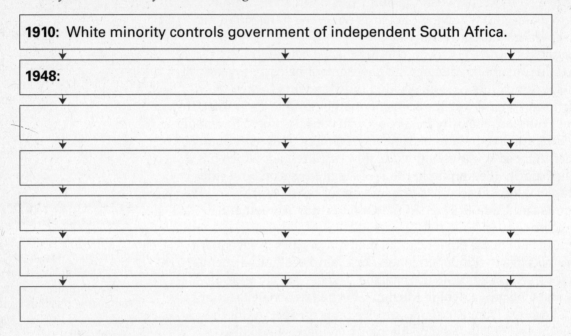

1910: White minority controls government of independent South Africa.
1948:

B. *As you read "Ethnic Conflicts Kill Millions," identify the causes and effects of the conflicts in Rwanda, Sudan, Burundi, and Darfur.*

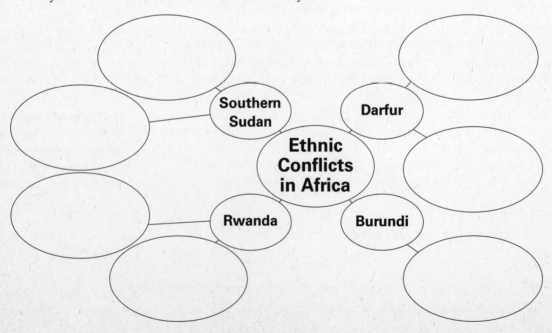

Southern Sudan

Darfur

Ethnic Conflicts in Africa

Rwanda

Burundi

CHAPTER 32 SECTION 2

Section Summary

STRUGGLES IN AFRICA

In the 1950s and 1960s, many new nations won independence in Africa. Several other African nations suffered internal conflicts and civil wars. In 1910, South Africa achieved self-rule from Britain. Most civil rights, however, were limited to white settlers. The black majority had few rights under a legal system of racial segregation called **apartheid.** Under apartheid, nonwhites faced many restrictions. For example, laws banned marriages between races and stipulated segregated restaurants, beaches, and schools.

The **African National Congress (ANC)** opposed apartheid and led the struggle for majority rule. In 1960 police gunned down 69 people during a protest in **Sharpeville,** a black township. The government then outlawed the ANC. **Nelson Mandela,** an ANC leader, was sentenced to life imprisonment.

In the 1980s, international demands for an end to apartheid and for Mandela's release increased. In 1984, Bishop **Desmond Tutu** won the Nobel Peace Prize for his nonviolent opposition to apartheid. In 1990, South African president **F.W. de Klerk** ended apartheid and freed Mandela, who was elected president in 1994.

South Africa's neighbors also experienced long conflicts to attain independence. Portugal granted independence to Angola and Mozambique in 1975. South Africa and the United States saw the new nations as threats because some liberation leaders had ties to the ANC or the Soviet Union.

After independence, ethnic conflicts plagued many nations. Historic resentments divided nations, and regional rivalries fed ethnic violence. In Rwanda, one of Africa's deadliest wars occurred. There, the **Hutus** were the majority, but the minority **Tutsis** dominated the country. In 1994, extremist Hutus slaughtered about 800,000 Tutsis and moderate Hutus. Another 3 million Rwandans lost their homes. In response, world leaders pledged to stop genocide wherever it may occur. Their power to do this, however, was limited. In Sudan, non-Muslim, non-Arab rebels in the south battled Arab Muslims from the north. This war, drought, and famine caused millions of deaths. Finally, southern rebels signed a peace agreement in 2004. In the same year, however, ethnic conflict spread to Darfur in western Sudan. This conflict raised fears of a new genocide.

Review Questions

1. Describe conditions under apartheid in South Africa.

_____

_____

2. What led to deadly war in Rwanda?

_____

_____

READING CHECK

Which two African countries gained independence from Portugal?

_____

_____

_____

VOCABULARY STRATEGY

What does the word *stipulated* mean in the underlined sentence? Note that *stipulated* refers to laws. The previous sentence has a reference to restrictions that non-whites faced. Use these context clues to help you understand the meaning of the word *stipulated*.

READING SKILL

Recognize Sequence Did the South African government outlaw the ANC before or after the protest in Sharpeville?

_____

_____

_____

<table>
<tr><td>CHAPTER
32
SECTION 3</td><td>## Note Taking Study Guide
CONFLICTS IN THE MIDDLE EAST</td></tr>
</table>

Focus Question: What are the causes of conflict in the Middle East?

As you read the section in your textbook, use the flowchart to record the sequence of events relating to the conflicts in the Middle East.

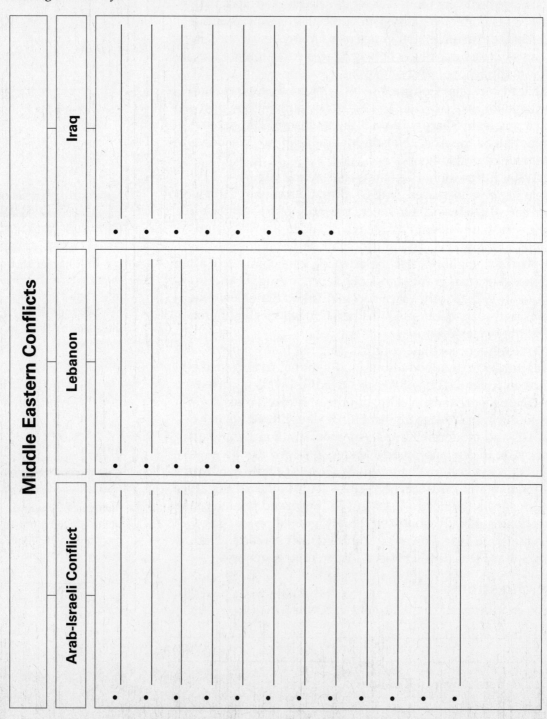

CHAPTER
32
SECTION 3

Section Summary
CONFLICTS IN THE MIDDLE EAST

For decades, the Middle East has been the location of conflict. Modern Israel was created in 1948 on land that had belonged to Palestinian Arabs. As a result, there has been repeated war and violence. In several wars against Egypt and others, Israel gained more land. This is called the **occupied territories.**

The Palestine Liberation Organization, led by **Yasir Arafat,** fought against the Israelis. In the occupied territories, Palestinians launched uprisings called **intifadas.** In addition, suicide bombers spread terror inside Israel. The Israelis responded with armed force, and Palestinian bitterness increased. Leaders, such as Israeli Prime Minister **Yitzhak Rabin,** pushed for peace. There were many stumbling blocks, however, such as disagreements over **Jerusalem,** a city sacred to Jews, Christians, and Muslims. During the early 2000s, new steps toward peace offered some hope, but serious obstacles remained.

Lebanon is home to diverse ethnic and religious groups. The government depended on a delicate balance among Arab Christians, Sunni Muslims, Shiite Muslims, and Druze. In 1975, Christian and Muslim **militias** battled each other, and both Israel and Syria invaded. By 1990, however, peace had been restored.

Conflicts also plagued Iraq. Iraq's Sunni Muslim minority dominated the country for centuries. The Kurdish minority and Shiite Muslim majority were excluded from power. In 1979 **Saddam Hussein** took power as a dictator. He fought a prolonged war against neighboring Iran in the 1980s. In 1990, Iraq invaded Kuwait. In response, the United States led a coalition against that invasion. In the Gulf War that ensued, Kuwait was liberated and Iraqi forces were crushed. Saddam Hussein remained in power and used terror to impose his will. The United States, France, and Britain set up **no-fly zones** to protect the Kurds and Shiites. The UN worked to keep Saddam Hussein from building biological, nuclear, or chemical weapons, called **weapons of mass destruction (WMDs).**

In 2003, the United States led a coalition that invaded Iraq and overthrew Saddam Hussein. Iraqi **insurgents** fought against the occupation that followed. In 2005, national elections were held for the first time.

Review Questions
1. How did Israel come to control the occupied territories?

_____

_____

2. What were the results of the Gulf War in 1990?

_____

_____

READING CHECK

Which groups in Iraq were excluded from power?

_____

_____

_____

VOCABULARY STRATEGY

What does the word *diverse* mean in the underlined sentence? Notice how in the next sentence four ethnic groups are mentioned. Use this context clue to help you understand the meaning of *diverse.*

READING SKILL

Recognize Sequence Circle the phrase in the sentence below that signals sequence.

In 1990, Iraq invaded Kuwait. In response, the United States led a coalition against the invasion.

Name_____ Class_____ Date_____

Focus Question: How have the nations of the developing world tried to build better lives for their people?

As you read this section in your textbook, complete the chart below with supporting details from the text about economic development and developing countries.

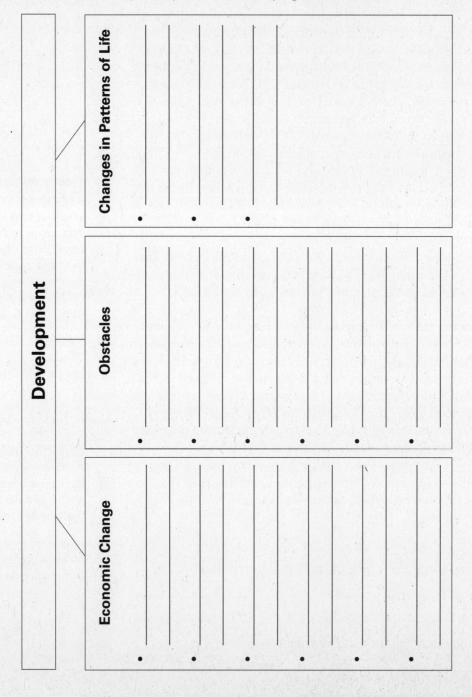

CHAPTER 33 SECTION 1

Section Summary
THE CHALLENGES OF DEVELOPMENT

After World War II, a central goal in Africa, Asia, and Latin America was **development,** or creating a more advanced economy and higher living standards. Nations that are working toward this are referred to as the **developing world.** They are also called the global South, because most of these nations are south of the Tropic of Cancer. Most industrialized nations are north of the Tropic of Cancer, so they are sometimes called the global North. Nations of the global South have tried to develop economically by improving their agriculture and industry. They have also built schools to increase **literacy.**

To pay for development, many countries in the global South procured large loans from industrialized nations. For centuries, most people in the global South had lived and worked in **traditional economies.** After gaining independence from European colonists, some of these countries experimented with government-led command economies. However, when these countries had trouble paying off their loans, lenders from the global North required many of them to change to market economies. Now many developing nations depend on the global North for investment and exports.

Beginning in the 1950s, improved seeds, pesticides, and mechanical equipment led to a **Green Revolution** in many parts of the developing world. This increased agricultural production, feeding many more people. It also benefited large landowners at the expense of small farmers. These farmers sold their land and moved to cities.

The global South still faces many challenges. Some developing nations produce only one export product. If prices for that product drop, their economies suffer. Also, the population in many of these countries has grown rapidly. Many people are caught in a cycle of poverty. When families are forced to move to cities, they often find only low-paying jobs. As a result, many children must work to help support their families. With so many moving to cities, many people are forced to live in crowded and dangerous **shantytowns.**

Economic development has brought great changes to the developing world. In many countries, women have greater equality. However, some religious **fundamentalists** oppose these changes and have called for a return to the basic values of their faiths.

Review Questions

1. What happened when nations in the global South had trouble repaying their loans?

_____

_____

2. What problems do people in the developing world often face when they move to cities?

_____

_____

READING CHECK

What is development?

_____

_____

_____

VOCABULARY STRATEGY

What does the word *procured* mean in the underlined sentence? Notice that *procured* refers to loans. Use this clue to help you figure out the meaning of the word *procured*.

READING SKILL

Identify Supporting Details
Record details that support this statement: "The global South faces many challenges."

_____

_____

_____

Name_____ Class_____ Date_____

Focus Question: What challenges have African nations faced in their effort to develop their economies?

As you read this section in your textbook, complete the concept web below to record the main ideas about challenges faced by African nations, and details that support those main ideas.

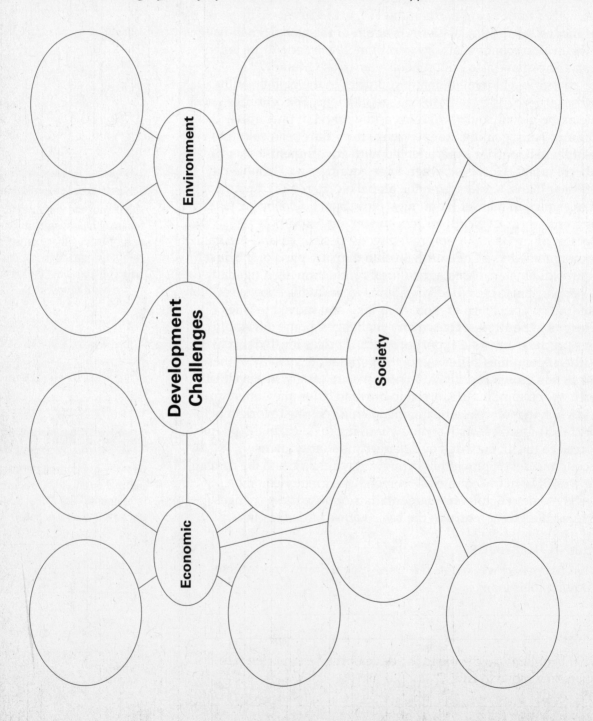

CHAPTER 33 SECTION 2

Section Summary

AFRICA SEEKS A BETTER FUTURE

After World War II, African nations had little capital to invest, so they had to make difficult economic choices. Some nations chose **socialism,** a system in which the government controls parts of the economy. The leaders of these governments hoped to end foreign influence in their countries and to close the gap between the rich and the poor. However, socialism sometimes led to large, inefficient bureaucracies. Other nations relied on capitalism, or market economies. These economies were often more efficient, but foreign owners of businesses took profits out of the country. Some governments tried to fund development by growing crops for export, rather than food crops. However, this forced them to import food to replace the food crops. <u>Governments then had to subsidize part of the cost of importing food from overseas.</u>

African nations faced many obstacles to development. Droughts led to famine in parts of Africa. This was especially true in the Sahel, where overgrazing and farming led to **desertification.** People in African nations also faced the devastating disease AIDS. In the early 2000s, more than 2 million Africans died of the disease each year. **Urbanization** has also created problems in Africa. This shift from rural areas to cities has meant hardship for many and has weakened traditional cultures and ethnic ties. However, in West Africa, the growth of urban markets has increased opportunities for women.

Another concern in Africa is environmental threats. Nearly 70 percent of Africa's animal habitats have been destroyed, causing many animals to become **endangered species.** Other animal species are being killed for their tusks or fur. One environmental activist, **Wangari Maathai,** has fought back by starting the Green Belt Movement. This organization promotes reforestation. It also helps local women with projects of **sustainable development** that aim to provide lasting benefits for future generations.

A close look at Tanzania reveals the problems that many African counties have faced. In the 1960s, the government embraced "African socialism." However, attempts to build on African traditions of cooperation failed to increase agricultural production. In 1985, new leaders introduced economic reforms. However, Tanzania remains poor and has had to rely on foreign loans to avoid economic crisis.

Review Questions

1. Why did some African nations choose socialism?

_____

_____

2. Why are many animal species in Africa endangered?

_____

_____

READING CHECK

What is urbanization?

_____

_____

_____

VOCABULARY STRATEGY

What does the word *subsidize* mean in the underlined sentence? *Subsidize* comes from a Latin word that means "aid" or "support." Use this clue to help you figure out the meaning of the word *subsidize.*

READING SKILL

Identify Main Ideas What is the main idea of this Summary?

_____

_____

_____

CHAPTER 33 SECTION 3 — Note Taking Study Guide

CHINA AND INDIA: TWO GIANTS OF ASIA

Focus Question: How do China and India compare in building strong economies and democratic governments?

As you read this section in your textbook, complete the table below to record the main ideas about reform and change in China and India.

Reform and Change in China and India

Type	China	India
Economic	• Free market • _____ • _____ • _____ • _____ • _____ • _____ • _____	• _____ • _____ • _____ • _____ • _____
Political	• _____ • _____ • _____	• _____ • _____ • _____

CHAPTER 33 SECTION 3

Section Summary

CHINA AND INDIA: TWO GIANTS OF ASIA

After Mao Zedong died, moderate leaders took control of China. **Deng Xiaoping** began a program called the Four Modernizations, which allowed some features of a free-market economy. Some private ownership of property was permitted, and entrepreneurs could set up businesses. Farmers were allowed to sell surplus produce and keep the profits. Foreign investment was also welcomed. These reforms brought a surge of economic growth, although a gap developed between poor farmers and wealthy city dwellers. After 30 years of reforms, China's economic output quadrupled.

Despite these economic reforms, however, Communist leaders refused to allow more political freedom. Demonstrators seeking democratic reforms occupied **Tiananmen Square** in Beijing in May 1989. When the demonstrators refused to disperse, the government sent in troops and tanks. Thousands were killed or wounded.

China continues to face many challenges. Its population is the largest in the world. The government started the **one-child policy** to prevent population growth from hurting economic development. Population growth slowed. Many rural workers have moved to cities, but they often live in poverty there. Pollution and HIV/AIDS are also problems. Critics of the government are jailed, and human rights abuses continue.

By contrast, India is the world's largest democracy. After gaining independence, India's government adopted a command economy, but development was uneven. The Green Revolution in the 1960s improved crop output, but most farmers continued to use traditional methods. In the 1980s, India shifted toward a free-market system. By the 1990s, several Indian industries were expanding rapidly.

Despite these improvements, India's population growth has hurt efforts to improve living conditions. The Indian government backed family planning, but it had limited success. More than one-third of Indians live below the poverty line. Many rural families moved to overcrowded cities like **Kolkata** and **Mumbai.** To help the urban poor, **Mother Teresa** founded the Missionaries of Charity.

Changes in India have brought improvements for India's lowest social castes and women. India's constitution bans discrimination against **dalits**, people in the lowest caste, but prejudice persists. The constitution also grants equal rights to women.

Review Questions

1. What impact have economic reforms had in China?

_____

_____

2. Name two groups that have benefited from changes in India.

_____

_____

READING CHECK

Which country, India or China, has had more success in limiting population growth?

_____

_____

_____

VOCABULARY STRATEGY

What does the word *disperse* mean in the underlined sentence? Notice that demonstrators occupied, or gathered in, Tiananmen Square and then refused to *disperse*. Use this clue to help you figure out the meaning of the word *disperse*.

READING SKILL

Identify Main Ideas In your own words, write the main idea of the first paragraph of this Summary.

_____

_____

_____

CHAPTER
33
SECTION 4

Note Taking Study Guide
LATIN AMERICA BUILDS DEMOCRACY

Focus Question: What challenges have Latin American nations faced in recent decades in their struggle for democracy and prosperity?

As you read this section in your textbook, complete this outline to identify the main ideas and supporting details about challenges faced by Latin American nations.

I. Economic and Social Forces
- **A.** Society
  - **1.** _____
  - **2.** _____
  - **3.** _____
  - **4.** _____
- **B.** _____
  - **1.** _____
  - **2.** _____
  - **3.** _____
  - **4.** _____

II. _____
- **A.** _____
  - **1.** _____
  - **2.** _____
  - **3.** _____
- **B.** _____
  - **1.** _____
  - **2.** _____
- **C.** _____
  - **1.** _____
  - **2.** _____
  - **3.** _____
  - **4.** _____
  - **5.** _____
  - **6.** _____
  - **7.** _____

(Outline continues on the next page.)

(Continued from page 304)

D. _____
  1. _____
  2. _____
E. _____
  1. _____
  2. _____

III. _____
  A. _____
    1. _____
    2. _____
  B. _____
    1. _____
    2. _____
    3. _____
    4. _____
    5. _____

CHAPTER 33 SECTION 4

Section Summary
LATIN AMERICA BUILDS DEMOCRACY

READING CHECK

What is liberation theology?

_____

_____

_____

VOCABULARY STRATEGY

What does the word *alleged* mean in the underlined sentence? This verb is often used in legal proceedings. The noun form is *allegation*. An *allegation* is "an assertion made without proof." Use these clues to help you understand the meaning of *alleged*.

READING SKILL

Identify Main Ideas and Supporting Details Outline the last paragraph in the Summary on the lines below.

_____

_____

_____

_____

_____

In the 1950s and 1960s, many governments in Latin America encouraged industries to manufacture goods that had previously been imported. This is called **import substitution.** More recently, government policies have focused on producing goods for export. Governments have also tried to open more land to farming, but much of the best land belongs to large **agribusinesses.** In many countries, a few people control the land and businesses, and wealth is distributed unevenly. Another problem is population growth, which has contributed to poverty. Many religious leaders have worked for justice and an end to poverty in a movement known as **liberation theology.**

Because of poverty and inequality, democracy has been difficult to achieve in Latin America. Between the 1950s and 1970s, military leaders seized power in Argentina, Brazil, Chile, and other countries. From the 1960s to the 1990s, civil wars shook parts of Central America. In Guatemala, the military targeted the **indigenous** population and slaughtered thousands of Native Americans.

The United States has had a powerful influence in Latin America. It has dominated the **Organization of American States (OAS).** During the Cold War, the United States backed dictators who were anti-communist. When socialist rebels called **Sandinistas** came to power in Nicaragua, the United States supported the **contras,** guerrillas who fought the Sandinistas. The United States has also pressed Latin American governments to help stop the drug trade. <u>Many Latin Americans alleged that the problem was not in Latin America but was based on the demand for drugs in the United States.</u>

By the 1990s, democratic reforms led to free elections in many countries. In Mexico, the Institutional Revolutionary Party (PRI) had dominated the government since the 1920s. However, in 2000, an opposition candidate was elected president. Argentina experienced 50 years of political upheavals beginning in the 1930s. **Juan Perón,** Argentina's president from 1946 to 1955, enjoyed great support from workers but was ousted in a military coup. The military seized control again in 1976 and murdered or kidnapped thousands. Mothers whose sons and daughters were missing protested and became known as the **Mothers of the Plaza de Mayo.** By 1983, the military was forced to allow elections.

Review Questions

1. Why was democracy difficult to achieve in Latin America?

_____

_____

2. Why did the United States support dictators in Latin America during the Cold War?

_____

_____

<table>
<tr><td>CHAPTER
34
SECTION 1</td><td># Note Taking Study Guide
INDUSTRIALIZED NATIONS AFTER THE COLD WAR</td></tr>
</table>

Focus Question: How did the end of the Cold War affect industrialized nations and regions around the world?

As you read this section in your textbook, complete the chart below to compare and contrast developments in industrialized nations after the Cold War.

Asia	
Russia/United States	Russia •___ •___ •___ •___ United States •___ •___ •___
Europe	• 1991 — Germany is reunified. •___ •___ •___ •___ •___

Section Summary
INDUSTRIALIZED NATIONS AFTER THE COLD WAR

READING CHECK

Which four Pacific Rim countries are called the "Asian tigers"?

_____

_____

_____

VOCABULARY STRATEGY

What does the word *inflation* mean in the underlined sentence? Think about what happens when you *inflate* a tire. In this sentence, *inflation* refers to prices. If prices are *inflated,* would you expect them to be higher or lower? Use these clues to help you understand the meaning of *inflation.*

READING SKILL

Compare and Contrast Compare and contrast the U.S. economy in the early 1990s with the economy in the early 2000s.

_____

_____

_____

The beginning of a new global economy began with the end of the Cold War. The division between communist Eastern and democratic Western Europe crumbled. Business and travel became easier. At the same time, new challenges emerged, including a rise in unemployment and in immigration from the developing world. One exciting change was the reunification of Germany. However, East Germany's economy was weak and had to be modernized.

In the 1990s, the European Economic Community became the **European Union** (EU). The **euro** soon became the common currency for most of Western Europe. By the early 2000s, more than a dozen countries had joined the EU, including some Eastern European nations. The expanded EU allowed Europe to compete economically with the United States and Japan. However, older members of the EU worried that the weak economies of Eastern European nations might harm the EU. Most Eastern European nations wanted to join NATO, too.

After the breakup of the Soviet Union, Russia struggled to forge a market economy. Unemployment and prices soared, and criminals flourished. In 1998, Russia **defaulted** on much of its foreign debt. High inflation and the collapse of the Russian currency forced banks and businesses to close. When **Vladimir Putin** became president in 2000, he promised to end corruption and strengthen Russia's economy. However, he also increased government power at the expense of civil liberties.

After the Cold War, the United States became the world's only superpower. It waged wars in the Middle East and started peacekeeping operations in Haiti and the former Yugoslavia. An economic boom in the 1990s produced a budget **surplus** in the United States. Within a decade, however, slow economic growth and soaring military expenses led to huge budget **deficits.**

The **Pacific Rim** nations have become a rising force in the global economy. Following World War II, Japan became an economic powerhouse and dominated this region. However, by the 1990s, Japan's economy began to suffer, and Taiwan, Hong Kong, Singapore, and South Korea surged ahead. These "Asian tigers" have achieved economic success, due in part to low wages, long hours, and other worker sacrifices.

Review Questions

1. When did the global economy begin to develop?

_____

_____

2. What economic challenges did Russia face after the breakup of the Soviet Union?

_____

_____

Name_____ Class_____ Date_____

Focus Question: How is globalization affecting economies and societies around the world?

As you read this section in your textbook, use the Venn diagram to compare the effects of globalization on developed and developing nations.

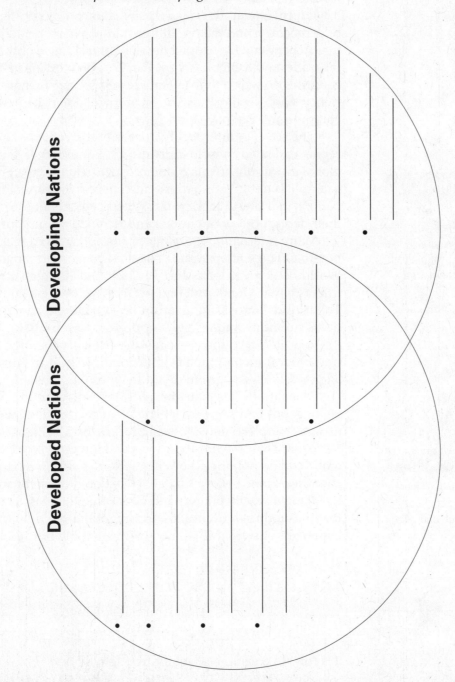

CHAPTER 34 SECTION 2

Section Summary
GLOBALIZATION

READING CHECK

What is globalization?

_____

_____

_____

VOCABULARY STRATEGY

What does the word *assets* mean in the underlined sentence? Think about what it means if someone says that you are an *asset* to the team. Use this clue to help you figure out the meaning of *assets*.

READING SKILL

Compare and Contrast Compare and contrast the effect of borrowing capital on rich and poor nations.

_____

_____

_____

Globalization defines the post-Cold War world. It is the process by which national economies, politics, and cultures become integrated with those of other nations. One effect of globalization is economic **interdependence.** This means that countries depend on one another for goods, resources, knowledge, and labor.

Improvements in transportation and communication, the spread of democracy, and the rise of free trade have made the world more interdependent. Developed nations control much of the world's capital, trade, and technology. Yet they rely on workers in developing countries, to which they **outsource** jobs to save money or increase efficiency. Globalization has also encouraged the rise of **multinational corporations** that have branches and assets in many countries.

One effect of interdependence is that an economic crisis in one region can have a worldwide impact. For example, any change to the global oil supply affects economies all around the world. Another example is debt. Poor nations need to borrow capital from rich nations in order to modernize. When poor nations cannot repay their debts, both poor nations and rich nations are hurt.

Many international organizations and treaties make global trade possible. The United Nations deals with a broad range of issues. The World Bank gives loans and advice to developing nations. The International Monetary Fund promotes global economic growth. The **World Trade Organization (WTO)** tries to ensure that trade flows smoothly and freely. It opposes **protectionism**—the use of tariffs to protect a country's industries from competition. Regional trade **blocs,** such as the EU in Europe, NAFTA in North America, and APEC in Asia, promote trade within regions.

Global trade has many benefits. It brings consumers a greater variety of goods and services. It generally keeps prices lower. It also exposes people to new ideas and technology. Nations involved in free trade often become more democratic. However, some people oppose globalization of trade. They claim that rich countries exploit poor countries. Some believe that globalization hurts indigenous peoples by taking away their lands and disrupting their cultures. Others say that the emphasis on profits encourages too-rapid development. This endangers **sustainability,** thereby threatening future generations.

Review Questions

1. What is the goal of the World Trade Organization?

_____

_____

2. How do consumers benefit from global trade?

_____

_____

Note Taking Study Guide

SOCIAL AND ENVIRONMENTAL CHALLENGES

Focus Question: How do poverty, disease, and environmental challenges affect people around the world today?

As you read this section in your textbook, complete the chart below to compare aspects of globalization.

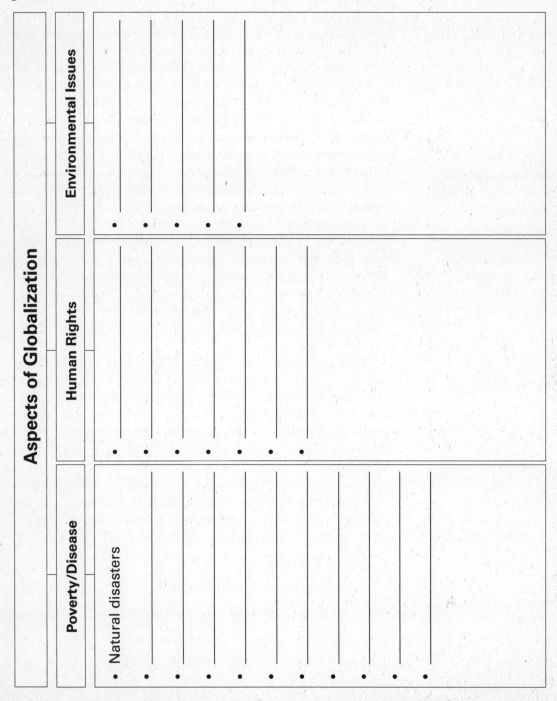

Aspects of Globalization

Environmental Issues

• • • • •

Human Rights

• • • • • • • •

Poverty/Disease

Natural disasters

• • • • • • • • • •

CHAPTER **34** SECTION 3	**Section Summary**
	SOCIAL AND ENVIRONMENTAL CHALLENGES

What is an epidemic?

_____

_____

_____

What does the word *inhibit* mean in the underlined sentence? The words *help* and *aid* are antonyms of *inhibit*. Use what you know about these antonyms to help you understand the meaning of the word *inhibit.*

Compare Compare the two theories about global warming mentioned in the Summary.

_____

_____

_____

Poverty, disasters, and disease are still challenges today. The gap between rich and poor nations is growing. Half the world's population earns less than $2 a day. Poverty is a complex issue with many causes. Many poor nations owe billions in debt and have little money to spend to improve living conditions. Political upheavals, civil war, corruption and poor planning inhibit efforts to reduce poverty. Rapid population growth and urbanization also contribute to poverty.

Natural disasters cause death and destruction around the world. One example is the **tsunami** in the Indian Ocean in 2004. Other natural disasters include earthquakes, floods, avalanches, droughts, fires, hurricanes, and volcanic eruptions. Natural disasters can cause unsanitary conditions that lead to disease. Global travel makes it possible for diseases to spread quickly. When a disease spreads rapidly, it is called an **epidemic.** HIV/AIDS is an epidemic that has killed millions. Natural disasters can also cause **famine.** Wars and problems with food distribution also contribute to famine. Poverty, disasters, and wars have forced many people to become **refugees.**

International agreements, such as the Universal Declaration of Human Rights and the Helsinki Accords, have tried to guarantee basic human rights around the world. However, human rights abuses continue. Women in both the developed and developing world often lack equal rights. Worldwide, children suffer terrible abuses. In some nations, they are forced to serve as soldiers or slaves. Indigenous people around the world also face discrimination and exploitation.

Industrialization and the world population explosion have caused damage to the environment. Strip mining, chemical pesticides and fertilizers, and oil spills are all environmental threats. Gases from power plants and factories produce **acid rain.** Pollution from nuclear power plants is another threat. Desertification and **deforestation** are major problems in certain parts of the world. Deforestation can lead to **erosion** and is a special threat to the rain forests. One hotly debated issue is **global warming.** Many scientists believe that Earth's temperature has risen because of gases released during the burning of fossil fuels. Others argue that global warming is due to natural fluctuations in Earth's climate.

Review Questions

1. What are some causes of poverty?

_____

_____

2. What environmental problem is a special threat to the rain forests?

_____

_____

CHAPTER 34
SECTION 4

Note Taking Study Guide
SECURITY IN A DANGEROUS WORLD

Focus Question: What kinds of threats to national and global security do nations face today?

As you read this section in your textbook, complete the chart below to compare threats to global security.

Threats to Security					
Nuclear Weapons	Nuclear weapons are unsecured in Soviet Union.				

CHAPTER 34 · SECTION 4

Section Summary

SECURITY IN A DANGEROUS WORLD

What is terrorism?

_____

_____

_____

What does the word *priority* mean in the underlined sentence? Notice the sentence that follows it. What did the United States do because security was a *priority?* Use this context clue to help you understand the meaning of the word *priority.*

Compare and Contrast Compare and contrast information about nuclear weapons before and after the Nuclear Nonproliferation Treaty.

_____

_____

_____

Weapons of mass destruction (WMDs) include nuclear, biological, and chemical weapons. During the Cold War, the United States and Russia built up arsenals of nuclear weapons. To ensure that nuclear weapons did not **proliferate,** or spread rapidly, many nations signed the Nuclear Nonproliferation Treaty (NPT) in 1968. However, the treaty does not guarantee that nuclear weapons will not be used. Four nations have not signed the treaty, and other nations, such as Iran and North Korea, are suspected of buying and selling nuclear weapons even though they are treaty members. Stockpiles of nuclear weapons in the former Soviet Union are a special concern. This is because the Russian government has not had money to secure the weapons properly.

In the 2000s, terrorist groups and "rogue states" began to use WMDs for their own purposes. **Terrorism** is the use of violence, especially against civilians, to achieve political goals. Terrorist groups use headline-grabbing tactics to draw attention to their demands. Regional terrorist groups, such as the Irish Republican Army (IRA), operated for decades. They commit bombings, shootings, and kidnappings to force their governments to change policies. Increasingly, the Middle East has become a training ground and source for terrorism. Islamic fundamentalism motivates many of these groups. One powerful Islamic fundamentalist group is **al Qaeda,** whose leader is Osama bin Laden. Al Qaeda terrorists were responsible for the attacks on the United States on September 11, 2001.

Al Qaeda's attacks triggered a global reaction. Fighting terrorism became a central goal of both national and international policies. In 2001, Osama bin Laden and other al Qaeda leaders were living in **Afghanistan.** When Afghanistan's Islamic fundamentalist leaders, the **Taliban,** refused to surrender the terrorists, the United States attacked Afghanistan and overthrew them. Because President Bush believed that Saddam Hussein of Iraq was secretly producing WMDs, the United States also declared war on Iraq. In addition, increased security at home became a priority. As a result, the United States created a new Department of Homeland Security and instituted more rigorous security measures at airports and public buildings.

Review Questions

1. Why are nuclear weapons in the former Soviet Union a special concern?

_____

_____

2. Why did the United States declare war on Iraq?

_____

_____

Note Taking Study Guide
ADVANCES IN SCIENCE AND TECHNOLOGY

Focus Question: How have advances in science and technology shaped the modern world?

As you read this section in your textbook, complete the chart below to compare the impacts of modern science and technology.

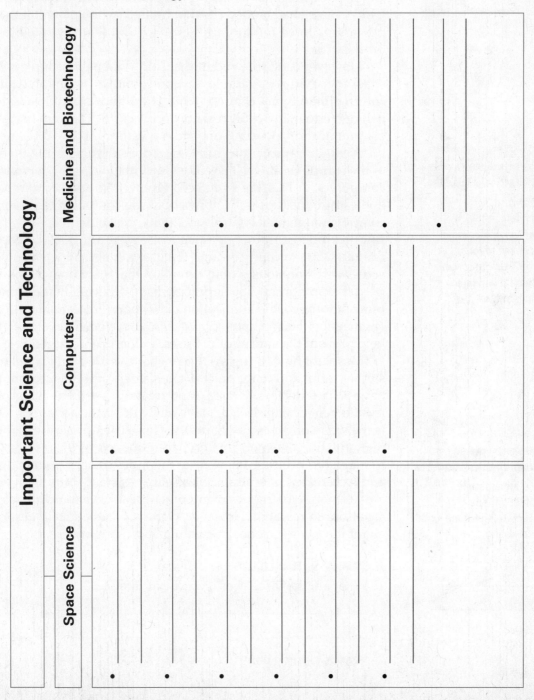

Important Science and Technology

- Medicine and Biotechnology
- Computers
- Space Science

CHAPTER 34 SECTION 5

Section Summary
ADVANCES IN SCIENCE AND TECHNOLOGY

READING CHECK

What is biotechnology?

_____

_____

_____

Since 1945, scientific research and technological developments have transformed human existence. One example is the exploration of space. During the Cold War, the United States and the Soviet Union competed in a "space race." This began in 1957 when the Soviet Union launched *Sputnik,* the first **artificial satellite.** By 1969, the United States had landed the first human on the moon. Both superpowers explored military uses of space and sent spy satellites to orbit Earth.

However, since the end of the Cold War, nations have worked in space together. For example, several countries are involved in the **International Space Station (ISS).** Thousands of artificial satellites belonging to many countries now orbit Earth. They are used for communication, observation, and navigation.

Another important technological development is the invention of the computer. It has led to the "Information Age." **Personal computers**, or **PCs**, have replaced typewriters and account books in homes and businesses. Factories now use computerized robots, and computers remotely control satellites and probes in space. The **Internet** links computer systems worldwide and allows people to communicate instantly around the globe. It also allows people to access vast storehouses of information that were unavailable before.

VOCABULARY STRATEGY

What does the word *manipulation* mean in the underlined sentence? It comes from the Latin word *manus,* meaning "hand." Use this word-origins clue to help you figure out the meaning of the word *manipulation.*

Other important developments have occurred in medicine and **biotechnology**—the application of biological research to industry, engineering, and technology. Vaccines have been developed that help prevent the spread of diseases. In the 1970s, surgeons learned to transplant human organs. **Lasers** have made many types of surgery safer and more precise. Computers and other technologies have helped doctors diagnose and treat diseases. The fields of genetics and genetic engineering have made dramatic advances. **Genetics** is the study of genes and heredity. <u>Genetic engineering is the manipulation of genetic material to produce specific results.</u> Genetic research has produced new drug therapies to fight human diseases and has created new strains of disease-resistant fruits and vegetables. Genetic cloning has many practical applications in raising livestock and in research. However, cloning raises ethical questions about the role of science in creating and changing life.

READING SKILL

Compare How have people benefited from advances in science and technology since the space race began?

_____

_____

_____

Review Questions

1. What are the three uses of artificial satellites?

_____

_____

2. Why is cloning controversial?

_____

_____

Concept Connector Study Guide

Belief Systems

Essential Question: What major belief systems have emerged over time?

A. Define *belief system.* _____

_____

_____

B. *Record information about the topics listed in the Cumulative Review or your answers to the questions in the Cumulative Review below. Use the Concept Connector Handbooks at the end of your textbook, as well as chapter information, to complete this worksheet.*

1. Animism (Chapter 1, page 25)

_____

_____

_____

_____

2. Judaism (Chapter 2, page 49)

_____

_____

_____

_____

_____

3. The Influence of Religion on Ancient Egyptian and Ancient Israelite Society
(Chapter 2, page 63)

_____

_____

_____

_____

4. Compare the Views of Ancient Egyptians and Ancient Indians
(Chapter 3, page 109)

_____

_____

_____

_____

_____

Concept Connector Study Guide

BELIEF SYSTEMS *(continued)*

5. Christianity (Chapter 5, page 181)

_____

_____

_____

_____

_____

6. The Great Schism (Chapter 9, page 299)

_____

_____

_____

_____

_____

7. Muhammad and the Idea of Brotherhood (Chapter 10, page 335)

_____

_____

_____

_____

_____

8. Shinto (Chapter 12, page 403)

_____

_____

_____

_____

_____

9. Impact of Missionaries (Chapter 24, page 779)

_____

_____

_____

_____

_____

Concept Connector Study Guide
BELIEF SYSTEMS *(continued)*

C. Sample Topics for Thematic Essays

Below are examples of thematic essay topics that might appear on a test. Prepare for the test by outlining an essay for each topic on a separate sheet of paper. Use the Concept Connector Handbooks at the end of your textbook, as well as chapter information, to outline your essays.

1. Describe the religion of ancient Egyptians, including their belief in an afterlife.

2. Compare ancient Greek and Roman religions.

3. Describe the role of Aztec priests in ancient Aztec society.

4. Describe the special covenant the Israelites believed that God made with Abraham and his descendants.

5. Discuss several major events or issues that encouraged the spread of Christianity.

6. Discuss the impact of the religion of Islam on daily life and how the Sharia helps unify Muslim people.

7. Describe the beliefs of Methodism, founded by John Wesley in the mid-1700s, and its effects on industrial workers at the time.

8. Describe the influence of religion on the partition of India and Pakistan, and its role in the continuing conflicts between the two countries.

Concept Connector Study Guide

Conflict

Essential Question: What issues cause groups of people or countries to come into conflict?

A. Define *conflict.* _____

_____

_____

B. *Record information about the topics listed in the Cumulative Review or your answers to the questions in the Cumulative Review below. Use the Concept Connector Handbooks at the end of your textbook, as well as chapter information, to complete this worksheet.*

1. The Persian Wars (Chapter 4, page 145)

_____

_____

_____

_____

_____

_____

2. Compare the Persian Wars and the Punic Wars (Chapter 5, page 181)

_____

_____

_____

_____

_____

3. Compare War Between Christians and Muslims in the 700s with the Crusades (Chapter 8, page 277)

_____

_____

_____

_____

_____

_____

Concept Connector Study Guide
CONFLICT *(continued)*

4. Examples of French-British Conflict (Chapter 14, page 467)

_____

_____

_____

_____

_____

_____

5. Compare the American Revolution with the Thirty Years' War
(Chapter 17, page 567)

_____

_____

_____

_____

_____

_____

6. European Revolutionaries in 1830 and 1848 (Chapter 20, page 653)

_____

_____

_____

_____

_____

7. Congress of Vienna and the Paris Peace Conference (Chapter 26, page 847)

_____

_____

_____

_____

_____

_____

Concept Connector Study Guide

CONFLICT *(continued)*

8. The Chinese Communists and the Guomindang (Chapter 27, page 879)

_____

_____

_____

_____

_____

_____

_____

_____

9. World War II (Chapter 29, page 959)

_____

_____

_____

_____

_____

_____

_____

_____

_____

10. The Recent Conflict in Northern Ireland and Earlier Religious Conflicts
(Chapter 32, page 1061)

_____

_____

_____

_____

_____

_____

_____

_____

_____

Concept Connector Study Guide
CONFLICT *(continued)*

C. Sample Topics for Thematic Essays

Below are examples of thematic essay topics that might appear on a test. Prepare for the test by outlining an essay for each topic on a separate sheet of paper. Use the Concept Connector Handbooks at the end of your textbook, as well as chapter information,, to outline your essays.

1. Describe the events of the Peloponnesian War, and discuss the outcome of this conflict.

2. Explain why nationalists in Europe fought against rulers during the revolutions of 1830 and 1848, and discuss the results of their struggles.

3. Describe the basic issues that led to the conflicts in the Balkans during the nineteenth and twentieth centuries and how the rest of the world has reacted to them.

4. Describe the issues that led to the partition of Africa by European powers in the late 1800s, and discuss how they served as the basis for conflicts between Africans and colonial powers between 1900 and 1975.

5. Compare and contrast the issues that sparked the Latin American wars of independence in the 1800s with those that created the movement for independence in Africa after World War II.

6. Describe some of the key features of the struggle between the Chinese Communists and the Guomindang (Nationalists) from the 1920s through the 1940s.

7. Analyze the issues that led to the breakup of the Soviet Union and the fall of communism in Eastern Europe in the 1980s and 1990s.

8. Describe and discuss the issues today that divide some Arabs and Arabs and Israelis in the Middle East.

Name_____ Class_____ Date_____

Concept Connector Study Guide

Cooperation

Essential Question: In what ways have groups of people or countries cooperated over time?

A. Define *cooperation.* _____

_____

_____

B. *Record information about the topics listed in the Cumulative Review or your answers to the questions in the Cumulative Review below. Use the Concept Connector Handbooks at the end of your textbook, as well as chapter information, to complete this worksheet.*

1. Iroquois League (Chapter 6, page 207)

_____

_____

_____

_____

_____

_____

_____

2. Roads and Trade Routes (Chapter 6, page 207)

_____

_____

_____

_____

_____

_____

_____

Concept Connector Study Guide
COOPERATION *(continued)*

3. **Development of Medieval Trade Routes; Glorious Revolution; American Revolution** (Chapter 17, page 567)

_____
_____
_____
_____
_____
_____
_____

4. **Coalitions Against Napoleon** (Chapter 18, page 603)

_____
_____
_____
_____
_____
_____
_____

5. **Tactics of Abolitionist Groups** (Chapter 23, page 745)

_____
_____
_____
_____
_____
_____
_____

Concept Connector Study Guide

COOPERATION (continued)

6. League of Nations (Chapter 26, page 847)

_____
_____
_____
_____
_____
_____

7. United Nations (Chapter 29, page 959)

_____
_____
_____
_____
_____
_____

8. European Community (Chapter 30, page 1009)

_____
_____
_____
_____
_____
_____

9. NGOs (Nongovernmental Organizations) (Chapter 34, page 1127)

_____
_____
_____
_____
_____
_____

Concept Connector Study Guide
COOPERATION *(continued)*

C. Sample Topics for Thematic Essays

Below are examples of thematic essay topics that might appear on a test. Prepare for the test by outlining an essay for each topic on a separate sheet of paper. Use the Concept Connector Handbooks at the end of your textbook, as well as chapter information, to outline your essays.

1. Choose two civilizations, such as Sumer, Egypt, the Indus Valley, and Shang China. Compare and contrast levels of cooperation in these two civilizations and explain how cooperation led to success.

2. Describe how the Iroquois League helped individual member nations by encouraging cooperation.

3. Compare and contrast the Glorious Revolution with the American Revolution. Discuss which groups cooperated with one another, which came into conflict, and the governments that were created as a result.

4. Discuss how Enlightenment thinkers in France, England, and other European countries cooperated to refine their ideas and to spread them across Europe and beyond.

5. Describe the new level of cooperation pledged by the members of the League of Nations after World War I, but why the organization could not prevent World War II.

6. Describe the uneasy cooperation among Allied leaders Roosevelt, Churchill, and Stalin during World War II.

7. Describe the cooperative goals of the European Community (Common Market) and the European Union, and how it has improved the economies of its members.

8. Select two challenges the world faces in the twenty-first century, and discuss what kinds of cooperation will be needed meet them. Consider economic, social, environmental, or security issues.

Concept Connector Study Guide

Cultural Diffusion

Essential Question: In what ways have migration and trade affected cultures?

A. Define *cultural diffusion.* _____

_____

_____

B. *Record information about the topics listed in the Cumulative Review or your answers to the questions in the Cumulative Review below. Use the Concept Connector Handbooks at the end of your textbook, as well as chapter information, to complete this worksheet.*

1. Cultural Diffusion in Early Human History (Chapter 1, page 25)

_____

_____

_____

_____

_____

_____

_____

_____

_____

2. Arabic Numerals (Chapter 3, page 109)

_____

_____

_____

_____

_____

_____

_____

_____

_____

Concept Connector Study Guide
CULTURAL DIFFUSION *(continued)*

3. Decimal System (Chapter 3, page 109)

_____

_____

_____

_____

_____

_____

4. Hinduism (Chapter 3, page 109)

_____

_____

_____

_____

_____

_____

5. Buddhism (Chapter 3, page 109)

_____

_____

_____

_____

_____

_____

6. Evolution of the Alphabet (Chapter 4, page 145)

_____

_____

_____

_____

_____

_____

Concept Connector Study Guide
CULTURAL DIFFUSION *(continued)*

7. The Spread of Roman Culture (Chapter 5, page 181)

_____

_____

_____

_____

_____

_____

8. The Spread of Christianity and the Spread of Buddhism (Chapter 5, page 181)

_____

_____

_____

_____

_____

_____

9. The Roman and Byzantine Empires (Chapter 9, page 299)

_____

_____

_____

_____

_____

_____

10. The Spread of Islam (Chapter 10, page 335)

_____

_____

_____

_____

_____

_____

Concept Connector Study Guide

CULTURAL DIFFUSION *(continued)*

11. **The Spread of Ideas and Culture as a Result of Buddhist and Christian Missionaries** (Chapter 12, page 403)

_____

_____

_____

_____

_____

12. **The Renaissance and Islam** (Chapter 13, page 441)

_____

_____

_____

_____

_____

13. **The Renaissance and the Tang and Song Dynasties** (Chapter 13, page 441)

_____

_____

_____

_____

_____

14. **Indian Influence on Southeast Asia** (Chapter 14, page 467)

_____

_____

_____

_____

_____

15. **Influence of Ancient Civilizations on Enlightenment Thinkers** (Chapter 17, page 567)

_____

_____

_____

_____

_____

Concept Connector Study Guide

CULTURAL DIFFUSION *(continued)*

C. Sample Topics for Thematic Essays

Below are examples of thematic essay topics that might appear on a test. Prepare for the test by outlining an essay for each topic on a separate sheet of paper. Use the Concept Connector Handbooks at the end of your textbook, as well as chapter information, to outline your essays.

1. Describe the importance of the Phoenician sea traders in the spread of culture throughout the Mediterranean region around 700 B.C.

2. Discuss the importance and role of the Silk Road as an agent of cultural diffusion.

3. Describe how Greco-Roman culture spread through the Roman empire during the *Pax Romana.*

4. Describe the spread of Buddhism from India to China. What was the role of merchants in this instance of cultural diffusion? How did Buddhism interact with traditional Chinese beliefs?

5. Describe how the migration to Ireland in the 1600s changed the political and economic structure of the country and the impact of the Great Hunger of the 1840s.

6. Describe the ways in which Chinese culture spread to Korea during the Koryo and Choson dynasties. Give at least two examples of how the Koreans adopted certain aspects of Chinese culture, and how they adapted these cultural influences.

7. Discuss how increased trade and the demands of a global economy have changed people's lives in today's developing countries.

8. Describe at least two examples of cultural diffusion in the world today.

Concept Connector Study Guide

Democracy

Essential Question: How has the practice of democracy developed over time?

A. Define *democracy*. _____

_____

_____

B. *Record information about the topics listed in the Cumulative Review or your answers to the questions in the Cumulative Review below. Use the Concept Connector Handbooks at the end of your textbook, as well as chapter information, to complete this worksheet.*

1. Roman Citizenship (Chapter 5, page 181)

_____

_____

_____

_____

_____

_____

2. Government by the People (Chapter 8, page 277)

_____

_____

_____

_____

_____

_____

3. The Magna Carta and the English Bill of Rights (Chapter 16, page 537)

_____

_____

_____

_____

_____

_____

Concept Connector Study Guide
DEMOCRACY (continued)

4. **The American Declaration of Independence** (Chapter 17, page 567)

_____

_____

_____

_____

_____

5. **The Declaration of the Rights of Man and the Citizen and the American Declaration of Independence** (Chapter 18, page 603)

_____

_____

_____

_____

_____

6. **The American Revolution and Revolutions in Latin America** (Chapter 20, page 653)

_____

_____

_____

_____

_____

7. **John Locke and the Expansion of Suffrage** (Chapter 23, page 745)

_____

_____

_____

_____

8. **The Curtailment of Citizen's Rights** (Chapter 29, page 959)

_____

_____

_____

_____

_____

Concept Connector Study Guide
DEMOCRACY *(continued)*

C. Sample Topics for Thematic Essays

Below are examples of thematic essay topics that might appear on a test. Prepare for the test by outlining an essay for each topic on a separate sheet of paper. Use the Concept Connector Handbooks at the end of your textbook, as well as chapter information, to outline your essays.

1. What do you think were the three most important steps in the development of democracy? Explain your choices.

2. How were the American and French Revolutions related?

3. Compare the beliefs of at least three cultures throughout history regarding power, authority, governance, and law.

4. How would you define citizenship, and how have different societies viewed the rights and responsibilities of citizenship?

5. How are contemporary democratic governments rooted in Enlightenment ideals?

6. What impacts did Greece and Rome have on the development of later political systems?

7. What forces led to the nineteenth-century failure of democracy in Latin America and Russia?

8. What role does democracy play in Latin America today?

Concept Connector Study Guide

Dictatorship

Essential Question: How have dictators assumed and maintained power?

A. Define *dictatorship.* _____
_____
_____

B. *Record information about the topics listed in the Cumulative Review or your answers to the questions in the Cumulative Review below. Use the Concept Connector Handbooks at the end of your textbook, as well as chapter information, to complete this worksheet.*

1. Mussolini and Hitler (Chapter 28, page 919)

_____
_____
_____
_____
_____
_____

2. Stalin and Other Russian Leaders (Chapter 28, page 919)

_____
_____
_____
_____
_____
_____

3. Communist Dictators and Other Dictators (Chapter 30, page 1009)

_____
_____
_____
_____
_____
_____

Concept Connector Study Guide

DICTATORSHIP *(continued)*

4. Mobutu Sese Seko (Chapter 31, page 1039)

_____

_____

_____

_____

_____

_____

5. Saddam Hussein (Chapter 32, page 1061)

_____

_____

_____

_____

_____

_____

_____

6. The Rise of Latin American Dictators (Chapter 33, page 1091)

_____

_____

_____

_____

_____

_____

_____

Concept Connector Study Guide
DICTATORSHIP *(continued)*

C. Sample Topics for Thematic Essays

Below are examples of thematic essay topics that might appear on a test. Prepare for the test by outlining an essay for each topic on a separate sheet of paper. Use the Concept Connector Handbooks at the end of your textbook, as well as chapter information, to outline your essays.

1. Compare and contrast the ways in which dictators gained control and the powers they had during the Roman republic and the Roman empire.

2. Discuss why many French people supported Napoleon, even though he was essentially a dictator.

3. Describe the conditions in Mexico that led to the revolution in 1910 against the dictator General Porfirio Díaz.

4. Describe the conditions in Italy that led to Mussolini's rise to power after World War I, and the ideas and methods that kept him in power until Italy's defeat in World War II.

5. Describe Hitler's belief in a "master race," and how he used it to gain power and promote war.

6. Compare and contrast the ideas of fascism and communism and the ways in which adherents gained and maintained power in Europe and Russia before World War II.

7. Compare Fulgencio Batista and Fidel Castro. What are the similarities and differences in how they came to power and how they ruled?

8. Describe the dictatorship in China since Mao Zedong died in 1976. What has been the country's approach to economic and political freedom in this period?

Concept Connector Study Guide

Economic Systems

Essential Question: What types of economic systems have societies used to produce and distribute goods and services?

A. Define *economic system.* _____

_____

_____

B. *Record information about the topics listed in the Cumulative Review or your answers to the questions in the Cumulative Review below. Use the Concept Connector Handbooks at the end of your textbook, as well as chapter information, to complete this worksheet.*

1. The Expansion of Towns in Medieval Europe (Chapter 7, page 239)

_____

_____

_____

_____

_____

_____

2. Mercantilism and Manorialism (Chapter 15, page 499)

_____

_____

_____

_____

_____

_____

3. Market Economy (Chapter 19, page 629)

_____

_____

_____

_____

_____

_____

Concept Connector Study Guide
ECONOMIC SYSTEMS *(continued)*

4. Centrally Planned Economy (Chapter 19, page 629)

_____

_____

_____

_____

_____

_____

_____

_____

_____

5. Mixed Economy (Chapter 19, page 629)

_____

_____

_____

_____

_____

_____

_____

_____

_____

6. Compare Socialism with Mercantilism (Chapter 19, page 629)

_____

_____

_____

_____

_____

_____

_____

_____

_____

_____

Concept Connector Study Guide
ECONOMIC SYSTEMS *(continued)*

7. **The Commercial Revolution During the Middle Ages and the Industrial Revolution** (Chapter 21, page 687)

_____
_____
_____
_____
_____
_____
_____
_____
_____

8. **Command Economies in Developing Countries and in Russia** (Chapter 33, page 1091)

_____
_____
_____
_____
_____
_____
_____
_____
_____
_____

9. **Economic Systems in the Twentieth Century** (Chapter 34, page 1127)

_____
_____
_____
_____
_____
_____
_____
_____
_____
_____

Concept Connector Study Guide

ECONOMIC SYSTEMS *(continued)*

C. Sample Topics for Thematic Essays

Below are examples of thematic essay topics that might appear on a test. Prepare for the test by outlining an essay for each topic on a separate sheet of paper. Use the Concept Connector Handbooks at the end of your textbook, as well as chapter information, to outline your essays.

1. Discuss the importance of trade in early civilizations and how the development of a money economy helped unite the Persian empire.

2. Describe the benefits and drawbacks of feudalism and the manor economy for peasants.

3. Describe the attitude toward merchants during the golden age of Muslim civilization, the merchants' success, and the development of new business practices.

4. List the regions involved in the triangular trade and how the Atlantic slave trade contributed to the economy of each one.

5. Contrast socialism with capitalism, and discuss the benefits early socialist reformers predicted would occur in the event that socialism replaced capitalism.

6. Discuss the role British mercantilism played in sparking the American Revolution.

7. Describe the economic changes in Eastern Europe after the fall of the Soviet Union and the challenges facing countries as they adapted from one economic system to another.

8. Contrast the Great Leap Forward of Mao Zedong in 1958 with the Four Modernizations of Deng Xiaoping in the 1980s, and discuss their results.

Concept Connector Study Guide

Empires

Essential Question: What factors allow empires to rise and what factors cause them to fall?

A. Define *empire.* _____

_____

_____

B. *Record information about the topics listed in the Cumulative Review or your answers to the questions in the Cumulative Review below. Use the Concept Connector Handbooks at the end of your textbook, as well as chapter information, to complete this worksheet.*

1. Characteristics of Successful Rulers (Chapter 2, page 63)

_____

_____

_____

_____

_____

_____

2. Empire-Building in India, China, Egypt, and the Middle East (Chapter 3, page 109)

_____

_____

_____

_____

_____

_____

3. Methods of Control in the Roman Empire and Han Dynasty (Chapter 5, page 181)

_____

_____

_____

_____

_____

_____

Concept Connector Study Guide
EMPIRES *(continued)*

4. Aztec and Inca (Chapter 6, page 207)

_____

_____

_____

_____

_____

_____

_____

5. Was Charlemagne Really King of the Romans? (Chapter 7, page 239)

_____

_____

_____

_____

_____

_____

_____

6. The Roman Empire and the Holy Roman Empire (Chapter 8, page 277)

_____

_____

_____

_____

_____

_____

_____

7. The Byzantine Empire (Chapter 9, page 299)

_____

_____

_____

_____

_____

_____

_____

Concept Connector Study Guide
EMPIRES *(continued)*

8. The Abbasid Empire (Chapter 10, page 335)

_____

_____

_____

_____

_____

_____

9. The Mughal Empire (Chapter 10, page 335)

_____

_____

_____

_____

_____

_____

10. Suleiman the Magnificent (Chapter 10, page 335)

_____

_____

_____

_____

_____

_____

11. The Mongol Empire (Chapter 12, page 403)

_____

_____

_____

_____

_____

_____

Concept Connector Study Guide
EMPIRES (continued)

12. The Ming Empire (Chapter 12, page 403)

_____

_____

_____

_____

_____

13. The Roman Empire and the Tang Dynasty (Chapter 12, page 403)

_____

_____

_____

_____

_____

14. The Qing and the Yuan Dynasties (Chapter 14, page 467)

_____

_____

_____

_____

_____

15. The Roman Empire and the Spanish Empire in the Americas (Chapter 15, page 499)

_____

_____

_____

_____

16. North American Colonies and Latin American Colonies (Chapter 20, page 653)

_____

_____

_____

_____

_____

Concept Connector Study Guide

EMPIRES *(continued)*

17. The Second Reich and the Holy Roman Empire (Chapter 22, page 717)

_____

_____

_____

_____

18. The Spanish Empire of the 1500s and the British Empire of the late 1800s (Chapter 24, page 779)

_____

_____

_____

_____

_____

19. Arguments Against Imperialism (Chapter 24, page 779)

_____

_____

_____

_____

_____

20. The Soviet Union and Other Empires (Chapter 30, page 1009)

_____

_____

_____

_____

21. Chechnya and Earlier Efforts to Break Away from an Empire (Chapter 32, page 1061)

_____

_____

_____

_____

_____

Concept Connector Study Guide
EMPIRES *(continued)*

C. Sample Topics for Thematic Essays

Below are examples of thematic essay topics that might appear on a test. Prepare for the test by outlining an essay for each topic on a separate sheet of paper. Use the Concept Connector Handbooks at the end of your textbook, as well as chapter information, to outline your essays.

1. Describe the main causes of the fall of the Roman empire.

2. Discuss the extent and the organization of the Inca empire and the reasons why it fell to Europeans in the 1500s.

3. Describe how the three great kingdoms of West Africa gained power and the reasons why they declined in power during the 1600s.

4. Describe the achievements of the Mongol empire in Asia, especially in China, during the 1200s and 1300s.

5. Discuss reasons why Napoleon was able to build an empire in the early 1800s, and the reasons for its fall.

6. Describe the results of the Congress of Vienna in 1815 and the forces that challenged the old empires during the next 30 years.

7. Describe reasons why Western powers were able to gain control over much of the world between 1870 and the beginning of World War I.

8. Discuss reasons for the fall of communism and the breakup of the Soviet Union in the 1980s.

Concept Connector Study Guide

Genocide

Essential Question: What factors have led groups of people or governments to commit genocide?

A. Define *genocide*. _____

_____

_____

B. *Record information about the topics listed in the Cumulative Review or your answers to the questions in the Cumulative Review below. Use the Concept Connector Handbooks at the end of your textbook, as well as chapter information, to complete this worksheet.*

1. Native Americans (Chapter 15, page 499)

_____

_____

_____

_____

_____

_____

_____

_____

2. Indigenous People in North America, Australia, and New Zealand
(Chapter 25, page 809)

_____

_____

_____

_____

_____

_____

_____

_____

_____

Concept Connector Study Guide
GENOCIDE *(continued)*

3. **The Holocaust and the Armenian Genocide** (Chapter 29, page 959)

_____
_____
_____
_____
_____
_____
_____
_____

4. **Genocide in Cambodia Compared with Earlier Genocides**
(Chapter 30, page 1009)

_____
_____
_____
_____
_____
_____
_____
_____

5. **Genocide in Rwanda Compared with Earlier Genocides** (Chapter 32, page 1061)

_____
_____
_____
_____
_____
_____
_____
_____

Concept Connector Study Guide

GENOCIDE *(continued)*

C. Sample Topics for Thematic Essays

Below are examples of thematic essay topics that might appear on a test. Prepare for the test by outlining an essay for each topic on a separate sheet of paper. Use the Concept Connector Handbooks at the end of your textbook, as well as chapter information, to outline your essays.

1. Discuss reasons why the Romans persecuted early Christians and how Roman attitudes changed during the 300s A.D.

2. Describe the factors that led to the dramatic decrease of Native American populations in Latin America in the 1500s.

3. Describe the early contacts between Europeans and Native Americans in North America and how westward expansion by colonists affected the Native Americans.

4. Discuss the effects of the Atlantic slave trade on the people of West Africa.

5. Describe the differences between Armenians and the Ottoman Turks in the late 1800s, and discuss the factors that led to the genocide of the early 1900s.

6. Discuss Nazi attitudes towards Jews and other ethnic groups and how these views were used to justify the events of the Holocaust.

7. Describe ethnic and religious differences among groups in the former Yugoslavia and how they led to attempted genocide in Kosovo in the 1990s.

8. Discuss the reasons why genocide occurred in Rwanda in the 1990s and the international response.

Concept Connector Study Guide

Geography's Impact

Essential Question: How have geographic factors affected the course of history?

A. Define *geography.* _____

_____

_____

B. *Record information about the topics listed in the Cumulative Review or your answers to the questions in the Cumulative Review below. Use the Concept Connector Handbooks at the end of your textbook, as well as chapter information, to complete this worksheet.*

1. Rivers and the Rise of Civilization (Chapter 1, page 25)

_____

_____

_____

_____

_____

_____

_____

_____

2. The Tigris and Euphrates Rivers (Chapter 2, page 63)

_____

_____

_____

_____

_____

_____

_____

_____

Concept Connector Study Guide

GEOGRAPHY'S IMPACT *(continued)*

3. The Aegean and Mediterranean Seas (Chapter 4, page 145)

_____
_____
_____
_____
_____
_____

4. Geographic Environments of Developing Civilizations (Chapter 6, page 207)

_____
_____
_____
_____
_____
_____
_____

5. The Ocean's Influence on the Vikings (Chapter 7, page 239)

_____
_____
_____
_____
_____
_____

6. The Importance of Rivers to Early Cultures (Chapter 9, page 299)

_____
_____
_____
_____
_____
_____

Concept Connector Study Guide
GEOGRAPHY'S IMPACT (continued)

7. **Geography and Cultural Development in Eastern Europe and Africa**
   (Chapter 11, page 363)

   _____

   _____

   _____

   _____

   _____

   _____

8. **The Impact of Geography in Japan and Mesopotamia** (Chapter 12, page 403)

   _____

   _____

   _____

   _____

   _____

   _____

   _____

9. **Location and the Relationship Between Latin America and the United States, 1800–1914** (Chapter 25, page 809)

   _____

   _____

   _____

   _____

   _____

   _____

10. **The Effect of Oil on the History of Saudi Arabia and the United States**
    (Chapter 31, page 1039)

    _____

    _____

    _____

    _____

    _____

    _____

Concept Connector Study Guide
GEOGRAPHY'S IMPACT *(continued)*

C. Sample Topics for Thematic Essays

Below are examples of thematic essay topics that might appear on a test. Prepare for the test by outlining an essay for each topic on a separate sheet of paper. Use the Concept Connector Handbooks at the end of your textbook, as well as chapter information, to outline your essays.

1. Discuss the role of river valleys in the development of early civilizations, such as Egypt, the Indus Valley, and Shang China.

2. Evaluate the importance of geography in the development of the ancient civilization of Sumer. What was it about this location that allowed civilization to begin there?

3. Select two cities or countries whose locations have helped in their military defense. Discuss each location and describe how geography made foreign invasions more difficult. You may consider ancient Greece and the Acropolis, Paris, the islands of Great Britain or Japan, or other locations.

4. Explain how the availability of natural resources helped Great Britain and the United States become leaders in the Industrial Revolution.

5. Explain how the geography of Indonesia (which was favorable for growing spices) affected the exploration of the world by Europeans in the 1400s and 1500s.

6. Describe how the location of the United States and Latin America led to the development of the Monroe Doctrine and the Roosevelt Corollary and how these policies shaped the relationship between the United States and Latin America.

7. Explain why the location of the Ottoman empire made it a desirable ally during World War I. How did its decision to join the Central Powers affect the war?

8. Describe how desertification affected early migrations in Africa and how it may affect Africa's future.

Concept Connector Study Guide

Migration

Essential Question: What factors cause large groups of people to move from one place to another?

A. Define *migration.* _____

_____

_____

B. *Record information about the topics listed in the Cumulative Review or your answers to the questions in the Cumulative Review below. Use the Concept Connector Handbooks at the end of your textbook, as well as chapter information, to complete this worksheet.*

1. Migrations of Early People (Chapter 1, page 25)

_____

_____

_____

_____

_____

_____

_____

_____

2. Indo-European Migrations (Chapter 3, page 109)

_____

_____

_____

_____

_____

_____

_____

_____

_____

_____

Concept Connector Study Guide

MIGRATION *(continued)*

3. Migration and Language (Chapter 11, page 363)

_____

_____

_____

_____

_____

_____

_____

_____

4. Westward Movement in the United States (Chapter 23, page 745)

_____

_____

_____

_____

_____

_____

_____

_____

_____

5. Factors in European Migration to the Americas (Chapter 23, page 745)

_____

_____

_____

_____

_____

_____

_____

_____

_____

Concept Connector Study Guide
MIGRATION *(continued)*

C. Sample Topics for Thematic Essays

Below are examples of thematic essay topics that might appear on a test. Prepare for the test by outlining an essay for each topic on a separate sheet of paper. Use the Concept Connector Handbooks at the end of your textbook, as well as chapter information, to outline your essays.

1. Describe at least three reasons why river valleys were "pull" factors in the migration of early peoples.

2. Select at least two instances between 1600 and 1950 where groups were "pushed" to migrate from one area to another. Describe the reasons why they migrated, and discuss how the groups adapted to the migration and how their move affected the area to which they moved.

3. Compare and contrast the "pull" factors that brought Europeans to the Americas between 1600 and 1800 with the "pull" factors that encouraged movement to the western United States between 1800 and 1900.

4. Identify and discuss at least three factors that "pushed" or "pulled" people into growing cities in Europe and the Americas between 1800 and 1900.

5. Identify and discuss at least three factors that cause people to migrate today. Give an example of each and describe the conditions that have encouraged migration.

6. Explain the role of religion in the partition of India in 1948 and in the migration of people that resulted.

7. Identify the "push" factor that brought the first large group of Europeans to Australia and the "pull" factors that drew others there during the late 1800s.

8. Evaluate how the potato famine in Ireland (which began in 1845) and the resulting migration of a million Irish people affected Ireland's relationships with the United States and Great Britain.

Name_____ Class_____ Date_____

Concept Connector Study Guide

Nationalism

Essential Question: How have people used nationalism as a basis for their actions?

A. Define *nationalism.* _____

_____

_____

B. *Record information about the topics listed in the Cumulative Review or your answers to the questions in the Cumulative Review below. Use the Concept Connector Handbooks at the end of your textbook, as well as chapter information, to complete this worksheet.*

1. Nationalism in the American Revolution (Chapter 18, page 603)

_____

_____

_____

_____

_____

_____

_____

_____

_____

2. Latin American Nationalism and French Nationalism (Chapter 20, page 653)

_____

_____

_____

_____

_____

_____

_____

_____

_____

Concept Connector Study Guide
NATIONALISM *(continued)*

3. Unification and Nationalism in Greece and Italy (Chapter 22, page 717)

_____

_____

_____

_____

_____

_____

4. Revolts in the Balkans (Chapter 22, page 717)

_____

_____

_____

_____

_____

_____

5. English Nationalism (Chapter 24, page 779)

_____

_____

_____

_____

_____

_____

6. Nationalism in the United States (Chapter 24, page 779)

_____

_____

_____

_____

_____

_____

Concept Connector Study Guide
NATIONALISM (continued)

7. Pan-Arab and Pan-Slav Nationalism (Chapter 27, page 879)

_____
_____
_____
_____
_____
_____
_____

8. Expansion in Japan, the United States, and Britain (Chapter 27, page 879)

_____
_____
_____
_____
_____
_____
_____

9. Hindu Nationalism of the BJP in India (Chapter 31, page 1039)

_____
_____
_____
_____
_____
_____
_____

Concept Connector Study Guide

NATIONALISM *(continued)*

C. Sample Topics for Thematic Essays

Below are examples of thematic essay topics that might appear on a test. Prepare for the test by outlining an essay for each topic on a separate sheet of paper. Use the Concept Connector Handbooks at the end of your textbook, as well as chapter information, to outline your essays.

1. Compare and contrast the ways in which nationalism helped Napoleon create an empire and how it also encouraged resistance against that empire.

2. Discuss the role of nationalism in the revolts by slaves, creoles, and others in South and Central America in the late 1700s and early 1800s.

3. Describe how Bismarck used nationalism to attack both the Catholic Church and socialists in the late 1800s and the results of those attacks.

4. Explain the effects of nationalist movements on the Hapsburg empire before and after 1848 and how the success of the Hungarians after 1866 continued to weaken the empire.

5. Describe the British response to nationalists in India before and after World War I and how Mohandas Gandhi helped inspire Indians to work for an independent nation.

6. Discuss how Mussolini used nationalism to gain and keep power in Italy.

7. Describe how Adolf Hitler used nationalism to help him gain control of the country and establish the Third Reich.

8. Describe the role of nationalism in the conflict that broke out in the former Yugoslavia in the 1990s.

Concept Connector Study Guide

People and the Environment

Essential Question: What impact have people had on the environment?

A. Define *environment.* _____

_____

_____

B. *Record information about the topics listed in the Cumulative Review or your answers to the questions in the Cumulative Review below. Use the Concept Connector Handbooks at the end of your textbook, as well as chapter information, to complete this worksheet.*

1. Stone Age Hominids and Neolithic Farmers (Chapter 1, page 25)

_____

_____

_____

_____

_____

_____

_____

_____

_____

2. Farming Methods (Chapter 6, page 207)

_____

_____

_____

_____

_____

_____

_____

_____

_____

_____

Concept Connector Study Guide

PEOPLE AND THE ENVIRONMENT *(continued)*

3. The Building of Tenochtitlán (Chapter 6, page 207)

_____

_____

_____

_____

_____

_____

_____

_____

_____

4. Geoglyphs (Chapter 6, page 207)

_____

_____

_____

_____

_____

_____

_____

_____

_____

5. Cliff Dwellings and Earthworks (Chapter 6, page 207)

_____

_____

_____

_____

_____

_____

_____

_____

Concept Connector Study Guide
PEOPLE AND THE ENVIRONMENT *(continued)*

C. Sample Topics for Thematic Essays

Below are examples of thematic essay topics that might appear on a test. Prepare for the test by outlining an essay for each topic on a separate sheet of paper. Use the Concept Connector Handbooks at the end of your textbook, as well as chapter information, to outline your essays.

1. Explain how the ability of people to produce their own food during the Neolithic Revolution led to changes in the environment and how people lived.

2. Discuss the relationship between the natural environment and industrialization in the period between 1750 and 1914.

3. Explain how British rule in India affected the natural environment.

4. Evaluate the positive and negative effects of automobiles on people's lives and on the environment.

5. Compare and contrast the conditions in North American and European cities during the Industrial Revolution with those in South American and Asian cities today.

6. Discuss how increased industrialization has threatened air and water quality and how governments have responded.

7. Discuss how nuclear power could help the environment as well as ways it could harm it.

8. Describe how global warming might harm the environment as well as how limiting emissions of greenhouse gases could hamper economic growth.

Concept Connector Study Guide

Political Systems

Essential Question: How have societies chosen to govern themselves?

A. Define *political system.* _____

_____

_____

B. *Record information about the topics listed in the Cumulative Review or your answers to the questions in the Cumulative Review below. Use the Concept Connector Handbooks at the end of your textbook, as well as chapter information, to complete this worksheet.*

1. Oligarchy (Chapter 4, page 145)

_____

_____

_____

_____

_____

_____

2. The Roman Republic and the Oligarchies of Ancient Greece
(Chapter 5, page 181)

_____

_____

_____

_____

_____

_____

3. Religion and Rulers in Egypt, China, and the Inca Empire (Chapter 6, page 207)

_____

_____

_____

_____

_____

_____

Concept Connector Study Guide

POLITICAL SYSTEMS *(continued)*

4. **Feudalism and Building a Strong Empire** (Chapter 7, page 239)

_____

_____

_____

_____

_____

5. **Absolute Monarchy Under Louis XIV and Imperial Rule in Ancient Rome**
(Chapter 16, page 537)

_____

_____

_____

_____

_____

6. **The Federal Government** (Chapter 17, page 567)

_____

_____

_____

_____

_____

7. **Enlightenment Ideas About Democracy and Totalitarianism**
(Chapter 28, page 919)

_____

_____

_____

_____

_____

_____

Concept Connector Study Guide

POLITICAL SYSTEMS *(continued)*

C. Sample Topics for Thematic Essays

Below are examples of thematic essay topics that might appear on a test. Prepare for the test by outlining an essay for each topic on a separate sheet of paper. Use the Concept Connector Handbooks at the end of your textbook, as well as chapter information, to outline your essays.

1. Describe the government, society, and religion of city-states in ancient Sumer and how those forces worked together to govern.

2. Compare and contrast democracy in ancient Athens with the American political system today, including the responsibilities of citizens.

3. Describe the government of the Inca empire and how its technical achievements in building roads led to effective government.

4. Describe the political system in England after the Magna Carta and the establishment of Parliament in the 1300s.

5. Compare oligarchy to autocracy. How are these two political systems similar? How are they different? Include an example of each from history in your essay.

6. Describe the relationship between the Industrial Revolution and the ideas of Karl Marx, and discuss the reasons why communism appealed to many workers of this time.

7. Analyze the conditions in Eastern Europe and the Soviet Union late in the Cold War that led to the collapse of communism and the breakup of the Soviet Union.

8. Describe the democratic political system in South Africa after the end of apartheid and the approval of a new constitution in 1997.

Concept Connector Study Guide

Revolution

Essential Question: Why have political revolutions occurred?

A. Define *revolution.* _____

_____

_____

B. *Record information about the topics listed in the Cumulative Review or your answers to the questions in the Cumulative Review below. Use the Concept Connector Handbooks at the end of your textbook, as well as chapter information, to complete this worksheet.*

1. The Transfer of Power in England, 1377–1688 (Chapter 16, page 537)

_____

_____

_____

_____

_____

_____

2. The German Peasants' Revolt of 1524 and the French Revolution (Chapter 18, page 603)

_____

_____

_____

_____

_____

3. Latin American Revolutions (Chapter 20, page 653)

_____

_____

_____

_____

_____

_____

Concept Connector Study Guide
REVOLUTION *(continued)*

4. **The Russian Revolution and the French Revolution** (Chapter 26, page 847)

_____

_____

_____

_____

_____

_____

_____

_____

_____

5. **European Colonial Independence Between 1946 and 1970 and the American Revolution** (Chapter 31, page 1039)

_____

_____

_____

_____

_____

_____

_____

_____

_____

6. **Recent Rebellions in Latin America and Earlier Revolutions** (Chapter 33, page 1091)

_____

_____

_____

_____

_____

_____

_____

_____

_____

Concept Connector Study Guide
REVOLUTION *(continued)*

C. Sample Topics for Thematic Essays

Below are examples of thematic essay topics that might appear on a test. Prepare for the test by outlining an essay for each topic on a separate sheet of paper. Use the Concept Connector Handbooks at the end of your textbook, as well as chapter information, to outline your essays.

1. Describe how plebeians helped change the Roman republic and how their opposition to rulers helped create the Roman empire.

2. Describe the system of government in England during the early 1200s, when rebellious barons forced King John to sign the Magna Carta, and the effect on government in the following years.

3. Describe China under Mongol rule and the reasons why Chinese leaders rebelled and established the Ming dynasty.

4. Discuss the basic dispute between monarchs and Parliament in England in the 1600s and how it resulted in the English Civil War and the Glorious Revolution.

5. Discuss the economic problems of the Third Estate before the French Revolution and how these problems inspired people to revolt.

6. Discuss the causes and effects of the revolution and civil war that put Vladimir Lenin in power in Russia by 1921.

7. Contrast the tactics used by Mohandas Gandhi during the struggle for independence in India with tactics used by other revolutionary leaders before World War II.

8. Describe the social and economic conditions in South Africa during most of the twentieth century and how other countries around the world helped bring about change there.

Concept Connector Study Guide

Science

Essential Question: How has science changed people's lives throughout history?

A. Define *science.* _____

_____

_____

B. *Record information about the topics listed in the Cumulative Review or your answers to the questions in the Cumulative Review below. Use the Concept Connector Handbooks at the end of your textbook, as well as chapter information, to complete this worksheet.*

1. Advances in Mathematics (Chapter 4, page 145)

_____

_____

_____

_____

_____

_____

2. Incan Surgery (Chapter 6, page 207)

_____

_____

_____

_____

_____

_____

3. The Ideas of Copernicus and Newton (Chapter 13, page 441)

_____

_____

_____

_____

_____

_____

Concept Connector Study Guide

SCIENCE *(continued)*

4. **The Scientific Revolution and the Scientific Ideas of the Late 1800s**
   (Chapter 21, page 687)

   _____

   _____

   _____

   _____

   _____

   _____

   _____

   _____

   _____

5. **Newton's Theories and Einstein's Theories** (Chapter 28, page 919)

   _____

   _____

   _____

   _____

   _____

   _____

   _____

   _____

   _____

   _____

6. **Louis Pasteur's Medical Advances and Those of World War II**
   (Chapter 29, page 959)

   _____

   _____

   _____

   _____

   _____

   _____

   _____

   _____

   _____

Concept Connector Study Guide
SCIENCE *(continued)*

C. Sample Topics for Thematic Essays

Below are examples of thematic essay topics that might appear on a test. Prepare for the test by outlining an essay for each topic on a separate sheet of paper. Use the Concept Connector Handbooks at the end of your textbook, as well as chapter information, to outline your essays.

1. Describe the sources of knowledge used by Greek scientists during the Hellenistic Age and the advances they made in mathematics, physics, and medicine.

2. Explain the important scientific advances of the Aztec, Inca, and Maya.

3. Describe science during the golden age of Muslim civilization and the advances made by Muslim scientists.

4. Discuss how the Scientific Revolution that began in the mid-1500s marked a profound shift in the thinking of Europeans and how that shift is still reflected in the work of scientists.

5. Describe how "germ theory" helped improve health in the 1800s, and discuss how new medical and health practices contributed to the growth in population.

6. Discuss the scientific knowledge that changed medical care in hospitals during the 1800s and how it improved health care, especially for poor people.

7. Discuss the effect of computers on society and modern life and the reasons why this period is sometimes called "The Information Age."

8. Describe some benefits of biotechnology and genetic engineering, as well as some issues that create debate about these topics.

Name_____ Class_____ Date_____

Concept Connector Study Guide

Technology

Essential Question: How has technology changed the way people live and work?

A. Define *technology.* _____

_____

_____

B. *Record information about the topics listed in the Cumulative Review or your answers to the questions in the Cumulative Review below. Use the Concept Connector Handbooks at the end of your textbook, as well as chapter information, to complete this worksheet.*

1. Paleolithic Stone Tools (Chapter 1, page 25)

_____

_____

_____

_____

_____

_____

2. Advances During Prehistory and Technological Advances in Egypt and Mesopotamia (Chapter 2, page 63)

_____

_____

_____

_____

_____

_____

3. Military Technology and the Ottoman and Safavid Empires (Chapter 10, page 335)

_____

_____

_____

_____

_____

_____

Concept Connector Study Guide
TECHNOLOGY *(continued)*

4. The Printing Press (Chapter 12, page 403)

_____

_____

_____

_____

_____

5. Gunpowder (Chapter 12, page 403)

_____

_____

_____

_____

_____

6. The Compass (Chapter 14, page 467)

_____

_____

_____

_____

_____

7. The Printing Press and the Steam Engine (Chapter 19, page 629)

_____

_____

_____

_____

_____

8. The Agricultural Revolution and the Industrial Revolution
(Chapter 21, page 687)

_____

_____

_____

_____

_____

Concept Connector Study Guide

TECHNOLOGY *(continued)*

9. **First and Second Phases of the Industrial Revolution** (Chapter 21, page 687)

_____

_____

_____

_____

_____

_____

_____

10. **Nuclear Power** (Chapter 29, page 959)

_____

_____

_____

_____

_____

_____

_____

11. **Coal Mines, Factories, and Railroads in Europe and North America in the 1800s and Hydroelectric Power in Africa Today** (Chapter 33, page 1091)

_____

_____

_____

_____

_____

_____

12. **The Telephone and Computer Technology** (Chapter 34, page 1127)

_____

_____

_____

_____

_____

_____

_____

Concept Connector Study Guide
TECHNOLOGY *(continued)*

C. Sample Topics for Thematic Essays

Below are examples of thematic essay topics that might appear on a test. Prepare for the test by outlining an essay for each topic on a separate sheet of paper. Use the Concept Connector Handbooks at the end of your textbook, as well as chapter information, to outline your essays.

1. Describe the new technology used during the Neolithic agricultural revolution and how it contributed to the beginning of civilization.

2. Compare the role of technology in ancient Rome to the role of technology in the United States. How did technology contribute to the success of both ancient Rome and the present-day United States?

3. Discuss new technology used by farmers during the Middle Ages and the changes in population and trade that resulted.

4. Discuss how improved technology helped Europeans explore the world beginning in the 1400s and to establish distant colonies.

5. Discuss how the use of steam power changed land and sea transportation during the 1800s and how it expanded business opportunities and personal travel.

6. Compare the benefits of industrialization with the problems it created.

7. Discuss how improvements in transportation technology have contributed to the success of Japan and "the Asian tigers" since the end of World War II.

8. Discuss the reasons why the United States used the atomic bomb in World War II and how its development by the Soviet Union within a few years affected world politics.

Concept Connector Study Guide

Trade

Essential Question: What have been the major trade networks in world history?

A. Define *trade.* _____

_____

_____

B. *Record information about the topics listed in the Cumulative Review or your answers to the questions in the Cumulative Review below. Use the Concept Connector Handbooks at the end of your textbook, as well as chapter information, to complete this worksheet.*

1. Phoenician Sea Traders (Chapter 2, page 63)

_____

_____

_____

_____

_____

_____

2. Phoenician Trade Network and the Silk Road (Chapter 3, page 109)

_____

_____

_____

_____

_____

_____

3. Trade in Ancient Greece and Phoenicia (Chapter 4, page 145)

_____

_____

_____

_____

_____

_____

Concept Connector Study Guide
TRADE *(continued)*

4. Traders and Merchants in Feudalism and the Manorial System
(Chapter 7, page 239)

_____

_____

_____

_____

_____

_____

_____

5. Trade in the Byzantine Empire, Russia, and Phoenicia (Chapter 9, page 299)

_____

_____

_____

_____

_____

_____

_____

_____

6. Coastal Peoples and Trade (Chapter 11, page 363)

_____

_____

_____

_____

_____

_____

_____

7. Chinese Trade in Southern China and Up Coast (Chapter 12, page 403)

_____

_____

_____

_____

_____

_____

_____

_____

Concept Connector Study Guide
TRADE *(continued)*

8. The Dutch Trading Empire (Chapter 14, page 467)

_____

_____

_____

_____

_____

_____

_____

9. Indian Trade in Southeast Asia (Chapter 14, page 467)

_____

_____

_____

_____

_____

_____

_____

10. European Approaches to Trade in the 1500s and 1600s (Chapter 14, page 467)

_____

_____

_____

_____

_____

_____

_____

11. Earlier Slave Trades and the Atlantic Slave Trade (Chapter 15, page 499)

_____

_____

_____

_____

_____

_____

_____

Concept Connector Study Guide

TRADE *(continued)*

12. Railroad Travel and Travel on the Silk Road (Chapter 19, page 629)

_____

_____

_____

_____

_____

13. The British and Dutch Trading Empires (Chapter 25, page 809)

_____

_____

_____

_____

_____

14. United States Trade in the Twentieth Century (Chapter 34, page 1127)

_____

_____

_____

_____

_____

15. Fears About Foreign Trade Dominance (Chapter 34, page 1127)

_____

_____

_____

_____

_____

16. Modern Free Trade and Mercantilism in the 1600s and 1700s
(Chapter 34, page 1127)

_____

_____

_____

_____

_____

Concept Connector Study Guide
TRADE *(continued)*

C. Sample Topics for Thematic Essays

Below are examples of thematic essay topics that might appear on a test. Prepare for the test by outlining an essay for each topic on a separate sheet of paper. Use the Concept Connector Handbooks at the end of your textbook, as well as chapter information, to outline your essays.

1. Discuss how the strong Roman military helped support trade during the *Pax Romana*, and how that trade then affected Roman civilization.

2. Describe the spice trade in the 1400s and how it helped spur European exploration.

3. Discuss the importance of trade in the Spanish and Portuguese conquests of Latin America and its effects on the lives of Native Americans and Africans.

4. Describe the triangular trade that began in the 1500s and its effects on each of the three regions it linked.

5. Describe the British trade in cotton before the Industrial Revolution and how it was changed by the factory system.

6. Describe the importance of trade in Latin American nations before and after independence. How did trade have both positive and negative effects?

7. How was a favorable balance of trade an important part of Japan's growth after World War II?

8. Describe the development of the Common Market and European Union, and evaluate their impact on trade among member nations.